LIBRARY OF NEW TESTAMENT STUDIES

299

formerly the Journal for the Study of the New Testament Supplement Series

Editor
Mark Goodacre

Dedicated to the loving memory of

Yap Boon Kiat, Natalie

(18 May 1974 – 2 January 2003)

Lover and best friend, confidante, soulmate, playmate

IDOLATRY AND AUTHORITY

A Study of 1 Corinthians 8.1–11.1 in the Light of the Jewish Diaspora

RICHARD LIONG-SENG PHUA

t&t clark

Copyright © Richard Liong-Seng Phua, 2005
A Continuum imprint

Published by T&T Clark International
The Tower Building, 11 York Road, London SE1 7NX
15 East 26th Street, Suite 1703, New York, NY 10010

www.tandtclark.com

British Library Cataloguing-in-Publication Data
A catalogue record for this book is available from the British Library

Library of Congress Cataloging-in-Publication Data
Phua, Richard Liong-Seng
    Idolatry and authority : a study of 1 Corinthians 8.1-11.1 in the light of the Jewish diaspora / Richard Liong-Seng Phua.
        p. cm. -- (Library of New Testament Studies 299)
    Includes bibliographical references (p.) and index.
    ISBN 0-567-03060-1
        1. Bible. N.T. Corinthians, 1st, VIII, I-XI, 1--Theology. 2. Idols and images--Worship--Biblical teaching. 3. Judaism--Relations. I. Title. II. Series.

    BS2675.6.I35P48 2005
    227'.206--dc22

                                                            2005050583

ISBN 0-567-03060-1 (hardback)

Typeset by ISB Typesetting, Sheffield
Printed on acid-free paper in Great Britain by MPG Ltd, Bodmin, Cornwall

CONTENTS

Acknowledgments   vii
Abbreviations   x

Chapter 1
INTRODUCTION   1
    1. Introduction   1
    2. Textual Evidence – Initial Analysis/Survey   1
    3. Survey of Interpretations of Conflicts in Corinth   6
    4. Summary and Conclusion   26

Chapter 2
IDOLATRY: DEFINITIONS AND PATTERNS   29
    1. Introduction   29
    2. An Analysis of Idolatry: Halbertal and Margalit (1992)   30
    3. Idolatry in the Septuagint (LXX)   35
    4. Summary and Conclusion   48

Chapter 3
CRITICISM OF IDOLATRY IN DIASPORA JEWISH LITERATURE   50
    1. Introduction   50
    2. Wisdom of Solomon 13–15   51
    3. Philo   57
    4. Josephus   68
    5. *Joseph and Aseneth*   77
    6. Sibylline Oracles   82
    7. Summary and Conclusion   88

Chapter 4
JEWS AND THE WORSHIP OF THE GODS   91
    1. Introduction   91
    2. LXX Exodus 22.27a   92
    3. Identification of the True God with other Gods – *The Letter of Aristeas*   96
    4. The use of Θεὸς Ὕψιστος: A Brief Survey   104
    5. Artapanus   111
    6. Jews' Participation in/Accommodation to Gentile Cults   116
    7. Summary and Conclusion   124

Chapter 5
PAUL VERSUS THE 'STRONG' ON IDOLATRY   126
  1. Introduction   126
  2. Idolatry of the 'Strong': A Brief Overview   127
  3. The γνῶσις of the 'Strong'   128
  4. The Use of δαιμόνιον   137
  5. Paul's Use of εἴδωλον   146
  6. The Distinction between εἴδωλα and δαιμόνια in Paul   148
  7. The Danger of Idolatry   153
  8. Summary and Conclusion   169

Chapter 6
PAUL'S APOSTOLIC AUTHORITY AND EXAMPLE   172
  1. Introduction   172
  2. Is 1 Corinthians 9 Paul's Defence of his Apostolic Authority?   173
  3. Evidence from 1 Corinthians 1–4   179
  4. The Double Purpose of 1 Corinthians 9: Authority and Example   185
  5. The Centre of Authority: Who is to Decide?   197
  6. Summary and Conclusion   199

Chapter 7
CONCLUSIONS   201
  1. Summary   201
  2. The Answers to our Questions   202
  3. A Possible Fresh Approach to Understanding Paul's Ethics?   205
  4. Historical Reconstruction: Ancient Judaism and Early Christianity   207

Bibliography   209
Index of References   222
Index of Authors   234

ACKNOWLEDGMENTS

This book is a slightly revised version of a doctoral thesis originally submitted to the Faculty of Divinity at the University of Glasgow. I wish to express my heartfelt gratitude and appreciation to Professor John M.G. Barclay who guided me with equal amounts of critical challenge, amazing skill and great patience throughout. The few years of learning under his wise supervision have taught me what makes a true and profound scholar, gentleman and friend, for he has consistently demonstrated himself to be one. All the flaws of this book, however, remain my responsibility.

I would also like to thank the editorial assistant Ms Rebecca Vaughan-Williams for her gracious assistance throughout, and Dr Mark Goodacre, the editor, for accepting my thesis for publication in this series and for all the helpful suggestions along the way.

Several organizations have made it financially possible for me to undertake my studies in Glasgow: Orchard Road Presbyterian Church, Singapore; Brash Trust; The Lee Foundation; and the Faculty of Divinity, University of Glasgow. The support of Dr and Mrs Christopher Khoo and that of the Bible study group of Mr and Mrs Tony and Jehanne Puah allowed my wife and myself to honour the commitments we had towards families and several poverty-stricken people. To the above organizations and friends, I wish to express my deepest appreciation.

Friends and leaders from our church in Singapore, Orchard Road Presbyterian Church, have been most encouraging: the former senior minister the Revd Derek J. Kingston; the Board of Elders and Deacons. The Revd Yap Wai Keong has been a true friend through thick and thin.

Human relationships are a very vital part of our stay in Glasgow. We have met many wonderful and caring people. Space does not permit, I shall therefore briefly mention some: the former pastor of Park Church Uddingston, the Revd Earsley White and his wife Silvia, extended gracious hospitality to us in ways beyond description; the profound friendships of the following have been sustaining, even now: Dr and Mrs David and Mary Graham; Mr and Mrs David and Jeanette Miller; Mr and Mrs Robert and Margaret Miller; Mr and Mrs David and Pauline Young; Mr and Mrs Kenneth and Cassie McClean; Mr and Mrs Ian and Liz Hutcheon; Mr and Mrs William and Isabel Bar; Mrs Elizabeth Thompson; Mrs Helen Ooi and many members of Park Church unreservedly extended their love and hospitality to us. Mr and Mrs David Batteridge, our landlord, provided a most conducive and warm environment in which my wife and I spent the best part of our lives together and where my entire research was completed.

Shortly after my viva, a deep personal crisis struck us that eventually led to the tragic death of my wife (I will elaborate more below). It has since been an extremely difficult time for me. During the last three years, a few friends have surrounded me with love and care; among them are Pastor Freddie Ong, the Revd Yap Wai Keong, the Revd Dr Anthony Ang, Mr Chan Chong Yew, Mr Andy Lew, Ms Lee Hwee Chin, Ms Joan Low, Ms Pauline Ong, Ms Joy Tong, and Ms Faith Wang. Friends of my late wife constantly offer care and encouragement, especially Ms Melissa Tan and Ms Lim Swee Keng. Five months after the death of my wife, Professor Kung Lap Yan of The Chinese University of Hong Kong, upon learning about my bereavement, flew to Singapore just to visit me, when he did not even know me. This was to turn into a profound friendship. Many friends at Trinity Theological College, where I now teach as a lecturer, have been most understanding and supportive. The Principal, Revd Dr Ngoei Foong Nghian, made special arrangements for me to join the college first as a guest lecturer and later as a full faculty member, and so provided the much needed space and finance not only during a time of intense grief but also when this manuscript was due. Our friends in Glasgow continued to support me at a distance and poured out their love in a most amazing way. To these friends and colleagues I am most grateful.

My mother-in-law, Madam Chong Oi Chan, who witnessed my wife's death suffers extreme pain losing a most doted daughter and yet does so much to encourage and comfort me, so do all my siblings. To them I owe so much.

Finally, I turn to the most important person in my life and in the whole journey of my doctoral studies, and her final exit. During a time when all her friends were actively and enthusiastically finding jobs and setting up their careers, Natalie packed up everything and left with a man for a totally unknown place. She left family, friends, the prospects of a good career and, without a single penny, joined me to go to Glasgow. Despite her weak health (which turned out to be strengthened by Glasgow weather!), she gave all her support. During our first year, she was so thrifty that we ended up spending only about £2,000! She fell quite ill during our first winter but did not once utter a single word of complaint. She endured all the loneliness and showered her love on a husband struggling for a PhD. It was in Glasgow that she first took to cooking and preparing all the wonderfully delicious meals for her hungry husband, including some of the most tasty traditional Asian pastries. She encouraged me when the path of research seemed rough and unpromising, and her lovely smiles and laughter simply kept me going. During our stay in Glasgow, she missed her mother so dearly and was totally devastated when she learnt, belatedly, about her mother's hospitalization. Similarly, she lost two uncles while we were in Glasgow. Natalie endured all this, and more, with patience and suffered very much because of me and this academic pursuit.

On 5 September 2002, Natalie joined me to return to Glasgow for the oral defence of the doctoral thesis, which was scheduled for 9 September 2002. When we returned to Singapore, Natalie suddenly became very ill the day after, that is, on 13 September 2002. Doctors could not tell exactly what she was suffering from, except that it was some form of mental illness. Natalie was in torment and slowly lost her ability to eat, sleep, write, watch television programmes, go out of the house; eventually she lost most of her emotions and speech. From 9 November 2002 onwards, she continually pleaded with me to help her end her life. She never recovered from her illness and, on 2 January 2003, she ended her own life by plunging down from our flat on the seventeenth floor. She landed on a tiny triangular plot of soft soil where there was a small plant, with solid concrete surrounding the plot. The miracle was that her body was fully preserved. I am reminded of Ps. 116.15, 'Precious in the sight of the LORD is the death of His saints'. Her suffering of three and a half months finally ended. Her departure breaks my heart forever. Natalie, who is my best friend, my lover, my soul, my life, and my all, will always remain in my heart and I will love her forever. This book is dedicated to the loving memory of her.

ABBREVIATIONS

AB	Anchor Bible
ABD	David Noel Freedman (ed.), *Anchor Bible Dictionary* (New York: Doubleday, 1992)
ANRW	Hildegard Temporini and Wolfgang Haase (eds.), *Aufstieg und Niedergang der römischen Welt: Geschichte und Kultur Roms im Spiegel der neueren Forschung* (Berlin: W. de Gruyter, 1972–)
BAGD	Walter Bauer, William F. Arndt, F. William Gingrich and Frederick W. Danker, *Greek-English Lexicon of the New Testament and Other Early Christian Literature* (Chicago: University of Chicago Press, 2nd edn, 1979)
BDB	Francis Brown, S.R. Driver and Charles A. Briggs, *A Hebrew and English Lexicon of the Old Testament* (Peabody, Massachusetts: Hendrickson, 1979)
BDF	Friedrich Blass, A. Debrunner and Robert W. Funk, *A Greek Grammar of the New Testament and Other Early Christian Literature* (Cambridge: Cambridge University Press, 1961)
Bib	*Biblica*
BIS	Biblical Interpretation Series
BNTC	Black's New Testament Commentaries
CBC	Cambridge Bible Commentary
CBQ	*Catholic Biblical Quarterly*
CIG	A. Boeckh (ed.), *Corpus Inscriptionum Graecarum* (4 vols.; Berlin, 1828–77)
CIJ	J.B. Frey (ed.), *Corpus Inscriptioinum Judaicarum* (2 vols.; Rome, 1936–52)
CPJ	V. Tcherikover (ed.), *Corpus Papyrorum Judaicorum* (3 vols.; Cambridge, 1957–64)
CRINT	Compendia Rerum Iudaicarum ad Novum Testamentum
EKKNT	Evangelisch-katholischer Kommentar zum Neuen Testament
ERE	J. Hastings (ed.), *Encyclopaedia of Religion and Ethics* (13 vols.; New York, 1908–1927. Reprint, 7 vols, 1951)
ExpTim	*Expository Times*
GAP	Guides to Apocrypha and Pseudepigrapha
GRBS	*Greek, Roman, and Byzantine Studies*
HTR	*Harvard Theological Review*
HUT	Hermeneutische Untersuchungen zur Theologie
ICC	International Critical Commentary
IDB	George Arthur Buttrick (ed.), *Interpreter's Dictionary of the Bible* (4 vols.; Nashville: Abingdon Press, 1962)
ISBE	Geoffrey Bromiley (ed.), *International Standard Bible Encyclopaedia* (4 vols.; Grand Rapids: Eerdmans, rev. edn, 1979–88)
JAL	Jewish Apocrypha Literature
JBL	*Journal of Biblical Literature*

JRS	*Journal of Roman Studies*
JSJ	*Journal for the Study of Judaism in the Persian, Hellenistic, and Roman Periods*
JSNT	*Journal for the Study of the New Testament*
JSNTSup	*Journal for the Study of the New Testament*, Supplement Series
JSOT	*Journal for the Study of the Old Testament*
LCL	Loeb Classical Library
LXX	The Septuagint
NCB	New Century Bible
NIB	*The New Interpreter's Bible*
NICNT	New International Commentary on the New Testament
NICOT	New International Commentary on the Old Testament
NIDNTT	Colin Brown (ed.), *New International Dictionary of New Testament Theology* (4 vols.; Grand Rapids: Eerdmans, 1975–85)
NIGTC	New International Greek Testament Commentary
NIV	New International Version
NJB	*New Jerusalem Bible*
NovT	*Novum Testamentum*
NRSV	New Revised Standard Version
NTS	*New Testament Studies*
NTT	New Testament Theology
Numen	*Numen: International Review for the History of Religions*
OGIS	W. Dittenberger (ed.), *Orientis Graeci Inscriptiones Selectae* (2 vols.; Leipzig, 1903-1905)
OTL	Old Testament Library
OTP	James H. Charlesworth (ed.), *Old Testament Pseudepigrapha* (2 vols.; New York, 1983, 1985)
RB	*Revue Biblique*
RBL	Review of Biblical Literature
REB	Revised English Bible
RSV	Revised Standard Version
SBL	Society of Biblical Literature
SBLDS	Society of Biblical Literature Dissertation Series
SBLMS	Society of Biblical Literature Monograph Series
SNTSMS	Society for New Testament Studies Monograph Series
SNTW	Studies of the New Testament and Its World
SP	Sacra Pagina
ST	*Studia theologica*
TDNT	Gerhard Kittel and Gerhard Friedrick (eds.), *Theological Dictionary of the New Testament* (trans. Geoffrey W. Bromiley; 10 vols.; Grand Rapids: Eerdmans, 1964–76)
TrinJ	*Trinity Journal*
TynBul	*Tyndale Bulletin*
VC	*Vigiliae christianae*
VT	*Vetus Testamentum*
WBC	Word Biblical Commentary
WUNT	Wissenschaftliche Untersuchungen zum Alten und Neuen Testament
ZNW	*Zeitschrift für die neutestamentliche Wissenschaft und die Kunde der älteren Kirche*

Chapter 1

INTRODUCTION

1. *Introduction*

1 Corinthians 8.1–11.1 is the lengthiest and key New Testament passage for examining and understanding the differences of opinion in early Christianity on idolatry, represented by three positions. How we explain these differences will help us understand where the battle lines are drawn in the conflict within early Christianity and in the relation between early Christianity and early Judaism. Why is idolatry so important as to warrant Paul's lengthiest discussion in 1 Corinthians? What exactly is at stake? And why are there differences of opinion?

One of the key issues in the interpretation and understanding of 1 Cor. 8.1–11.1 lies in the parties involved: the 'strong', the 'weak', and Paul. Are the parties Jewish Christians or Gentile Christians? Or is it a question of conflict between a Jewish Paul and Gentile Christians' (converts') opinion? Or is it a conflict between a Christian Paul and his Jewish opponents?

But is this a question of ethnicity? Most scholars have assumed that the 'strong' and the 'weak' were either Gentile or Jewish Christians, simply on the basis of their opinions/practices. However, the issue of idolatry in this passage is much more complex which may not require an equation of Judaism with Jewish ethnicity. Indeed, the 'strong' and the 'weak' need not be ethnic Jews even though they may subscribe to a theology that is informed by the Jewish scripture, while they may differ from each other in their practice. What seems clear is that the ethnicity of the parties involved does not necessarily correlate with their practice. The only party whose theology is informed by the Jewish scripture, whose practice is somewhat modified (i.e. Christian), and who is clearly an ethnic Jew is Paul.

This chapter will survey the scholarly opinions on 1 Cor. 8.1–11.1 and draw out their strengths and weaknesses, illuminating on how the passage may be viewed. The first step in my task is to carry out an initial analysis of the textual evidence concerning the parties of the 'strong' and the 'weak'.

2. *Textual Evidence – Initial Analysis/Survey*

a. *Two groups – the 'strong' and the 'weak'*

(i) *The 'weak' – real or hypothetical.*
Although the vast majority of scholars have accepted the existence of two groups in 1 Cor. 8.1–11.1, it was J.C. Hurd who first suggested that there were not two

groups in the church at Corinth.[1] For when the two terms are used they do not
refer to two parties (1 Cor. 1.25, 26–27; 4.10).[2] Nor is there any consistent use of
the term outside 1 Cor. 8, nor any evidence supporting the notion of two groups.
The problem of idolatry is basically between Paul and the Corinthians as a whole;
and Paul has created the hypothetical 'weak' so as to discourage the Corinthians
from eating idol-meat.[3]

Similarly, Gooch does not think that those passages indicating two groups
(e.g. 8.7–13; 9.22; 10.28; 11.18–22, 33–34) support the notion of these groups'
existence.[4] For 11.18–22, 33–34 have a different context, while the 'weak' of
9.22 are non-Christians. However, he offers no explanation for 10.28. And he
does not think 8.1–13 reflects the existence of the 'weak' either. Insisting on the
conditional nature of Paul's objections (e.g. 'lest in some way' [8.9]; 'if good is
an obstacle' [8.13]), Gooch concludes that Paul sets up a hypothetical case of the
'weak' ('if someone sees you' [8.10], and 'if someone says' [10.28]).[5]

Are the 'weak' real or hypothetical? In 1 Cor. 8.1–6 Paul seems to agree with
the basic position of the Corinthians. However, the ἀλλά in v. 7 proves otherwise.[6] For Paul points out that not everyone shares the 'knowledge' of the 'strong'.
This statement of Paul is neither conditional nor hypothetical; but a bare assertion
of a fact. The 'strong' Corinthians would know best whether or not all of them
possess the same knowledge of vv. 1 and 4.

Further, in 1 Cor. 8.9, the 'strong' are cautioned against letting their freedom
become a stumbling-block to the 'weak' (τοῖς ἀσθενέσιν), a reference to a specific
group. If Hurd and Gooch are right that Paul is setting up a hypothetical case
of the 'weak', then it would only serve as a justification for the 'strong' to eat
idol-meat, since there really are no 'weak' members: 'since there are no "weak"
members among us', they might say, 'we suppose we can therefore freely eat
idol-meat'. The only way to understand v. 9 seems to be to take the 'weak' to be
a real group.

1 Corinthians 8.10 states, 'For if others see you, who possess knowledge…'
Who are these 'others'? They are contrasted with 'you' (the 'strong'). The context shows they cannot be unbelievers, but those members who do not possess
the knowledge of the 'strong' and they are none other than the 'weak' referred to
in 8.9.

1 Corinthians 8.11 refers to the one who is 'weak' (ὁ ἀσθενῶν) and attributes
his/her destruction if he/she eats idol-meat to 'your knowledge' (τῇ σῇ γνώσει).[7]

---

1.   Hurd 1983: 125.
2.   Hurd 1983: 124.
3.   This idea is followed by Fee (1980: 176). However, in his commentary (1987: 378) he seems
to imply the existence of these 'weak' Christians.
4.   Gooch 1993: 61-68.
5.   Gooch 1993: 66. Cf. Hurd 1983: 117-25. See both Fee (1987: 385, and also his n. 50) and
Hays (1997: 143) for a persuasive and opposing view.
6.   Fee (1987: 378) observes that the strong adversative 'but' indicates that Paul is about to qualify
his statement.
7.   ἐν τῇ σῇ γνώσει...has strong textual support: P[46] ℵ[*] A (B) D[(2)] F G 33 *pc* latt; Ir[lat] (Cl).

Those who have knowledge in v. 11 are those of v. 10; and the 'weak' of v. 11 would be the 'others' of v. 10.

From the textual evidence of 1 Corinthians 8, it is highly probable that the 'weak' group is not hypothetical but real. Horrell argues, 'there are no compelling grounds to doubt that differences of opinion and practice existed at Corinth; indeed, much of Paul's exhortation would be rather pointless if it did not'.[8] We can thus proceed on this assumption of the existence of the 'weak' group. Who they are and what viewpoint they represent is less agreed, and is to be surveyed below.

(ii) *The 'strong' – a question of label.*
There is no dispute among scholars over the existence of the 'strong'. The issue is with who they are and what viewpoint they represent. This question will be left to a later section (2,c). We will for now look at the text to see what Paul calls them.

To be sure, Paul never refers to this group as the 'strong', whereas in Rom. 14.1–15.7 Paul specifically mentions two groups: the 'weak' and the 'powerful'. Is the use of the term 'strong' therefore justifiable? From 1 Cor. 8.1, it seems clear that this group of Corinthians possess knowledge, which refers to the knowledge of the 'One God' and the non-existence of idols. They may therefore be called the 'knowledgeable'. A further hint about the 'strong' is seen in 1 Cor. 8.9 – they believe they enjoy a liberty that allows them to freely eat idol-meat at pagan temples (8.10), at the homes of unbelievers (10.27), and that bought from the market (10.25). This is in contrast to the 'weak' who have difficulty with such meats.

Since Paul mentions the 'weak' (8.7b, 9, 10b, 11), we may assume that there is a group of the 'strong' in contrast to the 'weak'. And the texts above indicate the existence of a group which may be variously called the 'strong', the 'knowing', or the 'knowledgeable'. The reference to the group who have γνῶσις as the 'strong' is therefore made in this thesis for the sake of convenience. The term is chosen as a contrast to the 'weak'. By using this term, I mean no more than that the 'strong' behave in a certain way that is informed by their knowledge and they have a 'strong' conscience.

We now move to a closer look at the text to glean what may be deduced concerning the identities of the 'strong' and the 'weak'.

b. *The 'weak'*
Central to our understanding of the 'weak' and their identity is the passage in 1 Cor. 8.7, 9–13. We will look at 1 Cor. 8.7b first and only at 1 Cor. 8.7a later since the latter is linked to 1 Cor. 8.9–13. In 1 Cor. 8.7b, there is a hint that the 'weak' are former pagans since they were 'accustomed' to idols. The word translated here 'accustomed', συνηθείᾳ, has a variant reading, that is, συνειδήσει, found in the Western and Byzantine traditions. However, the former, συνηθείᾳ, is to be preferred to the latter, συνειδήσει, as it is well supported by ℵ* A B P

8.   Horrell 1997: 85.

Q33 81 1739 *al* while the latter is supported by ℵᶜ D G 88 614 *Byz Lect*, a
reading which according to Metzger 'arose through assimilation to the following
συνείδησει'.⁹ But are the 'weak' necessarily Gentiles? Scholars in general tend to
adopt this interpretation on the basis that Jewish Christians cannot have been
accustomed to idols.¹⁰ However, 1 Corinthians 8 does not explicitly state that the
'weak' are Gentile Christians. While Gentiles are accustomed to idols, the 'weak'
referred to above could possibly be 'liberal' Jews who accommodated themselves
to idolatry in the past, before their conversion to Christ (see Chapter 4 below).
Thus, we cannot be certain as to whether the 'weak' are Gentile Christians on the
basis of 1 Cor. 8.7.

We need to consider the συνείδησις of the 'weak'. What does Paul mean when
he refers to the weak συνείδησις? Robertson and Plummer explain it in terms of
an 'unilluminated conscience', that is, the 'weak' lack the knowledge of the
'strong' to enlighten them in their practice.¹¹ Fee defines this as the experiential,
emotional level of a person.¹² That is to say, although some people may have the
knowledge that there is only one God and idols are non-existent, emotionally
they are unable to let their 'knowledge' inform their practice because of their past
association with idolatry. But why is their conscience defiled (μολύνεται, 8.7)?
And why would they be destroyed (ἀπόλλυται, 8.11)? And why would their
conscience be wounded (τύπτοντες, 8.12)? There are two important points to
note. The first is by eating idol-meat the 'weak' face 'destruction'. This suggests
that the question of 'salvation' is involved here, which further suggests that the
'faith' of the 'weak' is undermined. The second is the two words 'defile' (8.7)
and 'wound' (8.12) probably indicate the same effect of eating idol-meat.

This leads to the consideration of 8.9–13. Because the 'weak' believe that the
idols still hold power, they think it wrong to eat idol-meat as such meats would
defile and hurt their 'belief' and 'conscience', destroying their 'faith' in Christ.¹³
In this case, the 'conscience' of the 'weak' may be described as a kind of 'spiritual condition' that undergirds their relationship with Christ which, if it is not
carefully handled, can also undermine that relationship. Paul is therefore worried
that the 'weak' would be drawn into the pagan cult.¹⁴ This makes sense for Gentile Christians who have 'turned to God from idols' (cf. 1 Cor. 12.2; 1 Thess.
1.9–10), that is, their συνείδησις has been significantly 'Judaized' when they
become Christ-believers. But these are the only cases Paul records. The use of ὡς
εἰδωλόθυτον in 8.7 also suggests a Jewish influence on the 'weak', as the term is
clearly a compound of εἴδωλον, and the suffix -θυτος.¹⁵ Further, in 1 Cor. 10.28,
Paul advises abstention from the food that has been specifically pointed out to be

9.   Metzger 1971: 557; similarly, Fee (1987: 376 n. 1). Cf. Murphy-O'Connor 1978b: 551.
10.   E.g. Fee (1987: 378); Hays (1997: 141); Conzelmann 1975: 147.
11.   Robertson and Plummer 1911: 168–69.
12.   Fee 1987: 379.
13.   Robertson and Plummer (1911: 169), 'they cannot eat ἐκ πίστεως (Rom. 14.23)'. Similarly
Héring 1962: 73.
14.   Hays 1997: 142.
15.   Cf. Büchsel 1964: 378–79.

sacrificial food. The term appears to be attributed to unbelievers and in that case it is ἱερόθυτον, thus suggesting that Paul in 8.7 is representing the 'weak' in their use of the term εἰδωλόθυτον. We cannot, therefore, conclude about the ethnicity of the 'weak' simply on the basis of their former idolatrous practice (see Chapter 4 below). All that can be said about the 'weak' is that they used to worship idols; but as Christ-believers they now believe it is wrong to continue their idolatrous practice.

c. *The 'strong'*
We will briefly examine a few important probable quotes from the Corinthians in 1 Corinthians 8–10, which will illuminate the identity of the 'strong'. 1 Corinthians 8.1 appears to be a quote from the Corinthian 'strong', 'we all possess knowledge'.[16] The fact that this is a quote from the 'strong' may be seen in Paul's immediate corrective statement, 'knowledge puffs up, but love builds up', and from 8.7a where a similar corrective statement is made. It is also seen in the use of οἴδαμεν ὅτι both here and in v. 4, which is a formula to introduce what the 'strong' have said.[17] It shows that the 'strong' are those who have a particular type of knowledge, which is probably summed up in 8.4: 'we know that there is no idol in the world and there is no God but one'. Apart from the οἴδαμεν ὅτι formula, Paul's qualifying statement in 8.5-6 further shows that 8.4 is a slogan of the 'strong'.[18] Verse 5 introduces Paul's criticism of the knowledge of the 'strong', with v. 6 acting as the basis of Paul's argument.[19] There are two clauses in 8.4. The first is the rejection of idols (οὐδὲν εἴδωλον ἐν κόσμῳ). The second seems to reflect the monotheistic nature of the *Shema* (οὐδεὶς θεὸς εἰ μὴ εἷς, cf. Deut. 6.4), suggesting Jewish influence. Although the Jewish influence of the second clause cannot be fully confirmed, since pagans can equally adopt the same belief, the word εἴδωλον in the first clause suggests it is more likely Jewish. Further, Paul's inclusion of the Christian confession in 8.6 suggests that he thinks the 'knowledge' of the 'strong' is inadequate.[20] Scholars agree that in 8.6 Paul is setting out the Christian tradition of redemption and creation in Christ.[21]

16.   This is well accepted by scholars; e.g. Robertson and Plummer (1911: 163); Héring (1962: 67); Barrett (1968: 189); Conzelmann (1975: 140); Murphy-O'Connor (1978b: 545); Fee (1987: 365); and Hays (1997: 136).

17.   Cf. BAGD on ὅτι. See also Fee (1987: 365 n. 31; 370 n. 6); and Robertson and Plummer 1911: 163, 166.

18.   Like 8.1a, 8.4 is well recognized by scholars as a slogan of the Corinthian 'strong'; e.g. Robertson and Plummer (1911: 166); Barrett (1968: 189); Conzelmann (1975: 142); Fee (1987: 370–71); Hays (1997: 138-39).

19.   So Conzelmann 1975: 143-44. Fee (1987: 370) agrees with this basic point that Paul is qualifying in vv. 5-6 what the 'strong' have said in v. 4 (see further 370-76); and Hays (1997: 139).

20.   Some scholars see 8.6 as clear evidence of Paul's belief in the pre-existence of Christ, e.g. Robertson and Plummer (1911: 168); Conzelmann (1975: 144–45). However, this is not the main point of 8.6 as Hays (1997: 140) rightly points out; it is in fact Paul's qualification of the 'knowledge' of the 'strong' with a Christological twist, thus setting out the basic principle of his argument throughout 1 Corinthians 8–10.

21.   E.g. Robertson and Plummer 1911: 168; Barrett 1968: 193; Conzelmann 1975: 145; Fee 1987: 375–76.

The clause πάντα μοι ἔξεστιν in 1 Cor. 6.12 and 10.23 reveals that the 'strong' claim they have ἐξουσία/ἐλευθερία. Robertson and Plummer think these are Paul's own words to mean all things '*indifferent*', which however have been misused by the Corinthians.[22] Others, however, generally take this to be a claim of the 'strong'.[23] The general consensus among scholars is that the 'strong' claim their 'freedom' in Christ to do what they like. Hence in both instances Paul negates this principle by arguing that not all things 'benefit' (6.12) or 'build up' (10.23). He implies in 6.12b that the Corinthians have allowed such things as food and sexual immorality to 'enslave' them. And in 10.23, he suggests the exercise of the 'rights' of the 'strong' does not benefit/edify the 'weak'.

The above textual evidence raises several questions about the 'strong': who are the 'strong'? Are they Jewish Christians who, after becoming Christ-believers, adopt a 'liberal' stance towards idolatry? Or are they Gentile Christians (including former God-fearers) who have come to view idols as nothing and therefore feel at liberty to eat idol-meat? Or could they be a combination of Jewish and Gentile Christians, both of whom have come to believe in Christ but are equally influenced by Judaism, as seen in 1 Cor. 8.4? Or should we proceed on the question of their ethnicity? In other words, can the ethnicity of the 'strong' be determined and depended upon to illuminate the issue of idol-meat in 1 Corinthians 8–10? Or should we not search for the answer concerning the issue of idol-meat in different places? In other words, should we not look at their belief and practice, instead of their ethnicity, to enlighten our understanding of 1 Corinthians 8–10? This leads to another set of questions. What is the basis of the viewpoint of the 'strong'? 1 Cor. 8.4 suggests that the Jewish *Shema* is the basis of their viewpoint. Does this suggest that the 'strong' might have been influenced by Judaism? If the 'strong' have been influenced by Judaism, can we find parallels to their behaviour in the literature of about the same period and in a similar social context (i.e. the Diaspora)? What about their claim that they have ἐξουσία/ἐλευθερία? If the 'strong' have Jewish influence, are there Jewish parallels to such claims? These are questions which we will seek to explore and answer in the course of our study below.

We will now proceed to survey the literature on the interpretations of the situation at Corinth in general, and of 1 Corinthians 8–10 in particular.

3. *Survey of Interpretations of Conflicts in Corinth*

a. *The influence of a Petrine party in Corinth*

(i) *F.C. Baur.*
It was F.C. Baur who in 1831 suggested that there were two opposing groups within early Christianity, namely the party of the older apostles and that of Paul.

---

22.   Robertson and Plummer 1911: 121, 219.
23.   Cf. Héring 1962: 97; Barrett 1968: 239; Conzelmann 1975: 108, 176; Fee 1987: 251–52, 478–79; Hays 1997: 101, 175.

Although the relationship between the older apostles and Paul appeared harmonious superficially, there were tensions and disagreements.[24]

Paul had built his Gentile churches without requiring them to keep the Jewish laws and traditions. This alarmed the Jerusalem apostles who sent representatives to Antioch to investigate, resulting in a confrontation between Paul and Peter.[25] This same problem continued at the Galatian church where Paul's opponents had confused the Christians with the requirements of the law.[26]

While in Ephesus, Paul heard news of a renewal of the Galatian experiences at the church in Corinth where his opponents were the itinerant pseudo-apostles who invoked or bore the name of Peter,[27] who never visited Corinth. Paul's opponents were in fact trying to infiltrate the Corinthian church where, knowing that imposing Jewish requirements would be ineffective in a predominantly Gentile church, they sought to attack Paul's apostolic authority.[28] These opponents were almost entirely Gentile Christians who attached themselves to Peter and fought the cause of the Jewish Christians.[29] This resulted in the division of the Corinthian church into parties of whom the majority remained faithful to Paul.[30]

For Baur, Apollos never posed a problem since he was a friend and successor of Paul.[31] The real problem lies with the parties of Peter and Christ, which are in fact the same party under different names: the Peter party was so called because Peter held the primacy among the Jewish apostles while the Christ party was so called because the members asserted direct contact with Christ to be the chief requirement of apostolic authority.[32]

Baur does not mention how this perspective may apply to 1 Corinthians 8–10. And it is not clear how the conflict affected the issue of idol food. Baur's thesis suggests that there is a Jewish influence in 1 Corinthians, including 8–10. However, Baur's thesis is not without problems. First, in 1 Corinthians 8–10 Paul does not explicitly reject Jewish requirements of the law. Had the same Judaising opponents from the Galatian church been present at Corinth, Paul would have countered them with further condemnation. However, there is neither such a condemnation nor any specific reference to the encounter at Galatia, nor the confrontation at Antioch. It appears that Baur's thesis may over-simplify the multiple kinds of conflicts in Pauline churches.

Further, as P.J. Tomson has demonstrated,[33] Jewish influence in Corinth in general and 1 Corinthians 8–10 in particular need not be read as a Jew versus Gentile conflict. Further, to read 1 Corinthians as continuing the Paul versus Peter saga in Galatia runs the danger of disregarding the different historical situations

24. Baur 1876: 127.
25. Baur 1878: 52–54.
26. Baur 1878: 56-57.
27. Baur 1878: 61; Kümmel 1972: 129.
28. Baur 1876: 259, 266.
29. Baur 1878: 64–65.
30. Baur 1876: 259.
31. Baur 1876: 260–61.
32. Baur 1876: 267.
33. Tomson 1990.

of the two churches and the possible developments in Paul's own thought (e.g. 1 Corinthians 5). Steven C. Muir, in reviewing Michael Goulder's *St Paul versus St Peter: A Tale of Two Missions*, which is very much supportive of Baur's basic thesis, has rightly criticized, '(t)he idea that any single theory or set of circumstances can explain all New Testament texts is, at the least, optimistic. It is undeniable that many New Testament texts have an underlying context of conflict, even polemic. It is arguable, however, whether the same group or groups are being engaged in each case.'[34]

The question of whether 1 Corinthians indicates a Pauline-Petrine divide is also rightly called into question by J.C. Hurd, who rhetorically suggests that scholars of 1 Corinthians 'more often than not' brought views to the epistle.[35] Indeed, a cursory comparison between 1 Corinthians and Galatians would indicate that the tone and language of Paul in 1 Corinthians differ sharply from those in Galatians, as D. Litfin has demonstrated in his analysis of 1 Cor. 1.1–9, that 'Paul considered the Corinthians to be fundamentally sound.'[36]

(ii) *T.W. Manson and A. Ehrhardt.*

Manson and Ehrhardt separately suggested a somewhat modified version of Baur's thesis, that Peter was the one behind the conflict between the Corinthians and Paul. Manson suggested that when Paul in 1 Cor. 3.10–17 mentions there is another trying to build on his foundation, it is either 'Peter himself or someone acting on his behalf' who was trying to mar the work of Paul and provide the alternative foundation (cf. Mt. 16.18).[37]

According to Manson, after James had taken over the leadership of the Jerusalem church from Peter, there is 'evidence of attempts to assert the authority of Peter in the sphere of Paul's work',[38] hence the Cephas party. The Christ party stood at the 'opposite extreme' to the Cephas party. They believed Christ to mean something like 'God, freedom, and immortality', where God meant a refined philosophical monotheism, freedom meant 'emancipation from the puritanical rigours of Palestinian barbarian authorities into the wider air of self-realization', and immortality meant 'the sound Greek doctrine as opposed to the crude Jewish notion of the Resurrection'.[39] Thus Paul in Corinth is fighting on two fronts.

While Mason's theory seems interesting, as he tries to make sense of the Cephas party and the Christ party, he has not provided any clear evidence in support of his claim. And if Paul is fighting on two fronts, we do not see two distinct arguments against the two.

Of particular relevance to 1 Corinthians 8–10, Manson posited that it was the Cephas party who raised the issue of idol-meat (i.e. in reference to the decree).[40]

34. Muir 2000: 2 (http://www.bookreviews.org/). This review cannot be found in the printed version of RBL. Thus, the page number here refers to that in the electronic version.
35. Hurd 1983: 96–107.
36. Litfin 1994: 178–79.
37. Manson 1962: 194.
38. Manson 1962: 196.
39. Manson 1962: 207.
40. Manson 1962: 200.

For Jewish or Jewish-Christian conscience and sensitivity about idolatry leads to the objection being raised.[41] For Paul, Jewish 'taboos' do not apply to a predominantly Gentile Christian community, and the decree is meant only for the church at Antioch. Thus, his way of dealing with the objection, even though he had to agree with the basic principle of Peter, was to insist on a Christian basis.[42]

The re-construction of Mason may work if the Corinthian community is predominantly Gentile which, however, is itself ambiguous. For, as we have argued in section 1, the question need not be one of ethnicity. Judging from the constant reference to the Old Testament, especially in 1 Corinthians 10, it is not entirely unreasonable to posit that even if the ethnic Gentiles were the majority they would have been heavily influenced by Judaism/s to varying degrees. This will be seen in our subsequent argument. Further, the 'Christian' basis is equally ambiguous, without explicit evidence, either.

Following almost the same line of argument, Ehrhardt puts forward the hypothesis that it was Peter who came to Corinth and insisted on the 'general validity' of the apostolic decree (Acts 15.20, 28–29).[43] And Paul not only accepted the decree but also strongly commanded it for the sake of the 'weak'.[44] On the basis of 1 Cor. 8.4, 7, 13, Ehrhardt concludes that: (1) Paul once ate sacrificial meat at Corinth; but (2) he abandoned this practice of eating idol-meat at Peter's remonstrations 'for conscience sake', though not 'entirely without a certain acerbity directed at the address of St. Peter'.[45]

Ehrhardt's conclusions are even less convincing. For his first conclusion, not only is there complete silence on Paul's part, but there is no implicit reference to his association with idolatry at all. In fact, Paul does not seem to be one who dodges his own mistakes. At least, he shows elsewhere that he is capable of admitting to his errors (cf. 1 Cor. 5.9–11).

Both Manson and Ehrhardt are in agreement that Paul had accepted the decree,[46] though each sees the acceptance a little differently.[47] They showed that there are multiple kinds of Jewish influence in Corinth. It was through Paul, or Peter, and the decree. However, there is no evidence of a Jewish party under Peter which insisted on the decree; nor is there any mention of the decree, nor of Paul's agreement or acceptance of it in the text. Paul's insistence that the 'strong' consider the 'weak' arises out of his concern for 'love' (1 Cor. 8.1–2, 13), rather than an acceptance of the decree. Manson's suggestion that the 'strong' held to a philosophical monotheism is weak in that the monotheism of the 'strong' seems distinctively Jewish (cf. 1 Cor. 8.4).

41. Manson 1962: 200.
42. Manson 1962: 202.
43. Ehrhardt 1964: 277.
44. Ehrhardt 1964: 277.
45. Ehrhardt 1964: 278.
46. Cf. Barrett 1982: 46.
47. Manson 1962: 200–202; Ehrhardt 1964: 278.

(iii) *C.K. Barrett.*
Following Manson, Barrett posits that Peter probably had been to Corinth.[48] He
had not demanded circumcision but 'attempted to impose a Judaic pattern of
thought and religious life upon a Gentile community'.[49] Thus, Peter had to be
vigorously resisted for he not only represented 'a legalistic perversion of the
gospel'[50] but also was 'a more dangerous potential cause of schism in Corinth'.[51]

The Jewish Christians under Peter sought to introduce the decree to the Corinthian church, a decree they themselves not only retained but also obeyed.[52] This
is seen in 1 Corinthians 8–10 where the Cephas party raised the objection against
eating idol-meat since it constituted a breach of the decree. And because the
Cephas party were teaching under the name and authority of Peter, Paul had to
devote some considerable space to a defence of his apostolic authority in 1 Corinthians 9.[53]

Barrett further argues that Paul was not a practising Jew with regard to
εἰδωλόθυτα.[54] And in permitting the eating of εἰδωλόθυτα he contradicted the
decree and thus was brought into controversy with the Cephas party.[55] The 'strong'
are, it seems, another group of Corinthians whom Barrett terms 'Gnostics' whose
main emphasis is γνῶσις. The 'Gnostics' adopted the following:[56] (a) a practical
γνῶσις about idol-meat, that they believed that since their bodies are not raised,
they could go on eating and drinking with full freedom (1 Cor. 6.13); (b) a strict
monotheism on a rationalistic basis; (c) a strict dualism in a rational and logical
way so as to refuse a separation between the liberty to eat and the liberty to
commit fornication; and (d) a moral indifference, drawing from their rationalistic
dualism.

Barrett argues that there is a group of Jewish Christians under Peter who
raised the issue of idol-meat because the 'gnostic' Christians had freely eaten
such meat. This group cannot be the 'weak' as the 'weak' cannot be of Jewish
origin due to their past association with idols.[57] Barrett therefore concludes, 'In
Corinth, and not here only, Paul had to walk the tightrope between the legalism
of Jewish Christianity and the false liberalism of gnostic rationalism... Paul's
attitude to the question of εἰδωλόθυτα was too closely bound up with the
gnostic wing for the main body of Christians to accept it.'[58]

48.   Barrett 1982: 21, 32.
49.   Barrett 1982: 21.
50.   Barrett 1982: 12.
51.   Barrett 1982: 32.
52.   Barrett 1982: 44.
53.   Barrett 1982: 53; cf. 1 Corinthians 9.
54.   Barrett 1982: 50.
55.   Barrett 1982: 52-54.
56.   Barrett 1982: 54–56.
57.   Barrett 1968: 194. Barrett, however, is not clear on this. In his commentary, he states that the
'weak' cannot be Jewish Christians. However, in his essay of 1982, he suggests that it was the Petrine
party who raised the objection. This means the 'weak' did not raise the objection. Why then did Paul
tell the 'strong' to consider the 'weak'? This weakness in Barrett's thesis is also raised by Gooch
(1993: 146).
58.   Barrett 1982: 56.

Barrett is right that there is a Jewish element in this passage, but there is no evidence that this is connected to the Petrine party or the decree. And if the 'weak' and the 'strong' are both Gentile, then where is the evidence of a Jewish party raising the objection to idol meat in 1 Cor. 8.1–11.1? The Jewish influence seems to be found in the monotheistic language of the 'strong', which is inspired by Judaism, not 'gnosticism' or 'rationalism'. This view of the Corinthian situation as represented by Baur, Manson, Ehrhardt and Barrett became quiet for some years before M. Goulder recently revived it.

(iv) *M. Goulder.*

In his book, *A Tale of Two Missions,* Goulder hypothesizes that there was a basic tension between Paul and the Jerusalem apostles,[59] the latter had required Gentile believers to keep certain aspects of the laws. Paul, however, adopted a liberal policy of requiring the Gentile believers to keep the moral commandments while ignoring the ceremonial commandments.[60] This tension exploded when some representatives from Jerusalem were sent to Antioch where Gentiles were eating meat that was not slaughtered according to the kosher law.[61] The same problem was also extended into Galatia where Judaisers sought to impose the law's requirements such as circumcision on the Gentile believers.

The basic tension was to continue into all other epistles. According to Goulder, the Corinthian church members were Greek people and thus great admirers of wisdom. When the Jewish opponents of Paul came and settled in Corinth, they presented their religion as the highest form of wisdom. He cites 1 Cor. 1.19–20 and 2.5, 13 as proof of this idea.[62] And when the Jewish missionaries arrived in Corinth, they began to teach the Corinthian Gentile Christians that many detailed rules could be derived from the law. Paul became worried, though not about the decree, as he concurred with it.[63] So he insisted on the *Bible and the Bible only.*[64] Thus the issue is between the Jerusalem apostles wanting to impose legal requirements and Paul resisting it. Because the Jewish Christians of the Corinthian church knew about the law and did not want to break it, when it came to food, these members would want to ensure that the meat was not tainted.[65] Thus, the issue at Corinth 'was between the Pauline and Petrine Christians on the interpretation of the law'.[66]

Although Goulder does not mention specifically the situation concerning εἰδωλόθυτα, the implication of his argument is clear. It seems that the 'strong' of 1 Corinthians 8–10 would be the Gentile Christians who were faithful followers of Paul. Being 'Gentile', they would have no scruples over the eating of idol-meat.

59.   Goulder 1994: 1–7.
60.   Goulder 1994: 1.
61.   Goulder 1994: 3.
62.   Goulder 1994: 25.
63.   Goulder 1994: 25–26.
64.   Goulder 1991: 530; 1994: 25–26.
65.   Goulder 1994: 26.
66.   Goulder 1991: 526.

However, the 'weak', the Jewish Christians who were representative of Peter, raised objection against the practice of these 'strong' Gentile Christians.

Goulder's thesis is questionable for several reasons. First, the evidence for Judaizing in Corinth is strikingly absent, compared to Galatians. Second, Goulder does not deal adequately with 1 Corinthians 8–10, perhaps because his thesis precisely does not hold here. For example, the Jewish 'wisdom' of 1 Corinthians 1–4 is quite different from the 'knowledge' of 1 Corinthians 8–10. Third, as Christopher Tuckett has shown, the general thesis is weak, and the evidence of 1 Cor. 8.7 is fatal to a reconstruction of the 'weak' as Petrine bearers of the decree.[67] And although there is no doubt that there were divisions between groups in the earliest churches, it is doubtful whether they were simply between Pauline and Petrine groups.[68]

The above theories argue for the influence of either a Petrine party or the 'apostolic decree' on the 'strong' or on Paul. Although theoretically, there could be such an influence, there is no positive evidence to support such a theory. The scruples of the 'weak' are Jewish, but these are new scruples, following their conversion. It appears that the view of every party in Corinth is 'Jewish' in some respects. And since Jews in antiquity represented a spectrum of practice and beliefs, we need to depart from the simple 'Jewish' versus 'Gentile' Christianity hypothesis and explore the hypothesis of movements and opinions as all 'Jewish' but in varying ways and to varying degrees.

b. *The Corinthians as Jewish Gnostics*

W. Schmithals suggested that the situation in the Corinthian church was one of conflict between Paul and his opponents over the latter's teaching, while the latter charged that Paul was not a true apostle.[69] According to Schmithals, 1 Cor. 9.24–10.22 did not belong to 1 Corinthians 8–10, while 1 Cor. 8.1–9.23 + 10.23–11.1 together form one fragment.[70]

Schmithals argued that the Corinthians held to a system of Gnosticism which was pre-Christian.[71] The system involved a 'Christ Gnosticism' of which the 'Christ' was 'man himself'.[72] Because the figure and name of the messiah were central in this system, it was a system of Jewish Gnosticism.[73] This system was influenced by Christianity which venerated Christ as the prophet promised by Moses.[74] This Jewish Gnosticism was what the opponents of Paul were preaching, whose theology was the 'doctrine of knowledge'.[75] They made up just one Jewish group (cf. 2 Cor. 11.22),[76] who had come into the Corinthian community

---

67. See Tuckett (1994: 201–19) for the detailed argument.
68. Davies 1994: 26–27. See further Muir (2000: 2), and Downing (1994: 465–66).
69. Schmithals 1971: 116, 142.
70. Schmithals 1971: 90–95.
71. Schmithals 1971: 36.
72. Schmithals 1971: 50.
73. Schmithals 1971: 36, 51.
74. Schmithals 1971: 51.
75. Schmithals 1971: 143.
76. Schmithals 1971: 115.

from outside and carried with them letters of recommendation. They were apostles who not only preached at synagogues, among the Gentiles, but also in the Christian communities. Not only σοφία, but above all γνῶσις was used as a *terminus technicus* for their preaching as seen in 1 Cor. 8.1.[77] They spoke of Gnosis in a Hellenistic sense, i.e. γνῶσις θεοῦ as the understanding of the being of God.[78] Thus, for them, Gnosis was gospel.[79] When it comes to idol-meat, Paul had forbidden participation in pagan cultic meals in his preceding letter (i.e. 1 Cor. 10.14–22). This had raised the question in the minds of the Gnostics in 1 Corinthians 8 whether it was permitted to eat meat that was sold in the market-place.[80] The Gnostics, at the time of writing their letter to Paul, thought all of them were 'strong' because of their possession of Gnosis.[81] Schmithals then argued that the Corinthian Gnostics, based on the above, were preaching 'another gospel' without Paul's realizing it at first.[82] He only realized it much later and thus was of the opinion that some of the Corinthians had unacceptably returned to paganism.[83] Paul was therefore addressing the incorrect view of the Corinthians concerning the gospel which to him tended towards paganism.[84] However, despite their acceptance of Paul's statements, the Corinthians' appeal to 'knowledge' remained typically Gnostic in form and content.[85] Thus for Schmithals the Corinthian idolatry may be traced to a pronounced Gnosticism.[86]

Schmithals is right in emphasising the Jewish aspect of the Corinthian epistles. However, his treatment of the text does not appear to be fair or justified. The text of 1 Corinthians 8–10, especially that of 1 Cor. 8.7, 9–13, speaks clearly of a situation in which some (i.e. the 'weak') in the church have had scruples over others' partaking of idol-meat. Thus, there are explicitly two groups (see above section 2, a). His suggestion that Paul was not aware of the problem and had not fully understood the Corinthians' situation is unfounded, and threatens to undermine any attempt to reconstruct the Corinthians' position.

Schmithals' extraction of 9.24–10.22 from the literary context of 8–10 and combination of 8.1–9.23 and 10.23–11.1 as one fragment lose the overall thrust of Paul's argument and are again highly questionable. In fact, 9.24 seems quite a natural flow from 9.23 as the passage (9.24–10.22) is an explanation of 9.19–23 by an analogy of athletic competition and the warning of the danger of idolatry.[87]

77. Schmithals 1971: 143.
78. Schmithals (1971: 146) explains that for the Jews γνῶσις θεοῦ would mean the knowledge of the will of God, on the basis on Hos. 6.6. However, he does not explain how the Corinthian Gnostics, who were of Jewish origin, came to speak of γνῶσις θεου= in a Hellenistic sense.
79. Schmithals 1971: 150.
80. Schmithals 1971: 143, 227.
81. Schmithals 1971: 229.
82. Schmithals 1971: 116.
83. Schmithals 1971: 225.
84. Schmithals 1971: 226.
85. Schmithals 1971: 229.
86. Schmithals 1971: 229.
87. See Conzelmann 1975: 161–62; Fee (1987: 365 n. 32; 433) for the unity of 1 Corinthians 8–10;

Schmithals' attribution of the idolatry of the 'strong' in 1 Corinthians 8–10 to a 'pronounced Gnosticism' in a Hellenistic sense is not helpful. The word γνῶσις in the context of 1 Corinthians 8–10 appears to be explicated in 1 Cor. 8.4 and we have to deduce its content from there. Besides, the γνῶσις in 1 Cor. 8.4 is about the monotheistic quality of God and the non-existence of idols. Thus, 'Jewish Gnosticism' has neither historical nor textual foundation.[88] Heinz O. Guenther has ably argued that the issue in 1 Corinthians 8–10 is not gnosis but idol-meat, and that to simply attribute the catchword 'gnosis' to Gnostics is 'ill-founded'.[89] Schmithals is right to indicate that the 'strong' are 'Jewish' in some sense (as 1 Cor. 8.4 suggests). But his general thesis is untenable and we need to explain how all three parties in Corinth can be 'Jewish' in different senses.

c. *Hellenistic Jewish philosophy*
R.A. Horsley has advocated a Hellenistic Jewish philosophy modelled after Philo and *Wisdom of Solomon*, by examining such terms as 'pneumatikos-psychikos', wisdom (Sophia), consciousness and freedom, resurrection, and gnosis in 1 Corinthians.[90] His main thesis rests on the distinction between 'pneumatikos' and 'psychikos', which he identifies as the 'perfect' and the 'child' respectively.[91] He posits that in 1 Cor. 15.44–50, the 'pneumatikoi' refers to 'heavenly persons' while 'psychikoi' refers to 'earthly persons'.[92] These two types of humanity are paradigms of different levels of religious/spiritual achievements,[93] which are seen in the Corinthians' self-designations such as 'wise', 'powerful', 'nobly born', 'kings', 'rich'.[94] These, argues Horsley, are the highest religious status established through an intimate relation with Sophia.[95] Sophia is the means, agent, and content of salvation,[96] which is found in the Hellenistic Jewish tradition (cf. Wis. 7–10; Philo, *Migr. Abr.* 28–40; *Her.* 247–83; *Poster. C.* 124–29; *Abr.* 255-76; *Virt.* 179–80; *Quaest. in Exod.* 2.39–40).[97] In order to attain such a spiritual level, one must escape from bodily matters and sensual perceptions. The Corinthians therefore see themselves as freed from all bodily pleasures as to be able to say, 'all things

and Hurd (1983: 131–42) for the detailed argument against partition theories. Most commentators seem to assume the unity of these chapters, although Weiss thinks otherwise. See below.

88.   Wilson (1972: 74) cautions against indiscriminate use of this term as it can be dangerous and misleading. Fee (1987: 365 n. 32) argues against calling the Corinthians 'Gnostics' as this is anachronistic 'since those systems do not emerge until the second century'.

89.   Guenther 1993: 55–56.

90.   Yeo (1995: 130) assumes a proto-Gnostic audience whose theology is that of Hellenistic Jewish Philonic type. Unfortunately, Yeo does not explain himself as clearly as he could have, except a few paragraphs stating more assumptions (131).

91.   Noting that Philo does not make a distinction between 'pneumatikos' and 'psychikos', Horsley looks to Philo's interpretation of Gen. 2.7 and argues for such a conclusion.

92.   Horsley 1976: 274.

93.   Horsley 1976: 278-80.

94.   Horsley 1976: 281; cf. Horsley 1977: 231 and 1980: 43.

95.   Horsley 1976: 281, 288; 1979: 46–51.

96.   Horsley 1977: 244; 1979: 48f.

97.   Horsley 1979: 48.

are possible for me' (cf. 1 Cor. 6.12; 10.23). Horsley argues that 'gnosis' is given by God to those who have attained the highest religious achievements and this 'gnosis' is the Philonic monotheism of the 'one God',[98] which provides the Corinthians a 'strong consciousness',[99] giving them the liberty/authority to freely eat idol meat. But the ignorance of this monotheistic confession equals the belief that idols are Gods.[100] Paul's response is an insistence that the effect of one's behaviour on others is the criterion for ethics,[101] which involves viewing Christ as the Sophia of God, thus allowing himself to assert and insist on the lordship of Christ to the Corinthians.[102]

Horsley's argument is quite similar to that of B.A. Pearson, who argues that the Corinthians' view of wisdom and Paul's differ. The former believe wisdom to be the attainment of a spiritual plane of existence at which they are a spiritual élite, whose terminology is found in Hellenistic Diaspora Judaism.[103] Paul's view of 'wisdom', however, is the salvific plan of God centred on the crucifixion of Christ.[104] 'Sophia' is understood as the 'Lord of glory', which comes about as a result of Hellenistic-Jewish-Christian confession of Christ as the exalted one.[105] They were interested in the exalted state of Christ on the basis of Phil. 2.9–11. Paul's concern, however, was the cross.

Horsley and Pearson are right in drawing on the Diaspora Jewish authors to clarify the situation at Corinth. The strength of their thesis is the distinction between Paul's idea and the Corinthians' idea of wisdom. By demonstrating the difference, while simultaneously showing that both parties were influenced by Hellenistic Judaism, Horsley and Pearson have opened up the possibility that similarity of background influence need not always lead to similarity of belief or practice.[106] But this understanding has a subtle weakness. And this is particularly pronounced with regard to 1 Corinthians 8–10, where Horsley hypothesizes that 'Sophia' is the content of the gnosis, which he further links to that found in 1 Corinthians 1–4. A closer examination of these two passages, however, shows that in 1 Corinthians 1–4 Paul is singularly opposed to the wisdom of the Corinthians, an opposition absent in 1 Corinthians 8–10. This contrast suggests a difference between the central ideas of the two passages.[107] Further, 'Sophia' is never an issue, nor is Christ replaced with 'Sophia' in 1 Corinthians 8–10.[108] The problem

98. Horsley 1978a: 575–76.
99. Horsley (1978a: 581) terms it interchangeably with 'inner consciousness' or 'awareness'.
100. Horsley 1978a: 576.
101. Horsley 1978a: 586.
102. Horsley 1980: 48-51.
103. Pearson 1973: 28.
104. Pearson 1973: 31.
105. Pearson 1973: 33.
106. Horsley 1998: 117.
107. See Pascuzzi (2000: 144–45) who argues against Horsley's attempt to explain the entire 1 Corinthians against one background as being 'shortsighted'.
108. Paul never once mentions in 1 Corinthians 8–10 the cross of Christ. Pearson's theory that the opponents of Paul were interested in the 'exalted state of Christ' therefore only helps to explain 1 Corinthians 1–4, 12, 15 and perhaps elsewhere, but not 8–10.

in 1 Corinthians 8–10 thus remains unresolved. Horsley's theory assumes that the 'weak' do not share the same monotheistic confession. However, not all who share the same confession would necessarily have 'strong consciousness' and be able to eat idol meat without scruples (see section 2, b, above and Chapter 4 below). Both Horsley and Pearson have not explored the possibility that all three parties, that is the 'strong', the 'weak', and Paul could well share the same belief about the 'one' God but have drawn different interpretations or conclusions about how the belief should be practised. To understand better the situation we need to look at other Jewish material to see if there are Jewish parallels to all the parties concerned in 1 Corinthians 8–10.

d. *Non-Jewish interpretation*
In the following, I will briefly summarize the central thesis of each scholar who adopts a non-Jewish interpretation of 1 Corinthians 8–10, with a similarly brief critique of each.

(i) *W.L. Willis.*
Willis argues that the earlier 'sacramental' and 'communal' interpretations of 1 Corinthians 8–10 are insufficiently proven.[109] Instead, religious 'meals' in the Graeco-Roman period were often social occasions and the gods were observers, not participants.[110] This is termed the 'social' interpretation. He concludes the following: (1) 'sacrifices and common meals were normative features of Hellenistic cults and associations'; and (2) since neither a 'sacramental' nor 'communal' interpretation is valid, in 1 Cor. 10.14–21 Paul is not warning against the dangers of pagan sacraments.[111] Hence Paul is concerned that the Corinthians not be partners with idolaters, not because of the partnership with demons the meals will effect,[112] but the effects it will have on the 'weak'.[113] Although Willis is right in pointing out the social aspects of religious meals in the Graeco-Roman setting, he fails to see that the social and religious aspects of such meals are often interwoven. Further, the fact that Paul's mention of partnership with the 'demons' is an unambiguous reference to Moses' Song in the Old Testament receives less than fair treatment from him. It is therefore not surprising that he does not consider the possibility of Jewish influence on the three parties in 1 Corinthians 8–10.[114]

---

109. Willis (1985a: 21–47) surveys extensively both literary and inscriptional sources and shows that these are not as weighty as his 'social' interpretation (47–61).
110. Willis 1985a: 20.
111. Willis 1985a: 62–64. He has five conclusions, the first two have already been mentioned, that of the invalidity of the 'sacramental' interpretation and the plausibility of the 'social' interpretation. His last conclusion includes two tangential discoveries which he concedes cannot be proven.
112. Willis 1985a: 191.
113. Willis 1985a: 184–192; 227–28.
114. See Cheung (1999: 309–11) for a strong refutation of Willis' overall thesis.

(ii) *D. Newton.*

One of Newton's aims is to listen to the Corinthians' viewpoints in 1 Corinthians 8–10, as he argues that there are ambiguities, boundary definition difficulties and conceptual differences in the ancient Graeco-Roman world of the Corinthians.[115] This results in differences of opinion, which could all be valid, not only between Paul and the Corinthians, between the Corinthians, but in all directions.[116] Paul is left with no possible solution but to shift the argument from the individualism of the Corinthians to the importance love and consideration for others.[117] While Newton's aim is to 'expose and dissect its (Corinthian situation's) underlying dynamic', his thesis seems to lean too much on the Graeco-Roman background of the Corinthian situation, while passing over the possible Jewish influence on the parties in 1 Corinthians 8–10 in almost complete silence. For example, Newton's treatment of εἴδωλα and the clause οὐδεὶς θεὸς εἰ μὴ εἷς fails to take into consideration their strong suggestion of Jewish influence. What is even more speculative is his suggestion that in 1 Corinthians 8–10 the devotion of the imperial cult is the issue. There is no clear evidence in support of this hypothesis which, moreover, is considerably weakened by the presence of the cult of Zeus in Corinth. Further, Paul's use of the Old Testament in 1 Corinthians 10 suggests familiarity with it on the part of the 'strong', whose slogan he quotes in 1 Cor. 8.4 that uses the term εἴδωλον (see below Chapter 6, section 3, b). All this further indicates Jewish influence, an area that needs investigation.

(iii) *B. Witherington III.*

In an earlier article, and later in his commentary, Witherington argues that it is doubtful whether εἰδωλόθυτον was a polemical term coined by early Jews to refer to idol meat.[118] Rather, it is a Jewish-Christian term quite possibly coined by Paul himself for the purpose of dealing with this issue.[119] Alex Cheung rightly criticizes Witherington's implicit view that Jewish attitude was irrelevant simply because the term was not used by early Jews.[120] The term, however, shares the root of εἴδωλον, which is primarily a Jewish term.[121] It was unnecessary, nor was it justified, for Witherington to make that supposition. The issue in 1 Corinthians 8–10, Witherington argues, has to do with members of different social statuses. The 'strong' were members of the well-to-do who wanted to be true Romans.[122]

115. Newton 1998: 22, 118–19.
116. Newton 1998: 22. Thus, Newton believes the issue in 1 Corinthians 8–10 is not about who is right or wrong, but about a wide spectrum of viewpoints and viable individual interpretations on Christian involvement in cultic meals.
117. Newton (1998: 276, 372–74; 379 n. 209) where he argues that Paul tried to mediate between the two parties by steering them away from individualism to community (see also 389, 393).
118. Witherington III (1993: 237–39; cf. 1995: 189) mistakenly argues that the term arose in early Christianity.
119. Witherington III 1993: 254.
120. Cheung 1999: 319. Cheung further criticizes Witherington's interpretation of the term ἱερόθυτον. See Cheung (1999: 320) for a more detailed statement.
121. See Büchsel (1964: 377–78) and Chapter 6, section 6 below.
122. Witherington III 1995: 195, 201.

By being present in pagan temples and eating idol meat, the 'strong' maintained their status. Their approach is therefore either very individualistic or very status conscious, which leads to Paul's concern about the social and moral effects of eating idol meat on the 'weak'.[123] Even though Witherington points out that v. 4 is reminiscent of the *Shema* and that v. 6 is Paul's adaptation of it,[124] he does not seem to think that the 'strong' have had Jewish influence. He maintains that the 'strong' were Gentile Christians who had read Paul's monotheistic teaching through an Epicurean lens.[125] Paul tries to correct their view by pointing out that Christian love is to be the guide to one's life and conduct. He challenges the conventions and exhorts the Corinthians to imitate him. Witherington is right to point out the possible background of the Jewish *Shema* behind 1 Cor. 8.4. However, the slogan of the 'strong' in v. 4 seems to suggest more than just an Epicurean understanding on the part of the 'strong'. The *Shema* and the term εἴδωλον both point to possible Jewish influence on the 'strong'. The scruples of the 'weak' similarly suggest that they have been influenced by the teaching of the *Shema*. Jerome H. Neyrey rightly points out that Witherington ignores the theory on the formation of 'boundaries' and fails to consider the important anthropological materials of Mary Douglas on the model of purity.[126] One may well make a connection between analysing 1 Corinthians 8–10 anthropologically and studying it in the light of Diaspora Judaism which will involve issues of purity. Witherington could at least demonstrate the kind of boundary between Jewish scruples and Gentile religious practices. His main focus, however, is that of a rhetorical reading of the Corinthian correspondence, thus missing out the important aspect and possibility of a stronger than expected Jewish influence on the parties in 1 Corinthians 8–10. We need to investigate how the parties in these chapters may have been influenced by Judaism to varying degrees.

(iv) *J. Murphy-O'Connor.*

Murphy-O'Connor's interpretation of 1 Corinthians 8–10 to some extent is similar to most of those who advocate a non-Jewish interpretation, that is, the mediation of the two factions by Paul via love.[127] He recognizes the existence of two parties. The 'strong' do not need any monotheistic arguments, nor do they need to justify their eating of idol meat.[128] In order to counter the criticism of the 'weak', they developed their slogans of 1 Cor. 8.1, 4 and 8.[129] The question arises then as to whether the 'strong' had the knowledge prior to developing their slogans. If so, what was this knowledge? Was it influenced by, or derived from, Judaism? And does it not suggest that the 'weak' were to some extent aware of what the slogans meant, which further means that the 'weak' similarly have had

---

123. Witherington III 1995: 196, 187, 200.
124. Witherington III 1995: 197–98.
125. Witherington III 1995: 188, and also his n. 9.
126. Neyrey 1997: 182.
127. Murphy-O'Connor 1978b: 556–74.
128. Murphy-O'Connor 1978b: 547; cf. 1978c: 391–96.
129. Murphy-O'Connor 1978b: 547–48.

Jewish influence? The 'weak' are Gentile Christians who have not fully imbibed their intellectual conviction of the 'one God', which Murphy-O'Connor argues is the fundamental element of Paul's preaching.[130] Murphy-O'Connor's theory is that Paul agrees with the basic position of the 'strong' but urges them to be sensitive about the social and moral reality of eating idol meat, particularly the concern for the 'weak'. Although Murphy-O'Connor rightly points out that the 'weak' have received Paul's preaching of the 'one God', he does not emphasize the fact that Paul's preaching is rooted in the Old Testament, which would mean the scruples of the 'weak' are Jewish. Nor does he discuss the possibility of Jewish influence on the 'strong'. There is again a need to consider the possibility of Jewish influence on the 'strong' and the 'weak', which the text of 1 Corinthians 8 seems to warrant.[131]

(v) *G.D. Fee.*

In both his essay and commentary, Fee consistently argues that the 'weak' are Gentile Christians.[132] Paul's concern in 1 Corinthians 8–10 is with the eating of idol meat in a pagan temple, before the idols, which Fee argues is a common Gentile practice in the Hellenistic world of the first century CE.[133] The situation in Corinth is that some Corinthian Christians have turned back to pagan temple attendance after Paul's departure from there. For Fee, the meaning of εἰδω-λόθυτον is to be found in the nature of idol-worship in pagan antiquity, not in Jewish abhorrence of it. The monotheistic statement of 1 Cor. 8.4 is for Fee the teaching of Paul and is therefore Jewish-Christian monotheism.

Throughout, Fee does not think that Jewish influence on the 'strong' and the 'weak' might be an important factor. Yet, in 1 Cor. 8.4, the slogan of the 'strong' resembles more the *Shema* rather than Paul's teaching, given the fact that Paul almost immediately corrects or modifies it with the inclusion of Christ (cf. 1 Cor. 8.6). Further, Fee's attribution of εἰδωλόθυτα to Hellenistic idol-worship appears unconvincing, given that ἱερόθυτα was the term used by pagans in referring to sacrificial food. Fee rightly points out that Paul's single concern in 1 Cor. 10.1–13 is to warn the Corinthians using Israel's history, not elaborate on her idolatry.[134] But this only serves to suggest that the 'strong' had knowledge of the Jewish scripture, which further implies Jewish influence. Fee argues that the 'weak' failed in their 'conscience' not because of Jewish scruples but because of pagan temple attendance.[135] However, if the 'weak' had been Gentiles, what then informed their belief? Could it not be Jewish scruples, since Paul would have preached with much of his teaching based on the Jewish scripture, as he does in 1 Cor. 10.1–13? And could it not be possible that the 'weak' have had Jewish

---

130. Murphy-O'Connor 1978b: 545.

131. Gooch (1993: 152) is right to criticize Murphy-O'Connor for not taking into consideration Paul's warning against the danger of participating in the table of demons, and his reference to the Israelites' examples in 1 Corinthians 10.

132. Fee 1980: 189; 1987: 370 n. 7.

133. Fee 1980: 184–85.

134. Fee 1980: 185–86.

135. Fee 1980: 189.

influence that caused them to have scruples about idol meat? And if Jews have been found to practise idolatry (see Chapter 4 below), does this mean that we cannot make conclusive statements about the ethnicity of the parties involved? This is a question that we will have to explore further below.

(vi) *P.D. Gooch.*
Gooch argues that idol food was a problem for Paul, who urged it as a problem for the Corinthians.[136] He argues that Paul advocates the exclusive allegiance to Yahweh by urging avoidance of any participation in idolatrous rites, including the eating of idol food.[137] To achieve this goal, Paul created a hypothetical 'weak' group and urged the Corinthians to consider this group.[138] Having surveyed the social importance of meals in the Graeco-Roman world, Gooch concludes that most of these meals would have involved religious rites. It was difficult to avoid such meals as they were means to maintain social relationships.[139] Paul's prohibition therefore created tremendous difficulties for the Corinthian Christians.

There are two kinds of eating which Paul prohibits: eating in contexts that effect partnership with demons and thus break partnership with the Lord; and eating that results in the breaking of others' partnership with the Lord.[140]

Gooch has rightly pointed out the twin concern of Paul and argued persuasively the reasons for Paul's prohibitions. However, his thesis works only because he treats the 'weak' as a hypothetical group. This has been dealt with in section 2 above. Like other scholars who adopt a non-Jewish, Hellenistic interpretation of 1 Corinthians 8–10, Gooch does not consider the possible Jewish influence on the 'strong' and the 'weak'.

The majority of the above scholars are inclined towards the idea of Paul mediating between the two parties, with the primary aim of discouraging the 'strong' from eating idol meat. This is somewhat similar to the rhetorical studies which argue that in 1 Corinthians 8–10 Paul is trying to reconcile the two parties. Among the more notable are Mitchell, and recently Yeo.[141] Little attention has been paid to the possible Jewish influence on the two parties. We will need to look at this aspect of Jewish influence and see if there are parallels to the positions of these parties in 1 Corinthians 8–10.

e. *Social/economic interpretation*

(i) *G. Theissen.*
In his various essays collected in *The Social Setting of Pauline Christianity*, Theissen posits that there is internal stratification among the Corinthians that

---

136. Gooch 1993: 61-72.
137. Gooch 1993: 129.
138. Gooch 1993: 66-68.
139. Gooch 1993: 27-46.
140. Gooch 1993: 75-78.
141. Mitchell 1991; Yeo 1995. Yeo's work is basically an effort to draw from Paul's strategy to inform a cross-cultural Chinese hermeneutic. His work assumes too much what the term 'Chinese' entails, which considerably weakens his argument.

divides the Corinthians into the lower and the upper classes, of which the lower-class members formed the majority of the church.[142] This is based in part on Paul's statement in 1 Cor. 1.26 which Theissen argues shows the 'wise, power-ful, nobly born' are of sociological significance.[143] The divisions in the church are the result of different social strata that bring with them various interests, customs and assumptions. Thus the 'socially strong' and the 'socially weak' differ on issues such as the Lord's Supper, idol meat, civil litigation among members and such like.

With the above ideas set out, Theissen then identifies the 'strong' and the 'weak' of 1 Corinthians 8–10 with the 'socially strong' and the 'socially weak' of 1 Cor. 1.26. The 'strong' were exposed to a variety of meats by virtue of their high social status, thus they had no scruples over idol meat. They were in fact former Gentile God-fearers sympathetic to Judaism while the 'weak' were the former Gentiles or Jews who had been accustomed to idols and thus would eat idol meat with a guilty conscience.[144]

Paul, according to Theissen, does not object to the basic position of the 'strong'. But at the same time he sees a need to mediate between the two parties by suggesting that the 'strong' accommodate the 'weak' on the basis of love and respect, while the 'weak' should respond to the 'strong' in subordination, fidelity and esteem. Theissen calls this 'primitive Christian love-patriarchalism'.[145] This sociological approach to 1 Corinthians 8–10 creates a situation in which all the parties involved in the dispute could resolve the main contention without anyone 'losing out'. The 'strong' could continue to eat idol-meat without losing the submission from the 'weak'. The 'weak', on the other hand, could reap benefits from the 'strong', not only in areas of perhaps social protection but also wealth and food. This also means the preservation of the ecclesiastical unity within the Corinthian church. Thus Paul too would not 'lose' the church to internal division as a result of the consumption of idol-meat.

This has been well received among scholars and is now termed as the 'new consensus'.[146] But Theissen's theory of internal stratification assumes that it was the issue of 'class differences' that resulted in most of the problems in Corinth. On the consumption of idol-meat in chs. 8–10, the class differences would have played out in this way: the 'strong' had access to meats, particularly fresh meats not only because of their wealth but also because of their connections to other high-status members of the society; while the 'weak' had not because of the lack

---

142. Theissen 1982: 69.
143. Theissen 1982: 71–72.
144. Theissen 1982: 102–104, 138. Theissen's basic thesis has won a number of followers, notably Meeks (1983: 68–70), Clarke (1993), Martin (1995), and Horrell (1996). All of these scholars make use of Theissen's thesis to draw different theses of their own. Meeks seeks to illuminate the situation of the 'first urban Christians', Clarke looks at the idea of 'secular' and 'Christian' leaderships and compares the two, Martin looks at the conflict between Paul and the 'strong' as arising from their different body ideologies, and Horrell seeks to show that Paul is using the Pauline 'symbolic order' with its centre as the cross of Christ to invert the values and status of the dominant social order.
145. Theissen 1982: 107. See also Theissen (2001: 65).
146. See, however, Theissen (2001: 66–68)

of finance and social connections to wealthy people.[147] Yet a closer look at 1 Corinthians 8–10 shows Paul's concern to be that of participation in idolatry, its consequences, and its implications on the 'weak'. And it does appear that 1 Corinthians 8–10 seems to suggest that the 'strong' and 'weak' of Corinth do interact to some degree, which indicates to us that the 'perceived' class differences might not have been a factor in Paul's discussion in 1 Corinthians 8–10.[148] Further, as we will see in Chapter 5 below, Paul seems to believe that idolatry has the potential of incurring God's wrath and so causing the loss of one's eschatological salvation. And Theissen's theory does not resolve this issue.

Theissen's interpretion of the Corinthian situation in general and 1 Corinthians 8–10 in particular has not gone unchallenged. Recently, Meggitt has ably put this theory under scrutiny and considerably challenged it. It is necessary to look at Meggitt's critical evaluation of Theissen.

(ii) *J. Meggitt.*

Meggitt has challenged the so called 'new consensus' in his book, *Paul, Poverty and Survival*, and argued that there are no social divisions of the 'élite' and 'non-élite'.[149] Instead, the Pauline communities 'shared fully in the bleak material existence that was the lot of the non-élite inhabitants of the Empire'.[150] His argument against Theissen's analysis cannot be examined here in full, except in relation to 1 Corinthians 8–10. On the parties in 1 Corinthians 8–10, Meggitt objects to Theissen's theory for the reason that (1) there is no evidence of the party of the 'strong' in 1 Corinthians 8–10; and (2) it is problematic to see the use of the word ἀσθενής in 1 Corinthians 1 as determinative of its meaning seven chapters later.[151] He does not rule out the possibility that the 'weak' of 1 Cor. 1.27 may be identical to the 'weak' of 1 Corinthians 8–10, although the association is less certain. However, if we allow the existence of the 'weak', we would need to consider who the others are who do not belong to the 'weak'. This has been set out above (see section 2, a, above). Meggitt provides no alternative.

Theissen has argued that the knowledge of the 'strong' is class-specific and that their 'gnosis' demands high intellect which required a high education, which Meggitt criticizes as ambiguous and weak.[152] Indeed, the 'knowledge' of the 'strong' seems to be religious and, as Meggitt rightly points out, is seen through 'a handful of rather clichéd slogans'.[153] What is even more important is Meggitt's criticism of Theissen's claim that 'a soteriology of knowledge' is also a class-specific trait. This idea roots 'salvation' in the saving power of discernment and,

---

147. Meggitt (1998: 111–12) has demonstrated from literary evidence that the 'non-élite' had equal access to meats at many cookshops and wine shops.

148. Meggitt (1998: 112–13) makes a similar observation, though within the context of 1 Cor. 10.27ff.

149. Meggitt 1998: 100–53.

150. Meggitt 1998: 153.

151. Meggitt 1998: 107–108.

152. Meggitt 1998: 114.

153. Meggitt 1998: 114.

for the 'strong', it is the knowledge that 'idols do not exist'.[154] Meggitt shows that different 'salvation cults' not only attracted the wealthy, but the poor as well.[155] Futher, his refutation of Theissen's notion of élite self-consciousness as misguided shows that spiritual élitism could be found among the non-élites. And this point is clearly seen in the scruples of the 'weak' over the consumption of idol-meat. Thus Meggitt demonstrates the inadaquacy of Theissen's overall thesis that there the 'strong' were the social élites while the 'weak' were the socially poor. Theissen's work neither addresses the question of idolatry and theology in 1 Corinthians 8–10 nor the question of authority (see Chapter 6) as an issue in the resolution of the problem.

Although Meggitt's work has raised many questions about Theissen's work, his division of the population in first-century Graeco-Roman world into two groups of 1 per cent élite and 99 per cent of destitute is not helpful in resolving the problems raised in 1 Corinthians.[156] With regard to 1 Corinthians 8–10, Meggitt's suggestion that meats were readily available to the non-élites of Graeco-Roman society would have difficulty explaining 1 Cor. 8.10, where Paul says that the 'weak' might be encouraged to eat idol-meat because of the attendance of the 'strong' at Gentile temples. For if the non-élites had ready access to meats, they would not have to resort to eating idol-meat. But more fundamentally, while the socio-economic explanation provides one possible perspective to some of Paul's statements in 1 Corinthians 8–10, the question of Jewish scruples, Christian theology, and the interaction between various views have not been adequately discussed, and must be addressed. In other words, if indeed the accessibility to meats was not an issue, then the question of the consumption of idol-meat might well be related to questions of theology and idolatry.[157]

Even if we grant that Theissen's social explanation of the differences between the two groups will work, which does not as Meggitt shows, it would have provided the sociological aspect only, without the aspects of Jewish influence on the parties involved. Although Theissen is right to indicate that there could be Jewish influence on both groups, he does not develop this aspect and we need to indicate how this could be, or to use Theissen's words, that is, what sorts of 'accommodated' and 'non-accommodated' Judaism are present? We will now turn to look at some works which advocate Jewish influence in 1 Corinthians 8–10.

---

154. Theissen 1982: 135.

155. See Meggitt (1998: 115) for details.

156. This dichotomy is particularly challenged by Martin (2001: 51–64) who also accuses Meggitt of various flaws such as methodological oversimplification, misrepresenting other scholars, erroneous handling of ancient sources and the like. This has been given a robust response from Meggitt (2001: 87–91). I agree with Meggitt that Theissen's response is richer and, I would add, weightier.

157. Although Theissen (1982: 122–23) does qualify himself that different convictions about 'humanity, the world, and God' are at the root of different human behaviour, and that a sociological analysis does not reduce such a 'theological quarrel' to mere social factors, his conviction is that such a conflict can and ought to be interpreted sociologically. This working presupposition is not an issue here; but the issue is how eventually the question of theology is addressed.

f. *Paul's position as Jewish or influenced by the Decree*

(i) *J.C. Hurd.*

Hurd posits that there is not a 'weak' party in the Corinthian church.[158] Paul is addressing the whole church and in 1 Corinthians 8–10 he lays down two prohibitions: (1) do not offend the weaker Christians; and (2) do not practise idolatry. The 'weak' were created hypothetically for Paul's own argument.[159]

Hurd sees the issue of 1 Corinthians 8–10 as arising from changes in Paul's own position. The prohibition of idol meat was not part of Paul's original teaching, as the Decree was not yet formulated.[160] Paul sent the regulations of the Decree to the Corinthians in his previous letter, which generated strong reactions from the Corinthians who charged that Paul was not being consistent. According to Hurd, Paul had accepted the Decree in order to win the recognition of the Jerusalem apostles, but remained silent about it in 1 Corinthians 8–10 because the mention of the Decree would undermine his hold over the Corinthian church.

Hurd's suggestion that Paul's position has been influenced by the Decree does not explain why Paul argues so strongly and vehemently against idolatry. Besides, the rigour in his argument concerning his authority in 1 Corinthians 9 does not suggest that he is trying to win the recognition of the Jerusalem apostles. In fact, he appears quite independent in asserting his apostolic authority. The entire argument of 1 Corinthians 8–10 gives the impression that Paul has the conviction of scripture, rather than the influence of the Decree. Paul's position could well be informed by his previous training in the Jewish scripture, albeit with new interpretations in the light of Christological insights.[161] Hurd seems to think that the Corinthians are ethnically Gentile. However, he does not address the possibility of Jewish influence on the 'strong', seen in their slogan of the 'one God' and use of the term εἴδωλον in 1 Cor. 8.4. It must be affirmed, though, that he is right that there is Jewish influence on Paul. We need to look at how the other two parties may have Jewish influence.

(ii) *J. Weiss.*

Weiss posits that 1 Corinthians 8 and 10.23–11.1 belong to a later letter, while 1 Cor. 10.1-22 constitutes part of Paul's previous letter mentioned in 1 Cor. 5.9-13. In the previous letter, Paul took a vehement stance against idolatry, which was shared by the 'weak', as a result of his Jewish superstition.[162] For Weiss, there are two groups whom Paul addresses. In 1 Corinthians 8 and 10.23–11.1, Paul has abandoned his fear of demons and now advocated that eating itself is morally indifferent. Thus Paul is taking the stance of the 'strong' in this letter. Where he appears to oppose the 'strong', it is for the sake of the 'weak', not because he thinks idolatry is dangerous.[163]

---

158. Hurd 1983: 147.
159. Hurd 1983: 148. See section 2 above.
160. Hurd 1983: 261.
161. See Gooch 1993: 141.
162. Weiss 1910: 264.
163. Weiss 1910: 212, 264.

Weiss' partition of 1 Corinthians 8–10 has been challenged variously and no longer appears convincing.[164] However, his suggestion that Paul had, in his previous letter, commanded against idol meat because of his Jewish scruples might help to illuminate 1 Corinthians 8–10. If Paul had shared the position of the 'weak' before, it would mean the 'weak' had had Jewish influence. This idea might illuminate our understanding of the 'weak': in what way were the 'weak' Jewish in their scruples? And if 1 Corinthians 8 and 10.23–11.1 represent Paul's liberation from Jewish superstition, what does that say about the 'strong', given their belief in the 'one God' and the non-existence of idols? We need to see in what way all parties here might be Jewish.

(iii) *P.J. Tomson.*

Tomson's thesis rests on his assumption that Paul is operating within a halakhic framework and tradition, and therefore teaches a 'rational, halakhic definition' of what constitutes idolatry and what does not.[165] Thus, unlike scholars who argue that Paul was inconsistent, Tomson argues from ancient Jewish idolatry laws and early Christian attitudes that it is unlikely Paul would condone eating idol meat.[166] Throughout, Tomson seeks to see Paul and explicate 1 Corinthians 8–10 in the context of Paul's Jewish Pharisaic background. The 'strong' have γνῶσις which allows them to eat idol meat. This γνῶσις, according to Tomson, is lacking in the 'weak' who are pagans.

Tomson is right to posit that Jewish theology lies behind Paul's teaching in 1 Corinthians 8–10, with different implications/practical conclusions drawn. However, his thesis is too heavily dependent on the Tannaitic halakha and therefore has not fully explored Paul's Christian convictions and how they impinge on his position. Further, the use of later rabbinic halakha to explain Paul runs the risk of anachronism, a point that has been noted by Cheung.[167] Is this geographically and chronologically appropriate?

While there are clear Jewish influences on Paul and, I shall argue below, on the parties involved, would it be possible for us to explore the possible Jewish parallels to the positions of the two parties, the 'weak' and the 'strong' in 1 Corinthians 8–10, by looking at the Diaspora? There are at least two advantages for doing this. First, the Corinthian church is a Diaspora community itself. Are there parallels to their behaviour regarding idol meat? Second, we have evidence of Jews living everywhere in the Mediterranean. Their survival depends to a large extent on how they interacted with their Gentile surroundings. But this also suggests that it might be possible for us to find Jewish parallels to the behaviour of the two parties.

---

164. Cf. Hurd 1983: 131–42; Gooch 1993: 138; and Cheung 1999: 85.
165. Tomson 1990: 217.
166. Tomson 1990: 151–86.
167. Cheung 1999: 307.

(iv) *A. Cheung.*

Cheung's basic thesis is that idol food is dangerous if, and only if, it is identified as such. This thesis is based on his argument that Paul's primary authority for his prohibition against idol food is the Jewish scripture, although Cheung also recognizes the possibility of the background of other Jewish works.[168] He further finds support for his thesis in the interpretations of Paul by early Christian authors.[169] Throughout his work, Cheung is concerned to show that Paul is Jewish in his attitude towards idol food, thus categorically arguing against Barrett and others.[170]

Cheung is certainly right to look at the Jewish scripture for the background of Paul's attitude. But this research agenda of his reflects an assumption of Judaism – Jews always reject idolatry – and a similar assumption about the 'weak' as Gentiles.[171] This assumption is unnecessary and, as I shall show below (Chapter 4), there is evidence that Jews in the Diaspora did not always abstain from idolatry. What 1 Corinthians 8–10 shows is that all the parties seem to have had Jewish influence to varying degrees. And we need to investigate this important question of the Jewish influence in 1 Corinthians 8–10.

4. *Summary and Conclusion*

We have looked at the textual evidence for two groups in 1 Corinthians 8–10 and concluded that there are indeed two parties of the 'strong' and the 'weak', contrary to Hurd and Gooch. We have also looked at the question of the identities of these two groups and shown that while it is possible to identify the opinions and practice of these groups, it is not possible to determine their ethnicity – the groups could all be Jewish. If this tentative hypothesis were to be proven plausible, which will be discussed in the following chapters, then it suggests that Judaism is not so simple as most scholars made it out to be. One of my tasks in this chapter was to survey the scholarly interpretations of 1 Corinthians 8–10, with particular focus on their view of the 'strong' and the 'weak'. We have looked at these in a thematic fashion and found that all parties in 1 Corinthians 8–10 have been identified as 'Jewish' in different ways and to varying degrees. And scholars who proposed a non-Jewish interpretation have not denied the presence of any Jewish influence, but merely looked at the Graeco-Roman background of dining. What is lacking is the attention that should have been paid to the explicitly Jewish slogans of the 'strong'.

There are various ways of looking at this phenomenon. All the parties, namely, Paul, the 'weak' and the 'strong', may be Jewish but not all hold to the same opinion about the 'one God' and the idols. For example, Paul says in 1 Cor. 8.7 that not all share the same view of the 'strong'. Even if all parties hold a similar opinion on the 'one God', not all of them may believe the same about the

---

168. Cheung 1999: 31–81.
169. Cheung 1999: 177–277.
170. Cheung 1999: 76–81.
171. Cheung 1999: 22 n. 20.

idols or the pagan gods. Even if they share similar beliefs about the idols as being non-existent, they need not adopt the same practice. Thus, for example, the 'strong' have no scruples about attending pagan temples and eating idol meat. But the 'weak' have difficulty with such a practice. As will be discussed below (Chapter 3), the position of the 'weak' seems to reflect Jewish opinion about idols, which gives them the scruples regarding eating idol meat. But the 'strong' adopt a completely opposite behaviour – they freely eat idol meat because of the belief that idols are non-existent. Similarly, Paul seems to believe in the non-existence of idols, but he continues to believe in the reality of demons. And he will not allow his behaviour to give room to any possible partnership with these demons.

There is a wide spectrum of views/practices among the Jews themselves. And this will imply that Judaism is to some extent multifaceted and we therefore cannot oversimplify Judaism by adopting a viewpoint that makes Judaism conform to one strand of view/practice.

The purpose and rationale of my book is to examine the issue of idolatry and authority in 1 Corinthians 8–10 by looking at the Jewish Diaspora communities and establishing parallels to the behaviour of the parties in these chapters. And in the process, I hope to show that the parties are all 'Jewish' in varying ways but differ in their practices. Thus, in the next chapter, we will look first at the examples of idolatry in the LXX (Chapter 2), using the model or definitions found in M. Halbertal and A. Margalit's *Idolatry*.[172] From here, we will move to examine the reactions of representative Diaspora Jewish authors against idolatry (Chapter 3). This will illuminate the position of the parties in 1 Corinthians 8–10 in which idols are said to be οὐδὲν ἐν κόσμῳ (cf. 8.4). While Chapter 3 will draw out the reactions to idolatry, Chapter 4 will be a discussion of Jews' accommodation to idolatry. I will look at the Jewish inscriptions and papyri, in addition to other Jewish authors, to survey these examples of idolatrous behaviour. This will set up parallels to the practice/behaviour of the 'strong' in eating idol meat as seen in 1 Corinthians 8–10.

These chapters will pave the way to a contrast between the positions of the 'strong' and Paul regarding idolatry: the 'strong' argue for the neutrality of food based on their theology, and adopt a non-traditional practice; but Paul sees eating idol meat in an idol temple as equivalent to entry into a partnership with the 'demons' (Chapter 5). Paul's position will be presented as one that is Jewish but modified with a Christian perspective that underpins his argument throughout.

One of the main aims of my work is to look at the question of authority, which is closely linked to idolatry – who decides what is idolatrous behaviour and what is not? The final chapter (6) will focus on 1 Corinthians 9 which, I will argue, fulfils Paul's double purpose of defending/re-affirming his apostolic authority and setting himself as an example to the 'strong', using precisely the authority that he has just re-affirmed. Because the law no longer functions as a 'final court of appeal' for a Diaspora church like the Corinthian church, the basis

172. Halbertal and Margalit 1992.

for authority and for what is distinctively Christian action will have to be found elsewhere. And it is here in 1 Corinthians 9 that Paul provides this basis. I will conclude the book with answers to our questions raised in this first chapter, offer a fresh approach to Paul's ethics, and draw implications for historical reconstruction of ancient Judaism and early Christianity as they relate to idolatry.

Chapter 2

IDOLATRY: DEFINITIONS AND PATTERNS

1. *Introduction*

Chapter 1 shows that while scholars have argued for different interpretations of 1 Cor. 8.1–11.1, there remains a need to explain how all three parties in the passage may be Jewish and how these positions may be illuminated by comparison with Diaspora Judaism.

Although discussions on idolatry almost always assume some kind of definition, none of the scholars surveyed in Chapter 1 has defined idolatry in a comprehensive way.[1] But the issue of idolatry is a subjective one – different people will define idolatry differently and thus practise according to what they think is or is not idolatry.[2] For example, does eating idol-meat constitute idolatry? Or does idolatry take place only when such eating involves actual idols? Thus, is a monotheist, who only views eating idol-meat but not visits to pagan temples as idolatry, committing idolatry when he or she conducts business transactions at a pagan temple? Similarly, a person may not think that eating idol-meat constitutes idolatry, only if one worships an idol. But to others who do not think so, that person is idolatrous.[3] Even within the Jewish tradition, idolatry does not seem to be a clearly defined category (see below). This shows that there is no single definition of idolatry. In order to understand the issues concerning idolatry, a multifaceted set of definitions will need to be established. Such definitions are important as they will enable us to identify what we are looking for in the texts we examine, and also to understand why some Jews accommodated to idolatry while others found it objectionable (see further Chapter 4 below).

Although Halbertal and Margalit's work, *Idolatry* (1992), spans across a much wider Jewish terrain and historical period, it draws from the biblical motifs and employs them philosophically to analyse the question of idolatry. And because their work looks at idolatry from a multifaceted perspective, it serves as a useful

---

1. To my mind, the one scholar who has pointed in the right direction is Derek Newton. His point that the passage of 1 Cor. 8.1–11.1 is complex with ambiguity, boundary definition difficulties and conceptual differences in opinion shows the need for a proper definition of idolatry (see Newton 1998: 21–23).

2. Newton (1998: 22) points out that 'the whole church in Corinth represented its multiple views to Paul', and rightly says, 'We cannot assume that the Corinthians held the same concepts and boundaries as Paul with regard to such concepts as idolatry, worship and Christianity' (1998: 23).

3. Batnitzky (2000: 3) rightly shows, from a modern philosophical perspective, how 'idolatry' as one religious category can be so diversely defined.

critical tool for understanding the Jewish texts on idolatry. Thus, I will employ their analysis and apply it to the discussion of idolatry in the base Jewish text, that is, the Septuagint. Because the LXX serves as the base Diaspora text for the Diaspora Jews, the discussion of idolatry in this text will enable us to trace the patterns of thought on idolatry which are at work here. The discussion will also enable us to understand how different Jews might interpret the LXX differently, when we look at the other Jewish texts later.[4]

In the subsequent discussion of other Jewish texts, inscriptions and papyri, we will continue to examine the issue of idolatry using the critical analysis as set out in Halbertal and Margalit's work. Thus, the task here must begin with an overview of Halbertal and Margalit's critical analysis.

2. *An Analysis of Idolatry: Halbertal and Margalit (1992)*

In their book *Idolatry*, Halbertal and Margalit address the central question – what is idolatry and why is it viewed as an unspeakable sin? What they are interested in are the various models of this concept in the monotheistic religions, especially in Judaism.[5] They look at the different concepts of idolatry by looking at the different models. This is done by looking also at the different concepts of God, for these concepts create different concepts of idolatry when reversed.

The sin of idolatry is first of all seen in the framework of anthropomorphic concepts of God through the biblical metaphor of marriage relationships. This is because the marriage relationships are exclusive and therefore provide a useful explanation for the sin of idolatry. The marriage metaphors are used to describe the relationship between Israel and Yahweh.[6] For example, the marriage metaphor in Hosea provides a description of the relationship between Israel and her God as one in which Israel as the wife has been 'unfaithful' to her husband, God (cf. Hos. 1.2; 2.9–11, 14–15).[7] What is involved is a 'jealous' God whose wife has 'betrayed' him. Such 'betrayal' is viewed as such because of God's 'jealousy', which has two sides to it: (1) Israel's 'betrayal' or 'unfaithfulness' constitutes a threat to his power; and (2) Israel's idolatry means humiliation for God. 'Unfaithfulness' or 'betrayal' defines idolatry when *another god or an alien cult other than Yahweh is worshipped*, which may also be seen as a form of 'rebellion'. In this case, the breach of the covenant would be viewed as idolatry.

Another aspect of idolatry concerns the ways God is represented. Not only is the worship of other gods forbidden, but *the representation of God by means of a statue or picture is also banned*. There are basically three types of representation:[8] (1) similarity-based representation, which refers to the representation of one thing by another because it is similar to it; (2) causal-metonymic representation, which refers not to a relation of similarity but a relationship of possession;

---

4.   One example is Josephus' use of Numbers 25 incident (see Chapter 3, section 4, b below).
5.   Halbertal and Margalit 1992: 1.
6.   Halbertal and Margalit 1992: 9–36.
7.   Halbertal and Margalit 1992: 11–23.
8.   Halbertal and Margalit 1992: 38–66.

for example a handkerchief of someone represents him/her not because it resembles him/her but because it belongs to him/her;[9] and (3) convention-based representation, which refers to the convention that permits something to be so called. For example, a cup is called a cup without (1) and (2) but because there is a convention that allows the word 'cup' to represent the physical object. The issue of representation arises with regard to the definition of idolatry through *misrepresenting* God by means of an object, or by treating the gods/demons as if they were the true God, thus confusing God with them. The second commandment explicitly prohibits representing God at all with an image (cf. Exod. 20.3–4). Since God cannot be represented, any physical representation of God will be viewed as an act of idolatry.[10]

Conventional representation in the sense of linguistic representation is permitted in the biblical tradition. However, there is a fine line between linguistic representation and similarity-based representation of God, that is, between speaking of God as a mighty king and drawing a picture of him as such. Although there are various arguments in favour of linguistic representation, Maimonides developed a strong objection that linguistic representations can be even more dangerous because they state propositions and make judgements. Thus, the distinction between these two types of representation should be abolished.

There is another view, that is, that the 'Torah speaks in the language of the people'.[11] This view rejects the types of representation mentioned above. It sees the Torah as speaking in the language in which the people have been brought up and taught. However, this view of language raises the question of the limitations of language in describing God. Further, there is always the danger that the use of language will distort, rather than accurately describe, the true God, since human language is limited and humans on their own do not know anything positive about God. This further raises the question of the appropriateness of a particular representation, be it linguistic, anthropomorphic, or otherwise.

There are two aspects to the problem of anthropomorphism: (1) does it provide an erroneous picture of God? And (2) does it provide a disrespectful and inappropriate picture of God? This leads to the cognitive level of idolatry.

Idolatry is here defined in terms of *cognitive error*. In this error, one internalizes idolatrous beliefs so that even though one may worship in a monotheistic setting, one is still an idolater.[12] In other words, the concept of idolatry is being transferred from the performance of alien ritual worship to *harbouring alien beliefs*.

---

9. Metonymic representation appears to be permitted in the biblical tradition as can be seen in the Old Testament such as the Temple and all that is in it, such as the Holy of Holies, the Ark of the Covenant, etc.

10. Halbertal and Margalit 1992: 45–49. Such representations are less likely to lead to any false conception of God. However, false conception of God can take place when one equates, for example, the Ark of the Covenant as powerful as if it were God himself. Thus, the issue is with *misrepresentation* of God.

11. Halbertal and Margalit 1992: 54–62.

12. Halbertal and Margalit 1992: 109.

This is explained as 'mental internalization', which 'refers to a description of the deity that uses mental expressions in a literal sense'.[13]

Another aspect of cognitive error is found in *false worship and false belief*. False worship may be defined in terms of 'wrong' kinds of action, that is, the action that renders to the true God what is meant for pagan gods or alien cults. False belief is closely linked to false worship – it precedes false worship. This leads to imagination, which Halbertal and Margalit define in terms of what provides us with objects for the error of false belief. But false belief and imagination further give rise to a lack of abstraction.

The lack of abstraction, it is argued, forces people to conceive of God in observable terms. And observable terms provide the potential for error. In view of the above, that is, false belief, imagination and lack of abstraction, *the question of intention* becomes an important factor in defining idolatry. For whom one intends the worship indicates whether it is idolatry; what kind of worship one intends for the true God also plays a part. In other words, if a worshipper intends the right kind of worship to the wrong god (or alien cult), it is considered idolatry. Similarly, if one intends the wrong kind of worship to the true God, it is equally considered to be idolatry.[14] This leads us to the question of what or who constitutes the 'right' or 'wrong' God.

Halbertal and Margalit argue that no description of God is adequate and that the 'right' God can only be identified through his proper name. The identification of the 'right' God is made impossible if we take Maimonides' view that any description of God will be false. However, if we take G.E. Moore's causal condition as the criterion, then tradition will guarantee the conception of the 'right' God' by the 'shared form of worship, and by the worshiper's intent to worship the God of his fathers'.[15]

The identification of the 'right' God leads to the question of idolatrous practice. The practice of idolatry may be simply the worship of any object other than God. But at times, it involves certain ways (methods) of worshipping God. In defining wrong worship, Halbertal and Margalit point out that the perspective of a practical definition of idolatry, based on the method of worship, means that there is a shift from the cognitive error to the practice of worship that 'regards every deviation from the accepted method of worship as a form of idolatry, even if it is God himself who is being worshipped'.[16] This perspective means that a form of worship can still be idolatrous even if no idol or false god is involved. This means it is necessary to answer the question, *what is worship*? Do those who forbid the worship of other gods deny their existence, or do they admit their existence but forbid their worship?

The issue for the monotheists is that there can be only the worship of one God. What constitutes 'correct' worship may be gleaned from the Old Testament incident of the golden calf. The story shows that the basic difference between idol

13.   Halbertal and Margalit 1992: 110.
14.   For a more in-depth discussion of 'intention', see Halbertal and Margalit 1992: 202–209.
15.   Halbertal and Margalit 1992: 162.
16.   Halbertal and Margalit 1992: 181.

worshippers and the worshippers of God is the difference in the method of worship. And it appears that while the Israelites in the wilderness did not worship an alien cult, they had misrepresented Yahweh with the image of a calf. Thus, one's intention of worshipping God may be acceptable but one's method may not.

The final issue dealt with by Halbertal and Margalit is that of idolatry and political authority.[17] They argue that religious language is filled with metaphors of political sovereignty describing God and his people. This is even more so in the biblical tradition where the covenant between God and Israel is perceived as that between a king and his vassals.

In contrast to the marital metaphor, in a political metaphor God is the king to whom his people must yield total loyalty. What is God's relationship to the system of human dominion? Is political loyalty to God so exclusive that any other political loyalty is considered a betrayal and thus idolatry? This limits the potential for establishing human political institutions. Israel under Samuel no longer could continue living under the burden of a holy political sovereignty so that they demanded a king. In fact, the failure of the prophets in their politics is precisely because of the uncompromising requirement of the exclusive heavenly sovereignty of God. The exclusivity of this political leadership of God was waived by God when Israel demanded a king (cf. 1 Sam. 8.6). But such a waiver was 'conditional on both the king and the people understanding that they are still subject to God and that the king is nothing but an agent: …'.[18] Thus, 1 Sam. 8.7-8 shows that even though there may be a king in Israel, he is only to be an agent, and that any rejection of a political leadership is in fact a rejection of God. And this rejection is compared to Israel's rejection of God and worship of other gods in the wilderness (v. 8). Thus the *failure to recognize the sovereignty of God*, that is, failure to be loyal to God, constitutes another definition of idolatry.

a. *Summary*
The above analysis enables us to see idolatry in two broad categories, namely, *the worship of other gods or alien cult*, and *misrepresenting*, or *dishonouring God (Yahweh)*. These two can take place simultaneously or independently.

(i) *Worship of other gods or alien cults.*
There are two further aspects of this first category. (1) The first aspect is 'unfaithfulness' in which idolatry is seen through the metaphor of the marriage relationship, which describes Israel or the people of God as the wife and God as the husband. Idolatry takes place when Israel turns away from God to other gods just as an unfaithful wife turns away from her husband to other men. It is therefore a form of rebellion against the true God. And since the true God always remains true, such 'unfaithfulness' would also also be a form of 'betrayal'. An example is Israel's worship of the Baal.

17.   Halbertal and Margalit 1992: 214–35.
18.   Halbertal and Margalit 1992: 219.

(2) The second aspect within the first category is disregarding ancestral customs and tradition. In the case of Israel, the breach of the covenant with God will be seen as a form of idolatry. Israelite religion is an ancestral tradition in the sense that it began as a family belief which gradually grew to become institutionalized, climaxing in the written code of the Torah. The belief was then passed down from one generation to another serving as a norm for each successive generation's individual as well as communal life and practice. The central motif of this tradition is embedded in the covenant, which is expressed in and through the Law given by Moses. And the tradition is accepted as being given by the one true God, therefore any act of worship that contradicts the ancestral tradition is deemed idolatrous.

(ii) *Misrepresenting/dishonouring God (Yahweh).*
The second broad category is that of *misrepresenting*, or *dishonouring* the true God (Yahweh). Under this category, idolatry may be defined in two ways. First, visually, that is, by representing God with an object. Thus, any effort in trying to represent God physically or visually by any form will be deemed idolatrous. An example of misrepresenting God visually is the golden calf event in Exodus 32.

The second definition is on the cognitive level. While idolatry has often been thought of as building and worshipping an idol, it in fact can happen without necessarily having an idol. The understanding of idolatry as cognitive error identifies three areas in which idolatry takes place. (1) One area refers to the 'wrong' kind of worship, which can be further defined in two ways. (a) The first is by intention. When a person worships the true God but with a wrong intention, that is, mentally the person has in mind some other gods, idolatry has taken place.[19] (b) The second is by action. A person may worship God with all the right conceptions of divinity but with an act that is inappropriate to the worship of God. For example, one may worship God with the acts of worship normally prescribed by the nations for their own cults or gods – such a worship constitutes the 'wrong' kind of worship.

Under the definition of 'wrong' kinds of worship, either wrong intention or wrong action will constitute idolatry. In other words, the right action with the wrong intention or the right intention with the wrong action would render the worship idolatrous. Both action and intention must be right in order that idolatry as 'wrong' kind of worship may not take place. This is a two-pronged approach in which monotheism is safeguarded and idolatry defined. An example of right belief or conceptions about the true God but with the 'wrong' actions may be seen in the act of eating idol-meat in the presence of the gods in 1 Corinthians 8–10.[20]

---

19.   Halbertal and Margalit (1992: 109) explain that a person may worship in a synagogue alongside his fellow monotheistic Jews and behave in a manner totally indistinguishable from a monotheist. However, his concept of divinity may be so 'distorted by errors and corporealizing' that his intentions in worship can only be described as worshipping an alien god.

20.   The 'strong' may hold the right view of God as one, but their action of eating idol meat in the pagan temple renders them idolatrous.

(2) Another area of cognitive error is that of confusing God with nature or mixing God with other gods/demons (δαιμόνια). When Israel views an object, be it a tree, or a stone, or the sun, and such like, and attributes power to it even though no actual worship of the object takes place,[21] idolatry is deemed to have taken place. In this case, it is different from representing God with an object such as the golden calf, or the 'wrong' kind of worship in terms of action or intention.

(3) The third area of cognitive error may be seen in Israel's failure to recognize the sovereignty and/or the uniqueness of God. For example, when Israel demands a king, it is seen as her failure to recognize God's rule over her and thus her failure to recognize God's sovereignty.

The above analysis of Halbertal and Margalit yields at least two achievements. (1) It has identified different definitions of idolatry which are interwoven in the Jewish tradition but are intellectually separable and of varying degrees of importance to different Jews.[22] Thus, in our analysis of the LXX and other Jewish texts, including 1 Corinthians, the Halbertal and Margalit analysis will be useful in identifying what are the different determining patterns of thought on idolatry for different Jews. Such patterns of thought are most likely the reasons for which different Jews acted they way they did regarding idolatry. (2) By indicating the complexities and subtleties in the definition of idolatry, the analysis reveals the possible spaces Jews might carve out for themselves which they might not consider idolatrous, but which are considered idolatrous by others. For example, a Jew may attend a pagan temple but claim to be worshipping the one God because he or she denies the existence of idols.[23] But others may still accuse him/her of employing the wrong method of worship, or having the wrong intentions (see Chapter 4 below). In other words, although the definitions yielded by Halbertal and Margalit's analysis are complementary, they do not form one single package.

The above definitions of idolatry will serve as a critical tool for analysing the various Jewish texts, including 1 Corinthians 8–10, in our subsequent chapters. We will begin with the LXX.

3. *Idolatry in the Septuagint (LXX)*

The LXX is a translation of the Hebrew scripture meant for the Greek speaking Diaspora Jews. It was an important part of their identity and a guide to their life as a people. It provided the language, history and authority to which Diaspora Jews of different kinds appealed. For example, Moses, the Law, and the different Jewish stories have been cited by different Jewish authors to argue for a particular policy, or advocate a particular value, or champion a particular cause.[24]

---

21. Most of the time, however, the people would tend to bow down and worship an object which they perceived as having power.

22. This will enable us to see the different emphases placed upon different definitions in different Jewish texts, and thus help us see on what grounds Jews identified an act as idolatrous.

23. See, for example, Halbertal (1998: 157–72), where he shows from the Mishnah *Abodah Zarah* how Jews carved out the space for themselves in which they justified their action or behaviour. See Chapter 4, section 6 below.

24. E.g. Philo, Josephus, Artapanus, 1, 2, 3, and 4 *Maccabees*, to name a few.

A survey of idolatry in the LXX would therefore serve as a foundation for the subsequent analysis of other Jewish texts. Such a survey would enable us to trace the different definitions and patterns of thought on idolatry in different periods of Israel's history operating in the LXX, and provide an important path towards the understanding of idolatry within Diaspora Judaism.

However, our discussion will only focus on texts which explicitly concern idolatry. Two reasons may be cited. First, the bulk of the material is simply too diverse for an exhaustive study to be done. It is, in any case, not the purpose of this thesis. Second, the above definitions require that the passages cited be analysed straightforwardly. Using the above definitions means that the texts cited have to be arbitrarily classified, and thus the process has to be very selective, that is, those closer to a particular definition will be placed under that definition, even though they may also appear to fit another definition. We will see that some of the texts chosen under a particular category refer to one period of Israel's history more than others. For example, under the category of 'worship of other gods (alien cults)', examples from the exilic period are cited more often. This could serve as a hint that Israel in exile turned to other gods more regularly or readily, perhaps because the people were in an alien land where interaction with alien cults was more frequent.[25] But texts on idolatry during the pre-exilic period tend to come under the second category: 'misrepresenting God', which again suggests that Israel before exile had frequently dishonoured Yahweh.

a. *The first two commandments*
That the first and second commandments are frequently cited in the many Jewish texts that critique idolatry shows these commandments to be foundational to the concept of 'monotheism'. However, do the first two commandments recognize the existence of other gods, but prohibit only the Israelites but not the Gentiles from worshipping these gods (monolatry)? Or do these commandments stipulate that only Yahweh is to be worshipped, and that all other gods are denied (monotheism)? It appears that there is evidence suggesting both possibilities. It is necessary to cite the two commandments here:[26]

The first commandment:

Ἐγώ εἰμι κύριος ὁ θεός σου, ὅστις ἐξήγαγον σε ἐκ γῆς Αἰγύπτου ἐξ οἴκου δουλείας. οὐκ ἔσονται σοι θεοὶ ἕτεροι πλὴν ἐμοῦ.

'I am the Lord your God, who brought you out of the land of Egypt, from the house of slavery. You shall have no other gods except me.' (Exod. 20.2)

25. Similarly, during the wilderness sojourn, Israel had engaged in idolatry, again perhaps due to their constant encounter with alien cults. One example is the Numbers 25 incident (see section 2, b below).
26. When the first commandment ends and the second begins is open to debate. However, Philo and Josephus represent the first two in the present arrangement (see Philo, *Dec.* 12; and Josephus, *Ant.* 3.91–92). Cf. Weinfeld (1990: 6–7) who reconstructs the ten commandments based on Philo and Josephus. For a thorough treatment of the various versions of the Decalogue, see Greenberg (1990: 83–119).

The second commandment:

οὐ ποιήσεις σεαυτῷ εἴδωλον οὐδὲ παντὸς ὁμοίωμα, ὅσα ἐν τῷ οὐρανῷ ἄνω καὶ ὅσα ἐν τῇ γῇ κάτω καὶ ὅσα ἐν τοῖς ὕδασιν ὑποκάτω τῆς γῆς. οὐ προσκυνήσεις αὐτοῖς οὐδὲ μὴ λατρεύσῃς αὐτοῖς. ἐγὼ γάρ εἰμι κύριος ὁ θεός σου,...

'You shall not make for yourself an idol nor likeness of anything in heaven above or on the earth below or in the waters under the earth. You shall not worship them or serve them. For I am the Lord your God...' (Exod. 20.4)

The first commandment, which sets the tone for the rest,[27] lays the foundational principle for the relationship between Yahweh and Israel: I am the Lord your God. And this is set within the historical context of deliverance from Egypt and the covenant into which Yahweh entered with Israel.[28] Yahweh is therefore the only God of Israel. The second is a logical deduction from the first: Israel is not to make any idols; nor is Israel allowed to worship or serve them. The question is whether these two commandments are meant only for Israel, or whether they extend beyond Israel to include Gentiles. In other words, are the first two commandments meant to advocate monotheism, or henotheism (or monolatry)?[29]

The first commandment seems to suggest that there are other gods, and Israel is barred from worshipping them because their Lord is Yahweh God. Thus, the commandment is applicable only to Jews and not to Gentiles. However, the second commandment prohibits idol-making, which presumably includes the physical representation of Yahweh, with the reiteration that Yahweh is God. The word 'idol' (εἴδωλον) here suggests that the ban covers the Gentile idols.

Houtman observes that the first two commandments do not prohibit the Gentiles from worshipping their gods. For Yahweh has entered into a relationship with Israel, not with the Gentiles. Thus, the concern here is with the right worship of Yahweh and thus the Decalogue requires 'monolatry' of Israel.[30] This means the temptation to worship other gods must have been real.[31] It also suggests that the first two commandments could be used by Jews to critique the Gentile gods: Yahweh alone is the true God, all Gentile gods are false. However, if Gnuse's thesis is tenable that monotheism as a religious concept developed over a period of time,[32] then it is entirely possible that not all Israelites had the same understanding

27.   The question of who God is in relation to Israel is of utmost importance to the significance of the rest of the commandments. Albeck (1990: 265) rightly concludes that the first commandment itself suggests that God is known through the commandments themselves, and that this commandment is actually a command to believe in God. Thus, Houtman (2000: 19) says that this commandment is the 'most fundamental' commandment for the entire Old Testament.

28.   Cf. Urbach 1990: 172–73.

29.   Henotheism is here taken to mean belief in one god who is not necessarily the *only* God. Monolatry, on the other hand, means the worship of one god, without excluding belief in others. Cf. Gnuse (1997: 62–228) where he argues for a developmental monotheism in Israel.

30.   Houtman 2000: 20.

31.   Thus, Childs (1974: 403) writes: '...in the first commandment the prohibition describes the relation of Yahweh to Israel by categorically eliminating other gods as far as Israel is concerned'. This statement, however, contradicts his earlier statement that 'Yahweh's exclusiveness in the sense that Yahweh alone has existence is not contained in the first commandment'.

32.   See Gnuse (1997: 129–76) who argues for a development of monotheism, which is arrived at

about monotheism and how Yahweh was to be worshipped.[33] For example, the golden calf incident shows that the Israelites thought the calf was their god who led them out of Egypt (cf. Exod. 32.4). Similarly, not all monotheists necessarily have the same understanding of the 'one God'. For example, the 'strong' in Corinth believe in the 'one God', to the exclusion of all idols. But for Paul, there are still gods in heaven and on earth and eating idol meat constitutes partnership with demons (cf. 1 Cor. 10.22; see Chapter 6 below). Thus, in the following, besides using Halbertal and Margalit's definitions, we will also see how the first two commandments are brought to bear on the issue of idolatry.

b. *Worship of other gods (alien cults)*

(i). *The metaphor of 'unfaithfulness'.*
Numbers 25.1–9 provides us with an account of the Israelites' worship of the Baal of Peor. The incident took place at Shittim which, according to Davies, was an ancient pre-Israelite sanctuary where 'worship was marked by strongly Canaanite features'.[34] It was also the last stop-over before the Israelites crossed over the Jordan (Num. 33.49). The story about Israel's idolatry is progressive. First, the Israelites entered into sexual relations with the Moabite women (LXX: ἐβεβηλώθη ὁ λαὸς ἐκπορνεῦσαι εἰς τὰς θυγατέρας Μωάβ; the Hebrew ויחל means 'profaned themselves'; v. 1). The women then invited the people to join them in sacrificing to their idols (LXX: τὰς θυσίας τῶν εἰδώλων). It should be noted that the LXX translates the Hebrew אלהיהן, which means 'their gods' are 'idols', thus showing the negative attitude of the author to other gods. And the description of the people's worship of these gods is that they ate (ἔφαγεν), presumably food sacrificed to Baal of Peor, and bowed down to the women's idols (προσεκύνησαν τοῖς εἰδώλοις αὐτῶν). The god to whom the Israelites rendered their worship is the Baal of Peor (v. 3). LXX translates ויצמד 'yoked himself' as ἐτελέσθη which carries the meaning of 'fulfilling' or 'performing' the requirements for the sacrifice of the Baal of Peor. The Israelites are therefore unfaithful and hence idolatrous. Although the passage does not describe the Israelites as 'rebellious', the Hebrew word צמד, which carries the meaning of 'bind', 'join', 'attach oneself to',[35] suggests that the people have abandoned Yahweh since they have 'attached' themselves to Baal. Thus, Israel's idolatrous act may be considered one of 'rebellion' against their God.

Jeremiah 3.1–23 records Israel's 'unfaithfulness' during the pre-exilic period in terms of a marriage relationship. Verses 1–2 describe a broken marriage relationship – a man divorces his wife because she has become another man's wife.

only during the Babylonian exile. Thus, during the pre-exilic Mosaic period there was no developed monotheism and Israel's monotheism began with much the same pluralistic cultic beliefs as the Canaanites.

33.   Thus, inscriptional evidence shows that Yahweh and Asherah were in some way related. See Meshel (1979: 24–35), cited in Gnuse (1997: 70 n. 19).

34.   Davies 1995: 285.

35.   *BDB* 855.

Israel is then said to be playing the harlot and so is worse than such a woman. Carroll argues that the language about the pollution of the land indicates that Israel's act of whoring is a reference to baalistic cults.[36]

Verse 6 says Israel has played the whore on every high hill and under every green tree, places where altars and sacred poles are set up for religious rituals made to the gods (Jer. 17.2). The same theme of an adulterous affair is again referred to in vv. 8–9 as a description of Israel and Judah. The theme is again repeated in vv. 11–14 and 19–20 where in v. 13, the idolatrous act is a 'promiscuous traffic' with foreign gods; and in v. 20 Israel's act is viewed as a treachery towards Yahweh. Thus, the passage revolves around the motifs of 'unfaithfulness' and 'treachery' on the part of Israel towards God. The sexual language used is an attempt by the author to express the seriousness of the broken relationship between Israel and God, thus showing the exclusivity of the relationship which does not and indeed cannot allow a third party's entry. The theme of 'whoring' is seen throughout Ezekiel 16, where Israel is accused of using what God has given her to make images for worship (16.15–18).[37] In 16.24–25, Israel is said to have built a 'room' or 'house' of or for the harlot, where בג is translated in the LXX as οἴκημα πορνικόν.[38] Ezekiel 20.23 points out that Israel's rebellion in idolatry is the reason for her eventual exile to the nations. Thus we are given the impression that Israel's fate as a whole results from her 'unfaithfulness' to God (cf. Ezek. 36.19).[39] This metaphor is founded on the first two commandments.

Ezekiel provides us with more material on Israel's idolatry during the pre-exilic times. Ezekiel 2.3–7 describes the prophet Ezekiel's vision of addressing the people of Israel with the message of God. He accuses the people of 'provoking God' (τοὺς παραπικραίνοντας).[40] And the phrase 'a house of rebellion' (οἶκος

36. Carroll 1986: 142.
37. Brownlee (1986: 230) suggests that the elements of oil and incense in Ezek. 16.18 are a clear reference to the anointing of Israel's idols. The author of Ezekiel tells us that the food supplied by God was given in sacrifice to the idols as a 'pleasing aroma' (ὀσμὴν εὐωδίας). Cf. Stuart (1987: 44) who comments on Hos. 2.8 that Israel uses what God has given her to spend on the worship of an alien cult, i.e. Baal. Hosea 2.13 further accuses Israel of forgetting the Lord and of burning incense to the Baal, a reference to the festivals (Stuart 1987: 51); and they were an occasion for Baal worship. Stuart (1987: 51) argues that the feast, the new moon, and the Sabbath were originally legitimate festival holidays but had been turned into 'the days of Baal' (τὰς ἡμέρας τῶν Βααλιμ).
38. Cf. Hos. 2.1–13, where Israel is likened to an adulterous mother and an unfaithful wife (LXX: 2.4, ἐξαρῶ τὴν πορνείαν αὐτῆς ἐκ προσώπου μου καὶ τὴν μοιχείαν αὐτῆς ἐκ μέσου μαστῶν αὐτῆς). This charge is repeated in v. 5; and throughout, Israel is accused of not acknowledging God as her provider by the metaphor of an unfaithful wife's failure to acknowledge her husband's provisions. Thompson (1977: 475–81) explains that the 'lovers' of Israel shows her failure to love Yahweh alone and thus Israel violates the covenant into which God has entered with her (cf. Ezek. 16.59).
39. Ezekiel 36.17–18 specifically refers to Israel's uncleanness in terms of her idols. Cf. 37.23 where Israel is said to be no longer defiling herself with her idols after God has restored her (LXX: ἵνα μὴ μιαίνωνται ἔτι ἐν τοῖς εἰδώλοις αὐτῶν). Similarly, Ezek. 43.7–9.
40. See Liddell and Scott (1940: 1320) where the word also carries the meaning of 'rebellion'; Cf. Ezek. 12.2–9, 25, where the word παραπικραίνω is used several times, in vv. 2, 3, 9, and 25, denoting that the house of Israel is one of rebellion. The text in Hebrew sets this out quite clearly:

παραπικραίνων; בית מרי), which is used three times in vv. 5, 6, and 7, introduces the things to be said about Israel's rebellion.

For example, Ezek. 5.5–12 describes the abominations committed by Israel
with the word βδέλυγμα (vv. 9, 11), which in the Old Testament refers to
'everything connected with idolatry' (cf. Ezek. 7.20).[41]

Israel's idolatry invites God's destruction of her high places (Ezek. 6.3–13).
Even those who will escape destruction have sought after their idols (Ezek. 6.9).
For Israel as a whole has offered a pleasing aroma to 'all their idols' everywhere
(Ezek. 6.13).[42]

In a strange vision, Ezekiel is personally shown the idolatry of Israel through a
dramatic experience of being lifted to a secret location where there is a chamber
in which all kinds of carvings are found – reptiles, animals, and all the 'idols' of
Israel. This is where Ezekiel purportedly witnesses the 70 elders commit idolatry
(Ezek. 8.11).[43]

Similarly, their women are said to weep for Tammuz (Ezek. 8.14) in the house
of God (οἴκου κυρίου). Tammuz was apparently a cult identified with Baal
Hadad.[44] Brownlee has observed that the weeping of the women could be linked
to the Cannanite festival in which weeping was carried out to call back the god
of rain and storm at a time of dry vegetation.[45] This could well be connected to
v. 12 where the elders are said to have moaned the abandonment of God. The
leaders have thus turned to alien cults.[46]

Idolatry continued during the exilic period, when Israel lived in Gentile lands.
For example second Isaiah called upon the exiled Israel in Babylon (Isa. 46.1–
13), where idols are transported (vv. 1–2), to listen to her God who bore and
carried her, and who would save her (vv. 3–4). It was a reminder to Israel of her
birth as a nation, the exodus, and the eventual salvation from the nations by
Yahweh God. But Israel has forgotten Yahweh and turned to the idols of the
Babylonians (vv. 5–7).

The rebellious house: (v. 2)   בית־המרי
                         (v. 3)   בית מרי
                         (v. 9)   בית המרי
                         (v. 25) בית המרי

41. BAGD 137–38.
42. The phrase 'under every leafy oak', יתחת כל־אלה עבתה, is omitted in the LXX. This, however,
does not alter the basic meaning of what the text is trying to say, i.e. Israel worships in every possible
place.
43. It is not certain whether the secret location is a reference to the temple in Jerusalem. The
description does not seem to fit it. It does not make any difference to the point we are making, that
even the 70 elders are seen to be idolatrous in their practice.
44. Brownlee 1986: 134.
45. Brownlee 1986: 136. Gray (1962: 516) notes: 'The Sumerian deity of spring vegetation;
known from the Gilgamesh Epic as the love of Ishtar, Goddess of love, who had betrayed him. The
anniversary of her betrayal was the occasion of an annual wailing for the God in the fourth month,
which was named for him.'
46. Many other examples can be found. E.g. Ezek. 20.1–31; 23.1–39 (political alliance with the
nations that extend to the religious area); 44.6–14.

Jeremiah records an incident in which the people of Israel in exile worshipped an alien cult of the 'queen of heaven' (Jer. 44.1–19; cf. Jer. 7.18). The story reports that the women, with their husbands' full knowledge and co-operation (v. 19), intentionally turned away from the word of God and worshipped and made offerings to the queen of heaven and poured drink offerings to her (vv. 16–17).[47] The 'queen of heaven' is also mentioned in Jer. 7.18. It is an expression used of the Babylonian-Assyrian Ishtar, goddess of the planet Venus. Thus, the people of Israel in exile continued in their 'unfaithfulness' by worshipping an alien cult.

In a description resembling the exilic promise of restoration for Israel, Hosea announces God's future restoration of Israel in the marriage metaphor, '…you will call me "my husband", and no longer call me "Baal"' (2.16, LXX: 2.18). Although Stuart notes that both words איש and בעל could have similar meaning, he reckons that the point of the oracle is based on the fact that בעל is the name of a specific god.[48] The translators of LXX (2.18) bring out the meaning more precisely by indicating 'Baal' to be a proper name. Thus, Hosea shows that Israel had at one time turned from Yahweh to worship Baal.[49]

The book of Amos views idolatry from a different angle from Hosea. Amos announces various reasons for Yahweh's punishment against Israel (cf. Amos 2.7, 10–12; 5.7, 10–15). Among the reasons cited are the altars at Bethel (cf. LXX 3 Kgdms 12.28–30). This is a cult that is considered alien. And in 5.25–26, Amos points out that Israel in the wilderness did not have to bring sacrifices to God. They remained the people of Yahweh. However, Israel as God's people engaged in alien cult worship. Two specific names of the cult are mentioned: Sakkuth and Kaiwan (v. 26, NRSV). The LXX translates the two gods as Μολοχ and Ραιφα. Μολοχ is the 'Canaanite-Phoenician god of sky and sun'; while Ραιφα is the 'constellation of the god Romphia'.[50]

The above shows the importance in the LXX of the metaphor of 'unfaithfulness' and the pervasiveness of the definition of idolatry as the worship of other gods/ alien cults. Such a pattern of thought could be used as a self-critique. But it could also be used by Jews to critique each other. Another aspect of this definition can be seen in the breach of the ancestral tradition.

---

47. The expression used in the LXX is τῇ βασιλίσσῃ τοῦ οὐρανοῦ, but in 7.18 the expression is τῇ στρατιᾷ τοῦ οὐρανοῦ. The former refers specifically to 'queen of heaven' while the latter refers to 'host of heaven'. The difference is subtle in that the 'host of heaven' may refer to the power of the heavens while the 'queen of heaven' is the one possessing the power. However, the Hebrew does not make any distinction. In both passages, the same expression למלכת השמים is used, which could be due to the fact that both texts refer to the same Babylonian-Assyrian goddess Ishtar.

48. Stuart 1987: 57.

49. Other examples in Hosea may be cited: Hos. 4.12–19 (Israel consulting a piece of wood); Hos. 8.2–6 (Israel making idols); Hos. 9.10 (worshipping an alien cult, a reference to Numbers 25); Hos. 10.1–6 (Israel increasing its number of altars); and Hos. 11.1–2; 13.1–16 (Baal worship; cf. Stuart 1987: 178).

50. On Μολοχ, see BAGD, 526; and on Ραιφα see BAGD, 118. See further Amos 8 for the other sins of Israel. Besides the prophecies of Hosea and Amos, we have the record of the prophecy of Zephaniah against Israel's worship of the Baal, under the leadership of the priests who are lumped together with the priests of Baal as a condemned lot (Zeph. 1.2–6).

(ii) *Idolatry as contrary to Jewish ancestral tradition (covenant)*. Examples of idolatry as contrary to Jewish ancestral tradition are not many and most of them are brief statements. In the following we will look mostly at short verses which reveal explicitly Israel's idolatrous acts as contrary to ancestral tradition.

The first text is in Deut. 32.16–17, which describes Israel's idolatry as going after 'strange gods', sacrificing to demons and deities they had never known. Verse 17 then says that these are deities 'whom your ancestors did not know' (οὓς οὐκ ᾔδεισαν οἱ πατέρες αὐτῶν), an indication that Israel had engaged in alien cult worship contrary to her ancestral tradition.

After Joshua's death, Judg. 2.11–13 describes the Israelites as having abandoned the God of their fathers, their ancestral tradition and having worshipped the Baals. Jeremiah describes Israel's idolatry in terms of Israel's failure to follow their ancestral tradition through a breach of the covenant (Jer. 11.10). This is further seen in Jer. 16.11, where Israel's failure to keep the law (νόμος) is cited as one of the reasons for her punishment. For Israel has made offerings to 'other gods' and the Baal (Jer. 19.4–5), acts which Israel's ancestors and their kings did not know (cf. Deut. 32.17 above). Israel has thus forsaken the covenant of God (Jer. 22.9), leading to her idolatry (cf. Jer. 44.1–29).[51] In the prophecy of Ezekiel, Israel's idolatry is described as a rejection (ἀπώσαντο) of God's ordinances, statutes (Ezek. 5.6),[52] and a failure to walk according to God's covenant (cf. Ezek. 11.12). What this means is that, while there was a body of laws, statutes and ordinances passed down from Israel's ancestors, the people lived in a way that was contrary to this body of ancestral tradition.[53]

Similarly, a few passages in the Minor Prophets also refer to idolatrous acts as contrary to the covenant or ancestral tradition. Hosea 8.1 says the people have broken the (Mosaic) covenant of God (παρέβησαν τὴν διαθήκην, cf. Hos. 6.7) and transgressed his law (cf. 7.13). Davies rightly points out that the imposition of the legal obligations of the covenant on Israel is presupposed.[54] Thus, Israel's ancestral tradition is embodied in the law.[55]

What our analysis shows thus far is that a prominent analysis and critique of idolatry in the LXX covers the twin theme of worship of other/alien gods and

---

51. Cf. Hos. 4.12–19, where Israel's idolatry is both attributed to and equated with the transgression of the people against the covenant (Hos. 6.7), their betrayal (Hos. 7.13) and abandonment (Hos. 4.2) of God.

52. The two terms ἀπώσαντο and οὐκ ἐπορεύθησαν refer to the same thing.

53. See further Ezek. 20.4–39. Ezekiel 20.19 equates obedience to the law of God with acknowledgement of him as Lord; conversely, disobedience to God's law is abandonment of his lordship. Cf. Ezek. 20.24 where Israel's idolatry is summarized as the failure to walk according to the requirements (τὰ δικαιώματα) and keep the commandments (τὰ προστάγματα), etc.

54. Davies 1992: 171–72.

55. Cf. Amos 2.4 where a pronouncement of judgement is made on Judah precisely because of her rejection of the law of the Lord (ἀπώσασθαι τὸν νόμον κυρίου) and her failure to guard his statutes (τὰ προστάγματα αὐτοῦ οὐκ ἐφυλάξαντο). See further examples in Mal. 2.10 and 3.7 where the covenant is breached. Stuart (1987: 178) comments: 'Israel "chose new gods" (cf. Josh. 24.15; Judg. 5.8), thereby breaking the most basic rule of the covenant, "You will have no other gods besides me" (Exod. 20.3)'.

breaking ancestral tradition. Such nexus of ideas reflects the basic concern of the first commandment, which prohibits the worship of other gods, on the basis of the 'covenant' relationship to God.

c. *Idolatry as misrepresenting/dishonouring God (Yahweh)*

(i) *Visual (anthropomorphic) representation of God.*
The first passage that speaks explicitly about idolatry as dishonouring God by misrepresenting him visually may be found in Exod. 32.1–15 (cf. Deut. 9.15–21), where the golden calf incident is recorded. The text makes it clear that the Israelites understood the golden calf to be their God who led them out of Egypt, suggesting that they had not turned from their God or worshipped an alien cult, but merely sought to worship God by means of the calf. What is idolatrous with the golden calf event is the fact that the people had misrepresented God with a physical thing, which contradicts the second commandment against representing Yahweh physically.

A second passage that deals with Israel's idolatry in terms of dishonouring and misrepresenting God can be found in 3 Kgdms 12.25–33, which reports Jeroboam's building of the two calves out of political expediency (v. 27). However, v. 28 clarifies that the two calves were meant to represent Israel's God who brought the Israelites out of the land of Egypt; they were not 'other gods' or 'alien cults'. Further, Jeroboam and the people seemed to understand that the location of worship was not exclusive to Jerusalem, and the method of representing God was not fixed either. Both places, Dan and Bethel, had long been consecrated as shrines for Yahweh (cf. Judg. 18.27–31 and Gen. 28.16–22; 35.1–4). Thus they were the logical places to locate these calves.

Many subsequent kings, including many who did right in the eyes of Yahweh, did not remove these calves. The common expression of Jeroboam's sin in the LXX, ἁμαρτιῶν Ἰεροβοὰμ υἱοῦ Ναβὰτ ὃς ἐξήμαρτε Ἰσραήλ (3 Kgdms 14.16), can be seen in 3 Kgdms 14.21–24 (Rehoboam), 15.1–8 (Abijam), 22.51–53 (Ahaziah). The LXX interprets the 'failure' to remove these calves with this expression, ἐποίησε τὸ πονηρὸν ἐν ὀφθαλμοῖς Κυρίου ('he did evil in the eyes of the Lord'; cf. 3 Kgdms 14.22; 15.34; 16.7, 19, 25, 30; 3 Kgdms 14.9).[56] Although Jeroboam made an acclamation similar to that of Exodus (Exod. 32.1, 4), the editor of the LXX turned the original singular form of the verb (brought) to plural so as to reflect that אלהים is not read as 'God' but 'gods'.[57] The editor thus exploited the fact that there were two calves to make it look like alien worship. The LXX similarly translates אלהים as θεοί (gods). However, even though the intention of

---

56. The repeated Hebrew expression... ויעש הרע בעיני יהוה ...is well captured in the LXX translation.

57. De Vries (1985: 162–63) observes that the present consensus on the calves is that they were not idols but ornaments or pedestals and that 'Jeroboam undoubtedly intended the occasion to be good, happy and holy'. His observation is that the reporter's change of the word 'brought' to a plural form is a reflection of the reporter's 'censorious attitude' and so the reporter could conclude that Jeroboam's act was an error. Although he is referring to the Hebrew text, the LXX text seems to translate this more clearly.

Jeroboam, his people, and that of the subsequent kings, was never to turn away from God, the fact that they misrepresented God with two calves renders their act idolatrous. For it was an explicit act that violated the second commandment.[58]

(iii) *Cognitive error.*
'Wrong' kind of worship. Judges 17.1–13 gives an account of a man named Micah who gave his mother a large amount of silver, part of which she turned into an idol of cast metal (v. 4). According to v. 6, it was a period of Israel's history when there was an absence of both political and religious leadership, resulting in a lack of standards of belief and practice.

However, the passage also reveals some form of tradition. This is seen in Micah's shrine (LXX: οἶκος θεοῦ; Hebrew: בית אלהים, both mean 'house of God'), and the ephod (a priestly garment) and teraphim (תרפים) which he made. Presumably, the shrine was meant for the teraphim and the ephod, the priest,[59] who was needed to preside over the rituals. Verses 7–10 tell us that Micah knew about the priesthood and was aware that the Levites were set apart for the service of God. So when a young Levite came to look for a place to live in, Micah immediately invited him to be his (Micah's) priest. The words which Micah says in v. 13 are significant, 'Now I know that the Lord will be good to me' (LXX: ἀγαθυνεῖ μου Κύριος). And this belief is attributed to the fact that he now had a Levite as his priest (LXX: ἐγένετό μοι ὁ Λευίτης εἰς ἱερέα).

What the story shows is that Micah tried his very best to keep some kind of religious tradition at home, despite the lawlessness. And further, the hope of Micah's mother for the Lord's blessing on Micah was raised as a result of her moulding a cast metal idol for her son.

The above passage indicates that idolatry as wrong kind of worship takes place here in terms of action, but not intention. In other words, Micah's intention was religious. His act of worship, however, was wrong in that he had rendered worship to a teraphim and not to God. It was not unfaithfulness since the teraphim was not an alien cult,[60] nor was there any hint that Micah betrayed or rebelled against his Lord. As mentioned earlier in the discussion of definitions, idolatry as the wrong kind of worship can be deemed to have taken place as long as one of the two elements - wrong action or wrong intention - is present.

---

58. A similar example of Israel's misrepresenting God is found in Hos. 8.2–6, which is an allusion to 3 Kgdms 12.26–30 and possibly to Exodus 32. In the Hosea passage, Hosea says that God rejects the 'bull' (8.4). This is a possible later imposition of a theological interpretation of the 'bull of Samaria'. Thus, in 8.6, the same critique of idols is levelled against the bull (cf. Hab. 2.18–19).

59. Harrison (1982: 117–18) suggests several possible uses of the ephod: (1) a component of the high priest's vestments (e.g. 1 Kgdms 2.28; 14.3; 22.18); (2) images rather than garments (e.g. Judg. 8.27 refers to a gold idol or image); (3) clothing for the images. Harrison points out that the third possibility is most probably unlikely as Micah probably wore the ephod, although it could be worn by Micah's son whom he made a priest (Judg. 17.5). Since Micah found a young Levite to act as his priest, it would be more possible that the ephod was meant for the young Levite.

60. Albertz (1994: 37–38) observes that the 'teraphim' are part of the Israelites' regular household cult; they are not to be confused with the gods. For him, the 'household cult' of Micah was lowly deities and the teraphim were meant to represent them (the deities).

4 Kingdoms 16.1–20 is a very interesting account of the wrong kind of worship. The story is set in the political context of Ahaz's dependence on Assyria. In v. 7 Ahaz sent a brief diplomatic message to the king of Assyria, requesting help, to which the latter responded positively and came up to Damascus and seized it (v. 9). Verses 10–18 make a shift from the political situation to a religious one, in which King Ahaz went up to Damascus, presumably at the invitation of the Assyrian king, where he saw the altar (v. 10). He immediately sent to Uriah a model of the altar, patterned exactly after the one in Damascus in all its details. Verses 12–16 give a detailed account of the offerings which Ahaz made at the altar and the instructions he gave to Uriah concerning the morning and evening offerings, including grain offerings and drink offerings of the people. Verses 17–18a further provide a brief account of Ahaz's 'renovation' or 're-arrangement' of the interior of the temple. The fact that Ahaz built an altar in exactly the same pattern as the one in Damascus suggests he was following the traditional approach in his offerings and was careful in all these undertakings.[61] In other words, Ahaz's action was right. Verse 18b reveals that all the religious acts of Ahaz were 'in deference to the king of Assyria' (NIV) (ἀπὸ προσώπου βασιλέως Ἀσσυρίων). He had rendered the 'right action' but with the 'wrong intention', thus rendering his act idolatrous.

Ezekiel 14.3–7 is a passage that speaks about the thoughts and intentions of the elders of Israel in acquiring idols, presumably to worship them. The various words used in the LXX to refer to these elders' intention are τὰ διανοήματα (thoughts [vv. 3, 4]; BAGD, 187), ἐνθύμημα (thought, [v. 5]; Liddell & Scott 1940: 567), and ἐπιτήδευμα (pursuit, way of living [v. 6]; BAGD, 302), none of which mean 'idol'. However, these different words have been used by the translators of LXX to translate the Hebrew word גלולים (idol), which is used throughout the passage in the Hebrew text. Brownlee observes that the 'verb עלה in its intransitive form is the language of thinking, either by way of remembering (Isa. 65.17; Jer. 3.16) or by way of planning and forethought (Jer. 7.31; 19.5; 32.35; Ezek. 38.10)'.[62] The above observations clearly show that for the LXX translators the intention of the elders was to be unfaithful and thus amounts to, or is equivalent to, idolatry.[63]

The above passages show that idolatry could be construed on the basis of the 'wrong' kinds of worship both in terms of the wrong action and the wrong intention.

Mixing God with nature/other gods (δαιμόνια) or attributing power to what is powerless/idols. The first and most explicit text that speaks about Israel mixing God with δαιμόνια is Deut. 32.16–17. This is set within the larger context of Moses' Song which recounts and interprets the history of Israel in the wilderness

---

61. Hobbs (1985: 217) comments: 'From this account the motivation of Ahaz was clearly not apostasy, since the organization of the sacrifice that follows is consistent with the other legislation on sacrifice in the Old Testament'.

62. Brownlee 1986: 201.

63. Similarly, the thought of worshipping wood and stone (ξύλοι καὶ λίθοι) in Ezek. 20.32 is in itself idolatry in that such an intention constitutes the wrong kind of worship.

(Deut. 32.1–43), where Israel is accused of sacrificing to δαιμόνια,[64] a reference to the 'golden calf' incident. Verse 16 uses such words like ἀλλοτρίοις, βδελύγμασιν, and in v. 17, the word δαιμόνια is used for the first time to refer to the calf as demons. The Greek δαιμόνιον also means 'demon', '(evil) spirit', which occupies a position between the human and the divine.[65] This is a clear critique of Israel's idolatry by interpreting it as the worship of the non-gods or 'demons'. In other words, Israel is here mixing or confusing Yahweh with what is not God.

The powerlessness of idols is well illustrated in Isa. 41.21–29, in which the idols are challenged to show proofs of their abilities.[66] In v. 23, the gods are challenged to shock Yahweh with their deeds, and are accused of being non-gods because they fail to do so. Similarly, in v. 25, Yahweh calls out to Cyrus to do his will, and issues a question in v. 26 as to who knows beforehand about Cyrus' rising. The question appears rhetorical: the questioner knows his audience's awareness of the answer to his question (v. 27). And therefore, the audience too ought to know that the gods are nothing (v. 24) and their works are a delusion (v. 29).[67] But by attributing power to the powerless idols, Israel is guilty of the sin of idolatry in terms of cognitive error.

The critique of idolatry is intensified in Isa. 44.9–20 where its larger context is the announcement of God's good news to Israel (Isa. 40.1–44.23). Isaiah 44.9–20 is part of a larger text (Isa. 43.22–44.28) which speaks of God's help to his people. The passage, which describes the idols, is sandwiched between two passages that speak of God as the Lord. A chiastic structure is seen here which serves to highlight the contrast between the idols and the true God of Israel, revealing on the one hand the absurdity of the idols and on the other the reality of Yahweh.

Although Isa. 44.9–20 concerns idol making, Isa. 44.22 clearly indicates that the fashioning of the idols was in fact the sin of Israel at one time: 'I have swept away your transgressions like a cloud, and your sins like mist; return to me, for I have redeemed you' (NRSV). Israel is asked to 'return' to God, presumably from her idols, because Yahweh has *redeemed* her (λυτρώσομαι), a salvation that Israel's idols are incapable of providing. Instead, the idols are fashioned according to a detailed step-by-step procedure: trees are grown; they are then cut down once they have grown strong; every part of it is used for some practical purpose

---

64.   Cf. Ps. 106.37–38, where the term δαιμόνια appears to be used interchangeably with other 'gods'. Even in the Song of Moses itself, the δαιμόνια seem to be an alternative designation for the gods of the nations.

65.   BAGD 169. For a treatment of the term in the LXX, see Chapter 6, section 4, a, below. The Hebrew expression יזבחו לשדים means 'they sacrificed to demons', of which שד, which means 'demon', is a loan word from Assyrian שדו, meaning 'a protecting spirit'. *BDB* 993.

66.   The Isaianic text shows a more intellectual critique of idolatry. This appears to be a base text upon which similar critiques of idolatry are carried out by *Wisdom of Solomon* and Philo (see Chapter 3, sections 2 and 3 below). By an intellectual critique of idolatry, the Isaiah text defines what is the 'alien realm' (Halbertal and Margalit 1992: 8) and so clarifies the 'cognitive error' of 'misrepresenting' God.

67.   LXX πόθεν meaning 'whence?' understands אך to be an 'interrogative particle'. Thus the translators of LXX turned the statement into a question, challenging the validity of the idols, as it answers ἐκ γῆς (v. 24).

(as fuel to set up fire [v. 15a]; part of it for warming oneself [v. 15b]; part of it for baking bread [v. 15c]; part of it for roasting meat [v. 16]). Verse 15d says, 'Then he makes a god and worships it, makes it a carved image and bows down before it'. The force of the ridicule is in v. 17 which says that the 'god' is made from the 'leftover' of all the wood! This is especially strongly contrasted with the end of v. 16 in which the idol-maker, after having satisfied himself with the food and the warmth from the fire, says, 'Ah, I am warm, I can feel the fire'. It pictures a useless and wasted block of wood being turned into a god, thus giving the impression of a convenient recycle of a waste product.

The cognitive error is made even more explicit in v. 17b where the idol-worshipper attributes power to a powerless block of wood (γλυπτόν) and confuses God with it, asking it for salvation. Verse 18 ridicules: they know nothing, their eyes and hearts can neither see nor understand. Verse 20 further describes such cognitive error as arising from a 'deluded mind' (σποδὸς ἡ καρδία). For the idols are a βδέλυγμα (an abomination, v. 19b) and a ψεῦδος (v. 20, a lie/falsehood).[68]

Failure to recognize God's sovereignty. Apart from Halbertal and Margalit, scholars generally do not view the failure to recognize God's sovereignty as an idolatrous error. However, a critical evaluation of Israel's failure to recognize God's sovereignty reveals that she no longer accepts the rule of God over her. This has implications on whether the first commandment will be kept (cf. Exod. 20.3). The monotheistic nature of Israel's religious status would thus become dubious. It also suggests that Israel is ready to break the exclusive relationship with Yahweh. There are several examples worthy of discussion.

Judges 8.22–28 records that the Israelites asked Gideon to rule over them (ἄρξον ἡμῶν, v. 22), indicating their failure to recognize Yahweh as their sovereign ruler. As v. 23 points out, Gideon corrected them that it was God who would rule over them (κύριος ἄρξει ὑμῶν). Gideon then asked for a share of the people's gold earrings, with which he made an ephod (a priestly garment) which the people 'worshipped' (ἐξεπόρνευσεν, v. 27).[69] Davies observes that the people, whose request to be ruled by Gideon was turned down, were now turning to the ephod which could be used either to put on an idol, or to represent Yahweh, or possibly to make a connection with the Ark.[70] The context of the story suggests that the ephod of gold was meant to represent Yahweh. And since the people would have understood the Ark to represent God's presence, they could possibly regard the golden ephod as serving similar functions.

---

68. See further Jer. 2.26–29; 8.19; 10.1–15; 18.15; Ezekiel 8; similarly, Zeph. 1.5 speaks of the people confusing God with nature.

69. The word ἐκπορνεύω (Liddell-Scott 1940: 518) literally means *commit fornication*. It is used in Exod. 34.15 as a metaphor for idolatry. The RSV translates ἐξεπόρνευσεν πᾶς Ἰσραηλ as 'all Israel played the harlot'.

70. Davies 1962: 118. In view of the marriage metaphor of 'unfaithfulness', Judg. 8.27 may be taken to mean that Israel performed some kind of worship to the ephod, which could, in this case, be an idol or an image (see Harrison 1982: 118; cf. Exod. 32.4 where Aaron asked for all the gold jewellery from the people and fashioned a calf out of the melted gold).

The exact purpose and meaning of the golden ephod are not clear in the text. However, the fact that the Israelites asked Gideon to rule over them constitutes a failure to recognize God's sovereignty, a factor very closely associated with idolatry.

Another example is found in Jer. 10.1–16 in which God is declared as the God of all nations (vv. 7, 10, 12, 16). The passage serves to contrast the idols and the true God of Israel by describing how idols are made. Although it appears similar to the critique in Isa. 44.9–20 (cf. Isa. 40.19–20; 41.7), it differs in function. In Jer. 10.1–16, the theme of God as God of all nations is repeated several times, indicating his sovereignty over all the nations. Thus, the passage does not mention Israel's idolatry but only serves to warn the people against following after these idols or worshipping them. While idols are totally dependent in that they have to be carried,[71] the true God is great and wise (Jer. 10.6–9). Yahweh is variously described: ἀληθινὸς θεός (the true God); θεὸς ζώντων (the God of the living); and βασιλεὺς αἰώνος (the eternal God). Verse 7 further declares that God is the 'king of the nations' (βασιλεῦ τῶν ἐθνῶν), thus affirming his universal sovereignty. Israel would have failed to recognize God's sovereignty over her if she turns to idols.

What the above shows is that idolatry in the LXX is not simply viewed from the angle of the worship of other gods, but also from various other angles such as the acts and intentions involved in the worship of God, how God is viewed, and whether God's sovereignty is compromised. Through these various articulations, the LXX shows that idolatry is as much a cognitive error, as it is an error in practice.

4. *Summary and Conclusion*

The discussion above reveals that the concept of idolatry is a multifaceted one which involves complex reasoning – an idolatrous act may have several definitions or a definition may cover various idolatrous acts and at times they are interwoven. These multifaceted definitions have the capability of guarding monotheism at different angles, and critiquing any act that may appear to be idolatrous in order to prevent any type or form of idolatry from taking place among the Israelites. These definitions set out by Halbertal and Margalit do not operate as a single package, as illustrated in the foundational Diaspora text of the LXX. For example, an act of worship involving an object may not be idolatrous in terms of 'unfaithfulness' because that object is not an alien cult but meant to represent Yahweh (e.g. golden calf). However, it becomes idolatrous under another definition, that is, idolatry as dishonouring God in terms of misrepresenting God visually (i.e. against the second commandment).

Even if the object is not anthropomorphic, it will come under yet another definition, that is, 'wrong' kind of worship – rendering an act of worship to an object that is not the true God.

71.   Jones (1992: 173) suggests that this is a possible reference to the procession of Bel-Marduk and Nebo his son, god of wisdom in Babylon.

The discussion above also reveals that a totally exclusivist monotheism is not a settled issue and can be exploited and therefore compromised. And the articulations in the LXX also reveal an interesting fact about Israel: idolatry is an ongoing practice *and* struggle in Israel as she interacts with her environment. For example, the golden calf incident during the wilderness and the two calves of Jeroboam which many successive generations of kings never removed might suggest that they had viewed the calves as legitimate or even as expressions of the monotheistic God of Israel. The lack of clarity and agreement on what constituted idolatry, despite the variegated approaches in dealing with idolatry in the LXX, indicates that the definition and critique of idolatry are crucial in determining Jewish boundaries. But the location and definition of such boundaries were not always clear to different Jews.

This ambiguity could be reflected in later Jewish history, which leads us to examine both sample Diaspora texts which castigate 'idolatry' (Chapter 3), and examples of Jewish accommodation to what others might consider 'idolatry', or of Jews speaking of God/the gods in terms which might arouse suspicion in others (Chapter 4). This ambiguity and variety might also illuminate the different positions in 1 Corinthians 8–10, which might all turn out to be Jewish in some sense, but in different ways and expressions.

While we cannot be sure how Diaspora Jews used the LXX with regard to idolatry, and whether they were in fact conscious of the definitions set out in this chapter, our discussion in Chapter 3 will demonstrate how the different definitions or aspects of them were operative in Diaspora Judaism, whether consciously or not.

Chapter 3

CRITICISM OF IDOLATRY IN DIASPORA JEWISH LITERATURE

1. *Introduction*

Our analysis in the previous chapter has demonstrated the complexity of idolatry and revealed that even within the LXX, there is a lack of clarity and agreement on what constitutes idolatry, despite its variegated approaches in dealing with the issue. Is this ambiguity also reflected in later Jewish history, especially in the Diaspora Jewish literature? To clarify the issue, we will look at the criticism of idolatry in the following representative Diaspora Jewish literature on idolatry: Wisdom of Solomon, Philo, Josephus, *Joseph and Aseneth*, and Sybilline Oracles.[1] There are good reasons for such a study and the choice of the literature.

First, such a study would illuminate the question of how Diaspora Jews viewed and reacted to idolatry. This will serve to highlight the different emphasis each places on the definitions set out in Chapter 2. This would enable us to see what were the base reasons for their rejection of idolatry, which will further illuminate the way idolatry was understood and defined by different parties in 1 Corinthians 8–10.[2]

The choice of the above Diaspora Jewish literature is made as the authors represent a variety of viewpoints on idolatry and emphasize its different aspects. In addition, since these texts date from a period close to that of the New Testament, what they say about idolatry may reflect the thinking on idolatry current at that time.

The focus of this chapter will be on the various emphases of the Diaspora Jewish authors and the definitions of idolatry particular to each. This will further strengthen the point made in Chapter 2, that the multifaceted definitions of idolatry are liable to the following: (1) intellectual separation of these definitions; and (2) subjective choice of the definitions by either individuals or groups.

---

1. The Epistle of Jeremiah is another Jewish text that criticizes idolatry. It is not included here as the material presented in this chapter is, to my mind, sufficient to illustrate my point. Further, space constraint and word length do not permit a full discussion of this Jewish work.

2. The fact that the Corinthian community was itself a Diaspora community, set within the Graeco-Roman world in which there were many gods and many lords (cf. 1 Cor. 8.5), means that a study of the criticisms of idolatry by the Diaspora Jews will shed light on our understanding of the situation in the Corinthian church where idol-meat was freely eaten by some, particularly when the 'strong', the 'weak' and Paul all show some degree of Jewish influence.

2. *Wisdom of Solomon 13–15*

The book of Wisdom is generally assumed to have been written by an Alexandrian Jew between 100 BCE and 30 CE,[3] although neither his exact identity nor his biography could be established.[4] The entire book appears to be the writer's efforts in encouraging his fellow Jews to take pride in their ancestral monotheistic belief of the one true God.[5] Throughout, the author seeks to persuade his readers that their belief is superior and thus their way of life a better option, by making a sharp contrast between the nations' gods and the true God,[6] revealing his categorical opposition to pagan culture and religions.

While there is a series of antitheses throughout the book, Barclay rightly concludes that the predominant theme is 'social conflict and cultural antagonism between Jews and non-Jews' and that it is 'an educated and deeply Hellenized exercise in cultural aggression'.[7] This is well attested throughout the book, not least in the chapters on idolatry (13–15).

Various structural outlines have been proposed.[8] Winston provides a relatively simple outline, while Grabbe provides the following more elaborate one:

A   Nature worship (13.1–9)
B   Idolatry (13.10–15.19)
    a   Introduction (13.10)
        b   Carpenter/wood (13.11–14.2)
           c   Apostrophe (14.3–6)
               Transition (14.7–11)
               d   Origins of idolatry (14.12–31)
           c´   Apostrophe (15.1–3)
               Transition (15.4–6)
        b´   Potter/clay (15.7–13)
    a´   Conclusion (15.14–19)

---

3.   Cf. Winston 1992: 121–22; Barclay 1996: 181–82, and 182 n. 3. Cf. Reider 1957: 12–14.

4.   See Clark 1973: 1–3.

5.   Winston 1979: 63.

6.   Collins (1997: 135) is right in saying that there is always an apologetic element in the attempts to extol the Jewish religion. Kolarcik (1999: 289–301) argues that the themes of 'universalism' and 'justice' can be seen throughout the book, in which the author expresses these themes by showing the relationship of God to the cosmos and the defence of the faithful. Cf. Collins (1997: 1–15) who rightly points out the inherent tension between natural theology and divine revelation in Wisdom.

7.   Barclay 1996: 184. Collins (2000: 200) does not find this conclusion justified, as he argues that there are Stoic and Cynic philosophical parallels to the polemic in Wisdom. However, the base foundation of the people in the ancient world may be traced to their religious belief. Thus, when one wanted to criticize another, the main area of criticism would seem to be that of religion. That the Gentiles have been found to be equally critical of the Egyptian animal worship does not therefore mean that the polemic in Wisdom cannot be viewed as 'cultural aggression'. There is no reason why one cannot borrow an idea from the Gentiles to criticize the Gentiles. Wisdom 13–15 certainly cannot be viewed as expressions of 'cultural convergence', as Collins sees it (2000: 202). Reider (1957: 9–12) looks at the entire book as a polemical work, of which the first five chapters are against the recalcitrant Jews while the rest of the book are against the vicious pagan idolatry.

8.   E.g. Winston 1979: 11; and Grabbe 1997: 23.

The above structure establishes two basic points of the writer of Wisdom: (1) the true God rules, saves, and extends his mercy; and, in contrast, (2) idols and images are dead, wrong, and despicable.[9] We will look at Wisdom 13–15 in greater detail, following Grabbe's outline.

a. *Nature worship (Wisdom 13.1–9)*

Wisdom 13 begins with nature worship, which is the result of a human tendency (13.2–3).[10] Humans worship the elements of nature because they are powerful (δύναμις) and influential (ἐνέργεια) (13.4). The word θεωρέω (13.5) means 'contemplate' or 'consider' when it is used of the mind.[11] However, the power of the elements means greater power of their creator.[12] By worshipping nature, the Gentile idolaters have gone astray (πλανῶνται, v. 6), confused nature with God and are thus in error (cf. v. 2). Cognitively, they have dishonoured God, whom they ironically fail to find behind these created things.[13] Thus, Reider correctly points out that the sense of v. 1 seems to be that '(A)ll men must be fools who can look upon the works of God and not recognize God in them'.[14] Such a failure serves as the basis for their rejection.

b. *Idolatry (Wisdom 13.10–15.19)*

(i) *Wisdom 13.10–19.*

The seeking of God leads to the making of 'gods', when people do not seek him in nature. Founded probably on Isa. 40, 41, 44 and 46,[15] Wis. 13.10–16 shows the absurdity of idols by describing the entire process of idol-making (cf. Isa. 44.9–20). First, the carpenter uses the wood for good purposes, and the leftovers are turned into idols, which are therefore 'dead' (νεκροῖς, vv. 10, 18), 'useless' (ἄχρηστον, v. 10; οὐθὲν εὔχρηστον, v. 13), 'worthless' (or 'cheap', εὐτελεῖ, v. 14), 'powerless' (ἀδυνατεῖ, v. 16), and 'lifeless' (ἀψύχῳ, v. 17).[16] Further, the

---

9.   Thus Schürer (III, 570) rightly says that essentially the contents of Wisdom warn against the folly of godlessness. Similarly, Grabbe (1997: 57) observes that harangues make up the bulk of the third part of Wisdom (i.e. Wisdom 13–15). See also Reider 1957: 10–11.

10.   Reider (1957: 160–61) is not convincing when he argues that the 'rulers of the world' in v. 2 refers to all sorts of gods, not just to sun and moon. Winston (1979: 250) takes the word πρυτάνεις κόσμου to refer to the sun and moon, although the term is also applied to the gods. In the context of Wis. 13.1–9, the author seems most certain to refer to the sun and moon.

11.   Liddell and Scott 1940: 364.

12.   This is essentially the point of the author in 13.4b. Cf. Reider 1957: 161.

13.   Reider (1957: 162), 'These men are unmoved by the world's beauty and endeavor to seek God, but somehow they fail to attain that end'. Cf. Collins 2000: 200.

14.   Reider 1957: 159. Cf. Collins (1997: 208–209) recognizes Wisdom as regarding the philosophers who worship nature as culpable, but goes on to say that they deserve respect when they seek to worship the true God, even though they fail in their attempt.

15.   Collins (2000: 200) says the polemic in Wis. 13.10–19 draws its inspiration from Isa. 44.9–20.

16.   These terms have at least two common features: (1) they are all negative; and (2) in contrast to the true God, they all have to do with the absence of life. The word ἄψυχος literally means 'lifeless', 'inanimate' (Liddell and Scott 1940: 143). The author's intention is clear: to show that idols are false and therefore no gods.

author attributes idol-making to the carpenter's idleness (ἀργία) and hence bore-dom, not to his devotion.[17] The idols made have various forms such as those of animals and of humans (εἰκόνι ἀνθρώπου), and are accommodated in a chamber, or shrine (οἴκημα), fastened on the wall, and nailed down for stability. Such an elaborate process is necessary as the idol is unable to help itself (v. 16),[18] thus exposing the passive inability of the idols and their absurdity. The passage shows a crescendo of polemic against idolatry.

(ii) *Wisdom 14.1–7.*
In 14.1–7, the idolater sets sail into the sea but encounters danger, from which he is saved when he entreats his idols. Here the author ridicules the idolater's god as but a piece of wood that is worse than a vessel. It is in fact the Father (πάτερ, v. 3) who, by his providence (πρόνοια, v. 3),[19] guides and saves (v. 4).[20] Thus, it is God, not the idol, who answers the idolater's prayer. He should have prayed to the true God but he did not.

(iii) *Wisdom 14.8–11.*[21]
In 14.8–11, the writer moves to a scathing attack on idols and their makers by pouring scorn and curses and pronouncing judgement on them. The hand-made idol (τὸ χειροποίητον, v. 8) is the ungodliness (ἡ ἀσέβεια, v. 9) of its maker who, together with its worshipper, call the perishable idols God (τὸ φθαρτὸν θεὸς ὠνομάσθη, v. 8).[22] Both idols and their makers are contradictory to God and his nature, and equally hateful to God (μισητὰ θεῷ, v. 9). The idol is pejoratively described as τὸ πραχθέν (that which was brought about) and its maker ὁ δράσας. Both will face punishment (κολασθήσεται) (v. 10), described as a visitation (ἐπισκοπή), for both are an abomination (βδέλυγμα, v. 11),[23] which is the result of misrepresenting the true God. Such idolatry results in the 'stumbling' (σκάνδαλα) and the 'snare' (παγίδα) of the human soul.[24]

---

17. Cf. Reider 1957: 164–65.
18. Cf. Ep. Jer. 27; Isa. 46.7.
19. Cf. Reider 1957: 167–68.
20. Verse 7: 'For blessed is the wood through which righteousness comes', may well be an allusion to Noah's ark (Reider 1957: 169). Winston (1979: 267) translates the verse correctly as 'blessed … through which righteousness survives'. Cf. Collins (1997: 210 n. 70), who rightly points out that the theory of a Christian interpolation is difficult.
21. Collins (1997: 210) takes 14.1–11 as a unified whole that forms a mockery of the sailor. But a closer look shows that in 14.8–11 the author shifts his emphasis from the idolater to the idols.
22. Could it be possible that the author is having in mind the second commandment, which bans the physical representation of Yahweh? Collins (2000: 201) observes a 'clear identification' of Israel in Wisdom. Reider (1957: 2) sees Wisdom 10–19 as an illustration of the power of wisdom from the ancient history of Israel. It is therefore possible that the author of Wisdom sees here a universal application of the first and second commandments.
23. Βδέλυγμα is a term frequently used in the LXX to refer to idols. Liddell and Scott 1940: 312. Reider (1957: 171) observes that '*Bdelugma* seems to be used in LXX for every opprobrious term applied to idols' (italics author's).
24. What these two terms mean may perhaps be gleaned from 14.12, where idolatry is accused of being the beginning of fornication and corruption of life. See further 14.24–28.

(iv) *Wisdom 14.12–21.*
In an extensive passage the author explains euhemeristically the origin of idolatry (14.12–21), which begins with the mind, and leads to moral decadence (ἀρχὴ πορνείας). It is the result of human error or, more precisely, humans' 'vain glory' (κενοδοξία) (v. 14). This is illustrated by the story of a grieving father who made an image of his recently deceased child and honoured him as a god (v. 15).[25] Over time, rules and rituals were introduced and passed down, which became a law to be kept (v. 16), and eventually became a national tradition (v. 17). The people from far away then sought to 'flatter' their monarch by erecting an image of him (εἰκόνα τοῦ βασιλέως), which soon attracted a great multitude who began to view this image of a man as an object of worship (v. 20).[26] The author calls such idolatry a hidden danger to life (τῷ βίῳ εἰς ἔνεδρον, v. 21), which he goes on to elaborate in the next section.

(v) *Wisdom 14.22–31.*
The consequences of idolatry are wholly negative and bring about only the abuse of the human life, body, institutions and the like. The idol worshippers have gone further by instituting rituals which are totally absurd, an indication that they are the wrong kinds of worship (14.23).

In 14.24–27, the author provides a catalogue of vices and attributes them to the worship of idols (εἰδώλων θρησκεία).[27] There is nothing positive about other religions or Gods, for they are the beginning (ἀρχή), the cause (αἰτία), and end (πέρας) of every evil (παντὸς κακοῦ) (v. 27).[28] And their devotees are equally evil (v. 28). The author describes the idolaters' celebrations as madness (εὐφραι-νόμενοι μεμήνασιν), their prophesying (προφητεύουσιν ψευδῆ) as lying, their living as unrighteous (ζῶσιν ἀδίκως), their swearing as false (ἐπιορκοῦσιν) and their invocation of the name of their Gods as light (ταχέως, literally 'hasty').[29]

---

25.   Collins (1997: 210–11) argues that this illustration of the origin of idolatry finds several parallels in various works, such as that of the fourth-century convert to Christianity Firmicus Maternus, the cult of Hadrian's Antinous, etc. Winston (1979: 270) rightly points out that the case of Firmicus Maternus is based on the widespread religious phenomenon of the Graeco-Roman world. While this may further reinforce the theory that the author sees an extension of the second commandment to the Gentiles, the use of a much later fourth-century work as a parallel runs the risk of anachronism.

26.   Winstons 1979: 279.

27.   According to Reider (1957: 174–75), this seems to be a description of the moral decadence of Greece and Rome. The murder, robbery and such like are also mentioned in Jer. 7.9 and Hos. 4.2. Cf. Philo, *Conf. Ling.* 12.

28.   Winston (1979: 280) translates ἀνωνύμων as 'unspeakable', 'not to be named'. Reider (1957: 176–77) is more correct in rendering it 'nameless', which is equivalent to 'without a name' and there-fore without existence. The description of the idols as 'dead', 'useless', 'worthless', 'powerless', 'lifeless', 'corpse' in 13.10–18 shows that the author in 14.27 is having similar thoughts about the idols.

29.   Reider (1957: 177) argues that v. 8 '(e)numerates four results of idolatry: madness (Bacchic frenzy), false ideals, injustice, and perjury'. Thus, we may deduce from the results of idolatry one of the reasons for Wisdom's condemnation of idolatry. For if idolatry leads to such serious conse-quences, then it not only fails to honour God but also directly advocates disobedience to the true God, which is the reason of their punishment.

With these negative terms the author conveys the idea that the results of idolatry are an evil and wicked society,[30] and so reveals his hatred for the religio-cultural practices of the Gentiles and his own surrounding Graeco-Roman world.[31] Thus far, the critique of idolatry in Wisdom seems to lie in the author's emphasis on the true God.[32]

(vi) *Wisdom 15.1–6.*
The theme of the true God continues in Wisdom 15, where the author contrasts the true God and idols showing that the former is sought after and therefore superior, while the latter are ridiculous because they are made.

In 15.1–6, the author begins with Σὺ δέ (but you…), changing the subject matter of 14.22–31, the consequences of idolatry, to the kind (χρηστός) and true (ἀληθής) God,[33] who is not only slow to anger (μακρόθυμος, literally 'patient') but also merciful (ἐλέει) (15.1). The emphasis here is on the four divine attributes mentioned in Exod. 34.6. Since the context of Exodus 34 is the re-writing of the laws, the reference to these divine attributes suggests the author has in mind the covenant motif, which primarily means those who seek after God are his (εἰδότες ὅτι σοὶ λελογίσμεθα, v. 2). And seeking after God involves not sinning (οὐχ ἁμαρτησόμεθα) which in the context here is a clear reference to idolatry, as vv. 4–6 show. In other words, belonging to God requires 'faithfulness' to his command to worship him alone.[34] And this leads to knowledge of God which is itself perfect virtue (ὁλόκληρος δικαιοσύνη) and the root of immortality (τὸ κράτος ῥίζα ἀθανασίας) (v. 3). In other words, the knowledge of the true God leads to salvation – 'we are yours' (v. 3).[35] Winston rightly points out that the covenant motif in Deut. 9.29, 'Yet they are your very own people', refers to Israel's status as Yahweh's children despite their sin.[36] Understood in a covenantal light, this is

30. So Reider 1957: 177.
31. While scholars have interpreted Wisdom as having different purposes, e.g. Collins (2000: 202) views it as one of convergence in Greek culture; Reider (1957: 9–12) sees it as a polemical work; and Barclay (1996: 184, 186) argues that it is 'cultural aggression', the basic conception that Wisdom reveals a distaste for the idolatrous evil practices of Alexandria is still valid. Even though Collins has sought to show from various Greek authors and the terms employed by Wisdom that the author of Wisdom is attempting to find common ground with his Greek counterparts, he precisely betrays the fact that it is still the idolatrous practices of the masses that Wisdom is polemicizing against.
32. That the author is having in mind the God of Israel may be seen in his allusions to Israel as a righteous people and his constant reference to the history of Israel as the paradigmatic example for the Gentiles. See Collins (2000: 200), who rightly points out the equation the author makes between Israel and the righteous. See further Wis. 2.23–24, where a clear reference to the creation is made (cf. Gen. 1.26; 2.17a, and 3.1–7), which again suggests that the God of Moses is in view here.
33. Reider (1957: 178) says, 'The writer passes now from the lifeless idols to the great living God of Israel…' Cf. Winston 1979: 281.
34. In the context of Exod. 34.17, Israel is specifically commanded not to visually or physically represent God.
35. One may argue that this is the question of the immortality of the soul, as Collins (1997: 186) does. But more importantly, knowledge of the true God in the context of covenant would imply a relationship with God himself.
36. Winston 1979: 281.

perhaps among the greatest benefits of worshipping the true God, which is totally absent between the idols and their devotees.

(vii) *Wisdom 15.7–13.*
Idol-making remains the theme in this section. Here, out of the same clay the potter makes vessels (γλυπτὰ δημιουργῶν, 'fabricated image') for various uses, both clean and unclean. Then with evil labour (κακόμοχθος) he forms a 'vain' God (θεὸν μάταιον) (v. 8). The term that the author uses to describe the image is κίβδηλα (v. 9), which, as a metaphor, means 'fraudulent' and 'dishonest',[37] suggesting the idols are only a counterfeit of the true God, meant to deceive others into believing them to be the true God. Thus, the idol-maker's hope is worthless (εὐτελεστέρα, v. 10) because idol-making is a sin (v. 13). The reference to Gen. 2.7 in v. 11 further suggests that the idol-maker has erred cognitively in that he has not 'discerned' (ἠγνόησεν) his creator.[38] This again highlights the author's emphasis on the true God.

(viii) *Wisdom 15.14–19.*
In 15.14-19, the author begins with an attack on the enemies and oppressors[39] of God's people as most foolish (ἀφρονέστατοι) and as having a soul more feeble (τάλανες) than that of an infant (v. 14). For they reckoned all idols as gods (v. 15). The critique of idols here in v. 15 resembles that of Ps. 115.4–7 where an intellectual critique of the idol is made, tracing its origin to the handiwork of humans. But because humans are unable to form a God like himself (v. 16), the idol is a dead thing (νεκρόν, v. 17). But the Egyptian animal worship by far receives the author's worst condemnation (v. 18),[40] particularly the animals they

37. It also means 'adulterated things'. See Liddell and Scott 1940: 956. Cf. Reider 1957: 181.
38. Reider (1957: 181) comments: 'He wilfully ignored his Maker, cf. Isa. 1.3'. The assumption of the author of Wisdom seems to be that the idol-maker should have known but failed to acknowledge the true God who created (πλάσσαντα, v. 11) him. This shows an expectation on the part of the author that all humanity ought to know the true God and creator, which further implies a possible view of a universal application of the first and second commandments.
39. Who are these oppressors? Reider (1957: 183) thinks they are the nations that have oppressed Israel, such as the Egyptians. The author may have had the thought that idols were introduced into Israel by the Gentile nations. If this is the case, he could well have in mind the religious influence of the Graeco-Roman world on the Jews. Thus, v. 18 serves the purpose of countering the particularly bizarre Egyptian animal worship.
40. This is unlikely to be an effort of the author of Wisdom to seek acceptance among the cultured Greeks of Alexandria (Collins 1997: 213; 2000: 200–202). For the conception of Wisdom concerning the true God differs from that of the Greeks. And if we were to take into consideration Wis. 15.14–19, it would appear that the author is extending the conception of 'faithfulness' in worshipping the true God to the Egyptians. Rather than attempting to gain acceptance among the cultured Greeks of Alexandria, the author is more likely criticizing pagan idolatry and the Egyptian animal worship from a culturally superior position of belonging to the 'true' God of the Jews. Although Collins is right to say that the author sees wisdom as universal, it is the true God to whom the author of Wisdom seeks to direct the attention of all people. And if Wisdom has in mind the God of Israel, as Collins himself has shown (2000: 201), and as we have seen in 15.3 the possible covenant motif, one wonders how the author is able to gain acceptance among the Greeks who were unlikely to accept the religion of the Jews.

worship, which the author considers the most hateful (τὰ ἔχθιστα, v. 18) and are therefore excluded from the praise and blessing of God (v. 19).[41]

c. *Conclusion*
The above analysis shows the author's attitude towards idolatry to be negative. He mounts a relentless attack not only on the idols, but also on the entire process of idol-making and the maker, while speaking positively about the God of the Jews (15.3). Throughout, the author critiques idolatry on the cognitive level, showing two basic reasons for such critique: (1) the true God cannot be represented; (2) idols have no real existence and are therefore powerless. Those who attribute to idols what rightly belongs to the true God, that is, power and life, are guilty of the sin of idolatry and therefore face the prospect of punishment. The second definition of idolatry as misrepresenting/dishonouring the true God seems to be operative in Wisdom, of which two aspects have received greater emphasis: (1) misrepresenting the true God visually; and (2) confusing God with nature.

3. *Philo*

Philo was born between 25 and 20 BCE and died around 50 CE in Alexandria.[42] His writings reveal that he had an excellent training in the Jewish scripture, which served as the foundation of his philosophy, alongside an extraordinary Greek education that familiarized him with Greek philosophies.[43] However, he preferred the tranquil life of contemplation to the complex and harsh reality of politics.[44] In him, we witness an epitome of a devout Jew who saw his life as deeply rooted in, and therefore committed to, the Jewish community, particularly that of Alexandria.[45] But he was also always concerned about the Jewish people universally.

For Philo, the most important source of one's life is the Torah, whose author is the Ruler, the Maker, the Divine, and Father of all.[46] Thus Philo categorically opposes any effort in representing God. Not surprisingly, therefore, we are able to find a philosophical and intellectual critique of idolatry and polytheism.[47]

---

41.   Reider (1957: 184) points out that the clause 'they have escaped etc.' in v. 19 is unclear. However, the author might have intentionally left it unclear so as to create a double insult, that is, both the animals and their devotees are excluded from God's praise and blessing.

42.   See Sandmel (1979: 3) and Barclay (1996: 159) for the dating of Philo's year of birth and also Barclay's n. 74.

43.   Sandmel (1979: 15) observes that 'There is universal agreement among scholars that the Greek culture reflected in Philo is both broad and penetrating, the result of reading and study in intensity and depth. He quotes some 54 classical authors directly and accurately.' See also Borgen (1997: 17) and Barclay (1996: 159–61) for similar comments, including those about Philo's Jewish background; cf. *Spec. Leg.* 1.314.

44.   Cf. Barclay (1996: 161–62) for a brief discussion of Philo's preference for a contemplative life; see also *Spec. Leg.* 3.1–6; cf. *Abr.* 20–25, 85–87; *Vit. Cont.* 18–21.

45.   That he was a prominent member of the Jewish community is see from, e.g., *Leg. Gai.* 182. See Borgen 1997: 14–15.

46.   Sandmel 1984: 23.

47.   Cf. Wolfson (1948: 27–32) who devotes a considerable amount of space to the discussion of polytheism. A somewhat truncated discussion can be found in Borgen (1997: 208–12).

We will discuss five main passages from Philo.[48] The first is *Op. Mund.* 170–72 where a foundation statement about God is made. The second is *Dec.* 52–81 where Philo makes a sharp attack on three levels of idolatry. The third is *Spec. Leg.* 1.12–31 where Philo repeats his vehement attack on idolatry but with a slight change. This is followed by a discussion of the fourth, *Vit. Cont.* 3–8, which provides a gradation of idolatry. The fifth and final treatment will be the piecemeal sections taken from *Legatio ad Gaium* in which Philo relates the event leading up to the violation of the temple at Jerusalem and hurls sharp and harsh criticisms at the emperor Gaius.

a. De opificio mundi *170–72*

De opificio mundi, On the Creation, is a treatise prior to Philo's treatment of the Laws (*Op. Mund.* 3). In this treatise, he gives an account (almost a commentary) of the creation based on Scripture,[49] and ends with a summary about the Maker of the world's origin in 170–72.[50] According to Philo, there are five things or conceptions that are fairest and best of all. The first is the eternal existence of God (170), of which both his existence and eternity are emphasized. This point is made with atheists in mind.[51] The second conception is the unity of God (θεὸς εἶς ἐστι, 171) that opposes polytheism.[52] For Philo, polytheists practise mob-rule (ὀχλοκρατία), when they view all the earthly creatures and animals as gods. The third conception is the creation of the world (γενητὸς ὁ κόσμος), which refutes those who believe the world is eternal.[53] The fourth is the singularity of the world (εἶς ἐστιν ὁ κόσμος), whose Maker makes it as unique as himself; those who teach a plurality of worlds therefore lack knowledge.[54] For such a notion suggests the wrong conception that God is not unique himself. The fifth conception is about the fatherly nature of God, which is his forethought (προνοεῖ). This constitutes the law of nature (172).

For Philo these five conceptions are foundational to the bliss and blessedness (μακαρίαν καὶ εὐδαίμονα) in one's life. Although this is not an explicit

---

48.   Many passages in Philo treat the question of idolatry or polytheism and it is not possible to include all of them, besides those cited here, other examples include *Dec.* 156; *Spec. Leg.* 1.56; *Vit. Cont.* 3–8; *Poster. C.* 165; *Vit. Mos.* 2.193–96, 205; *Fug.* 180; *Congr.* 15; *Omn. Prob. Lib.* 105; *Abr.* 267; *Praem. Poen.* 162.

49.   Borgen (1997: 68) observes that more than a third of *De opificio mundi* 'is devoted to arithmological excursus on the tetrad and the hebdomad' so that the treatise reveals 'an extensive use of Pythagorean-like speculations on numbers'. Cf. *Op. Mund.* 47–52, 89–128.

50.   Borgen (1997: 79) refers to these as the 'right ideas' about God. It is most appropriate to describe this as Philo's creedal statement; see Barclay 1996: 164–65.

51.   This is a criticism of the Sceptic view which doubts the existence of God. Cf. Borgen 1997: 68. Philo views polytheism as a step leading to atheism (*Praem. Poen.* 162); see also Goldenberg 1998: 51.

52.   Philo most likely has in mind the Greek and Egyptian Gods; cf. *Dec.* 53; *Vit. Cont.* 3–6; see also Wolfson 1948: 27–28. In *Migr. Abr.* 69 polytheism and atheism are equally profane.

53.   This is also called the Aristotelian view; cf. *Aet. Mund.* 10.

54.   The Epicureans believe in a plurality of worlds and deny the doctrine of providence. Cf. *Post. C.* 2 where the doctrines of the Epucureans also posit that God has a human face.

condemnation of idolaters, Philo probably would not deny that the reverse will be true, namely that idolaters will lead a miserable life.

b. De decalogo *52–81*

There are three main strands of critique here: that of nature worship; that of idol-makers and idol-worshippers; and that of Egyptian animal worship.[55] And Philo discusses his critiques in an ascending order with increased intensity.

(i) *Nature worship (52–65).*

Philo begins with a foundational principle – the transcendent source of all that exists is God (52). However, this principle is lacking among humanity in whom is a great delusion or deception (πλάνος τις ου μικρός),[56] expressed in nature worship.

For example, humans have deified (ἐκτεθειώκασι) the four elements of nature (53–58) – earth, water, air, and fire; also the sun, the moon, planets, stars, heaven and the whole world (53) – and have given them names of Greek and Roman gods,[57] and therefore concealed (παρεκαλύψαντο) the true God.[58]

Such deification of nature comes from the myth-makers (55),[59] who contradict Moses' instruction against treating any part of the universe as the omnipotent God (58). According to our definitions of idolatry, nature worship is, cognitively, a mixing of God with nature thus reducing God to 'not being' (οὐκ ὄντα).[60] Philo terms this 'profanity' (ου θεμιτόν), a result of the lack of capacity for instruction (ουκ ειδότες ἀδιδάκτω τῆ φύσει); the failure to learn (οὐ σπουδάζοντες μαθεῖν) and therefore the inability to know the truly Existent One (τὸν ὄντα ὄντως).

For Philo, nature worship is equivalent to honouring a king's subordinates, and nature worshippers are most senseless, foolish and 'unjust' (61). In so doing they are giving equal measure to what is unequal; and have deliberately forgotten the Maker (λήθη, 62).[61] They therefore ought to reject (ἀπωθεῖν) such imposture (τερθρείαν) and not to worship (μὴ προσκυνεῖν) the brothers (τοὺς ἀδελφούς). For Philo, the created order and humans share one Father (πατὴρ ἀπάντων

55.   Cf. Goldenberg 1998: 52. This is similar to the critique in Wisdom, a pattern which will be discussed below.

56.   Cf. *Congr.* 15; *Virt.* 214 states that the removal of the One God is 'delusion'.

57.   So Borgen 1997: 209–10.

58.   The true God is here described as the highest (ἀνώτατον) and the most august (πρεσβύτατον), the begetter (τὸν γεννητήν), the ruler of the great world-city (τὸν ἄρχοντα τῆς μεγαλαπόλεως), the commander-in-chief (τὸν στρατάρχην) of the invincible host, the pilot (τὸν κυβερνήτην) who regulates (οἰκονομεῖ) safety.

59.   The making of myths is μυθοποιία; cf. *Leg. All.* 1.43; *Sacr.* 13, 76; *Fug.* 121; *Spec. Leg.* 1.79; see Wolfson (1948: 32–34), who rightly argues that Philo sees in the second commandment a prohibition not only against idolatrous worship but also against all deities invented by myth-makers. Cf. Wis. 13.1–9.

60.   Elsewhere, i.e. *Vit. Mos.* 2.193–96, the Egyptians are accused of nature worship by setting up earth against heaven and by even deifying the Nile as if it were the counterpart of heaven; see also *Fug.* 180 and Wolfson 1948: 30.

61.   Cf. *Virt.* 179 which states that the best of all is God, but Him they forget.

εἶς), who is the Maker of all (ὁ ποιητὴς τῶν ὅλων).⁶² Thus, nature worship is 'brother worship'!

Humans, however, are to serve the uncreated (τῷ ἀγενητῷ) and the eternal (τῷ ἀιδίῳ), and to engrave in themselves the first and most sacred of command-ments, which is the acknowledgement and honour of the One God (65).⁶³

(ii) *Idol-makers and idol-worshippers (66–76a).*

In 52–56, the second commandment serves as the basis for Philo's critique of idolatry. In 66–76a, he is applying it more universally, and as a critique of all forms of idolatry.⁶⁴ Thus, in 66, he first makes a distinction between those who worship nature and those who worship idols. Taking a similar stance as Wisdom (13.6–7), Philo thinks that the former have a lesser offence than the latter, which he elaborates more extensively.

First, they misrepresent God by making images and figures with wood (ξύλα), stones (λίθους), silver (ἄργυρον), and gold (χρυσόν), including 'other works of human hands' (τὰ ἄλλα χειροκμήτων), which are likely anthropomorphic representations of God (cf. *Det. Pot. Ins.* 125). These sever the idolaters from the rightful conception of God (67),⁶⁵ resulting in their utter lack of security in the certainty of truth. They are blind (τυφλοί) to the truth of God and more mis-erable than the physically blind (68). Such people should receive no pity, only punishment (τοῖς δὲ κόλασις ὡς μοχθηροῖς).⁶⁶

Further, the idolaters should have deified the sculptors and painters,⁶⁷ who receive less concern than the idols which the idolaters embellish and serve (70–71).

Indeed, embellishing and beautifying idols which idolaters regard as gods is one thing, offering prayers and sacrifices to these idols by their own makers is worse (72). Philo, again sarcastically, argues that they might as well worship their own hands; or if that were to appear egotistical, they could always worship their hammers, anvils, pencils, tongs, and other tools. By mentioning the tools neces-sary for the making of the idols, Philo shows that the tools are of better and greater use, without which the idols would not even have been formed! Thus, the futility and the sin of idolatry are being exposed, making those who engage in idol wor-ship even more preposterous.

---

62.   Thus Borgen (1997: 233) is not altogether accurate when he says the 'brothers' referred to the stars. Certainly it includes the stars, but other created things as well!

63.   This is in sharp contrast to the errors of those who deify the elements and other planetary balls; cf. Borgen 1997: 233.

64.   See for example the treatment of the golden calf by Philo in *Vit. Mos.* 2.161–73, *Spec. Leg.* 3.125. Elsewhere, i.e. *Spec. Leg.* 1.54, Philo warns that any betrayal of the One God leads to the utmost punishment.

65.   *Abr.* 268 states: 'Faith in God, then, is the one sure and infallible good, consolation of life, fulfilment of bright hopes, dearth of ills, harvest of goods, inacquaintance with misery, acquaintance with piety, heritage of happiness, all-round betterment of the soul which is firmly stayed on Him Who is the cause of all things and can do all things yet only wills the best'.

66.   Writing in a hyperbole, Philo argues that even 'an infant knows' (ἔγνω νήπιος) that the crafts-man is superior to what he has made. He argues that the craftsman is the father of the craft since he has made it.

67.   Cf. *Abr.* 267 on the creation of sculptors and painters.

More vehement is the critique of 73–74, in which Philo describes the idolaters as demented (ἀπονοηθέντας), who should seek to be like their images which are totally useless and powerless. This description is clearly an echo of Ps. 115.5–8 where v. 8 likens the idol-makers to their idols, so are those who trust in idols like them (cf. Isa. 44.9–20). Thus, Philo's critique targets idol-makers, their idols, and idol-worshippers. Philo further insults the pagan shrine and temple by calling them a temple-prison (εἰρκτὴν τὸν ἱερόν): idols are prisoners and their worshippers prison-guards!

One clear proof of the idolaters' impiety is their indignation at calls to imitate their idols (75). Such a reaction could be due to the possibility that idolatry in itself is impious, and that these idolaters know in their hearts that idols are useless and truly foolish. Or it is possible that the idolaters hold a high regard for their idols that any suggestion to be like their idols would be tantamount to blasphemy, which further highlights their impiety.

Philo does not see anything positive in idolaters, or any sincerity or devotion in idolaters towards their idols. He therefore attacks them because what they do – idol-making and idol-worshipping – goes against the teaching of the Torah which to him is universally applicable.[68]

Thus Philo concludes that humans who have souls must not worship the idols which have no souls (76a). For it is out of place (ἄτοπους) and therefore unnatural and disgusting for humans to turn to the service of what their hands have made.

(iii) *Egyptian animal worship (76b–81).*

For Philo, the Egyptian animal worship is by far the worst form of idolatry. For the Egyptians not only venerate all kinds of animals, but also invent legendary tales about them (μυθικοὶ πλάσματα).[69] He reserves his strongest criticism yet for the excess of such worship, which includes the fiercest and most savage of all animals, namely lions and crocodiles, and the venomous asp (ἀσπίδα, a small poisonous snake, possibly the Egyptian cobra, perhaps similar to the present day North African cobra).[70] They are a deliberate and careful choice resulting from a thorough ransacking of the two elements.[71] Such animal worship shows the Egyptians hold a wrong conception of God.[72] And Philo insults it further by saying that

68. Thus Barclay (1996: 174) comments: 'In this sense Jews are the one truly worshipful community in the world; they are the nation with the clearest vision of God, the people thus naturally most God-beloved'. See also *Vit. Mos.* 2.189; *Plant.* 55–60; *Migr. Abr.* 113–14; *Abr.* 98. Cf. Borgen (1984: 235) who states that Philo's purpose in writing the *Life of Moses* was to tell the Gentile readers about the supreme law-giver whose laws they should accept and honour. It is therefore clear that Philo views Judaism as universally applicable.

69. Although Philo grants that the Egyptians might deify their domestic animals (bulls, ταύρους; rams, κριούς; and goats, τράγους) since they provide the means of livelihood (77), he does not therefore endorse it. His reasoning here is probably a rhetorical ploy and no more. It is unlikely that having criticized so much the physical misrepresentation of God he should now allow the deification of animals.

70. In *Poster. C.* 165, he condemns the Egyptian animal worship as utterly nonsensical.

71. ἀφ' ἑκατέρου, literally, after each of the two, i.e. elements, γῆς and ὕδατος.

72. In addition, there are other less savage and grotesque animals than lions and crocodiles which the Egyptians deify such as dogs, cats, wolves, birds, fish, etc. But they are no less ridiculous

first-time visitors to Egypt who witness such worship are likely to die from laughing (80), for animal worshippers are like beasts in human shape (ἀνθρωποειδῆ θηρία).[73] The deification of animals shows the worshippers have stooped low and degraded themselves to a level lower than the animals, but failed to worship the true God.

c. De specialibus legibus *1.12–31*[74]

This part of the treatise treats the first two commandments. The first (12–20) follows the line of the discussion in *De decalogo*; the second (21–31) follows the same except that Philo further interprets idolatry symbolically (e.g. idolatry of wealth). However, the treatment found in *De decalogo* involves three levels of critique; whereas in *Spec. Leg.* 1.12–31, only the first two are treated while Egyptian animal worship is left out. Meanwhile, Philo adds two other aspects of idolatry: that of idolatry of wealth (23–27), and the idolatry of personages (28–31).

(i) *Nature worship (12-20).*

In this passage, Philo goes into another lengthy discussion of nature worship, in which he calls the action of nature-worshipppers 'a going astray' (πλάνον, 15–16). For they recognize the gods as absolutely powerful (αὐτοκράτορας, 13) and the cause of all events. But citing Moses, Philo points out that the universe was created as the greatest city (πόλις ἡ μεγίστη), and the heavenly bodies are like magistrates and subjects (ἄρχοντας καὶ ὑπηκόους), which are not absolutely or unconditionally powerful, but are lieutenants (ὑπάρχους) of the one Father (ἑνὸς πατρός).[75] They operate perfectly as they have been modelled after the principles of the Maker's governance (μιμουμένους τὴν ἐπιστασίαν). Thus nature worshippers have confused God with nature, mistaking the created things for the cause of all events in the universe.[76] This is precisely what the first commandment warns against: not recognizing the true and eternal God as Ruler of all,[77] whom Philo describes as not only the God of gods (οὐ μόνον θεὸς θεῶν),

---

(καταγέλαστοι, 79). Philo elsewhere describes this form of worship as 'the folly (ἠλιθιότητα) of Egypt' (*Spec. Leg.* 1.79). Cf. Wolfson 1948: 31

73.   The word περινοστέω means to go around, to visit or inspect. It could mean that as the visitor, who is probably a tourist of some sort, looks on while the idol-worshippers go around visiting and inspecting their idols, thus they seem (δοκεῖν) beasts in human shape.

74.   Borgen (1984: 239) rightly points out that Book 1 provides the interpretation of the first and second commandments, and prohibits idolatry and gives details on the knowledge and the worship of God.

75.   They are at most 'his agents and subordinates', so Barclay 1996: 431; cf. *Conf. Ling.* 168–73.

76.   The instruction of Moses in Deut. 4.19 is repeated here (15) and it teaches that any act which deifies the heavenly gods is considered going astray (πλάνον). For it directly contradicts the teaching of Moses, and is consequently defined as idolatry at the cognitive level.

77.   Cf. 16–18, where Philo argues that the astral bodies must not be supposed to have absolute power as if they were gods. The reason is simple: God alone is absolutely powerful. The heavenly bodies may have the rank of subordinate rulers (τὴν ὑπάρχων τάξιν, 19), but they are not God. They rule or operate according to the laws of nature as given by God the Maker. Thus, Philo is careful not to contradict his own statement in *Op. Mund.* 171 where he describes the world as unique as the Maker.

who holds authority and sovereignty over all the gods, but also the Maker of all (πάντων δημιουγός).[78] The point which Philo makes here is carefully defined: if anyone renders the worship of the Eternal Creator to a created thing, that person stands 'damaged in the understanding', 'deranged' (φρεωβλαβής) and is guilty of the highest degree of impiety (ἀσεβείᾳ τῇ μεγίστῃ). This is a blanket charge since nothing other than the one true eternal Maker is to be worshipped, and all forms of worship to anything other than the true God are impious.

(ii) *Idol-making and idol-worshipping (21–31)*.

Philo goes on to a critique of idol-making. The treatment here differs from elsewhere in that Philo adds another category of idolatry: the love of wealth (23–27). The next category is the deification of personages (28–31). That all these three categories may be classified under idol-making and idol-worshipping seems clear as each is the making of something into a god for worship and honour.

Physical representation of God (21–22). Philo's harsh critique is first of all levelled against visual or physical representation of God (cf. *Vit. Mos.* 2.205). He cites the second commandment and argues against any physical representation of God with gold or silver (22). However, idolaters part with their silver and gold, and sculptors carry out the job of making idols as if they were 'competent to fashion gods'. It is a misrepresentation of God and thus a violation of the second commandment and a degradation of the true God.

Love of wealth (23–27). The love of wealth is capable of leading people to a point equivalent to religious devotion to a divine image (ἄγαλμα θεῖον). Therefore the non-literal aspect of the prohibition issued by the second commandment is valuable for promoting morality (23). Morality in relation to wealth, Philo argues, is dependent upon one's religious morality.[79] For those who love money, silver and gold, wealth would appear to be a source of blessing and happiness. But this also suggests a departure from the true God who alone must be worshipped.

Philo cites an example of the poor and needy begging for wealth at their neighbours' gate, and describes this behaviour as paying homage to neighbours' wealth (24), which he likens to people attending grand temples to bestow worship on their gods.[80]

By seeing a non-literal prohibition on wealth in the second commandment and in Lev. 19.4, Philo is actually making an application of the biblical prohibition on idolatry to wealth, thus turning an obsession with wealth into idolatry, the crux of

---

78. Goldenberg (1998: 52–54) states that Philo does not see any value in other gods for he only finds the Jewish religion, its scripture and its laws to be the most supreme, hence his rejection of all pagan religious worship.

79. Borgen (1997: 213) observes that the foundation of the ethical aspect of life and virtues is the worship of the God who is. Thus, there is a close relationship between idolatrous worship and immoral behaviour. Cf. *Virt.* 181–82.

80. Although this appears more like a violation of the first commandment, Philo views this as a conceptual error in that these people, by their very behaviour have made wealth represent God when they seek after it as if it was God.

which seems to be the 'desire for money' (φιλαργυρία, 24) and the 'divine honours' (τιμὰς ἰσοθέους, 25) assigned to wealth.

Conceptually, the obsession of the poor and the needy with wealth makes it like a god, which is elusive and unreliable (24). This could suggest a 'misrepresentation' of the true God. Thus it is deemed idolatrous.

Invention of personages (28–31). In 28, Philo charges that the myth-makers build their false imaginations against the truth (cf. *Congr.* 15) when they invent new gods.[81] The translation by Colson of the new gods as 'personages' requires explanation.[82] Do the 'personages' refer to important figures such as heroes of the past who are being venerated? Or are they mere characters imagined and invented from pure fantasy? Philo throws light on this point in *Spec. Leg.* 2.164, where he refers to the plurality of the gods and describes them as the 'vain invention of the tribe of poets...' (τὸ ποιητικὸν γένος ἐμύθευσε...). It thus appears that Philo has in mind the 'invented' myths, rather than the venerated past heroes or emperors.

'(T)o promote their seductiveness', the myth-makers incorporate melody, music with all the metre and rhythm so as to deceive the audience (cf. *Det. Pot. Ins.* 125). Philo attacks not just the sculpture and the painting associated with it, but also the whole purpose of the myth-makers whom he accuses of deceiving and of making the soul unsteady and unsettled. Thus, he exposes the deception of the myth-makers. This is contrasted with Moses who repeatedly teaches that God is one, the Framer and Maker of all things (θεὸς εἷς ἐστι καὶ κτίστης καὶ ποιητὴς τῶν ὅλων) and the Lord of created things (ὁ κύριος τῶν γεγονότων) (30).

A further contrast of this one God is the truth that 'stability and fixity and lordship are by nature vested in Him alone' (τὸ βέβαιον καὶ πάγιον καὶ τὸ κῦρος ὡς ἀληθῶς περὶ αὐτὸν μόνον πέφυκε). Philo concludes that those who cling to the God who IS live![83] By inference, those who do not cling to the true God but deify others will die! Philo is therefore at odds with the pagan religion and all attempts to represent the true God.

The above Philonic critique suggests that Philo sees idolatry as having different grades, which seems to parallel his 'graded' critique in *Vit. Cont.* 3–8.[84]

---

81. There is no mention of the word 'pesonages' in LCL, except the word πάντες. However, the description of θεοὺς καινούς suggests that the πάντες refers to some form of gods and, with the description of the inventors as οἱ μυθογράφοι, we may follow Cohn's suggestion of adding μῦθοι before πάντες.

82. LCL, Philo, vol. 7, 114 n. 2.

83. Deut. 4.4, Colson's observation of the meaning of the original is that those who took God's side remain alive. Cf. *Fug.* 56 and *Spec. Leg.* 1.345.

84. Similarly, there seems to be a parallel between Philo's critique of idolatry (in *Dec.* 52–81 and *Spec. Leg.* 1.12–31) and that found in Wisdom 13–15.

d. De vita contemplativa *3–8*.
Although Colson does not consider *De vita contemplativa* to 'rank high' among Philo's works,[85] the section 3–8 is important as it reflects Philo's view that there is a gradation of idolatry. For Philo, the different grades seem to connote different degrees of seriousness. The first is termed the 'elements' (τὰ στοιχεῖα) which comprise earth, water, air, and fire (*Vit. Cont.* 3; cf. *Spec. Leg.* 1.12–20; *Dec.* 52–65). While these elements are powerful in themselves, Philo describes them as 'lifeless' (ἄψυχος). And they are 'laid' there by God (*Vit. Cont.* 4). This is a strong word of critique as it shows the unreasonableness of the people who not only revere the elements, but also the celestial stars. But the elements and the celestial host are the result of the Architect who is perfect in knowledge, a clear reference to God (*Vit. Cont.* 5). The second level of idolatry moves a little lower, that of the demigods (*Vit. Cont.* 6) (cf. *Spec. Leg.* 1.28–31).[86] For Philo, the claim that one is a god is ridiculous as he believes one cannot be both mortal and immortal. The argument is further bolstered by his reference to human birth, youthful passions and sexual liaison with women, which suggest that Philo views immortality to be incompatible with mortality because of the latter's human limitations. The third level of idolatry concerns the worship of actual idols of previously shapeless wood and stone (*Vit. Cont.* 7), hewn by quarry-workers and wood-cutters (cf. *Spec. Leg.* 1.21–27; *Dec.* 66–76a). The fourth level is that of the Egyptian animal worship, which is 'hardly decent even to mention' (*Vit. Cont.* 8) (cf. *Dec.* 76b–81).

The gradation of the idolatry in *De vita contemplativa* and the parallel critique of idolatry found in Wisdom might suggest that either depended on the other for their critique, or possibly that both drew on the same source.[87] It is possible that both Philo and the writer of Wisdom depended on the same biblical record such as Jer. 10.1–16 and Isa. 44.9–20. However, the range of critiques of idolatry in the LXX, Philo, and Wisdom might also suggest that there is no fixed tradition in terms of the source. It would be helpful to tabulate the four passages (*Dec.* 52–81, *Spec. Leg.* 1.12–31, *Vit. Cont.* 3–8, and Wisdom 13–15) on idolatry and compare them. Such a tabulation enables us to see the similarities and differences between Philo and the writer of Wisdom, as well as the different critiques of idolatry by Philo.

---

85. Cited in LCL Philo, vol. 9, 104. See Schürer (III, 756ff.).

86. See the discussion on *Legatio ad Gaium* in which Gaius is compared to a demigod. Cf. Wis. 14.15–21.

87. Winston (1979: 248) puts it the other way, that although both Philo and Wisdom may derive from a common Jewish-Hellenistic apologetic tradition, it is likely that one could be dependent upon the other.

De decalogo (52–81)	De specialibus legibus (1.12–31)	De vita contemplativa (3–8)	Wisdom of Solomon (13.1–15.19)
(1) nature worship (52–65): – deification of the natural elements as 'error'	(1) nature worship (12–20): – 'going astray'	(1) worship of the elements (3–5)	(1) nature worship (13.1–9)
(2) idol-makers and worshippers (66–76a): – misrepresenting God	(2) idol-making and worshipping (21–31): – physical misrepresentation of God (21–22) – wealth (23–27)	(2) demigods (6)	(2) idol-making and worshipping (13.10–19; 14.1–7, 12–21; 15.7–17)
(3) ————	(3) personages (28–31): – myths	(3) idol-making and worshipping (7)	(3) origin of idolatry (14.12–21): – veneration of humans/demigods
(4) Egyptian animal worship (76b–81): – 'folly of Egypt'	(4) ————	(4) Egyptian animal worship (8)	(4) Egyptian animal worship (15.18–19)

The above table shows that idol-making and worshipping is a common theme which invites condemnation. But of greater condemnation is the Egyptian animal worship, since in each critique of the different idolatrous acts, the intensity of condemnation grows towards Egyptian animal worship. Thus, in the three texts in which animal worship is mentioned, it is placed at the lowest of all categories. However, from the gradation of idolatry, it seems clear that there is a variety of critique of idolatry within a common shape, and thus it may be possible that there is no fixed tradition behind the critique.

e. Legatio ad Gaium

In *Legatio ad Gaium*, Philo reacts to a situation in which the Jewish community was being threatened, particularly the sanctity of the temple in Jerusalem during the reign of emperor Gaius. Even though the event was extremely complex, the main target of Philo's severe criticism was Gaius.

The tragic tale started with the emperor Gaius who, after a series of extreme murderous acts to ensure the security of his throne and to remove all those whom he disfavoured (22–65), wanted to be thought of as a god (75–80). He took on the insignia of the images of the gods (81) and attacked the honours paid to these gods (93–97). However, Philo meticulously sets out the symbolic meanings of all the ornaments of the gods (98–113) and questions Gaius's qualification to be likened to any of them (114). However, because of the people's praises Gaius thought he was really God (162) and so bestowed upon himself the divinity by setting up a statue of himself under the name of Zeus (181) and demanded that all should acknowledge his divinity (117–18). The Jews, however, refused on the basis of their laws and their knowledge of the one God (115), and became the prime suspects of opposition and a target of the Alexandrians' hatred. This led to the pogrom of 38 CE during which images of Gaius were forcefully introduced into the synagogues (120–36).

When his efforts to be made God were delayed (203, 276–329), Gaius decided to order a colossal statue of himself to be built in Rome. Then calculatingly and carefully he moved to install statues of himself in cities in Alexandria before finally proceeding to the temple in Jerusalem (337–38).

Philo attributes the desecration of the synagogues and the temple to Gaius's great inconsistency of conduct (346) and attacks his act in no uncertain terms (347–48). First, Gaius is accused of annexing ether and heaven (αἰθέρα καὶ οὐρανόν), a result of his dissatisfaction with all his possessions. Second, he is accused of treating God as worthy of nothing (τὸν θεὸν οὐδενὸς ἄξιον). Third, by installing his own statue in the temple hallowed for God (θεῷ καθιερω-θέντα), Gaius was taking away what properly belonged to God, that is, his sovereignty![88] These, Philo charges, are the origin of a great flood of evil. While idolatry discussed earlier is fundamentally erroneous, it is worse still to think and make oneself God.

Thus, Gaius failed to stay within the bounds of human nature (75), but over-stepped them in his eagerness to be thought of as a god.[89] But his belief that he was the shepherd of his people was but 'a mythical fiction' (μυθικὸν πλάσμα, 77) and the 'most godless assumption of godship' (τὴν ἀθεωτάτην ἐκθέωσιν). It is the most grievous impiety, infidelity and ingratitude to the Benefactor of the whole world (118).

Gaius' act was equally idolatrous at the cognitive level in that he not only failed to recognize that God was sovereign over the temple, but also transferred that sovereignty to himself![90]

f. *Conclusion*

The above discussion yields the unambiguously negative attitude of Philo towards idolatry. It also reveals the grounds on which he bases his critique of idolatry. From our analysis above, Philo's basis for rejecting idolatry at all levels is first of all his conception of the true God – the God of the Jews is the Eternal existent God who is one (*Op. Mund.* 170–71), the Framer and Maker of all things, Father and Ruler. And the logical result is his insistence on a universal application of the commandments of the Jewish Scripture, which he extends even to the Gentiles.[91] Thus, any act or conception that contradicts the conception of divinity defined by Philo, regardless of the ethnicity of the persons involved, will be deemed idola-trous and deserving the most vehement critique and condemnation.

We may trace his critique to the definitions of idolatry set out in Chapter 2 above. Philo seems to adopt the second broad category of the definition of idolatry, that is, misrepresenting the true God with an object. And at the cognitive level,

88.   Cf. *Spec. Leg.* 1.67 where Philo asserts that there is to be only 'one temple for the One God', the defilement of which recorded in *Legatio ad Gaium* means that no trace of the reverence and honour due to God is left (*Leg. Gai.* 347).

89.   Cf. Borgen 1997: 22, citing Smallwood 1976: 174–80, 236–45.

90.   A most blasphemous act which is punishable by death; cf. *Spec. Leg.* 1.54; *Vit. Mos.* 2.206.

91.   Cf. Borgen (1997: 209) who comments on *Dec.* 52–57 that the 'two first commandments of the Decalogue serve as basis' for the criticism of idolatry.

three particular aspects of idolatry stand out: (1) the intention of seeking after what is no god to the extent that one replaces the true God, for example with wealth; (2) the mixing of God with nature (such as nature worship); and (3) the failure to recognize God's sovereignty, for example when Gaius imposed on himself the status of the Divine.

4. *Josephus*[92]

Josephus is reckoned to be the 'single most important source for the history of the Jewish people in the first century CE',[93] and since he lived in the turbulent years between 37/38 CE and sometime after 90 CE, a period that coincides with the New Testament times, he makes a relevant example of a Diaspora Jew whose attitude towards idolatry and the reasons for his rejection deserve our attention. How does Josephus view idolatry? And what grounds does he offer for rejecting idols and idolatry? In the following, we will see that Josephus upholds strongly the notion of the one God, which also serves as his basis for rejecting idolatrous ideas and behaviour. Josephus' view of idolatry and his reasons for its rejection are important as he had been accused of treason when he insisted on keeping the spoils which the Galilean revolutionaries took from plundering a royal caravan and on returning them to the owner at a later time (*Life* 126–44); when he later allowed a royal delegate who was imprisoned to flee (*Life* 388–89); and when he not only failed to take his own life under a suicide pact with his soldiers but went on to live in Rome with a royal pension (*Life* 387–88).[94] Although such aspects of Josephus' life could be construed as evidence of 'apostasy', or even 'unfaithfulness' to God, from which Josephus is now repenting, Mason has ably demonstrated the implausibility of such a theory.[95] Further, Josephus' critique of idolatry and his reasons for the critique show otherwise.

We may mention two basic as well as overarching purposes (at least in *Antiquities of the Jews* and *Against Apion*): that of warning the Jews against 'unfaithfulness' to the Jewish ancestral tradition; and that of promoting the Jewish nation by retelling its story,[96] thus correcting wrong or false notions about the Jewish

92.   Literature on Josephus is voluminous. See Schürer (I, 43–63) for an introduction to his works. Attridge (1984: 185–232) provides a good summary of Josephus and his works. Barclay (1996: 346–68) provides a thorough discussion of Josephus' social context and the works of Josephus.

93.   Attridge 1984: 185.

94.   See Feldman (1984: 779–87) for a survey of scholarly opinions on Josephus' life. Bilde (1988: 36–52) argues that Josephus sees himself not as a traitor but a prophet of God who is saved by the grace of God and acts as God's messenger to Vespasian. And it is 'possible to read this narrative in the context of important themes in the rest of his writings', if the emphasis is placed on God's grace and Josephus' characteristics as God's servant. But this seems too simplistic a theme on which Bilde seeks to hang all of Josephus' works.

95.   See Mason 1998: 66–68.

96.   See Barclay 1996: 356–57. Cf. Mason (1998: 80–88) who argues that *Antiquities of the Jews/Life* aim at providing interested Gentiles 'an alternative political constitution and as an alternative philosophical system' (80). However, the Numbers 25 incident which is not discussed at all by Mason poses a difficulty to his thesis: how could the Jewish law serve as an alternative constitution if

faith and the Jewish race and therefore defending Judaism.[97] This twin purpose will guide our following discussion.[98]

a. *Josephus' Summary of the Law (*Antiquities *4.200–201, 207;* Apion *2.190–93)*

Josephus places particular emphasis on the oneness of God which is seen in the 'one holy city' (ἱερὰ πόλις ἔστω μία), 'one temple' (νεὼς εἷς ἐν ταύτῃ ἔστω), and 'one altar' (βωμὸς εἷς) (*Ant.* 4.200).[99] This oneness of God serves as the basis for forbidding the building of altars and temples at other venues, thus maintaining God's uniqueness and holiness:[100] θεὸς γὰρ εἷς καὶ τὸ Ἑβραίων γένος ἕν (4.201).

Josephus claims that he does not criticize other gods out of respect for the word 'god', and explains that Jews should do the same (*Apion* 2.237). The reason why he goes on to criticize the Greek religions is that he is left with no choice,[101] for the accusers of the Jews' provoked him into it (*Apion* 2.238).[102] Thus, this is probably a rhetorical ploy. And the oneness of God is often the basis for his critique of other gods.

In another treatment of the law (*Apion* 2.190–93; cf. *Ant.* 3.91), Josephus argues that the theme of God is stated simply in the laws: he is the creator, the 'beginning, the middle, and the end of all things' (*Apion* 2.190). This effectively

---

the Jews themselves were not fully convinced but were easily lured by Gentile women? Further, the resolution of the problem does not seem to have come from 'reason', but 'violence'! It is thus safer to posit that Josephus seeks to promote the Jewish law but at the same time warns against the surrounding temptations to Jews and the challenges to the Jewish ancestral tradition.

97.   Thus, in his *Against Apion* he seems not only to refute his opponents but primarily to demonstrate the purity and superiority of the Jewish law and the faithfulness of the Jewish people to this law; cf. Barclay 1996: 366–68; Mason (1996: 187–224) argues that *Against Apion* aims primarily to 'encourage potential converts to Judaism' (222). To this, we may add, 'in addition to a thorough defence against the enemies' charges'.

98.   Attridge (1984: 185) notes: 'Each of these works relied in one way or another on earlier sources which Josephus recast to serve several apologetic purposes. Any use of his writings must take account of these various tendencies...' Cf. Barclay 1996: 346.

99.   This is a reference to Exod. 20.25. See Durham (1987: 319–20) for a discussion of the verse.

100.   This may be Josephus' apologetic against any ridicule of the Jewish peculiar form of worship (all the detailed aspects of the sacrifice mark them out), the Jewish peculiar object of worship (which is invisible to the eye), and the Jewish peculiar insistence on just one temple; cf. *Apion* 2.79.

101.   Bilde (1988: 116) observes that Josephus is not able to restrain himself in criticizing the ridiculous Greek religion. He is of the opinion that the traditional Jewish accusation against other gods is a set feature, i.e. a *topos*, in Jewish apologetic literature, and is also a feature here in Josephus.

102.   The ban on deriding the gods is found in Philo too (cf. *Vit. Mos.* 2.26, 205; *Spec. Leg.* 1.7, 53). There he explains with several points which Goldenberg (1997: 385; 1998: 68–69) summarizes as follows: (1) The name 'God' should never be taken lightly, even where it is wrongly applied (*Vit. Mos.* 2.203–205); (2) Praise is always better than attack (*Quaest. in Exod.* 2.5); (3) Religious polemic leads to social violence and should therefore be avoided (also *Quaest. in Exod.*); and (4) Mockery of idols can provoke blasphemy against the true God, while respect towards idols can elicit praise of the true God (*Spec. Leg.* 1.53). However, the ridicule and vehement attack on idolatry and other gods by both of these Jews show they only pay lip service to this point.

means that the God of the Hebrews encompasses all things. No one is fit to make an image of God, for God is inconceivable, unrepresented, invisible, and unimaginable (*Apion* 2.191). Thus, it is impious to represent God; conversely, the worship of God is most saintly, and a 'practice of virtue' (ἀσκοῦντας ἀρετήν) (*Apion* 2.192).

The one temple and one God receive further emphasis in *Apion* 2.193, εἷς ναὸς ἑνὸς θεοῦ. Josephus thus shows that the one God and one temple are the central themes of the Jewish law.[103] They serve as the perspective from which Josephus carries out his apologetics.

b. *Josephus' account of the Midianite women* (Antiquities *4.126–54*)
Josephus' account of Israelites' sexual and religious liaison with the Midianite women is an expansion of Numbers 25. It reflects an important purpose,[104] and sheds light on Josephus' attitude towards the Gentile gods.

It begins with Balaam providing advice to King Balak of Midian on how he may overcome the Israelites (*Ant.* 4.126–30).[105] The method appears relatively simple. The king should send attractive Midianite women to befriend Israelite men (*Ant.* 4.129), charming and luring them with their beauty until they were 'overmastered by their passion' (*Ant.* 4.130).[106] The women should then withdraw from the Israelites, laying down the condition for their continued liaison with the women: the Israelites should 'renounce the laws of their fathers' and their God and 'worship the gods of the Midianites and Moabites' (*Ant.* 4.130).

This advice of Balaam is not found in the Bible. In Num. 25.1–2, no such strategy is in view. Josephus apparently offers an explanation of the Israelites' behaviour so as to shift the blame onto the Midianite women. The king followed Balaam's advice and the Midianite women succeeded in their plan (131–36). The address of the Midianite women is worth examining, as well as the Israelites' behaviour.

First of all, the Israelites possess customs and a way of life alien to all (ἀλλο-τριώτατα), seen particularly in their food and drink. What is noteworthy is that Josephus attributes to the Midianite women the description of the Israelites' food

---

103. Thus, Bilde (1988: 182) demonstrates that the fall of Jerusalem and of the temple became the essential theme in *The Jewish War*. Similarly, in *Antiquities of the Jews* and *Against Apion*, the themes seem to be the Jewish religion and the Jewish people.

104. Cf. *Ant.* 1.17 where Josephus says that he will set out the details of what is written in the Scriptures, neither adding to nor omitting any of it. But, as Feldman (1984: 788) correctly remarks, 'Anyone who takes the trouble…to read even a small portion of Josephus' narrative will immediately see how false Josephus has been to his pledge'. Indeed, Josephus' account of the Midianite women represents one such example.

105. Feldman (2000: 376) points out that in Philo (*Virt.* 34–35) the advice comes from the Midianites rather than from Balaam. Who was the originator of the advice is not as important as the point of the story. Thus, although van Unnik (1974: 245–46) rightly observes that Josephus expands much more on the seduction of the Israelite youths by the women, but deals only briefly with the Phinehas story, the latter in no way is less important as Josephus holds him up as a paragon of a law-abiding Jew. See further discussion below.

106. Cf. Philo (*Vit. Mos.* 1.54.296–99; *Virt.* 34–40) for a similar expansion of the seduction story.

as peculiar (ἰδιοτρόπους) and their drink as 'not common' (μὴ κοινά) (*Ant.* 4.137),[107] thus suggesting that the Jewish way of life was generally perceived to be distinct and unique by the Gentiles.

The Midianite women's condition for the Israelites and the latter's unconditional declaration to worship the women's god (cf. *Ant.* 4.137) suggest that Josephus wanted to press home the point that the surrounding pagan world posed a threat to the Jewish faith, custom and way of life. It was thus a possible warning to the Jews of his time.[108] We see Josephus making the women the main blameworthy party for the Israelites' failure to keep their faith and customs, turning the host (the Midianites) into 'alien' people and giving the impression that these 'aliens' and their customs and gods are bad because they lead young men (i.e. Israelite youths) astray. In this way, what goes against the notion of the one God and the Jewish race is being criticized. But the Israelite youths are equally wrong, and in a more fundamental way because they have transgressed the laws of their fathers (παρέβησαν τὰ πάτρια, *Ant.* 4.139). The word παραβαίνω in this context means 'to pass beside', 'to go beyond', 'to overstep' and 'to transgress', thus suggesting that the Israelites have passed by the side of their ancestors, or have gone beyond and overstepped their ancestors. They now believe that there are gods (*Ant.* 4.139). It is a gradual process: from mental acceptance of the plurality of gods to crossing cultural and religious barriers of worshipping other gods to partaking of strange meats (*Ant.* 4.139).[109]

Thus the Israelites are accused of contradicting their law (ὁ νόμος αὐτῶν ἐκέλευε ποιοῦντες διετέουν, *Ant.* 4.139). The combination of τοὐναυτίον and διετέλουν forms a sharp critique of the Israelites' behaviour: they incessantly opposed that which their law commanded. This is described as 'lawlessness' or 'transgression of the law' (παρανομίαν) and a 'sedition' (στάσιν), which leads to the ultimate danger of complete destruction of the Israelites' institutions (*Ant.* 4.140).[110] In other words, it is 'unfaithfulness' to the Jewish ancestral tradition, which is what our first definition of idolatry means.

Although Moses's response appears mild (*Ant.* 4.141–44),[111] Josephus reveals his perception of the Israelites when he says Moses advised them to mend their

107. Such a description of the Israelites' lifestyle and custom has to come from non-Israelites as Josephus would not like it to come from the people of God.

108. Van Unnik 1974: 261.

109. ξενικοῖς means 'foreign', 'alien'. Does it mean those meats were idol-meats? The context seems to suggest that the meats were offered by the Midianite women who brought them to the party. However, a phrase like this which follows immediately the description of the Israelites making sacrifices to the gods appears more likely to refer to meats from the sacrificial table.

110. Van Unnik (1974: 251) observes the parallel in King Solomon (1 Kings 11) and the striking similarity in terminology between the two events. Thus, he rightly comments that '(Great) stress is laid upon the fact that this is a transgression of the Mosaic Law, the specific Law of the Jews that had strongly warned against such practices'. Feldman (2000: 380) argues that Zimri's open challenge to not only Moses but Judaism's refusal to 'open itself to other religious views' explains why Josephus regards his (Zimri's) rebellion as much worse than that of Korah which he refers to in *Ant.* 4.12.

111. Feldman (2000: 381) observes the difference between Josephus' description here and that found in Numbers 25. In Numbers 25 God instructs Moses to execute the chiefs of the people. But

ways, not to violate the laws but resist their passion (*Ant*. 4.143).[112] And their liaison is described as a 'drunken riot' (παροινεῖν, *Ant*. 4.144).[113]

What is interesting is that unlike Numbers 25, Moses does not order the execution of the Israelite youths. But Josephus changes the story by making Phinehas take the law into his own hand and kill Zambrias and his wife (*Ant*. 4.152–53).[114] Thus Phinehas' act in killing Zambrias appears to be self-motivated. This helps to indicate that idolaters deserve the worst form of punishment, which requires no legitimation by Moses. For the crime itself and the motivation of Phinehas were sufficient for the act.[115] Josephus' emphasis on the temptation and the dire consequences of succumbing to it is obvious (*Ant*. 4.140).[116]

By making such a connection between Numbers 25 and the temptations of the Graeco-Roman world, Josephus points to the 'tempters' and their 'temptations' as leading to idolatry. Thus, Greek religion and Egyptian type of worship will receive a sharp critique later (cf. *Apion* 2.239–49). But, at the same time, Phinehas is held up as a model of a law-abiding and law-upholding Jew after whom Jews, indeed the rest of the Israelites, ought to pattern their lives (cf. *Ant*. 4.154).

c. Against Apion *(2.66–67, 80–81, 239–54, 73–77)*[117]

In *Against Apion*, Josephus sets out to refute Apion's various charges against the Jews. One of these charges revolves around the Alexandrian citizenship of the Jews. And in *Apion* 2.66, Apion is said to have challenged the Jews' Alexandrian

here in *Antiquities of the Jews* Josephus' Moses 'takes away the initiative from God' and shows much patience and restraint.

112. Feldman (2000: 381) is of the opinion that Moses' speech 'in effect equates moderation with obedience to authority', a concept of obedience (πειθοῖ, *Ant*. 6.160) which Josephus seems to try and convey, as also seen in his enumeration of 'his own canon of the cardinal virtues'. This could explain why Moses appears mild, patient and restrained: a reflection of a God who is patient and restrained, unless the people persist in breaking the law.

113. Cf. van Unnik (1974: 253) where he shows that such a method of resolving internal strife is often found in the works of Greek historians.

114. Feldman (2000: 384) makes the unlikely suggestion that Josephus was strongly opposed to zealotry that he omits the reward of a covenant of peace as recorded in Num. 25.10–13, even though he also concedes that Josephus does praise Phinehas in general. A careful reading of *Ant*. 4.152–54 shows that although Josephus devotes much less space to Phinehas, the description of him is positive throughout.

115. In *Ant*. 4.152, Josephus states that the action is to prevent 'the lawlessness from going further if those who started it were not punished', and in 4.154, he further describes those others who followed Phinehas as claiming for virtue and striving for honour (φιλοκαλεῖν, 'to love the beautiful', Feldman 2000: 384). Thackeray's suggestion that Josephus owes this idea to Thucydides who coined the phrase: οἱ ἀρετῆς τι μεταποιούμενοι, is not convincing as Josephus further describes the action of the rest of the men as brave and that many of the transgressors died as a result.

116. Cf. van Unnik 1974: 252.

117. As our main objective is to examine Josephus' critique of idolatry and his grounds for doing so, the methods and rhetorical skill of Josephus are therefore not our concern here. For a study of the polemic and apologetic methods of Josephus in *Against Apion*, see Kasher 1996: 143–86; cf. Bilde (1988: 112–21) where he also proposes the disposition of *Against Apion*. See particularly the recent essay of Barclay (1998b: 194–221) where he carefully analyses Josephus' argument against Apion.

citizenship by asking why the Jews did not worship the same gods as the Alexandrians.

Josephus replies with two basic points. The first is a critique of the Egyptian animal worship, of which the Egyptian gods are but hostile animals, while the Egyptians themselves have no settled opinion about their own religion (*Apion* 2.66). There is therefore no reason for the Jews to worship the Egyptian gods.

The second point is the ethnic origin of the Jews. Josephus reasons that the Jews are one 'single and united' race loyal to their religious laws (cf. *Ant.* 4.201). Thus, in defence of the sanctity of the temple against the allegation that the Jews worship a golden head of an ass (*Apion* 2.80),[118] Josephus rhetorically counters that it is at the very least not worse than the animals the Egyptians worship as gods (*Apion* 2.81). Since the golden head of an ass was apparently one of the most despicable things to the Egyptians,[119] his counter-argument turns the critique of the golden ass into a critique of Egyptian animal worship, and with a counter claim that the Jews had the 'purest type of religion' (*Apion* 2.82),[120] as evidenced by the fact that Antiochus Epiphanes and others did not find an ass' head when they invaded the temple (*Apion* 2.83–84).[121]

The Egyptians ascribe to crocodiles and asps honour and virtue (*Apion* 2.86)[122] by, for example, regarding the bite of a snake or the attack of a crocodile as a reflection of one's worth before God. Josephus criticizes this as lacking sense and being unreasonable, for instead of bringing good, the Egyptian gods bring pain. Josephus further exploits the idea of pain by arguing that the adoption of Egyptian customs would lead to the annihilation of all humanity as all the wild beasts, being regarded as gods, would have overrun the earth (*Apion* 2.139). Josephus thus denigrates the Egyptian customs and animal worship as potentially destructive.

As part of his argument against his accusers, Josephus downplays the significance of the Greek religions by arguing that their advocates have been censured by their admired sages (*Apion* 2.239). For they go about representing the gods

118. Different versions have been put forward. One version says it is a golden ass head (*Apion* 2.112–14, a version reported by Mnaseas of Patara, quoted by Apion and here preserved by Josephus); another says it is a statue of Moses seated on an ass, holding a book in his hands (Posidonius 34/35.1.3); yet one other version says it is an entire ass, not just the head (Tacitus, *Hist.* 5.4.2, first century CE, cf. Plutarch, *Quaest conviv.* 4.5.3), see Bar-Kochva (1996: 310ff) for the origins and development of the slander; cf. Feldman (1993: 499–501) who provides a truncated account of the theory.

119. Cf. Feldman (1993: 145) who mistakenly points out that Apion's charge appeared inconsistent since the Egyptians themselves worshipped animals as gods, as such he is inconsistent that he should object when others did likewise. For the Egyptians never worshipped an ass. Josephus is perhaps merely being rhetorical here.

120. Cf. *Apion* 2.83–85 where Josephus cites several historians as well as conquerors who agreed with this particular aspect of the Jewish religion.

121. It was in fact Antiochus, according to Apion, who found an ass' head in the temple when the former invaded it. Josephus' argument seems to depend on the various emperors who occupied the temple (*Apion* 2.82–83) but found no ass' head. Antiochus' finding in fact revealed that there was not an ass' head. Apion's source, according to Josephus, is dubious (*Apion* 2.82).

122. See similar critique above in Wis. 15.18–19; and Philo, *Dec.* 76–80.

according to their own choice: ἀριθμῷ μὲν ὁπόσους ἂν αὐτοὶ θελήσωσιν ἀποφαινόμενοι (*Apion* 2.240).[123] The term ἀποφαίνω carries the meaning of representing and displaying. Josephus thus makes the proponents of Greek religion out to turn their gods into a display! He uses terms such as ἐξ ἀλλήλων... γινομένους and παντοίους to describe the Greek gods as giving birth to one another, giving the impression of disorderliness and confusion.[124]

Further, he compares the Greek gods to animals (*Apion* 2.240), despite the Greeks not worshipping animals. But because Josephus claims that the Greeks assigned to their gods different localities and habits like the different species of animals, he lumps them together with the Egyptian animal worship and so levels a sharp critique against the Greek religions.

The critique of the Greek religions intensifies with a critique of Zeus, whom Josephus accuses of being a 'tyrant and despot' (τύραννον...δεσπότην, *Apion* 2.241),[125] being in enmity with his own family. Even the Greek intellectuals censure and ridicule the gods (*Apion* 2.242) for they are limited, ever quarrelling, fighting and wounding each other, and sometimes being harmed by humans. All this implies that the qualities and nature of the gods are very much the human projection of their own world.

In *Apion* 2.244, Josephus shifts his criticism to a moral one: the sexual behaviour of the gods. First of all, the 'noblest' (ὁ γενναιότατος) and 'chief' (πρῶτος) of all the Greek gods appears like a sex maniac who goes around seducing and impregnating women only to leave them dead (*Apion* 2.245). Thus, the chief Greek god appears morally weak. Besides, the 'chief' is incapable of providing salvation, and is emotionally unstable, as he cannot restrain his tears (*Apion* 2.246).

In a similar vein, he scornfully hails insults at the legendary tale about fornication in heaven with the gods standing by as envious spectators (*Apion* 2.246).[126] The eldest of these gods, who is the king among them (ὁ βασιλεύς), could not control his passion for his consort (τὴν γυναῖκα) that he had to quickly retreat into his own chamber! The Greek gods are therefore morally base.

As mentioned, Josephus claims that the Greek intellectuals similarly disapprove of their own religion (cf. *Apion* 2.242). For the Greek religion is considered

123. Although the Greeks do not worship animals like the Egyptians, the gods they worship represent various human aspirations by the functions they perform. Ferguson (1993: 143) provides a table of the various Greek gods' names, their functions and their Roman names (or counterparts). Cf. Price 1999: 1–46.

124. See, however, Grant (1986: 54–71) who gives a systematic exposition of most of the gods, their functions and deeds. Cf. MacMullen 1981: 1–18.

125. A 'tyrant' and 'despot' are terms used for a dictator, one who oppresses, exploits, controls, even kills his subjects. Kindness and benevolence are never associated with a 'tyrant' and a 'despot', nor is freedom.

126. In addition to these sexually immoral gods, Josephus highlights the fact that other gods are enslaved to humanity. For example, the gods are hired as 'builders' (οἰκοδομοῦντες), 'shepherds' (ποιμαίνοντες), with some imprisoned like criminals (*Apion* 2.247; cf. Homer, *Iliad* 21.442–45, 448–49). This is further strengthened by the criticism that worshippers of these deities seek after their own benefits and advantages (cf. *Apion* 2.249).

'irregular' (ἀνωμαλίας) and 'erroneous' (πλημμελείας), and therefore false. Such falsehood is due to the Greek law-makers' ignorance of the true nature of God, leading to their failure to formulate correct knowledge (*Apion* 2.250). Further, they are frivolous towards religion by allowing poets to introduce gods according to their own choices and passions, and by letting orators decide the names of various foreign gods on the register (*Apion* 2.251). And finally, great licence is granted to idol-makers to design and make their own gods (*Apion* 2.252).[127] Josephus concludes that some of these gods have grown old who once flourished, while new ones are continually introduced as objects of worship (*Apion* 2.254).[128] Throughout it is the human will (βουλή) that determines the fate of the gods, who have no will of their own.

What about the Jews? What is the difference between the Jewish religion and the pagan ones? One of the charges of Apion against the Jews is the latter's refusal to erect statues of the emperors, which Josephus counters in *Apion* 2.73–77, where he argues that the Romans do not require their subjects to violate their national laws and are content to receive honours which the subjects' national laws so far allow (*Apion* 2.73–74).

Further, Moses does not forbid honours paid to the Roman authority but only prohibits the physical representation of God. And he offers two reasons for the ban: (1) it is profitable neither to God nor to humanity; (2) God is not a creature (*Apion* 2.75–76). Thus, the Jewish religion differs from the Greeks'. Further, the Greeks' homage to their emperors is but an extension of their insincere religious practice. In contrast, the Jews pay homage to the emperors because Moses never forbids it (*Apion* 2.77). Accordingly, the Jews offer perpetual sacrifices on behalf of the emperor and worthy people, but not to them. In addition, their honour to the emperors is secondary to that which they render to God. Thus, a line is carefully drawn between honouring the emperor and worshipping God.

Josephus' defence against the charge that the Jews do not erect statues of the emperors thus revolves around the superiority and prominence of the Jewish law, which even the Roman authorities recognize. Such a defence is twofold: (1) it is a declaration of the faithfulness of the Jews in keeping their ancestral laws and tradition; and (2) it is a rejection of the Greeks' insincerity and a ridicule of the commonness of their worship.

d. *Conclusion*

The above discussion shows a twin purpose in Josephus' critique of idolatry: (1) that of warning the Jews against 'unfaithfulness' to the Jewish ancestral tradition; and (2) that of promoting the Jewish nation and thus of persuading non-Jews

---

127. This resembles the critique of Isa. 44.9–17 save the difference in Josephus' brevity. Cf. Philo, *Dec.* 52–80, *Vit. Cont.* 3–8, Wis. 13–15.

128. The same applies to their temples: some have become desolate, probably having gone out of fashion, while new temples are built, 'according to individual caprice' (κατὰ τὴν τῶν ἀνθρώπων βούλησιν ἕκαστος). The criticism here is levelled against the gods, their temples, and their worshippers who are fickle and fashionable.

about the purity and goodness of Judaism.[129] It is therefore not surprising that Josephus holds strongly to the Jewish notion of monotheism.[130] And his emphasis on the 'one God', 'one temple', and 'one holy city' enables us to see why he critiques the Greek religion and the Egyptian animal worship. Thus, for Josephus, the surrounding Graeco-Roman world poses a threat to the Jewish identity and way of life. This is seen in his use of the Numbers 25 incident, in which he adopts a particular stance towards idolatry, which can be explained by the definitions of idolatry set out in Chapter 2.

The particular aspect of idolatry as an act contrary to the Jewish ancestral tradition is seen to be operative in Josephus. In his use of the Numbers 25 story, Josephus repeatedly refers to the Israelite youths as having 'transgressed' the law and violated the ancestral customs. In other words, idolatry is to Josephus an act of 'unfaithfulness', which is the first category of definition set out by Halbertal and Margalit. The flip side of this definition is the worship of 'alien' gods. In the case of Numbers 25, the people have turned to the gods of the Midianites, which are 'alien'.

Josephus' use of Phinehas and his approval of the latter's act are telling. Three points may be said about Phinehas' act: (1) death will be the rightful destiny for those who apostatize; (2) the annihilation of the law-breakers (or the 'unfaithful') is a legitimate act; and (3) Phinehas' act is a model for all law-abiding Jews. Such a view of Phinehas lies in Josephus' view of the law. Throughout, Josephus views the law as the regulator of the covenant relationship between the true God and the Jews.[131] This leads us to his next area of emphasis: the law and the true God.

Throughout his critique of idolatry and the Greek religions, Josephus holds a universal conception of the God of the Jews as the ruler of the universe (*Apion* 2.185), who is the only true God whose laws are universally applicable (*Ant.* 1.20),[132] indeed, even to the Gentiles and their religions.[133]

---

129. Throughout, Josephus demonstrates a negative attitude towards the pagan customs and religions. And while he would prefer not to digress to the investigation of other peoples' gods and religious traditions (*Apion* 2.237), he would aggressively defend the superiority and purity of the Jewish faith and the Jewish people as a race.

130. Cf. Hurtado 1998: 9–14.

131. See Spilsbury (1998: 172–91), who shows that the relationship between God and Israel is a covenantal one but best understood through the patron-client model of relationships: God provides Israelites numberous benefactions, of which the law is the greatest. Israel's response should be wholehearted gratitude to God and obedience and loyalty to the law.

132. Thus, Mason (1998: 85) ably argues, '…Moses treated the constitution of the universe before framing his law, just so that his laws alone would be seen to be based upon universal truths, the laws of nature'. Cf. *Apion* 2.167, 190, where God's sole rulership is embodied in the first commandment, which thus serves as his basis for critically attacking and rejecting idolatry.

133. Cf. Mason (1998: 87–90) who argues that Josephus is offering the Jewish law as an alternative philosophical system to his Gentile audience.

5. *Joseph and Aseneth*[134]

According to Gen. 41.45, Pharaoh gave Aseneth, the daughter of Potiphera, priest of On, to Joseph as his wife. The biblical account is silent about how the couple met and how Joseph, a Hebrew, ended up marrying the daughter of a pagan priest. In *Joseph and Aseneth*, however, we have a detailed account of the couple's encounter in which Joseph is described as a powerful man of God while Aseneth is described in negative terms, not least her religious belief and practices.[135] However, the couple were eventually married, after Joseph's stunning confrontation of Aseneth over her idolatry, and Aseneth's eventual conversion following divine intervention.

While the text may be a demonstration of the use of the Hellenistic form by the author to carry out an attack on Hellenistic religions,[136] the particular aspect of attack on idolatry calls for a more careful and closer scrutiny. This is because idolatry seems to be the barrier between Joseph and Aseneth, and indeed the deciding factor that caused Joseph to distance from Aseneth, which triggered Aseneth's repentance, resulting in their marriage.

There are good reasons for viewing *Joseph and Aseneth* as Jewish,[137] despite suggestions of it as work of a Christian redactor.[138] The figure of Joseph and the issue of idolatry provide sufficient grounds for viewing this story as Jewish. The story serves as a good example of the practice of idolatry, of religious aggression by the monotheistic Joseph, and reveals the attitude of the author towards idolatry and his grounds for rejecting it. We will begin with a sketch of the story.

a. *The story: a sketch*[139]
The story begins with the dispatch of Joseph to gather grain. He comes to the territory of Heliopolis and requests accommodation at the house of Pentephres (3.1–3), who has a virgin daughter with unsurpassed beauty, named Aseneth (1.4). However, she arrogantly despises and scorns every man (2.1). Upon receiving news of Joseph's impending arrival, her father Pentephres makes the proposal to Aseneth to marry her to Joseph (4.7–8), which she quickly rejects (4.9–11).

---

134. The question whether the longer or the shorter recension is the priority remains unresolved. Kraemer (1998: 50–58; 1999: 234–65), has tried to argue for the priority of the shorter version. Collins (2000: 104) has rightly argued that her (Kraemer's) case has not been fully worked through. Burchard's reconstruction of the longer recension will be followed here.

135. Schürer (III, 546) states that *Joseph and Aseneth* 'is a romantic love story in which the author has put a midrashic elaboration of Gen. 41.45, 50–52 and 46.20 into the form of a Hellenistic romance'. For a thorough review of scholarly work on such questions as language, date, provenance, genre, message, and audience of the story, see Chesnutt (1995: 20–93). On *Joseph and Aseneth* as a 'recycling' of Aseneth, see Kraemer (1999: 234–65).

136. Cf. Barclay 1996: 204.

137. See Schürer III, 549; Gruen 1998: 92–93; and Collins (2000: 104–105) argues that the Jewish provenance of *Joseph and Aseneth* has stronger basis; cf. also Tromp 1999: 266–71.

138. Collins 2000: 104, and also his nn. 190–91.

139. Cf. Gruen (1998: 89–92) who provides a longer summary of the story than what is given below.

She flees her parents' presence in order to avoid meeting Joseph (5.1–2). In a subtle twist, the author creates the opportunity for both to meet: Joseph looking up and so seeing Aseneth (7.2), who was looking down from a large window. With some elaborate explanation, the two are willing to meet each other. However, Aseneth's greeting of a kiss is rejected by Joseph, who sees a distinction between himself, a man who worships God, and Aseneth, an 'alien' woman who is idolatrous (8.5).[140]

Aseneth is totally devastated despite Joseph's blessing (8.8–9). Utterly shaken and feeling desperately rejected, Aseneth discards all her idols and spends the next seven days in tearful fasting, repenting of her idolatry and sin (10–13).[141] At the end of the fast, a heavenly being descends and instructs her on what she should do (14.1–15). This is followed by the angel's announcement of her acceptance to God and her marriage to Joseph (15.2b–6). Her conversion from Egyptian idolatry to the God of the Hebrews is confirmed by the announcement of her changed name: she will be called City of Refuge (πόλις καταφυγῆς, 15.7).[142] And the angel will inform Joseph of Aseneth's repentance and their eventual marriage (15.9–10).

Further, the angel miraculously gives Aseneth a portion of the honeycomb so that she may eat the 'bread of life', drink 'a cup of immortality', and be anointed with 'ointment of incorruptibility' (16.16). This is in sharp contrast to 8.5, where Aseneth is described as having eaten from the table bread of strangulation, drunk a cup of insidiousness and anointed herself with ointment of destruction.

Everything happens as announced. The two are united in a wedding personally organized and solemnized by Pharoah (19.4–11).[143]

b. *Idolatry in* Joseph and Aseneth
With the story sketched out, we will focus on the idolatry of Aseneth which is described as follows. She has a chamber (θάλαμος), the first among ten, big and splendid (μέγας καὶ εὐπρεπής, 2.2) which is beautifully decorated, where she keeps all her idols.

On the walls of the chamber are countless Egyptian gods (οἱ θεοὶ τῶν Αἰγυπτίων ὧν οὐκ ἦν ἀριθμός),[144] including idols of gold and silver (χρύσοι

140. This has been described by Boccaccini (1991: 254) as the 'irreconcilability of Jews and Gentiles', the only road to a possible relationship between Joseph and Aseneth is the latter's conversion. This is a very powerful way in which the author shows idolatry to be negative and how giving up an idolatrous lifestyle can lead to a relationship with a 'man' who is also described as 'son of God'.

141. The author clearly is trying to show that the idols are the root of Aseneth's misery.

142. See Burchard (1985: 226 n. l) for the significance of Aseneth's change of name. The change of name signals a change in status for Aseneth. She is now the one through whom many people would repent and receive their divine protection. The author thus contrasts the different statuses of those who worship the Most High God and those who worship idols.

143. The second part is deliberately left out, as it is not my concern here. For an analysis of the second part of the tale, see Barclay (1996: 204–16) and Collins (2000: 108–10) who hold opposing views.

144. They are most likely statues of animals worshipped by the Egyptians. Cf. Wis. 15–18; Philo, *Dec.* 76–79.

καὶ ἄργυροι). All these Aseneth worshipped (ἐσέβετο), feared (ἐφοβεῖτο) and to them she performed daily sacrifices (θυσίας...καθ' ἡμέραν).

Further, Aseneth's linen robe has all sorts of idols that match those in the chamber, with the names of the Egyptian gods engraved on all the bracelets and stones, and all the faces of the idols carved on them (3.6).[145] The author describes it as a microcosm of the first chamber, thus indicating the extent of Aseneth's idolatry.

The author's critique of Aseneth is seen in Joseph's condemnation of idolatry and of Aseneth. In 8.5–7, Joseph charges Aseneth with being an 'alien' or 'strange' woman whom he will not kiss. The author describes the pair in contrasting terms, using possibly the language of religious rituals or symbols: Joseph is a man who worships God, blesses God, eats blessed bread of life, drinks a blessed cup of immortality and anoints himself with blessed ointment of incorruptibility, while Aseneth is the direct opposite who, as an 'alien' woman, blesses the dead and dumb idols, eats from the table of strangulation, drinks from a cup of insidiousness, and anoints herself with ointment of destruction.[146] Thus, the author shows that the religion of Aseneth is inferior to that of Joseph, and its 'strangeness' will lead eventually to destruction. The descriptions not only serve to define Aseneth's religion, but also act as a wholesale condemnation of it. We see this clearly when the two are placed side-by-side in a tabular form.

Acts	Joseph: A worshipper of God	Aseneth: A 'strange' woman
blesses	τὸν θεὸν τὸν ζῶντα	εἴδωλα νεκρὰ καὶ κωφά
eats	ἄρτον εὐλογήμενον ζωῆς	ἄρτον ἀγχόνης
drinks	ποτήριον εὐλογήμενον ἀθανασίας	ποτήριον ἐνέδρας
anoints	χρίσματι εὐλογημένω ἀφθαρσίας	χρίσματι ἀπωλείας

The contrast above shows that a 'strange' or 'alien' person is an abomination to the Lord God of Joseph (8.7).[147]

145. The author's use of the Jewish term εἴδωλα shows that the author views other gods pejoratively. More importantly, the conception of the one God Most High seems to be behind the author's antagonism against Aseneth's religion.

146. It is not clear what these rituals or symbols are. They could be either Jewish or Christian ceremonies. However, as Goldenberg (1998: 152 n. 87) has noted, no one has successfully identified these ceremonies. Philonenko (1968: 93, cited by Collins [2000: 233 n. 99]) takes it to be a reference to the initiation rite to Judaism. Chesnutt (1995: 130) posits that these are the pious habits of the righteous like Joseph. Burchard (1965: 126–33) is of the opinion that the formulaic reference to bread, wine and oil refers to the whole of the Jewish lifestyle, rather than to a ritual. He further argues (1985: 212), correctly, that the point is not to justify or institutionalize any meal, but to explain why such a person as Joseph does not kiss a 'strange' woman. In view of the uncertainty of these elements, it is best not to draw any conclusion about them. *Pace* Collins (2000: 232–33) who argues that 'the formulaic language can be referred to the everyday rituals of Jewish life'. The following tabular illustration is not meant to say anything about the meal, but to demonstrate the kind of comparison Joseph is making between himself and Aseneth which condemns Aseneth as an idol-worshipper.

147. Cf. Barclay (1996: 208–209) who carefully sets out the subtle play of the word ἀλλότριος in the story in which an 'alien' Aseneth is rejected, however moral or virtuous or physically attractive

The inferiority and worthlessness of Aseneth's religious belief and practice are further highlighted in Joseph's prayer for her in 8.9. The prayer refers to the Lord God as that of Israel and claims that he is the Most High (ὁ ὕψιστος), powerful one (ὁ δυνατός), the one who gives life (ὁ ζωοποίησας) to all. What is even more important to our discussion of idolatry is that Joseph's prayer implies that Aseneth is living in darkness, her belief is erroneous, and that she is without eternal life! We see this in the claims that God calls people from darkness (ἀπὸ τοῦ σκότους) into light (εἰς τὸ φῶς), from error (ἀπὸ τῆς πλάνης) into truth (εἰς τὴν ἀλήθειαν), from death (ἀπὸ τοῦ θανάτου) into life (εἰς τὴν ζωήν). Why does Aseneth need the blessing of this Most High God of Joseph unless she lacks what God is able to give? Thus Joseph pleads for her spiritual renewal (ἀνακαίνισον αὐτὴν τῷ πνεύματι σοῦ) and prays that she would be made alive by becoming a worshipper of God. Although idolatry is not explicitly attacked, the idolatrous Aseneth is described as totally and absolutely hopeless, helpless and worthless without the Lord God of Israel.[148] And the author subtly implies that the commandment to worship the true God of Israel is universal, hence the universal condemnation that accompanies its disobedience.[149] The contrast between the God of Joseph and the idols of Aseneth is also worth noting: the God of Joseph is the Most High (ὁ ὕψιστος),[150] while Aseneth's gods are 'alien gods' (ἀλλότριοι);[151] the God of Joseph is 'living', while Aseneth's gods are 'dead and dumb' (νεκρὰ καὶ κωφά); the God of Joseph is 'one', while Aseneth's idols are without number (οὐκ ἦν ἀριθμός).

The words and prayer of Joseph are so powerful as to cause Aseneth to repent of her gods and spurn all her idols (9.2). But this also shows that Aseneth's idols and gods are quite useless and weak as to be easily spurned and abandoned (cf.

---

she might be, because '[t]he only legitimate forms of kinship are with those who, through birth or marriage, share the religious orientation of the Jew'.

148. But it is precisely with a drastic action such as turning from her idols to the true God is any relationship with Joseph justified (Gruen 1998: 90). Collins (2000: 234) views this in terms of group membership whose requirement is acknowledgement of the true God, not ethnic descent.

149. In this case, Collins (2000: 234) suggests that the law is reduced to 'monotheism, rejection of idolatry, chastity before marriage, and avoidance of social or sexual intimacy with "aliens" – that is, people who worship other gods'. The behaviour of Joseph as described certainly speaks of one who sees himself as separated because of his association with the Most High God, that is, he worships the true God and thus must keep himself pure and free from an 'alien' woman (8.5), as Barclay (1996: 208) correctly points out.

150. See Chapter 4, section 4 below for a discussion of θεὸς ὕψιστος.

151. This is an interesting term used to critique Aseneth's idols as it is a carry-over of the Old Testament biblical language. For the author not only describes Aseneth as an 'alien woman', but the gods too are 'alien'. The term ἀλλότριος, according to Liddell and Scott, carries the meaning of being the opposite to 'one's own', that is, belonging to another. Thus an 'alien woman' (ἀλλοτρία γυνή) could also mean 'another man's wife'. In its reference to the gods, it has the meaning of 'foreign', 'strange', so that the 'alien gods' of Aseneth are in fact 'foreign gods', or gods belonging to another. Thus, in the use of this term, the author of *Joseph and Aseneth* clearly has in mind a universal conception of the true God, which he applies universally to even the Gentiles (see n. 147 above). In view of our definition of idolatry, this would fit well with the first category of the definition of idolatry as turning to 'alien' gods. See conclusion below.

10.1–13.14). And 10.12–13 shows that the idols can be discarded and ground to pieces; and all pagan gods, sacrifices and the like can be destroyed, discarded and removed. One of the most significant comments of Aseneth is seen in 10.13b, when she throws all the sacrificial food away: 'By no means must my dogs eat from my dinner and from the sacrifice of the idols, but let the alien dogs eat those' (10.13b). The food that has been sacrificed to the idols is considered so defiled and tainted that it is not even appropriate to feed it to the dogs. It is fit only for 'alien' dogs (οἱ κυνὲς οἱ ἀλλότριοι, 10.13). The word ἀλλότριος, used here for 'alien' dogs, is also used in 8.5 to describe Aseneth as an 'alien' woman, presumably because of the 'alien' gods she worshipped (cf. 11.7). Thus, the 'alien' dogs here may be a parallel to the 'alien' gods.

The next attack on idolatry is seen in Aseneth's soliloquy in 11.3b–14, set in the context of Aseneth's effort to harness enough courage to address the God of Joseph (cf. 11.7). In 11.7–9, we have a syllogism:

v. 7   the Lord God hates all those who worship idols and alien gods;
v. 8b I (Aseneth) worshipped dead and dumb idols;
v. 8a Therefore the Lord God has come to hate me too.

In v. 7, idols and alien gods, like in earlier passages, refer to the Egyptian animal statues. Hence, the God of Joseph hates all idol-worshippers who, together with their idols, constitute objects of divine hatred. Aseneth's confession of her idolatry in v. 8 serves as another attack on Egyptian idolatry: they are 'dead and dumb idols' (εἴδωλα νεκρὰ καὶ κωφά). Her partaking of the food and drink offered to these idols is condemned as defiling her mouth. Such defilement is blamed for Aseneth's lack of boldness to address Joseph's God (v. 9).[152] The syllogism leads to the logical conclusion that the Lord God of Joseph has also come to hate Aseneth since she is an idol-worshipper.

In her second soliloquy, Aseneth begins with the acknowledgement that she is a 'wretched woman' (11.16), an orphan and desolate, a state in which the true God is absent (cf. 12.8).[153] And she again accepts that she has worshipped idols and that her participation in eating the sacrificial food and her blessing the idols have defiled her mouth (11.16). The connection is made between idol worship and defilement, serving as a critique of idolatry.

Once Aseneth has gathered sufficient courage, she begins to address God in confession of her sin. In 12.4–5, Aseneth confesses her sin as lawlessness and irreverence (ἠνόμησα καὶ ἠσέβησα, 12.4), in terms of her idolatrous belief and practice. 12.5 repeats her previous statements that her mouth is defiled by sacrificial food and by participation at the table of the Egyptian gods. For these idols

152. Aseneth's soliloquy seems to echo the words of Joseph in 8.5–7. Either Joseph knows Aseneth's idolatrous practices because they are commonly carried out by the Egyptians everywhere, or Aseneth is so influenced by what Joseph has said that she is agreeing with Joseph. It could be that Aseneth, being of nobility, has more elaborate and 'refined' practices which Joseph would have been aware of since they would, in all probability, have been carried out in Pharaoh's palace. Being so much in love with Joseph, Aseneth is now prejudiced against her own religious practices.

153. Burchard (1985: 218 n. 'o'): 'Doubtless life often was like that when a person decided to become a Jew. The counterpoint is that it is expected that God will be a new and better father'; cf. 11.3.

and gods of the Egyptians are 'dead and dumb', a repeat of her previous agreement with Joseph's words (cf. 11.8; 8.5). It is of great importance that Aseneth is reported to be the one making the condemnation and carrying out the attack on her idols. 13.11 thus forms an important understanding of the critique: it is Aseneth herself who has now recognized that all the gods which she used to worship are 'dead and dumb' idols (13.11; cf. 21.13–14). What this suggests is that when one comes into the knowledge of the true God one will be enlightened and therefore see the stupidity and futility of idolatry.

c. *Conclusion*

It is noteworthy that the biblical story of Joseph and Aseneth precedes the giving of the ten commandments, which would have made any critique of the kind of idolatry in *Joseph and Aseneth* more difficult. What we have, therefore, in *Joseph and Aseneth* is a clear reading of the first commandment, which imposes a ban on acknowledging other gods or beings other than the God of the Jews, into an earlier event. Thus, there is the element of timelessness in the application of the commandment in the critique of idolatry.

What our discussion above, therefore, means is that the author of *Joseph and Aseneth* has turned the Lord God of Joseph into the God universal by whom all other gods and idols may be critiqued. And the contrast between Aseneth's 'alien' gods (21.13) and Joseph's 'true' God is repeatedly emphasized. This aspect of the author's critique reflects the first category of the definition of idolatry: other gods are 'alien' gods. Any worship of 'alien' gods is therefore considered idolatrous. By using a man of God to pour scorn on an 'alien' or 'strange' woman whose gods are equally 'alien' or 'strange', the author shows us his reason for rejecting 'other' or 'alien' gods: only the God Most High, the God of the Jews, is the true God. Therefore, any failure to worship this true God through 'alien' worship constitutes a rebellion.

6. *Sibylline Oracles*

Sibylline Oracles are a widely attested phenomenon in the ancient world. Although there is no satisfactory or conclusive evidence as to the etymology of the word 'sibyl', it is quite possible that the word was originally the proper name of a prophetess.[154] She was regularly depicted as an old woman who uttered ecstatic prophecies, often treated with great respect because of her age, which is assumed to be granted by the Divine together with divine wisdom.[155]

---

154. It is understood that in the earliest attestations, that is, from the fifth and fourth centuries BCE, the word 'sibyl' referred to a single individual; cf. Collins 1983: 317.

155. See Collins (1983: 317) for an interesting legend about the Sibyl. Barclay (1996: 216) comments: 'The Sibyl was considered a woman of immense longevity whose age accorded her great authority, while her ancient origins gave to her "prophecies" of historical events the impression of accurate prediction'. See further Schürer III, 618.

Although a number of Sibyls were reported by various people from the fourth century BCE,[156] the Sibylline Oracles which we shall examine below (Books 3 and 5)[157] are the Jewish (with occasional Christian)[158] concoctions and therefore different from those of the fourth century BCE.[159] While no conclusion has been drawn as to the various Sibyls and their oracles, Books 3 and 5 are generally recognized as having originated from Egyptian Judaism.[160] This is seen in the references to the seventh king of Egypt (3.193, 318, and 608), the various references to Egypt (3.155–61; 5.52–110, 179–285), and the Books' interest in such things as the temple, the expectation of a saviour figure and the eschatological adversary (e.g. 3.611, 75–92; 5.493–504, 512–53). Book 3 dates between 163 and 145 BCE,[161] while Book 5 dates most probably after 80 CE and before 130 CE given its reference to the Nero legend and the destruction of the temple.[162]

While Sibylline Oracles often predict woes and doom, they carry with them the agenda of political propaganda, mostly with a religious twist, that is, with reference to the will of the gods and the question of right worship.[163] Our discussion of The Egyptian Sibylline Oracles below will be confined to how the two books view idolatry, their grounds for rejecting idolatry, and what definitions of idolatry are at work here.

a. *The critique of idolatry in Sibylline Oracles*

(i) *Book 3.*
In her attack on idolatry in 3.29–39, the Sibyl proclaims the creator God (3.8) as the one God (εἷς θεός), sole ruler (μόναρχος), ineffable (ἀθέσφατος), lofty (αἰθέρι ναίων) (3.11); self-begotten (αὐτοφυής), invisible (ἀόρατος), and omniscient (ὁρώμενος αὐτὸς ἅπαντα) (3.12).[164] This God is not made by a

156. Collins (1983: 317 n. 10) cites Aristotle's *Problemata* 954a and Heracleides Ponticus in Clement, *Strom.* 1.108.1.

157. See Collins (1984: 365–73) for the introductory comments on the two books.

158. For examples, 3.776 and 5.256–59. See further Collins 1974: 88.

159. See Grabbe 1992: 563.; Barclay 1996: 216–18; Collins 2000: 83–87, 96–97, 143–50; Gruen 1998: 268–69.

160. Book 4 is accepted as an example of Jewish adaptation of an older Sibylline oracle (Collins 1984: 363); which was composed in about 80 CE, which Grabbe (1992: 563) thinks is an old Hellenistic oracle in its core, non-Jewish and dates from the second century BCE. Books 3 and 5 are the most certain in terms of their Egyptian provenance. See Collins (1983: 355–56 [on Book 3], and 390–91 [on Book 5]) for their Egyptian provenance and their Jewish attestation.

161. See Collins (1983: 354–55) for more details. Gruen (1998: 269–71, and 269 n. 96) provides a good summary of it, but cautions against placing too much emphasis on time and place as it may miss the apocalyptic character of the Sibyl's message. In our case, the time and place are relevant. The time falls within the Second Temple and is therefore close to the time of our New Testament text in question, and the place being the Diaspora enables us to see how idolatry is viewed by Diaspora Judaism.

162. See Schürer III, 643–45; Collins (1974: 80–87) gives a helpful treatment on the speculation of the return of Nero. Cf. Barclay (1996: 225) who sees the central motif of Book 5 to be 5.398–401, where the destruction of the temple is given a vivid description.

163. Cf. Collins 1983: 320.

164. Although Schürer (III, 633) views 3.1–96 as belonging to Book 2, Collins (1983: 354) considers it the conclusion of a different Book. See also Collins (1984: 365). However, he considers 3.1–92 as

sculptor's hand, nor by a cast of gold or silver, nor the human crafts (3.13–14). Such conception of God reflects a traditional Jewish position, seen particularly in Isa. 40.18–26 and Wis. 13.10–19. While it is God who reveals himself (3.15), humanity has wandered in vain (3.9), and is not mindful of the immortal creator (3.10).

The wandering is seen in the worship of animals, idols and attendance and service at the godless temples (3.32).[165] These idol-worshippers do not fear God (3.33)[166] but rejoice in the evil of stones and forget the judgement of the immortal saviour (3.34–35).[167] They view idols as the representation of their gods. However, the Sibyl would not accept this as the true God is the creator who cannot be fashioned (cf. 3.13–14).

In an ingenious combination of the evil of murder, impiety, double-tongued-ness (deceit and gossip?), and adultery, the Sibyl lumps idol-worshippers together with all kinds of evil (3.36–38; cf. Wis. 14.22–29).[168] They are therefore wicked and equal to shameless 'looters' (3.39–40). There is nothing positive to be said about idol-worshippers who as a result of their idolatry face eschatological destruction (3.46–59).[169]

In 3.57–59, we are told of the present religious life of the people: cities are 'embellished' with temples, stadia, markets and images of gold, silver and stones.[170] Such terms describe the cities in the Graeco-Roman world where everyone is free to practise one's religion and where organized pagan activities

the conclusion of a different Book while 3.93–96 constitutes the fragments of another Book (Collins 2000: 84). Gruen (1998: 271–72) does not seem to see any value in looking for a 'main corpus' in Book 3 and argues that '[t]he significance of the composition transcends any specific era'. Barclay (1996: 218) takes a middle course that takes note of the secondary nature of 3.1–96, without arguing for a specific location of 3.1–96 or dismissing the possibility of it belonging elsewhere. It is necessary to recognize that 3.1–96 does contain references to events after 68 CE. Thus, we would reckon the fact that 3.1–96 is incorporated in Book 3 is assumed to be considered at least by the editor or compiler as relevant to the sibyl's argument, particularly with regard to idolatry.

165. The sitting at the doors of the temples could be that either the people are waiting for their turn to enter the temples and offer sacrifices, a form of queuing, or they are voluntary helpers sitting as guards or guides. In either case, they give themselves to the service of the idols, instead of serving the great true God. It could also be cultic rituals which involved the eating of idol food (cf. 2.96 where the people are instructed not to eat sacrificial food, εἰδωλοθύτων δ᾽ ἀπέχεσθαι; and 2.59 where they are warned against worshipping idols).

166. Collins (1983: 362 n. 'f'), citing Geffcken, agrees that it should be οὐ τρέμετε instead of τηρεῖτε.

167. This is an obvious repetition of earlier statements in 3.29. However, it is now taking on a greater force as the ensuing verses would show.

168. Wis. 14.27: 'For the worship of idols with no name is the beginning, cause, and end of every evil'.

169. Cf. 3.59 where, after describing the idolatry of both Rome and Egypt, the Sibyl says, 'so that you may come to the bitter day' (ἵν᾽ ἔλθητ᾽ εἰς πικρὸν ἦμαρ). Cf. Hab. 2.18–19 where a critique of idolatry is levelled against Babylon, following a prediction of its woes.

170. The images could be found everywhere, streets, marketplaces, and obviously temples. Stambaugh and Balch (1986: 88–89) point out that Hellenistic architecture of public buildings was prominent in all Greek cities so that even Palestine was without exception. In fact, much of the temple in Jerusalem was built in Greek style. See further Koester (1982: 67–73).

are rampant and alive, thus portraying idols and their places of activity and worship as trouble-causing evils that bring about end-time destruction.[171] The readers are left with the idea that idolatry constitutes the chief reason for their eschatological destruction because it is dishonouring to God.[172] The desolation of the land and its consequences and the eventual exile of the Jewish people (3.275–79) are all due to the following reasons which may be summarized: (1) the disobedience to the holy laws of the immortal God in the heart (3.275–76);[173] (2) the worship of unseemly idols (3.276–77); (3) the lack of the fear of God;[174] and (4) the unwillingness to honour God (οὐκ ἔθελες τιμᾶν, 3.279). The attack on idolatry here moves one level deeper. It is not just the act of idolatry, but the more fundamental attitude of the 'will' not to honour God.[175]

By explicating the above reasons for the troubles facing Judaea, the Sibyl exposes the serious consequences of idolatry and holds it solely responsible for the plight of the Jewish people. Thus, idolatry deserves the utmost condemnation.

The 'Great God' receives a further treatment in 3.545–54, where acts contrary to the 'Great God' are negatively portrayed (3.547–48, 554). The Sibyl suggests that the way to seek the face of the 'Great God' is to avoid such an error (πλάνον, 3.548), and cites a eulogy of the Jews: the Jews do not honour the works of humans (3.586–89), but fully honour the temple of the 'Great God' (3.575), eat sacred food in a holy manner (3.576–79), keep the law (3.580–84), worship the immortal God (3.591–94), and are morally holy (3.595–600).

The Sibyl thus sets up a contrast between all the Gentiles, their nations and the Jewish people who worship the true God. The former face terrible judgement (3.601–605) for their failure to piously honour God. But the latter will enjoy salvation (3.702–31). The Sibyl's attitude towards idolatry is totally scornful while her view of the worship of the true God is absolutely exclusive. Her emphasis

---

171. Cf. 3.221–33 where in a long discourse in praise of the Jews, the Sibyl sidetracks into a list of vices of which the Jews are never guilty. The views there are indicative of the Sibyl's attitude towards pagan religions, which take various forms, i.e. sorcery and astrology. The Sibyl views them as erroneous.

172. Similarly, the Sibyl cites idolatry as the reason for the future exile of the Jews. It is on the basis of post-exilic material that the Sibyl has made her pronouncement. In 3.282–94, we are able to see post-exilic elements which provide the hope in the Sibyl's oracles. See further below.

173. The word φρήν is used to describe such a disobedience. It carries the meaning of 'the heart or the mind' as the seat of thought (Liddell and Scott 1940: 871). In other words, the disobedience begins at the cognitive level and is thus the beginning of all the errors.

174. The 'fear of God' is an important theme in the Old Testament. In Prov. 1.7 the fear of God is linked to the acquisition of wisdom. And in Eccl. 12.13, the fear of God and the obedience to his commandments are one and the same thing. In 3.278, the Sibyl refers to God as the 'immortal begetter' of gods and all humanity, thus suggesting that the gods and humanity owe their existence to the true God. Humanity therefore ought to know and worship the true God, not idols.

175. There could be many reasons for the people's unwillingness to honour God. It could be the burden of the laws. It could be the lure of pagan religions. Or it could be the uncertainty of the Jews as a nation, a race and a people. The Sibyl does not seem to be bothered by the reason. For the truth of the immortal God as the begetter of all is a far better reason to worship and honour him than any other reasons not to.

throughout is the 'Great God' of the Jews and his 'honour', making him and the lack of honour for him the ground for rejecting all other gods and idols.

(ii) *Book 5.*[176]

Here, Sibyl declares the destruction of Egypt and renews her attack on Egyptian idolatry in 5.75–85. The idolaters are accused of being wicked and their persistent idolatry 'enduring evil' (5.75). They 'worship stones and brute beasts' instead of honouring God (5.77; cf. 3.29–32).[177] 5.78–79 reveals many other senseless, foolish and, by law, unmentionable things worshipped by the Egyptians. Idolatry is therefore unlawful and a crime.

Following a similar tradition as Isaiah (cf. Isa. 44.9–20), the Sibyl describes the idols pejoratively as being brought about by human hands (5.80). She uses the word κόπος to characterize the making of idols, which carries the meaning of 'toil', thus giving the impression that idol-making is a wearisome activity,[178] a result of human wicked notions (5.81–82). This description portrays the Egyptian gods as mere material (5.83), and are consequently lifeless (ἀψύχους), dumb (κωφούς) and easily destroyed (ἐν πυρὶ χωνευθέντας) (5.84).

In a lengthy praise of the Jews (5.238–85; cf. 3.573–600), the Sibyl combines a prediction of mortals' acknowledgement of God with an announcement of the happy ends of the righteous, which she declares as the end of the Egyptian animal worship (5.278–80).[179]

In a similar vein, she announces the disasters that are coming to the nations, which she says are meant to make humans take note of God (5.352). From 5.353 to 5.356, the Sibyl describes the idolaters as 'hostile' (δυσμενέας, 5.353), who will receive no mercy (οὐκ ἐλεήσει). Their sacrifices are unacceptable (5.354) and their object of worship offensive.[180]

The solution offered by the Sibyl is to love God, the wise eternal begetter (5.360). The contrast is clear and simple: God is wise; idols are unwise; God is eternal; idols are lifeless; God is the begetter of all; idols are made. The purpose of the Sibyl in condemning idolatry seems to be to show that the God of the Jews is the one true and eternal God so that others (i.e. the pagans) might be drawn to him.[181] The sibyl's grounds for rejecting idolatry are therefore a combination of

176. It is an accepted fact that Book 5 consists of six oracles or collection of oracles. See Schürer III, 644; and Collins 2000: 143. The following discussion will be confined to idolatry.

177. See our discussion of Wis. 15.18–19, Philo, *Dec.* 76–79 and *Vit. Cont.* 3–8 above. The Sibyl's critique differs from those of Wisdom and Philo who level their critique at an intellectual level. By virtue of her name and style, that is, the Sibylline Oracles, the Sibyl's critique tends to be one of speaking out oracles with little or no intellectual or philosophical discussion.

178. Liddell and Scott 1940: 978–79.

179. Although this may be a prediction of the mortals' turning to God, the words at the end of 5.80 speak much against Egyptian animal worship: στομάτευσσι κενοῖς καὶ χείλεσι μωροῖς (with vain mouths and foolish lips). Both words, κενός and μωρός denote both emptiness and futility, in addition to vanity and folly.

180. I.e. Hermes (ἀψύχοις θ' Ἑρμαῖς) and gods of stone (τοῖς λιθίνοισι θεοῖσιν) (5.356).

181. In 3.669–709 we read of the defence of the temple by God himself through a cosmic display of wrath against those who seek to destroy it. Such wrath of God eventually leads to the 'conversion'

several conceptions of God, among which are wisdom, eternity, and creatorship of the imperishable God.

It is not surprising that Isis receives equally vehement attack (5.484). According to Ferguson, Isis is the 'most important of the mother goddesses of the Hellenistic world to whom culture and mysteries were attributed'.[182] Three things are said about Isis: she will remain by the streams of the Nile alone; be a maenad on the sands of the Acheron (i.e. Hades); and no one will remember her. She will lose her followers as she belongs to the past. And instead of being worshipped, she is now a follower of Dionysus. She will be a speechless maenad (μαινὰς ἄναυδος, 5.485) who is as good as dead (ἀχέροντος).[183] By this critique, the Sibyl condemns Isis to oblivion (5.486).

Serapis is next in line to be attacked. A saviour god, he would now be unable to save himself as he reposes on many raw stones, an indication that he suffers from a heavy casualty (κεῖση πτῶμα μέγιστον, 5.488), due largely to the fact that his followers are now turning their attention to the imperishable God. In other words, the Sibyl is suggesting that Serapis will lose out in the contest against the imperishable God. For his followers are aware that he is nothing (5.491). Following such a condemnation of Isis and Serapis, the Sibyl continues to predict that the Egyptians would recognize their ancestral custom to be terrible (5.494).[184] And many Egyptians would convert to the imperishable God (5.497). The fact that the true God of the Jews is 'imperishable' is sufficient ground for rejecting all other gods and idolatry. And the Sibyl applies this conception of God universally,[185] suggesting that the nations too could turn to this imperishable God and be saved from their future disasters.[186]

b. *Conclusion*

The above discussion of Sibylline Oracles 3 and 5 demonstrates the widespread condemnation which idolatry receives from the writer of the oracles. The Sibyl reveals her attitude towards the pagan religions as one of intolerance. But this intolerance must be viewed from the perspective that she holds the belief that there is only one God, who alone is self-begotten and cannot be represented

of some who would offer worship in God's temple and meditate on the law of the Most High God (3.718–19). See Barclay 1996: 220–21.

182. Ferguson 1993: 249. Cf. Apuleius, *Metamorphoses*, in which Isis is given special significance through the transformation of Lucius back into a man, and the novel of Apuleius ends on a strong religious note. See also Price (1999: 140–41) for a discussion of the religious commitment.

183. Ἀχέροντος means Hades; but literally it means 'river of woe, one of the rivers of the world below' (Liddell and Scott 1940: 141).

184. Cf. 5.495–96 provides the results of the teaching of Egyptian ancestral custom, which are ridiculed, despised and degraded: the Egyptian gods are made from stone and earthenware, and are therefore devoid of sense.

185. For example, 5.264–65 refers to the conversion of the Greeks to the true God and their conformity to the laws.

186. Cf. 5.274–85 where the Sibyl predicts the failure of crops in yielding their harvest until all humans turn to the 'immortal eternal God', who is the 'ruler of all'. And the Jews are cited as the example for the nations as they piously put their faith in the 'one begetter' who alone is 'eminent'.

(cf. 3.11–15). The true God of the Jews is further described as 'immortal', 'eternal', 'imperishable', 'the great God', 'the begetter', and 'ruler of all'. It is against the background of such a theological foundation that she carries out her critique of idols, idol-worshippers, and the Egyptian animal worship.

There must be no representation of the true and great God, a principle based on the second commandment. And idol-making is viewed by the Sibyl as an attempt to represent God, and the worship of idols and animals considered a 'going astray' or 'wandering' from the great God (e.g. 3.29, 721). Thus, on the basis of the second commandment idolatry is defined and critiqued.[187] It appears that the second broad category of the definitions of idolatry as misrepresenting God, both visually and cognitively, seems operative here. By applying the conceptions of God universally, that is, Yahweh the true God of the Jews is now the 'great God' of all humanity, the sibyl rejects the worship of all idols as dishonouring the true God and all visual images of divinity as idolatrous.

7. *Summary and Conclusion*

This chapter serves to highlight the reactions of the Diaspora Jews against idolatry. While they are not exhaustive, they represent the Diaspora Jewish attitude towards idolatry and reflect the different grounds on which idolatry is rejected. We may summarize as follows. The Jews in the Diaspora in general view idolatry negatively and, on the basis of the Jewish scripture, pour scorn on and ridicule idols as stupid and absurd, and criticize the idol-makers as equally stupid. There appear to be some common emphases among all the Jewish authors; but there are also differences in emphasis. In fact, what we have seen above reflects different emphases on the different aspects of idolatry. And our definitions of idolatry as set out in Chapter 2 are not always taken as a package. In other words, some Jewish authors would emphasize some aspects of the definitions while others emphasise the other aspects.

What appears to be the common grounds of the above Diaspora Jews for rejecting idolatry are: (1) the true God of the Jews; (2) the Jewish law (i.e. the Jewish ancestral custom/covenant), particularly the first two commandments; (3) the Isaianic tradition that critiques idols and idol-makers.

For example, Philo and Wisdom appear to emphasize the definition of idolatry as misrepresenting God visually and at the cognitive level. Philo argues philosophically and draws heavily on the Jewish scripture to press home his points and advocates the Torah as the basis for condemning idolatry. Philo's approach to idolatry further includes one's passions. For example, his description of Gaius' efforts in making himself a God reveals that he views those efforts as Gaius' passions for idolatry. Similarly he refers to the passions of the poor in begging for alms (especially money) at the gates of the wealthy as idolatry. The author of

---

187. Although the first two commandments are not explicitly stated, the frequent reference to the law or holy law of the great God must be taken to include the ten commandments; cf. 3.275–76 where humanity's disobedience is to the 'holy laws' of the immortal God.

Wisdom, on the other hand, adopts an approach that is basically a polemic targeted at an inner circle. Through their critiques we are able to see that Philo and the author of Wisdom seem to view the Jewish conception of the true God as universally applicable to all humanity.

Josephus differs from Philo and the author of Wisdom in both his approach and emphasis. For Josephus, the approach to idolatry can be seen in his constant application of the scripture to the life in the Hellenistic world. He selects from aspects of the Jewish scripture to argue against the idolatrous Hellenistic way of life. He neither approaches idolatry from a purely intellectual perspective, nor aims at the inner circle of Jews. Rather, he uses scripture but at the same time embellishes the biblical account so as to make it fit his contemporary world. This is seen particularly in his use of the Numbers 25 incident. The behaviour of the Israelite youths is described as a 'transgression' against the ancestral customs and laws. Such an emphasis provides the ground for his rejection of the Israelite youths' behaviour as idolatrous – the second aspect of our first category of definition of idolatry. But Josephus also emphasizes the second category of the definition of idolatry – misrepresenting/dishonouring God. Idol-making, Egyptian animal worship, the Greek gods, and emperor worship all receive severe critique from Josephus.

Joseph and Aseneth represents yet another approach which critiques idolatry through a comparison between the true God of the Jews and the idols of Aseneth. This comparison and contrast is further seen in the lives of both Joseph and Aseneth, the praiseworthy God of Joseph and the condemnable idols and Egyptian gods of Aseneth. One of the key terms used for condemning idolatry in *Joseph and Aseneth* is 'alien', which describes the gods and idols of Aseneth, while the God of Joseph is the true God. And throughout, Joseph is described in favourable terms while Aseneth is a miserable person until her conversion. What we see here is an emphasis on the 'alienness' of idolatry, which fits the first category of the definition of idolatry set out by Halbertal and Margalit in Chapter 2. The 'God Most High' also receives a strong emphasis, and this conception of God serves as a ground for the author to reject idolatry.

The last Jewish author is that of the Sibylline Oracles in which the Sibyl pours scorn on idols and idolatry. This last author represents a less intellectual negation and critique of idolatry, compared to Philo and the author of Wisdom. The approach of the Sibyl differs from all the above Jewish authors, which does not discuss, but simply makes 'prophetic' and 'polemical' utterances against, idolatry. The Sibyl simply states 'propositions' without elaboration, and is not concerned with the intellectual aspect of her critique. Throughout, the true God is described as the great God who cannot be represented. And this conception of the true God is that he is 'immortal', 'eternal', 'imperishable', 'the great God', 'the begetter', and 'ruler of all'. The second category of misrepresenting/dishonouring the true God receives much emphasis. .

The interesting point to note is that all the Jewish authors discussed above seem to employ the first two commandments to varying degrees, some explicit and others not so explicit. To this end, the Numbers 25 incident is being used with a twist by Josephus who added many more details not found in the LXX. The story, which is so well embellished, serves to highlight that the covenant God of Israel is the reason for Jews to reject other gods.

In a similar vein, those LXX texts on 'idolatry' discussed in the previous chapter, such as Ezek. 2.3–7, Jer. 2.1–23, Isa. 46.1–13, often use the language of 'whoring' to describe 'unfaithfulness'. What we see in the above Jewish authors who criticize idolatry as 'unfaithfulness' is that there is an absence of such language. Instead, the criticism tends to be direct and the grounds are usually made explicit. The use of the Isaianic tradition in Isa. 44.9–20 is also worth mentioning at this point. This LXX text is being used as a basis for almost all the criticisms of idols, their origin, and the idol-makers. And when this is seen together with the second commandment, our Jewish authors have indeed demonstrated a clear basis for the rejection of idolatry.

While the above Diaspora Jews reflect a negative attitude towards idolatry, there are possible loopholes that are liable to exploitation. For example, both Philo's and Wisdom of Solomon's critiques and emphasis can leave room for idolatry, as it is entirely possible for a person who does not make any objects for worship, nor confuse the true God with nature, to visit the temple of Pan.[188] Similarly, while Josephus appears to have covered quite a wide area of idolatry, the whole question of action and intention is left out. In other words, Jews who remain relatively free from Josephus' criticism can possibly accommodate to idolatry in terms of their intention or action. For example, they may confuse God with nature or demons at the cognitive level, without actually becoming idolatrous in the way Josephus defines or critiques idolatry. It seems that Josephus' emphasis is mostly on the direct worship of idols, so that the lack of emphasis on association with idols, such as eating idol food at the pagan temple, creates a loophole for Jews to accommodate to idolatry without appearing to be so. As for *Joseph and Aseneth*, the simple and direct account of the story allows Jews to misrepresent God visually, since it is the 'alien' gods that the author is opposing. In the case of the Sibylline Oracles, the lack of emphasis on the possibility of Jews turning away from Yahweh to 'alien' gods leaves room for Jews to accept that while there is only one true God, he can be the same God as that of other religions, for example, Zeus. Conceptually, one can think of the great God of the Jews as the same as the gods of others, just that he has a different name.

While there are loopholes/chinks, at times, what is ambiguous can also be exploited. For example, the use of a pagan juridical formula which invokes the name of a pagan god can be ambiguous enough for some Jews to have no difficulty with its use. These will be our discussion in the next chapter.

188. See Chapter 4, section 6, a, below.

Chapter 4

JEWS AND THE WORSHIP OF THE GODS

1. *Introduction*

We have seen in the last chapter that Jewish authors in the Second Temple period generally reflect a negative stance towards idolatry and concluded that they view idolatry as an act of unfaithfulness to the true God and a break from their ancestral tradition. The worship of idols is seen as a disloyal and dishonouring act to the covenant God of Moses. Most of them hold the theme of the true God and the law, while some also reflect the Isaianic tradition in their critique of idolatry. These authors argue vehemently against idolatry and oftentimes ridicule both the Gentile idols/gods and the idol-makers.

While such a view suggests a Diaspora Judaism that was clearly anti-Gentile and anti-idolatry, we need to ask whether this defines Judaism on idolatry as a whole, or whether it represents only one aspect of Judaism with other sections of Judaism adopting a different stance. In Chapter 3 we have noticed that the definitions of idolatry set out by Halbertal and Margalit are not always adopted as a package, and that there are loopholes/chinks in the different emphases of the Diaspora Jews whom we examined. In other words, there were different views about what constituted idolatry. Moreover, there is evidence, both literary and archaeological, to suggest that there remain ambiguities in the definitions of idolatry. Even within the LXX, idolatry is not always clearly defined, with the exception of the first two commandments which in themselves are limited in scope. The differences in emphasis and ambiguities mean that different Jews could behave in a manner they do not consider idolatrous but which is considered idolatrous by others.

In this chapter, we will examine some of these examples to see how they may enlighten our understanding of Second Temple Judaism and how they may serve as parallels to the 'strong' in 1 Corinthians 8–10, who display a benign attitude towards the Gentile gods, and their willingness to attend Gentile temples and participate in cultic meals. In other words, are there Jewish parallels in the Second Temple period in terms of thought, attitudes, or actions, or a combination of these, to those of the 'strong' in 1 Corinthians 8–10?

We will begin with an examination of Exod. 22.27a, its understanding by Philo and Josephus, and whether it might serve as a parallel to the understanding of the 'strong'. This will be followed by a discussion of *The Letter of Aristeas* which will show that it is possible for Jews to adopt an accommodating attitude towards other gods, at a cognitive level. We will then discuss the use of the term

'Theos Hypsistos' among Jews and Gentiles, which will reveal a possible conceptual overlap about God between Jews and Gentiles. This will raise the question whether at a cognitive level an accommodating attitude and conceptual overlap about God might also serve as a parallel to the 'strong'. Next, we will examine Artapanus who represents an example of a Jew who accommodated to other religious traditions, particularly the Egyptian cultural and religious traditions. Finally, we will look at actual examples of accommodation and participation by Jews in idolatry from literary and inscriptional sources. These discussions will raise the question of how ambiguities in different definitions of idolatry might be exploited, ranging from a cognitive/conceptual level to a practical level. And such ambiguities may also raise the question as to how those Jews who accommodated to idolatry could serve as parallels to the 'strong' in 1 Corinthians 8–10.

2. *LXX Exodus 22.27a*

a. *What does the LXX ban in Exodus 22.27a teach?*
The Hebrew text of Exod. 22.27a is אלהים לא תקלל, which is rendered in most English translations as 'you shall not revile God' (NJB, REB, RSV, NRSV), with the exception of the King James' Version and the Vulgate which follow the LXX: 'Thou shalt not revile the Gods'.[1] However, the LXX translates it as follows: θεοὺς οὐ κακολογήσεις... The use of the plural θεοί in the LXX is intriguing and calls for a closer look.

In Exod. 20.2, the singular θεός is used while the plural θεοί is used in Exod. 20.3, even though the same Hebrew word אלהים is used in both verses. Similarly, the Hebrew אלהים is used in Exod. 23.32 and is translated in the LXX as θεοί, with the context clearly pointing to the gods of the nations. But there is no clear indication in Exod. 22.27a that points to the gods of the nations so that the rendering of אלהים as θεούς in the LXX seems puzzling. Why did the translators do this?

Van der Horst argues that the translators 'wilfully made the text say what it now says', that is, one should not criticize other people's gods whom the Jews encountered daily in Alexandria.[2] His suggestion that the background to the LXX rendering is a genuine desire for tolerance towards other religions is highly plausible.

What is clear is that Exod. 22.27a (LXX) prohibits 'cursing' (in the Hebrew) or 'criticizing' (in the Greek) other people's gods. And those who read the Greek version of the Pentateuch were mostly Hellenized Jews who did not speak or read Hebrew. Could it be possible that the LXX command was meant to advise the Jews at least not to criticize the gods of the Gentiles? And if this is possible, could it not be possible that on this basis the 'strong' in 1 Corinthians 8–10 were exercising a certain restraint towards other people's gods, at least in terms of speech? But this is preceded by another question: were the 'strong' aware of the LXX prohibition? Could what Exod. 22.27a commands serve as a parallel to the non-critique of idols on the part of the 'strong'? Before proceeding to this, we will discuss Josephus' and Philo's use of the LXX ban.

1.   Van der Horst 1994: 112.
2.   Van der Horst 1994: 112–13.

b. *The use of the LXX ban in Exodus 22.27a by Philo and Josephus*

In *Spec. Leg.* 1.53, Philo advises proselytes against reviling the gods whom others acknowledge so that others would not reciprocate in kind and so profane the true God. Further in *Vit. Mos.* 2.203–205, Philo explains Lev. 24.15–16 (LXX) in the light of Exod. 22.27a by saying that anyone who names the name of the Lord commits a sin punishable by death, whereas anyone who curses God bears only the guilt of the sin. Since the two sins appear to have disproportionate punishments, that is, naming the Lord's name receives a more severe punishment than cursing God, the former must refer to the only God while the latter the gods. Then, in *Quaest. in Exod.* 2.5, Philo's answer to why Exod. 22.27a forbids reviling other gods provides three reasons: (1) praise is always better than curse (or revilement); (2) criticism of each other's gods always leads to war, whereas the Law is peaceable; and (3) restraint from reviling others' gods may lead to a reciprocation in kind from others, i.e. they may speak well of the true and living God.[3] Thus, Philo's plea to God-believing Gentiles not to revile other gods seems to be motivated by a belief in peace between different religious traditions, and a desire always to ensure that the true and living God is well spoken of. His concerns are therefore different from those in *Dec.* 93.[4]

Josephus is another Jewish author who applies the LXX ban in Exod. 22.27a as it is. In *Apion* 2.237, he declares his preference to pay attention to the Jewish Law over the investigation of Gentile religious traditions. He explains that even Moses explicitly bans the derision or blasphemy of others' gods out of respect for the word 'God'. Elsewhere in *Ant.* 4.207, Josephus cites the Law as prohibiting the blasphemy of the gods others revere. In an earlier citation, *Ant.* 4.202, the blasphemy of the one true God is punishable by death, whereas in *Ant.* 4.207, no such punishment is suggested at all. This means there is still a difference between blaspheming the true God and the gods, a position similar to that of Philo. The reason for the different punishments is again due to the fact that the true God is distinguished from the gods.

While it is not clear why LXX renders Exod. 22.27a the way it does, it is sometimes explained from an apologetic angle. For example, in *Quaest. in Exod.* 2.5 Philo asks, 'Do they still accuse the divine law of breaking down the customs of others?' and goes on to say that not only does the Law lend support to those who worship different gods, but it also 'muzzles and restrains its own disciples'.

---

3.   Goldenberg (1997: 385), on the basis of *Spec. Leg.* 1.53 and *Vit. Mos.* 2.205, adds one more: the name 'God' should never be taken lightly, even when it is wrongly applied; see also Golderberg (1998: 68).

4.   In *Dec.* 93, Philo states that those who take an oath should ensure that their soul is pure from lawlessness, their body from pollution, and their tongue from evil speaking. With regard to the tongue, he says that 'it would be sacrilege to employ the mouth by which one pronounces the holiest of all names, to utter any words of shame' (οὐ γὰρ ὅσιον, δι' οὖ στόματος τὸ ἱερώτατον ὄνομα προφέρεται τίς, διὰ τούτου φθέγγεσθαί τι τῶν αἰσχρῶν). Although Philo is making this point in connection with oath making, in the light of his comments on the ban in Exod. 22.27a, it may indicate, for Philo, that the use of the tongue for honouring the true God and its use for reviling other peoples' gods are incompatible. For such use of the tongue only makes one's honour and praise of the true God οὐχ ὅσιον!

Such an idea of the Jewish Law giving support to Gentiles who worship different gods while restraining its own followers provides an example of Jewish tolerance towards idol-worshippers. And it suggests that there were Jews who might be more inclined towards a more positive interpretation of the Scriptures when other gods were mentioned. Philo's own view might serve as a basis for other Jews to be self-restrained. And it is not unreasonable to suggest that the rendering of אלהים of Exod. 22.27a in LXX as θεούς was apologetically motivated. Interestingly, even though Philo and Josephus cite the same apologetic purpose for the LXX ban, as shown above, they continue to find excuses for reviling others' gods.[5] But others who read them might judge their comments on Exod. 22.27a worthy of consideration and perhaps acceptance.

Goldenberg has argued that the ban was not obeyed by the Jews,[6] as may be seen in the violent destruction of the Gentile shrines during the Maccabean revolt. He further cites Goodenough's argumentation that the excuse of not being familiar with the Greek translation of the Torah is not available to Jews in Alexandria and Cyrene who behaved equally violently towards the Gentile religious institutions later, when tensions between Jews and pagans broke out into open war. He concludes that the lack of references about the obedience to the LXX ban suggests that the Jews might not even be aware of the ban. However, the fact that the LXX contains so much criticism of idolatry shows that the violent actions against pagans and their gods need not be an indication of the lack of awareness of the ban. Moreover, social circumstances might make one less inclined to observe the ban. For example, Josephus and Philo know about the ban but pay mere lip-service to it, as seen above. Thus, the LXX ban can be used or ignored – it is liable to be used in a situation of social-religious accommodation.

c. *Were the 'strong' aware of LXX Exodus 22.27a?*

There are at least four possible reasons for their awareness. First, if the 'strong' in Corinth had Jewish influence, they would have been exposed to the Jewish Scriptures which, in all probability, was the LXX,[7] since Jews in the Diaspora mostly knew Greek and not Hebrew.[8]

5.   E.g. Josephus, *Apion* 2.74; 2.237–38; Philo, *Spec. Leg.* 1.12–31. Even in *Quaest. in Exod.* 2.5 itself, Philo criticizes others' religious traditions by saying that they are 'deluded about their own native gods and because of custom believe to be inerrant truth what is falsely created error...'; cf. *Dec.* 52–81.

6.   Goldenberg 1997: 387.

7.   The LXX version of the Hebrew Scriptures which the 'strong' know would probably be the Alexandrian version, i.e. the work of the Alexandrian Jews, since that translation is our earliest known translation of the Old Testament; the other versions such as those of Aquila, Theodotion and Symmachus belong to a date much too late to fit in the period under our discussion. The earliest possibility would be Aquila's translation. But since he is known to have studied under R. Akiba who began teaching only in 95 CE, his (Aquila's) translation would not even have come into existence during the period when the 'strong' in Corinth and Paul had their exchange over the issue of idolatry. For a good survey of the various Greek translations of the Old Testament, see Swete (1914).

8.   An example is the Jews of Alexandria in Egypt. Feldman (1993: 51–52) points out that less than a century after the founding of the city by Alexander, the Aramaic speaking Jews began to speak Greek, pray in Greek, sing Greek Psalms, write in Greek, produce Greek literature and think in Greek.

Second, the decision of the translators of the Hebrew Bible in rendering the Hebrew אלהים as the plural θεούς would have been a familiar one, so that Greek speaking Jews were more likely to be aware of the ban. This is because, as van der Horst has noted, the translators' rendering of the Hebrew אלהים as θεούς was inspired by apologetic motives, that is, to paint Moses in a good light.[9] This is due, perhaps, to the negative portrayal of Moses by Gentile writers such as Manetho who represented Moses as a leprous Jew who led the invasion of Egypt (*Apion* 1.227–50).[10] Given the religious tension between Jews and Gentiles, such apologetic efforts would have been commonplace.

Third, the constant charges and accusations of pagans against the Jews would have made any serious-minded Jew want to search for an answer or at least some guidance about other gods.[11] The LXX ban in Exod. 22.27a could serve as an alternative for Jews who wished to seek harmony with their Gentile neighbours. Further, the fact that both Philo and Josephus have independently made use of Exod. 22.27a (LXX) indicates that inter-religious relationships were a hot issue and that some Jews in the Diaspora would in general be more willing to restrain themselves as much as possible, so long as they were allowed to remain loyal to their ancestral tradition.[12] Thus, the self-discipline of the 'strong' in terms of their speech can be seen in their not openly criticizing Gentile religious traditions;

Hence the Egyptian Jews found it necessary to have the Torah translated into Greek. According to Swete (1914: 21), the Pentateuch LXX would likely date from the period of the third and second centuries BCE, on the basis that some peculiar words and forms of the LXX are found to be common with Egyptian Greek during this period. See also Schürer (III, 474ff.) for a discussion of the development of the LXX and its subsequent history. The Roman world by the first century was thoroughly hellenized (Fee 1987: 2), not to mention that Corinth was historically Greek. Further, there is no evidence for the use of Hebrew by Diaspora Jews till later, possibly in the second century CE when the Hebrew language increasingly gained influence and recognition among Hellenistic Jews.

9.   Van der Horst 1994.113–14.

10.   Gager (1972: 117) argues that such an identification of Moses with the invaders became a permanent fixture in Alexandrian literature. This is an interesting observation as other writers such as Lysimachus (Josephus, *Apion* 1.304–11) and Apollonius Molon (*Apion* 2.145), together with Apion, are also represented in Josephus as denigrating Moses, although Josephus probably summarized their positions. Although these represent only those anti-Moses elements, they could have spread to other parts of Asia Minor and such anti-Moses elements were later seen in authors such as Quintilian, Tacitus and Juvenal. For a discussion of their treatments of Moses, see Gager (1972: 80–86).

11.   Philo (*Leg. Gai.* 120) reports that the masses in Alexandria hated the Jews for sometime so that when the issue of emperor worship became a subject for further hatred and, indeed, the mob attack on the Jews, the masses simply let loose. Feldman (1993: 114) observes that among other factors the more immediate was the Gentiles' accusation against the Jews of being unpatriotic as they refused to engage in the veneration of the imperial cult. Further, we are told that Apion, in arguing against Jews' citizenship in Alexandria, accuses the Jews of not worshipping the same gods as the Alexandrians (Josephus, *Apion* 2.66). Jews in other Hellenistic cities faced similar problems from their Gentile counterparts so much so that two Roman emperors Caesar and Augustus had to pass various decrees to protect the Jews and allow them the right to practise their religion; see for example Josephus, *Ant.* 14.185–267 and 16.160–79. See also Schürer III, 116–17 nn. 33 and 37.

12.   Goldenberg (1998: 63ff.) observes that during the same period of Jewish opposition to other religions there was a parallel track which shows them that other Jews sought various means of accommodating to the religions of their neighbours.

their statement in 1 Cor. 8.4 that 'idols are nothing in the world' should be understood as part of an internal dialogue between them and Paul, which does not
constitute a public criticism of Gentile gods.

It is necessary to raise another question. If the Jewish-influenced 'strong'
Corinthians were obedient to the LXX ban, why did they not also obey the second
commandment which bans the worship of other gods and idols? In other words,
their obedience to the LXX command and their attendance at Gentile temples do
not seem to match. Could it be that their understanding of the true God actually
differs from those who are opposed to idolatry? We shall now turn to consider
this possibility.

3. *Identification of the True God with Other Gods* – The Letter of Aristeas

The Letter of Aristeas represents an example of a Jewish accommodating attitude
to the religious traditions of Gentiles. This is seen in Pseudo-Aristeas' attempt at
identifying the God of the Jews with Zeus, which could be considered an act of
dishonouring God, based on some of the definitions of idolatry set out in Chapter
2 above, particularly that of cognitive error, that is, mixing Yahweh with other
gods. This does not mean, however, that Pseudo-Aristeas has abandoned his Jewish distinctions, as may be seen throughout the letter. But it is in the midst of the
'letter' that Pseudo-Aristeas' accommodating stance is subtly revealed, particularly
sections 15–16 where his openness to Gentile religions is the most explicit.

The Letter of Aristeas seems to suggest that the event described in the letter
took place during the reign of Ptolemy II Philadelphus (285–246 BCE) but the
story is now recognized as a legend among scholars.[13] The work, though legendary, also reflects possible historical actuality in that a translation of the Jewish
Law into Greek in Alexandria in the third century BCE is known.[14] Thus, while the
contents of the letter may not be historical, the author would probably have
written after the mid third century, and possibly come from Alexandria.[15] The
date of the letter remains in dispute. Collins has argued that the letter may be
dated in the time of Physcon, around early to mid second century BCE, based on
the mention of the liberation of Jewish slaves in the beginning of the letter.[16]

---

13.   Collins 1983: 98 n. 92; cf. Boccaccini (1991: 164) who rightly points out that the translation
of the Law is only a frame for 'a quite complex, profoundly consistent, and articulated system of
thought that still asks to be explored and identified in its entirety'. Thus, even though a legend, *The
Letter of Aristeas* still serves as a window through which one can gain insight into Jewish thought.

14.   Schürer III, 677.

15.   It is most probably dated between the early and mid-second century BCE; see below. The idea
that the author is probably an Egyptian who comes from Alexandria is based on his detailed knowledge of Ptolemaic court life; see Bickermann 1930: 280–98; cf. Fraser 1972: 698–703 and Gruen
1998: 211.

16.   Collins (1983: 82–84) bases this argument on the explanation that after the death of
Philometor, the Jews from the land of Onias continued to support Cleopatra II against Physcon (see
Fraser 1972: 119–23). However, since Physcon triumphed, the Jews were in a difficult situation. It was
not until 118 BCE when a decree of amnesty was issued. Collins therefore suggests that the account of

Thus, Collins and others follow Bickermann who argues for a date between 145 and 127 BCE.[17]

Although the name Aristeas is Greek,[18] his Jewish identity is easily discernible in his concerns with the law (31, 144, 139–40), and the importance he attaches to Jewish separateness (181–84, 139), not to mention one of the central themes of the letter: the translation of the Law.

The purpose of the letter has not been totally clear. At the outset, Pseudo-Aristeas appears to tell how the Jewish Law was translated into Greek. But this does not seem to be the only reason for the letter.[19] Some scholars have posited that the author is defending Judaism against the Gentile world as may be seen in the pro-Jewish, pro-law effort in Aristeas' description of the king's ready acceptance of every answer to his questions during the question-and-answer session before each day's banquet.[20] Others are of the opinion that Pseudo-Aristeas is addressing the letter to a Jewish audience.[21] Bartlett concludes that Pseudo-Aristeas' letter would be an encouragement to both Jews and Gentiles in Alexandria to be mutually respectful of each other, and a reassurance to Jewish leaders in Palestine that under a friendly Hellenistic regime their counterparts in

the liberation of the Jewish slaves in Pseudo-Aristeas may have been meant as a subtle appeal to the king by commending the generosity of his ancestor, or designed to reassure the Jews of the general goodness of the monarchy and to suggest that the threat to Jews was due to other factors such as the greed of the soldiers or the impulse of the mob (*Ep. Arist.* 14, 27).

17. Bickermann 1930: 280–98. Cf. Schürer III, 679–84, and Gruen 1998: 210, and n. 76.

18. There are various reasons for the adoption of a Greek name. He is apparently a very acculturated Jew in Alexandria as may be seen in the display of his well-educated command of the Greek language and the plentiful literary *topoi* in the letter. Thus, Gruen (1998: 211) comments that Pseudo-Aristeas is an intellectual (202) who is well acquainted with the procedures at the highest levels, familiar with royal practices with regard to the issuing of decrees, understands the court protocol, is thoroughly conversant with the court arrangements required for formal banquets, knows the secretarial exactness of the records of Ptolemy's 'every word and deed'; and whose collection of all the various materials, documents and speeches indicates him to be a writer of 'unusual imagination'. The Greek name in itself reflects Pseudo-Aristeas' acculturation. The other reason is possibly that by working through a Greek name, the author creates for himself a narrator who is both directly involved in the story as well as a nearby observer. There is therefore a certain degree of freedom for the author to move forward and backward, depending on when and what he wants to say or comment. It allows him to be a party involved in the political conversation as well as a bystander-commentator. The use of a pseudonym may be more effective, therefore, when the author wants to say positive things about his own race, that is the Jews, and their Law and traditions, not least when the pseudonym is that of a pagan!

19. The story, as it progresses, seems to digress into an exalted praise of the Temple, the priesthood, Jerusalem and Judaea, the high priest's vestments, and the like in an exaggerated description (e.g. the description of the water supply within the Temple, 88–89; cf. Stinespring 1962: 549).

20. Cf. Bartlett 1985: 11–16.

21. Bartlett (1985: 12–13) is of the opinion that Pseudo-Aristeas is defending the authority of the Greek translation of the law, together with the whole Diaspora, against the negative attitude of the Palestinian Jews who are ever ready to accuse the Diaspora Jews of what to them is a compromising tendency in matters of the law. Barclay (1996: 148 n. 49), however, points out the implausibility of this theory as it does not make sense for Pseudo-Aristeas to disguise himself with a Greek name. Cf. Gruen 1998: 212–14.

Alexandria could still live in conformity to the Law.[22] Barclay argues that at a
time when Jews were becoming increasingly prominent, Pseudo-Aristeas creates
a narrative to describe the kind of respect Jews in élite circles could enjoy and to
explain the reasons for the Jews' differences in matters of religion, morality and
diet.[23] Thus, it is possible that *The Letter of Aristeas* is a fictional story created by
Pseudo-Aristeas for apologetic as well as reconciling purposes, among others.[24]

It may be that some of these reasons coexist side by side and they provide a
larger framework for understanding Pseudo-Aristeas' acculturation and open
attitude to others' religious traditions. The question before us is: how does Pseudo-
Aristeas display his openness to Gentile religions when he has actually filled the
'letter' with so much exaltation of the Jews and Judaism? Yet precisely because
Pseudo-Aristeas is such an acculturated Jew who at the same time remains committed to his Jewish tradition, his willingness to accommodate the religions of the
Gentile world in which he lives through the creation of a literary figure is even
more impressive. In the following I shall examine some of the texts in the letter
and show how they may reflect an accommodating stance on the part of the author.

a. *Religious accommodation in Pseudo-Aristeas*

At the beginning, Aristeas, a creation of the author, introduces himself as one of
the officials in Ptolemy's court who was also one of the members of the embassy
sent to Judaea. While discussing the proposal to send an embassy to Judaea,
Aristeas took the opportunity to request from the king the release of the Jews
captured as slaves during the king's father's reign (12–14). Aristeas' address,
contained in two simple sections (15–16), reveals much about Pseudo-Aristeas'
attitude towards Gentile deities. First he equates the God of the Jews with the god
who directs Ptolemy Philadelphus' kingdom (15). This may be variously
understood. It could mean that the God of the Jews is equally worshipped by the
king, although on the basis of this statement alone, it is unlikely. It could also
mean that the God of the Jews directs all other kingdoms without regard to these
kingdoms' religious devotion. It could also mean that there is no difference
between the gods of the different religious traditions. But this may be as good as
saying that there is only one God whom all worship except that different peoples
and cultures express their belief in this God differently. Section 16 clarifies what
Pseudo-Aristeas intends to suggest.

In section 16, Aristeas says, 'the God who is overseer and creator of all things
whom they (the Jews) worship is he whom all humanity worship, but we, O king,

---

22. Bartlett 1985: 16; cf. Gruen (1998: 220–21) who rightly points out that *The Letter of Aristeas*
is a complex, multi-layered, piece of work which is not driven by any single purpose.
23. Barclay 1996: 148–49.
24. Bartlett 1985: 16; cf. Barclay 1996: 148–49 and 149 n. 51. Gruen (1998: 221) argues against a
synthesis between Judaism and Hellenism promoted by scholars such as Tcherikover (1958: 70, 82),
Hengel (1974: 264–65) and others (see Gruen 1998: 221 n. 137). He proposes that *The Letter of
Aristeas* implies that Jews are not only fully at home in the Hellenistic culture, but they have also
surmounted it. Thus, Gruen does not think that *The Letter of Aristeas* is apologetic in the sense that it
is directed at outsiders.

call differently as Zeus and Dis' (τὸν γὰρ πάντων ἐπόπτην καὶ κτίστην θεὸν οὗτοι σέβονται, ὃν καὶ πάντες, ἡμεῖς δέ, βασιλεῦ, προσονομάζοντες ἑτέρως Ζῆνα καὶ Δία, 16).[25] This is probably the most explicit statement that reveals Pseudo-Aristeas' attitude. The implication is clear. The God of the Jews is not only being universalized in this statement, but more significantly, he is being made as not quite unique since the Greeks are said to address him with different names.

Although putting the words in the mouth of a Gentile Aristeas lessens the significance of the equation, it may perhaps be the only way in which a Jew like the author of *The Letter of Aristeas* could make that equation. Otherwise, as Goldenberg rightly points out,[26] since Jews do 'seem generally to have drawn the line at actually calling their God by the name of a Gentile deity', it would have been probably rejected by most Jews reading the letter, if not all. And the fact that the author has put himself into a Gentile persona might suggest that he does not wish to be known as a Jew. Further, since the author is a Jew, such an equation, though made through a Greek figure, must reflect the author's own accommodating attitude towards the Gentile religions! In theory, Pseudo-Aristeas' accommodation seems to be at the conceptual level, that is, identifying the Jews' God with the Gentiles' god. But in practice, he is able to write a pseudonymous 'letter' in which to express his religious openness.

In section 19, the other court officials are represented as advising the king to release the enslaved Jews as a thank-offering to 'the Most High God' (τῷ μεγίστῳ θεῷ, 19; cf. 37). This phrase, 'the Most High God', could mean that the author views the god of these Gentile officials as 'the Most High', or that 'the Most High God' of the Jews is the one whom these pagans worship. The former would imply that Pseudo-Aristeas is pluralistic; while the latter suggests that he sees the God of the Jews in the gods of the pagans. In either case, there is an attitude less strict than that seen in Philo and Wisdom; and in either case the exclusivist and negative stance appears to be absent. Further, Philadelphus is made to express an intention to do a 'pious action' and to dedicate a thank-offering to the Most High God (37). The author's positive description of the king's religious actions not only reveals his positive perception of the king, but more significantly his attitude towards Gentile religions.

In section 42, Eleazar the high priest reads King Philadelphus' letter to the whole people 'in order that they might know your pious reverence for our God' (ἵνα εἰδῶσιν ἣν ἔχεις πρὸς τὸν θεὸν ἡμῶν εὐσέβειαν). This is a subtle recognition that non-Jews are just as capable of worshipping the true God and therefore capable of righteousness. As it is, Pseudo-Aristeas has made clear that the king worships Zeus (16). But here in section 42, he seems to make a distinction by making Eleazar say 'our God' (τὸν θεὸν ἡμῶν). This is in reference to what the king does for the Jews in terms of the gifts and offerings for the Temple

25. Shutt (1985: 13) provides a mistranslation: 'These people worship God the overseer and creator of all, whom all men worship including ourselves, O King, except that we have a different name. Their name for him is Zeus and Jove.'

26. Goldenberg 1998: 65.

(40). Thus, the king views his 'pious action' as done unto his god, that is, Zeus; while the high priest views it as reverence for 'our God'![27] While it appears that Pseudo-Aristeas is concerned to emphasize 'our god' as against 'their God', this could be reversed to say that he wants to show that the king's god is equally 'our God'! But he has to show this through the high priest, since in the person of a Gentile, he cannot speak for the Jews.[28] Such is the careful twist of the author which exposes his accommodating attitude towards the Gentile god.

The question arises, then, as to what we may make of the critique of idolatry and of the Egyptian animal cults by the high priest (134–38). To be sure, such a critique reflects Pseudo-Aristeas' negative view of idolatry and the Egyptian animal cults. But it in no way reflects his critique of Zeus. In fact, seen against the background of the equation of the Jews' God and the Greek Zeus, the critique might suggest to us what Pseudo-Aristeas thinks of Zeus. God is one; and by the name of Zeus, he remains one! In other words, he is committed to the oneness of God: Zeus is God, but not the idol that represents him! The critique of idolatry by Eleazar therefore makes no difference to Pseudo-Aristeas' accommodation to the Gentile god; it in fact strengthens his position and therefore allows him greater room to manoeuvre! This is particularly so since he can interchange between the true God and Zeus without being thought of as being unfaithful to the Jewish tradition.

As the story unfolds, Pseudo-Aristeas' accommodation becomes even more apparent. In section 139, Eleazar says that Moses, having given thought to all the details, 'fenced us round with impenetrable barrier and iron walls'. Thus the Mosaic Law is described as a fortress whose purpose is to ensure that Jews do not have any contact with the other nations. And purity of the body and the soul is defined against that understanding of contact. In section 140, Eleazar further says that even the Egyptian priests acknowledge the Jews as 'people of God' (ἀνθρώπους θεοῦ). Such a description is reserved only for those who fear the true God (εἰ μὴ τις σέβεται τὸν κατὰ ἀλήθειαν θεόν), not to the rest of humanity. Yet, this position of Eleazar is softened by his very engagement in receiving the Gentile embassy from Egypt and sending a team of translators to Alexandria. It suggests a greater than expected tolerance towards non-Jews. For if Eleazar is of the opinion that the Mosaic Law is meant to keep the Jews from Gentile contamination, his willingness to send his team shows that the fear is at

---

27.   Although one may argue that Eleazar is referring to the gifts and offerings for the Temple, without reference to the 'pious action' and 'thank-offering' of the king in releasing the captured Jews, yet it precisely shows that Eleazar has chosen only that aspect of the king's action which speaks well of his piety. And there is no reason to think that the king would have such clear separation of ideas about his god and the Jews' God since in section 16 he has not been made to disagree with the equation of Aristeas.

28.   Indeed, in the person of a Gentile, Pseudo-Aristeas can speak positively of the Jews, their city and their Temple. But the question of the oneness of God is a sensitive one and being a Jew, he has to be extremely careful with what he says. In the end, the mutual reference to 'God' between the Gentile king and the high priest, both representing positions of authority, helps to express Pseudo-Aristeas' openness on this matter, as he says, 'just as my careful labour has shown' (καθὼς περιείργασμαι, 15), i.e. the mutual recognition of the true God.

least minimal. And given Eleazar's careful position, his choice of the translators would probably correspond with what he thinks are 'people of God' (cf. 121). This, we see in his description of the men in his reply to the king as: 'good and true' (καλοὺς καὶ ἀγαθούς, 46). And the willingness of these men of high quality to go to Philadelphus' court seems to show that they have no fear of Gentile contamination.[29] This self-contradiction of Pseudo-Aristeas can in fact be explained through the answers of the translators to all the king's questions, which will be looked at below.

The reception of the translators is equally telling. Upon the arrival of the translators and the Law, the king makes obeisance seven times (177) thanking not just the representatives from Judaea but more importantly thanking God 'whose oracles these are' (οὗτινός ἐστι τὰ λόγια ταῦτα, 177). Although this is a description of the king's favourable attitude towards the team of translators and the Law, it raises the question as to which god the king is thanking. The phrase 'whose oracles these are' suggests that Philadelphus is thanking the Jewish God. But his devotion is to Zeus, which implies that Pseudo-Aristeas is allowing a conceptual interchange between the king's own god and the Jews' God. The equation of section 16 between the God of the Jews and Zeus indicates such a possibility. Such accommodation is seen no more clearly than in the prayer of Elisha, the oldest of the translators, asking for good things to be granted to the king, his family and all those who support him. The prayer implies that the king is righteous enough to warrant favourable treatment from the Jews' God. And Elisha and those present who applauded at the prayer (186) probably viewed the king favourably in terms of his religious life, which reflects Pseudo-Aristeas' own accommodating attitude towards the Gentile king's religious behaviour.

The translators' constant praise of the king's rule and his commitment to justice and truth betrays the author's belief that those who worship the true God can also be found among Gentiles. The use of the word 'God' appears as if the king understood what the translators meant when they mentioned 'God'. Thus, the author turns 'God' into a common denominator between the Gentile king and the Jews.

In the first series of questions which the king asked, the last one received an answer which included the author's view of the king's counsels: they are good and are all fulfilled by God to your profit (τελειοῦται δὲ ὑπὸ τοῦ θεοῦ πάντα σοι καλῶς βουλευομένῳ...συμφερόντες, 199). There are two possible interpretations. It could mean that Pseudo-Aristeas recognizes that the God of the Jews is also the God of the pagans, if the God of the Jews is meant here. Alternatively, Pseudo-Aristeas may be recognizing the validity of other gods, if another god is meant here. If the former is meant, which probably it is, it shows

---

29. Barclay (1996: 147) argues that Aristeas is not guilty of self-contradiction since Philadelphus accommodates the dietary requirements of his guests and foregoes his normal religious practices, which suggests that 'if Jews and Gentiles are to mix in friendly social intercourse, it has to be *on the Jews' terms*'. However, we are also told that accommodating guests in matters of drink and food is a practice of the court so as not to create any discomfort (182). In other words, it is possible that Philadelphus' accommodation of his guests' dietary requirements is more a diplomatic move accorded to all guests, whether they are Jews or not.

Pseudo-Aristeas' openness to the possibility that pagans are just as capable of receiving favour from the 'true God' of the Jews. If the latter, then it shows that Pseudo-Aristeas is willing to accommodate Gentile gods.

In the answer to the question, 'what is the most essential quality of a ruler?' we see Pseudo-Aristeas' subtle connection between God as a lover of righteousness and the exhortation to the king to honour righteousness (209). Pseudo-Aristeas seems to view righteousness rather differently from the covenantal perspective so that even a Gentile king who acts righteously would be approved by God.[30] And the words of Eleazar in section 42 and the translator's answer in sections 232–33 to the question, 'how one might be free from grief' also reveal relatively clearly that the king's piety (εὐσεβεῖ, 233) is linked to 'righteousness' (τῇ δικαιοσύνῃ, 232). This suggests that Pseudo-Aristeas conceives of the king as approved by God,[31] although the king worships his own god (cf. 16).

Further, in answering the king's question on what is wise counsel, the translator credits Philadelphus with practising piety (τὴν εὐσέβειαν ἀσκοῦντι, 255) and states that it ensures the fulfilment of all the king's resolutions. Such a recognition of Philadelphus' practice as piety shows that Pseudo-Aristeas himself recognizes piety outside Judaism. This suggests the possibility that piety is seen by Pseudo-Aristeas as universal and that the God to whom and for whom one practises piety may not necessarily be as important as the act itself. If these two possibilities are allowed, then Pseudo-Aristeas' accommodating attitude would become more obvious.[32]

What the various examples of the answers so far reveal is that there seems first of all a common understanding of the word 'god'. Even though the translators would have known to what god Philadelphus devotes himself since they are learned men, the author puts them in a very friendly position with positive words uttered about the king and his religious and moral life. The way the translators refer to God, as if the king understood and accepted their God even though he has a different god, suggests that the author has a higher purpose: the encouragement of mutual recognition of each other's contributions, even religious ones. Thus, based on such an analysis, Pseudo-Aristeas would appear to display an attitude that is basically open, although he is careful to note the difference of the God of the Jews from the idolatry of the Greeks and the Egyptian animal cults

30. If we take the Jewish law observance as the key to defining 'righteousness', then to accord 'righteousness' to a Gentile is certainly going against the norm.

31. Cf. 280 where the king is praised for having been given a crown of righteousness by God.

32. Remaining examples may be briefly mentioned: God grants the king right judgement (267) and gives him good counsel (270; cf. 271–72), the gift of kind-heartedness (274), an alert understanding and powerful judicial ability (276). For the king models his deeds after God (281). One may argue that these are said out of political expediency. However, if we understand this to be fictional, then the kind of things said about the king would reflect an accommodating and friendly Pseudo-Aristeas not only towards the king, but also towards the god of the Gentile king! Thus, God is the one who fulfils the king's desires (283). His actions of care, restraint, and decency are honoured by God (285) who directs all the king's actions (287). He has conferred on Philadelphus the gifts of governing the country (290) and given him a pure mind that is untainted with evil (292). There is thus a conceptual overlap in Pseudo-Aristeas between the Jews' God and the Gentiles' gods.

(cf. 134–38). As mentioned earlier, Pseudo-Aristeas seems to view Zeus as the name with which the Greeks address the true God. But he rejects the idols which the pagans use to represent Zeus.

It is possible to detect Pseudo-Aristeas' principle in this accommodation elsewhere in the letter, besides the fact that he is a highly acculturated Jew.[33] In section 227, Philadelphus' question, 'with whom should we vie in generosity?' is given the following answer. Humanity in general would be quick to think that generosity is to be accorded to those who agree with themselves. However, the translator opines that a keen and open-hearted generosity is due to those who disagree with us so that we may win over our dissenters to what is right, which is at the same time to their own interest. By such a principle of 'kindness to thy dissenters', Pseudo-Aristeas seeks to win others to what is right. The author's accommodating stance is seen further in his care in using the phrase 'what is right' (τὸ καθῆκον, 227) rather than 'the true God'! By this, the translator's advice to the king can also be given to Jews. It is equally possible for the Jews to be turned to τὸ καθῆκον according to non-Jews. The neutrality of τὸ καθῆκον makes accommodation towards each other's values a mutual attitude. Those who face dissenters must entreat their God to help them win over their dissenters. And the author does not make clear who this God is, except that he rules the minds of all people (τὰς γὰρ ἀπάντων διανοίας κρατεῖ, 227). And if we recall what Aristeas says in 15–16, it is not impossible that the question as to who the god is remains an open one.

b. *Conclusion to* The Letter of Aristeas

The Letter of Aristeas demonstrates the accommodating stance of a Jew towards the Gentile religious tradition – the equation of the God of the Jews with the god whom all people worship, except that they call the god they worship by Zeus and Dis. The same attitude is also seen in various examples such as the king's 'pious action' and the translators' overall positive description of the king's religious life.

Pseudo-Aristeas' accommodation suggests that not all Jews responded negatively to Gentile culture and religious traditions, particularly those in the Diaspora who had come to terms with the reality of the religiously pluralistic environment in which they lived. Could this be a parallel to the 'strong' in 1 Corinthians 8–10 and their religiously pluralistic environment?

The examination of *The Letter of Aristeas* shows that some Jews adopted a more open and accommodating stance towards pagans and their god/s. The example of Pseudo-Aristeas' equation of the God of the Jews with other people's gods suggests that there is a possibility of a conceptual identification/overlap of

---

33. Cf. Barclay 1996: 147–48. In Barclay's important and influential work, *The Letter of Aristeas* serves as part of the evidence of cultural convergence in the Jewish Diaspora. Barclay employs different scales that depict the different kinds and the different degrees of Hellenization and carefully differentiates the two categories of assimilation and acculturation (1996: 92–98). He carefully analyses the letter and concludes that Pseudo-Aristeas 'produced a document which demonstrates both the extent of his acculturation and the limits of his assimilation' (see 1996: 149–50 for details).

the true God with other gods.[34] Is it possible that this might parallel the concept of the one God held by the 'strong' in Corinth? Like Pseudo-Aristeas, is there also a conceptual identification/overlap in the thought of the 'strong' concerning the true God and other gods? Even though our definitions of idolatry in Chapter 2 would have classified Peudo-Aristeas' identification of the true God with Zeus under idolatry by mixing the true God with other gods, what Pseudo-Aristeas is doing precisely reveals that at the conceptual level what constitutes idolatry can be ambiguous and such ambiguity can be exploited.

The above questions about the 'strong' regarding a conceptual overlap call for further discussion of other evidence, both literary and inscriptional, which points to that possibility by showing the use of Theos Hypsistos by both Jews and Gentiles to refer to their Gods.

4. *The Use of* Θεὸς Ὕψιστος: *A Brief Survey*

The term ὕψιστος usually means, in the superlative sense, 'highest', 'loftiest'.[35] Thus, θεὸς ὕψιστος is often taken to mean the 'highest God' or 'the most high God'. This could imply that the 'Most High God' is at the top of a divine hierarchy of gods, at least to the worshipper.[36] However, Jewish usage of the term appears to be inclined towards the absolute sense, that is, *the* god who alone is the true God, rather than the superlative sense.[37]

In the LXX, ὕψιστος occurs 110 times. Apart from a few topographical uses, ὕψιστος is always a term for the God of the Hebrews in the LXX, that is, it is a

34. In Aristobulus' citation of Orphaeus (Fragment 4, Eusebius, *Praeparatio Evangelica* 13.13.5), Orphaeus speaks of the oneness of the only God who is the strong and mighty God, and refers to this god as Zeus and describes him as ruler of all. What is important is that Aristobulus is citing Orphaeus in support of what he has to say about the God of the Jews (cf. *Orph.* 24)! This further strengthens our argument that there is a possible conceptual overlap of the true God and other gods among some Diaspora Jews. Similarly, in the citation of Aratus (*Praeparatio Evangelica* 13.13.7) we read that the name Zeus was deliberately removed, not because of any repulsion against its use, but because the reference to Zeus by the Gentiles is understood as a reference to God. Collins (2000: 189) rightly points out that Aristobulus' claim that the Greeks borrowed from Moses implies that the God of the Jews and the gods of the Gentiles are one. The removal of the name of Zeus was perhaps meant to universalize that reference. See, however, Barclay (1996: 152) who argues that Aristobulus is 'explicitly concerned with proper speech and thought about God'.
35. Liddell and Scott 1940: 852.
36. Trebilco (1991: 128) points out that the epithet 'the Highest' was used by pagans to indicate that the god they were worshipping was the 'most important god'; cf. Nilsson (1963: 102) who claims that it would seem natural for the Greeks to refer to Zeus as the High God since Zeus was recognized as the king of the gods, although a few pages later he also says that people deemed it unnecessary to call the High God by the name Zeus (106). Nock *et al.* (1936: 64) do not see the Gentile use of θεὸς ὕψιστος and Zeus Hypsistos as being influenced by Jewish usage; on the other hand, Levinskaya (1996: 84–95) argues that the idea of Theos Hypsistos being influenced by Gentile usage has been exaggerated by modern scholars and that examples of Hypsistos being used with a Gentile deity are relatively few.
37. Levinskaya (1996: 98) observes that the translators of LXX definitely have in mind the absolute sense of ὕψιστος.

term for Yahweh, and is usually the translation of עליון or עלי. The designation עליון is a reference to God as the 'Highest' or 'Most High' in the Old Testament.[38] Thus it serves as a proper name for Yahweh. Ὕψιστος, when used to translate this Hebrew designation, would clearly mean 'Most High' in the absolute sense. The use of ὕψιστος in the LXX in referring to Yahweh often takes the forms of ὁ θεὸς ὁ ὕψιστος and κύριος ὁ ὕψιστος. It is perhaps reasonable to assume, then, that for the translators of the LXX, the θεός of the Hebrew people is also the ὕψιστος and vice versa.[39]

The term's use can also be seen in Jewish authors. Philo uses the term, either when quoting the LXX or when referring to the Jewish God. In *Leg. Gai.* 157 and 317, Philo refers to the benevolence of Caesar in not only allowing the Jews complete freedom to offer sacrifices, but also charging the expenses to his own account. It is here that Philo refers to the God of the Jews as ὁ ὕψιστος θεός.[40] Elsewhere, the term is used as a title for the God of the Jews when non-Jews are being addressed. This can be seen, for example, in Agrippa's letter to Gaius (Philo, *Leg. Gai.* 278) and the description of Flaccus' failure to maintain the peace which resulted in the persecution of the Jews (Philo, *Flacc.* 46). But the most interesting use of the term that might shed light on the position of the 'strong' in 1 Corinthians 8–10 is found in Philo's comment on Gen. 14.18 in *Leg. All.* 3.82 in which Philo appears to be aware of the potential misunderstanding of the term ὕψιστος. He first explains that the use of the term ὕψιστος in referring to God does not mean there is a range of exalted deities (οὐχ ὅτι ἐστί τις ἄλλος οὐχ ὕψιστος). For Philo, the θεός ὕψιστος in Gen. 14.18 is to be understood in the absolute sense. His further elaboration is a close parallel to 1 Cor. 8.4.

Philo, *Leg. All.* 3.82	1 Cor. 8.4
οὐχ ὅτι ἐστί τις ἄλλος οὐχ ὕψιστος	οὐδὲν εἴδωλον ἐν κόσμῳ
not that there is some other not most high	an idol (or image) is nothing in the world
ὁ γὰρ θεὸς εἷς…καὶ οὐκ ἔστιν ἔτι πλὴν αὐτοῦ	οὐδεὶς θεὸς εἰ μὴ εἷς
for God is one…and there is none beside him	there is no God but one

38. E.g. Num. 24.16; Deut. 32.8; Ps. 18.14; 2 Sam. 22.14; Pss. 9.3; 21.8; 46.5; 50.14; 73.11; 77.11; 78.17; 83.19; 87.5; 91.1, 9; 92.2; 107.11; Isa. 14.14; Lam. 3.35, 38; see also Bertram (1972: 615–17) for its Semitic usage.

39. There are other examples of Jewish literary use of the term as a reference to Yahweh: *Sib. Or.* 3.519, 574, 719; *Ph. E. Poet*, Fragment 3; *Ezek. Trag.* Exagoge 239; *passim T. Abr.*

40. Levinskaya (1996: 95–96 n. 76) has suggested that the Roman authorities probably used the term to designate the God of the Jews. However, she concedes that Philo may not be citing the documents verbatim. Even though she argues that both Josephus (*Ant.* 16.163) and Joannes Lydus (*De mens* 4.53)* use the term in their quotation of Augustus' and Julian's decrees respectively, it could well be that ὁ ὕψιστος θεός was used in both decrees because that was seen as the way Jews referred to their God, if those decrees were indeed cited verbatim. In the absence of overwhelming evidence, it would be better not to draw a conclusion as Levinskaya has done. Trebilco (1991: 239 n. 12) observes that Celsus and Julian both used the title but they were both familiar with biblical usage. The latter is cited by Levinskaya as part of her argument (1996: 96 n. 76). *This is a questionable citation as *De mens* 4.53 does not refer to such a decree, nor mention the term.

Such a parallel is interesting in that it shows that the 'strong' in the Corinthian church could well have had Jewish influence in terms of their concept of the one God similar to that of Philo above. What is important is that while Philo's position resulting from such a belief is that of condemnation of all other gods,[41] the 'strong' in Corinth appear to be more accommodating as may be seen in their participation in Gentile cults, or presence at Gentile temples.

In a similar vein, Josephus uses the term rather rarely and, whenever he uses it, cautiously. Trebilco observes that Josephus uses the term when quoting the decree of Augustus.[42] In *Ant.* 16.163, Augustus is represented as having decreed that Jews may follow their own customs as they did in the time of the high priest Hyrcanus. Hyrcanus is here designated as ἀρχιερεὺς θεοῦ ὑψίστου. Thus, θεὸς ὕψιστος appears to be used as a reference to the God of the Jews in Josephus, in a rather careful way. Perhaps, the limited use of the term in Josephus might suggest that he, like Philo, wants to avoid any misunderstanding that the term might generate.[43]

In *Joseph and Aseneth*, the use of ὕψιστος seems to be exclusively reserved for referring to the God of Joseph. At various points when ὕψιστος is used by Jews or the 'heavenly man', it is clearly in reference to the God of the Jews.[44] However, others who are non-Jews or pagans use the term too. It is not clear whether the writer or author of *Joseph and Aseneth* intends to convey the idea that even pagans recognize the God of the Jews as the Most High when he puts the term in their mouths. But the description of Aseneth destroying and discarding all her idols (10.13) and the address of the God of Joseph as the Most High in her first soliloquy (11.1) indicate that ὕψιστος is here meant to refer to the God of the Jews only, to the exclusion of other deities. Like Philo, the author of *Joseph and Aseneth* seems to adopt a position which allows or requires the understanding of the term to deny and reject other religious traditions and practices.

Thus far, we have looked at the literary evidence which demonstrates the Jewish use of ὕψιστος or θεὸς ὕψιστος in the absolute sense which at the same time is considered by those who use it to deny and reject the religious traditions and practices of pagans. There are also Jewish inscriptions in which the term θεὸς ὕψιστος is found.[45]

This language of dedication is seen in two inscriptions which concern the dedication of a prayer-house or proseuche (προσευχή) to the Most High God (θεῶι ὑψίστωι, *CPJ* III, Appendix, no's. 1433 and 1443). The first is located in Hadra, Alexandria in second century BCE and the second in Athribis in second or first

41. See, for example, *Dec.* 52–81, *Spec. Leg.* 1.12–31, and *Vit. Cont.* 3–8. See further *Spec. Leg.* 2.165 where Philo makes a stunning statement that all the Greeks and Barbarians worship the same one God, 'the Father of gods and men and the Maker of the whole universe,...'. Yet, his conclusion is that all should therefore 'cleave' (ἀνῆφθαι) to the one true God and not invent new gods.

42. Trebilco 1991: 130.

43. Trebilco 1991: 130.

44. E.g. *Jos. Asen.* 8.10; 14.7; 15.6–8, 13; 16.7–8; 19.2; 22.5; 23.10.

45. Trebilco (1991: 133–37) provides a list of all the known θεὸς ὕψιστος inscriptions which are Jewish. I shall discuss only those relevant ones in terms of dating, i.e. those which fall within the Second Temple period, before the second century CE.

century BCE. Horbury and Noy rightly remark that the use of the word 'pro-seuche' to refer to the building makes its Jewishness unambiguous.⁴⁶ Together with the dedicatory language of θεὸς ὕψιστος, it is without doubt that the God of the Jews was meant.

Two inscriptions originating from the island of Rheneia, the burial place of the inhabitants of Delos, contain an appeal to God for vengeance on the murderers of two girls (*Inscriptions de Délos* no. 2532; *CIJ* 725). Both are almost identical and date no later than the end of the second or the beginning of the first century BCE.⁴⁷ The malediction appears to reflect the belief of the person or persons making the prayer. The appeal is addressed to the Most High God (τὸν θεὸν τὸν ὕψιστον). The interesting point is that the next line actually reveals what this Most High God was to the dedicant: τὸν κύριον τῶν πνευμάτων καὶ πάσης σαρκός (the Lord of the spirits and of every flesh). A number of lines down, the Most High God is addressed as 'the one who watches over all things' (κύριε ὁ πάντα ἐφορῶν). Although it is not explicitly stated that this Most High God is the true God, the description indicates that the θεὸς ὕψιστος in this prayer is to be understood in the absolute sense in that this highest God is the creator, thus the true God, at least to the dedicant.

There are a number of inscriptions from Delos which make use of θεὸς ὕψιστος to refer to the God of the Jews. Trebilco lists five of these inscriptions which have been found in a building claimed to be the synagogue at Delos and constructed in the first half of the first century BCE.⁴⁸ Two of the inscriptions will be highlighted and discussed here since their dating falls definitely within the period under our consideration.⁴⁹ The first is a dedication dated in the first century BCE which is about a woman named Laodice who was cured of a disease (*CIJ* 728). It reads: Λαωδίκη θεῶι Ὑψίστωι σωθεῖσα ταῖς ὑφ' αὐτοῦ θαραπήαις εὐχην (Laodice to the Highest God, who cured her of her infirmities, a vow).⁵⁰ The second is similarly dated in the first century BCE, about a man named Lysimachos who dedicates a thank-offering to the Highest God (Λυσίμαχος ὑπὲρ ἑαυτοῦ θεῷ Ὑψίστῳ χαριστήριον, *CIJ* 729). From the inscriptions alone, it cannot be absolutely determined that they are Jewish, since dedications to 'Theos Hypsistos' could also be rendered to 'Zeus Hypsistos'. However, we

---

46. Horbury and Noy 1992: 14. Schürer (II, 440 n. 61) points out that the term occurs in Gentile worship to refer to a place of prayer which may have had Jewish influence. Levinskaya (1996: 207–25) discusses the various criteria for distinguishing Jewish inscriptions and the meaning of the term προσευχή and draws two conclusions: (1) there is no clear evidence that the Gentiles ever borrowed the term to designate their places of worship; and (2) there was only one occasion when the term was used by a Judaizing group 'precisely because the term was markedly Jewish'. Thus, the term προσευχή seems to be exclusively used by Jews alone.

47. Schürer III, 70.

48. Trebilco 1991: 133–34; see further Trebilco (1991: 241 n. 30) for the entire list of the inscriptions and the various scholarly works that have been carried out on them.

49. Two have the possibility of being in the second century CE, while a third, namely *CIJ* 726, does not use the term θεὸς ὕψιστος at all; thus they will be left out of our discussion.

50. Cf. Trebilco 1991: 134.

have seen in an earlier discussion on two inscriptions,[51] that Jews on Delos addressed their God, Yahweh, as θεὸς ὕψιστος. Further, Trebilco points out that the building from which these inscriptions were discovered was unlikely to be the temple of Zeus since '"Zeus Hypsistos" had his own sanctuary on Mount Cynthus on Delos'.[52] In addition, one of the inscriptions found in the same building but which is not discussed here (*CIJ* 726, dated first century BCE) contains the words ἐπὶ προσευχῆι, of which προσευχή is almost an exclusively Jewish term.[53] If the building was a synagogue and the inscriptions were Jewish, the 'Theos Hypsistos' on them would quite certainly refer to the God of the Jews. Even though it is possible for Jews who dedicate their thank-offerings to 'Theos Hypsistos' to conceptually think that their 'Theos Hypsistos' is the same as 'Zeus Hypsistos',[54] it is most likely that they would view their God as the only true God, rather than the one at the top of the pantheon of gods. In other words, 'Theos Hypsistos' is most likely understood in the absolute sense.

Two inscriptions further show 'Theos Hypsistos' to be used by Jews to refer to Yahweh. In *CIJ* 690, a manumission inscription from Gorgippa in the Bosporan kingdom, dated 41 CE, reads: θεῶι ὑψίστωι παντοκράτορι εὐλογητῳ (To God Most High, almighty, blessed). While this beginning line suggests that this is a Jewish inscription, the concluding line, which is a Gentile juridical formula, reads: ὑπὸ Δία, Γῆν, Ἥλιον (under Zeus, Earth, Sun). Further, the words παντο-κράτωρ and εὐλογητός are common Jewish terms.[55] The fact that this dedica-tion is made in the προσευχή also indicates that this inscription is Jewish.[56] Since this inscription can be judged to be certainly Jewish, the 'Theos Hypsistos' would most certainly refer to Yahweh.

In an undated inscription found at Sibidunda in Pisidia,[57] the dedicant describes the θεὸς ὕψιστος also as the holy refuge (θεῷ Ὑψίστῳ καὶ Ἁγείᾳ κατα-φυγῇ). It is to be noted that καταφυγή is found in the LXX as a description of God as the 'Refuge'.[58] In other words, the dedicant had followed after the fashion of the LXX in calling and describing God as his καταφυγή. This indicates that the θεὸς ὕψιστος, to the dedicant, most likely refers to Yahweh.

It appears that in the above inscriptions, 'Theos Hypsistos' is used by the Jews to refer to (a) Yahweh, that is, the God of the Jews; and (b) the true God, that is, in the absolute sense of the word ὕψιστος, rather than in the superlative sense. In other words, it is reasonable for us to conclude that most Jews would regard their

51. I.e. *CIJ* 725 and *Inscriptions de Délos* no. 2532, cited in Schürer (III, 70).

52. Trebilco 1991: 134.

53. Mazur (1935: 21), cited in Trebilco (1991: 134 and 241 n. 33); see also Levinskaya (1996: 213–25) for her treatment on the meaning of the term προσευχή. Schürer (II, 440) claims that the term συναγωγή did not pass into the language of the Diaspora until the first century CE. This would suggest that Jews used the term προσευχή to refer to their prayer-house before that time. See also Barclay (1996: 26 n. 22) for a discussion of the two terms. See n. 46 above.

54. See section 3, a, above for the discussion on *Ep. Arist.* 15–16.

55. Lifshitz (1975: 67) in prolegomenon of *CIJ* I.

56. See Levinskaya (1996: 225) whose conclusion has already been cited in n. 46 above.

57. Bean (1960, no. 122), cited in Trebilco 1991: 136.

58. E.g. Exod. 17.15; Pss. 9.10; 17.3; 143.2; Jer. 16.19.

God, that is, Yahweh, as the true God. How they apply this belief with regard to other people's gods is something that cannot be determined easily. They could, in applying such a belief, reject all other religious traditions and practices as evil and demonic (as Paul has done, 1 Cor. 10.20). Or, they could accept that all other religious traditions and practices are equally valid for they are directed to the true God, since there is no other god (as the 'strong' have done, 1 Cor. 8.10; 10.14, 20–21).

Besides Jewish inscriptions using the term 'Theos Hypsistos', there are also Gentile inscriptions which make use of the same term. For example, we are told that there were two altars to Zeus Hypsistos in Olympia (Pausanias 5.15.5). And according to Nock *et al.*, the title Zeus Hypsistos is found at various points in the Greek world, including Theos Hypsistos, and at times, Hypsistos alone is used to refer to a god.[59] Nock *et al.* tabulate the evidence under three columns: Ζεὺς ὕψιστος, θεὸς ὕψιστος, and the third column refers to the use of both terms.[60] From the table we are able to see that the statue of Zeus Hypsistos has been found in Corinth, votive inscriptions of Zeus Hypsistos are found in Edessa (including a cult association, 51 CE), Imbros, Anchialos, Philippopolis Corcyra, Lagina, Pana-mara. These are not dated except Edessa. Further, the votive inscriptions of Theos Hypsistos and Zeus Hypsistos are jointly found in Athens (undated), and dedications (first century BCE) and prayers to Theos Hypsistos are jointly found in Delos while a precinct wall and altars are found to have been set up to Zeus Hypsistos on Mount Cynthus in Delos, near Semitic shrines.[61]

What do we make of those Gentile inscriptions which used the term 'Theos Hypsistos' or 'Hypsistos'? Could the Gentiles who used the term have been influenced by their Jewish counterparts? Trebilco argues that the epithet ὕψιστος or the term θεὸς ὕψιστος was used for Gentile deities throughout the Roman Empire.[62] This generalization has been dismissed as unwarranted by Levinskaya who argues that there are in fact only a few inscriptions which definitely used the term.[63] However, Levinskaya suggests the possibility of Jewish influence on Gentile choice of a title, and that it could also include some Jewish ideas of divinity. She explains that this could account for the absence of images of the gods in

59. Nock *et al.* 1936: 55; apparently, they are sometimes treated as equivalents.
60. Nock *et al.* 1936: 56–59.
61. Not all of those mentioned by Nock *et al.* are cited here as some are dated in the second century CE while others third century CE. These examples are sufficient to show that the epithet ὕψιστος is widely used by Zeus worshippers. For a more thorough survey of the evidence, see Cook 1925, 2, ii: 876ff.
62. Trebilco 1991: 128.
63. Levinskaya (1996: 92–93; and also her nn. 58–63) provides her list as follows: several times Helios is called Theos Hypsistos; once Apollo was so called; Hypsistos was used with the name of Attis and in the dedication πατρὶ θεῷ Σαμοθρᾶκι ἀθανάτωι ὑψίστωι; Isis was called the Most High in one dedication while another dedication was to Thea Hypsiste in Lydia. The comment of Nock *et al.* (1936: 59) strongly argues against the position of Levinskaya: '... Zeus Hypsistos has a temple at Thebes, a statue at Corinth, possibly a priestess at Argos, a precinct at Iasos, a priest (shared with Agathe Tyche) at Mylasa, not to mention a cult association at Edessa. The cult under this name has therefore in these places full standing.'

most of the Gentile dedications to Theos Hypsistos. She argues that it is possible for Jews or Gentiles under Jewish influence, when they witness Gentile dedications to Zeus the Most High, to find it necessary to honour in the same place the God of Israel.[64] But if Gentiles could make use of a Jewish term for Yahweh to render dedications to their gods, then it suggests that these Gentiles might have viewed the Theos Hypsistos of the Jews to be no different from their deities. Or it could be that these Gentiles might be God-fearers,[65] although this cannot be proven.[66] One such example is the inscription found recently near Acmonia,[67] which begins with a Gentile formula (Ἀγαθῇ Τύχῃ, with good fortune) but whose dedicants, Onesimus and his spouse, set up the monument to the Most High God (Θεῷ Ὑψίστῳ). The Gentile formula, unlike that of *CIJ* 690, is not a legal necessity. Thus, the use of the Gentile formula makes the inscription unlikely to be Jewish. At the same time, the use of a common Jewish term for Yahweh suggests Jewish influence. Trebilco observes that there was a sizeable Jewish community at Acmonia and in nearby Apamea and that the Jews at Acmonia did call their God by the term 'Theos Hypsistos'.[68] He therefore suggests that the dedicants were linked to the Jewish community and appeared to fit the category of 'God-fearers'. It is not certain who the dedicants of this inscription were. They could be Gentile God-worshippers, or worshippers of Gentile deities, or both.

What is noteworthy is that Gentile usage of 'Theos Hypsistos' might hint at the possibility that it does not concern the Jews, or constitute an offence to the Jews, that Gentiles are using the same term or epithet to refer to their deities. It is possible that Jews could view the Gentile usage of θεὸς ὕψιστος as legitimate since to them Gentiles are in fact addressing the one true God of the Jews, when they use the term. Although this theory cannot be proven, it is certainly possible. The reverse is equally possible, that is, as a result of the Gentile usage of θεὸς ὕψιστος, some Jews might think that their God is the same as the Gentiles' god, except that Gentiles sometimes address the true God by a different name (cf. *Ep. Arist.* 15–16). Could this be true of the 'strong' in 1 Corinthians 8–10 since, according to Pausanias (2.2.8), the cult of Ζεὺς Ὑψιστος was officially recognized in Corinth? Although the term ὕψιστος is never used in 1 Corinthians 8–10, indeed in the entire epistle, our discussion at least indicates that (1) Jews could use a term recognizable among the Gentiles, with the possibility of mutual recognition of the term; and (2) there were Jewish ways of referring to the 'one God' which could have non-exclusive practical consequences. This may lead to a more

---

64. Levinskaya 1996: 94.

65. Trebilco 1991: 138.

66. Kraabel (1981: 113–26) has argued that there was never a circle of God-fearers associated with ancient Judaism and that were it not for the book of Acts 'God-fearers' would have been unknown to us. This position has been ably challenged and proven wanting by Overman (1988: 17–26, and also his n. 9), and others such as Wilcox (1981: 102–22) and Finn (1985: 75–84).

67. Trebilco 1991: 138, 243 n. 54.

68. Trebilco 1991: 138.

accommodating attitude towards Gentile religious traditions and practices among some Jews.

Could there be a conceptual overlap between Gentiles and Jews about the true God when they used the term θεὸς ὕψιστος, even though they may differ in their conceptions of God? And could this be an area of ambiguity in the definitions of idolatry which can be exploited?

While the idea of θεὸς ὕψιστος in the absolute sense could serve as a parallel to Paul's position, it could equally serve as a parallel to the view of the 'strong' with regard to the true God. Is it not possible that both the 'strong' and Paul hold similar views about the true God, but draw opposing conclusions about the religious traditions and practices of the Gentiles? Could it be that for the 'strong' in 1 Corinthians 8–10, Gentile worship is in fact directed to the one true God since 'there is no God but one', but that Paul views Gentile worship as directed to demons, not to the true God (1 Cor. 10.20)? Are there different practical implications for both the 'strong' and Paul, that is, the practical implication of the position of the 'strong' is that they are accommodating towards others' religious traditions and practices – the one true God is inclusive; whereas the practical implication for Paul is that worship of the true God appears to have to conform to Paul's definition of what constitutes true worship and the place where worship is considered valid – the one true God is exclusive?

Besides the example of *The Letter of Aristeas*, the use of θεὸς ὕψιστος between Jews and Gentiles, Artapanus also serves as an example of an accommodating Jew. In fact, Artapanus goes further to suggest that Egyptian religious traditions originated from Moses.

5. *Artapanus*

Nothing certain can be known about Artapanus,[69] although the name is of Persian origin.[70] Scholarly opinion is now agreed that Artapanus is an Egyptian Jew, who may not have come from Alexandria.[71] Fraser argues that Artapanus appears to be familiar with the native life of Egypt and the purely priestly traditions, he could have been a Jew of mixed descent and possibly a resident of another centre such as Memphis.[72] This theory is possible, although it is not necessary to tie him to any centre, as Collins rightly says.[73]

The date of Artapanus is generally cast between 250 BCE and 100 BCE. Within this period any date is possible. However, the tendency is to place him sometime in the second century BCE.[74]

---

69. Holladay 1983: 189.

70. Fraser 1972: 985 n. 199.

71. Collins (1983: 33) is right in saying that it cannot be doubted that Artapanus wrote in Egypt, but by Egypt we need not think of Alexandria since Artapanus has little in common with the known Jewish literature of Alexandria.

72. Fraser 1972: 706, 985 n. 199; cf. Holladay 1983: 189.

73. Collins 1983: 54 n. 48.

74. Collins 1985: 890–91; cf. Barclay 1996: 127, 446.

The work of Artapanus is scarce, only three fragments, preserved by Alexander Polyhistor. This means there is probably some redactional effort involved.[75] The paucity of his work, however, does not in any way minimize Artapanus' importance and significance in our understanding of Egyptian Judaism. On the contrary, Artapanus' work differs from those other Jewish authors who in general appear to adopt a comparatively more exclusivist stance. Within his work, we not only see efforts of cultural convergence or integration, but also, and not least, the religious accommodation of a Jew towards the Egyptian cults, despite the fact that he displays tremendous pride in the Jewish tradition represented in Moses.[76] He seems much more accommodating to other cults outside Judaism.

From the beginning of his work, we witness a relatively friendly disposition, particularly in the portrayal of Moses, towards the Egyptian cults. In the following analysis of Artapanus, I shall confine myself to Artapanus' accommodating stance towards the Egyptian religious tradition.

Although Artapanus represents a Jewish effort to glorify the Jewish people and culture, there seems no hostile stance towards the Gentile religions and the gods. Instead, we read that the family of Joseph built both the temples in Athos and Heliopolis (23.4). While this may be a way in which Artapanus seeks to show the Hebrews' contribution to the Egyptian religious culture, thus glorifying the Hebrew people, it reveals Artapanus' openness to the use of Gentile religious institutions to magnify what to him is a positive aspect of the Hebrews.[77] Moses is turned into the teacher of Orpheus (γενέσθαι δὲ τὸν Μώϋσον τοῦτον Ὀρφέως διδάσκαλον, 27.4) by Artapanus. But Holladay has rightly pointed out that the relationship of Musaios to Orpheus normally is that of a son or a disciple.[78] In other words, Musaios is never the teacher of Orpheus![79] Since Orpheus is traditionally understood to be the one who transmits sacred wisdom to the Greeks which he gained during the Egyptian travels, by making the alteration, Artapanus makes Moses the source of Greek wisdom. Such an alteration of a tradition shows that Artapanus' accommodating stance can be extensive: he is prepared to go to the extent of making a claim that is not totally correct.[80] But it reflects his positive attitude to the sacred wisdom of the Greeks!

75.   Collins 1985: 889.

76.   Gruen (1998: 157–59) argues that Artapanus used a range of sources, both Gentile and Jewish, and shaped and moulded them to his own taste, so that Moses is reinvented as a 'cultural hero' for the Egyptians; Moses also doubled as a 'military hero' (159) who was victorious in the war against the Ethiopians.

77.   Athos is unattested as a city in Egypt. Collins (1985: 898) observes that this may be the biblical Pithom in Exod. 1.11. Cf. Holladay 1983: 230 n. 27. If Athos has any connection with Pithom in Exod. 1.11, then Artapanus might well be concluding that the Hebrews also built the temple since they had built cities there. As for Heliopolis, Holladay (1983: 230 n. 28) makes the association with the Jewish temple in Leontopolis. This, however, is not certain.

78.   Holladay 1983: 232 n. 45.

79.   For a broader treatment of Orpheus, see Ferguson (1993: 151–53).

80.   Thus Gruen (1998: 160) rightly states that Artapanus exhibits 'a light touch…a caprice and whimsy that tempered liberally with the Scriptures and inverted or transposed Gentile traditions to place the figures of Jewish legend in the center'.

More intriguing is Artapanus' attribution of all kinds of inventions in Egypt to Moses, even the Egyptian religious cult (27.4)! But, first of all, he (Moses) was called Μουσαῖος. The term is linked to Μοῦσα, which in the plural is also the term for the goddesses of song, music, poetry, dancing, and such like. Artapanus does not appear to have any reservation in so calling Moses. Even though the term Μουσαῖος is the name of a pre-homeric mythical Greek poet and seer of Attica,[81] either meaning would equally expose the accommodating stance of Artapanus.

While Moses is greatly exalted in Artapanus' efforts in glorifying the Jews, a strict Jew would hardly expect Artapanus to attribute the Egyptian animal cults to Moses,[82] the kind of religious cult that has invited vehement attack from the writer of Wisdom, Philo, and Josephus. In 27.4, Moses is said to have divided the city (τὴν πόλιν) into 36 nomes and to each of these he assigned the god to be worshipped (ἑκάστῳ τῶν νομῶν ἀποτάξαι τὸν θεὸν σεφθήσεσθαι), and the gods include cats, dogs and ibises.[83] The term σεφθήσεσθαι denotes the rendering of awe and fear, and as passive infinitive it serves to explain or spell out the function of all the gods: to be worshipped! In 27.12, we read further that Moses made a recommendation of bringing in a breed of oxen for the religious purposes of the king. And the king, in trying to ensure that he was the origin of Egyptian animal cults, ordered that those animals which Moses consecrated be removed and buried. Although the phrase, κατακρύπτειν θέλοντα τὰ τοῦ Μωϋσου ἐπι-νοήματα, reflects the king's self-centred and conceited efforts, it speaks about Moses much more than about the king! It is consistent in showing that Moses' ideas gave rise to the Egyptian religious cults and they cannot be suppressed. Such description about Moses as the founder of Egyptian polytheism goes against the Pentateuchal representation of Moses as the lawgiver of Israel and enforcer of the ten commandments. One wonders how, if Artapanus' chief concern is the glory and honour of the Jewish people, such descriptions can go down well with the Jews themselves.[84] The interesting point to note is that such notions about Moses, if viewed from the standpoint of the definition of idolatry in Chapter 2 above, would come very close to being idolatrous. This is particularly so since Moses is viewed as the one to whom Yahweh gave the covenant. By attributing the Egyptian religious tradition to Moses, Artapanus comes close to making Moses idolatrous!

81. Holladay 1983: 231 n. 44.

82. Collins (1985: 893) suggests that Artapanus' attitude must be seen in the light of his 'euhemeristic tendency' to explain Gentile cults. His argument that the legitimization of the Egyptian cults is done only in an attenuated sense is not convincing. For that would reduce Moses' own importance, since he attributes these cults to Moses. And if Artapanus represents what he calls 'competitive historiography', then Artapanus cannot attenuate the legitimization of Egyptian cults; but on the contrary, he probably heightens the cults' importance, at least to the Jews, since it was Moses who introduced them! See Barclay 1996: 130–32.

83. Freudenthal (1875: 147) notes similar language in 27.12 as well as in Diodorus Siculus 1.89.5: καθ' ἕκαστον δ' αὐτῶν καταδεῖξαι τοῖς ἐγχωρίοις σέβεσθαί τι ζῶον; this is cited in Holladay (1983: 233 n. 49).

84. Schürer (III, 523) says that Artapanus seems more interested in the glory and honour of the Jewish nation than in the purity of divine worship.

However, this is precisely an area of ambiguity which is being exploited here. It shows an accommodating Artapanus even though he remains committed to the God of the Jews (cf. 27.21–22, 25–26).[85]

Further, Moses' contributions are so great that the masses came to love him and accord him the worth of divine honour. He was called Hermes because of his ability to interpret the sacred writings (27.6). Artapanus does not leave us in any doubt, that Moses was the one who assigned the sacred writings to the priests (τά τε ἱερὰ γράμματα τοῖς ἱερεῦσιν, 27.4), thus his ability to interpret them should be a natural one. Holladay cites Gentile parallels in Artapanus' portrait of Moses and the claims made for Hermes can be found in other writings such as Plato, *Phdr.* 274–75, Diodorus Siculus 1.16.1 and others.[86] He argues that the portrait has apologetic value in that it responds to 'pagan charges that Jews had produced no figures who had made genuine contributions to humanity',[87] but this does not explain why Artapanus should turn Moses into Hermes. We should note that the attribution to Moses of the subsequent founding of a city named the city of Hermes (27.4) suggests that Moses is elevated to a status on par with Hermes (cf. 27.9), who was a 'messenger of the gods'.[88] Thus, Moses is turned into a 'messenger of the gods'.

Even if Holladay's hypothesis stands that it is an apologetic stance, what Artapanus says also means that he holds a relatively open attitude towards the Egyptian religious cults.

In a later passage, in 27.32, Artapanus reports the Egyptians as being favourable to Moses, despite his less than friendly acts towards Egypt when he tried to liberate the Jews. After witnessing what Moses' rod was able to do, the Egyptians set up a rod in every temple. What is even more interesting is the less favourable attitude of the Egyptians towards Isis. They did the same for Isis as they did for Moses' rod. But the two were carried out with different reasons. For Moses, the reason is that he introduced the gods to be worshipped, and was now introducing a rod that would work wonders. The reason for Isis is her ability to perform wonders – which was due to Moses' rod. This portrayal of Moses as being greater than Isis successfully transfers to Moses what is attributed to Isis.

---

85.   Thus, Artapanus remains a pious Jew. Collins (1983: 35) observes that Artapanus' piety is 'conspicuously similar to that of Hellenistic paganism'. However, since the biblical material forms the basis of Artapanus' reinterpretation, the implication is that the biblical material is equally similar to Hellenistic paganism, an implication that is hard to deny, nor is it an implication easy to defend. Collins (1983: 37) further argues that because the issue to Artapanus is not religion, Moses does not attempt to convert the Gentiles to the worship of God; no reason is therefore given for the Jews' persecution. And the divinity of Egyptian cults receives positive attitude from Artapanus, rather than condemnation. But Collins does not take into consideration Moses' prayer to God concerning the Jews' sufferings (27.21), and his reply to the king that the Lord of the universe had commanded him to liberate the Jews, when the king summoned and enquired of his reason for returning to Egypt (27.22). And the fact that Artapanus attributes the Egyptian animal cults to Moses shows that religion remains an issue.

86.   Holladay 1983: 232 n. 46.

87.   Holladay 1983: 233 n. 46.

88.   Ferguson 1993: 143.

It must be emphasised that Artapanus in no way minimizes or reduces the uniqueness of the Hebrew God. Whereas the Egyptian cults are explicable in terms of their origin, the God of the Hebrews remains the 'master of the universe' (τὸν τῆς οἰκουμένης δεσπότην, 27.22). And when the Egyptians and the Hebrew people faced each other, it was the former who together with their gods were destroyed by fire and water (27.37). The basic difference between Artapanus and the Jewish authors like Philo and Josephus is that Artapanus does not object to portraying Moses as one worthy of divine honour, nor does he abstain from making positive remarks about the Egyptian animal cults. Indeed, he views them as culturally beneficial to humanity.

The above shows that while Artapanus remains committed to the Jewish people as superior and to the God of the Jews as the master of the universe, he displays an attitude that appears accommodating to other gods. His accommodation to other religious traditions allows him not only to view them reasonably positively, but also gives him the relative freedom to even attribute the Egyptian animal cults to Moses. In Artapanus, we do not see an attitude that vilifies Gentile religious traditions. Unlike Philo, Josephus, the writers of Wisdom and Sibylline Oracles who pour scorn on idolatry and draw a clear line between the Jewish tradition and the Gentile cults, our examination of the texts above shows Artapanus to be accommodating in his attitude towards the Gentile cults.

We see further that, while *The Letter of Aristeas* identifies the God of the Jews with Zeus and revolves most of its discussions around this identification, Artapanus goes beyond Pseudo-Aristeas by making Moses the origin of the Egyptian religious traditions. In other words, Artapanus brings the two religious traditions together, that is, Jewish tradition and Egyptian religious tradition, and gives the impression that there is little difference between them. But the fact that Moses' God is portrayed as powerful, identifying Moses as the origin of the Egyptian religious tradition would imply that there is power in the Egyptian religions, thus attributing power to what is for other Jews powerless. And by bringing the two religious traditions together under one man, namely Moses, Artapanus runs the risk of confusing the true God with other gods. Both of the above can be seen as idolatrous under our definitions of idolatry. But Artapanus seems to exploit the fact that Moses is not God, and therefore being accommodating in his view and descriptions of Moses need not be idolatrous.[89] Could such a similarly friendly disposition towards other religious traditions be seen among the 'strong' in Corinth?

Both *The Letter of Aristeas* and Artapanus represent the cognitive level of Jews' open attitude towards other people's religious traditions. We will now look at the literary and inscriptional sources that reveal actual participation and accommodation of the Jews to idolatry.

---

89.   Although it is not entirely clear how Artapanus is viewed by other Jews, his presentation of Moses as culturally superior would most likely be well received by most Jews. The ready acceptance by Aristobulus of the notion that Moses was Orphaeus' teacher further suggests that Artapanus may not have been too negatively viewed, even though he was preserved by Polyhistor, a Gentile.

6. *Jews' Participation in/Accommodation to Gentile Cults*

In reality, Jews in the Diaspora did not always adopt an exclusivist stance, nor did they consistently adopt a condemning attitude towards Gentile cults, although evidence for such alternative behaviour/attitude is not altogether abundant. This could be due to the possibility of avoiding official censure or condemnation or worse still punishment. However, the evidence available from inscriptions and papyri might be telling; and it is possible that such evidence might represent some kinds of Jews who continued to view themselves as Jews and at the same time saw no contradiction in participating in Gentile cults. There are also literary sources which reflect such participation, but mostly in a rather disapproving manner such as Philo and Josephus. In the following, I shall look at some inscriptions and papyri as well as hints from authors like Philo and Josephus that show Jews' participation in Gentile cults.

There are clearly different or varying degrees of participation but participation nonetheless. It is necessary to clarify, at the outset, that by participation we do not mean that it always involves actual worship or the ritual of worship. The participation in Gentile cults revealed by inscriptions and Jewish authors may involve visitation to Gentile temples without clear evidence of actual participation in the worship of the cults. Or it may involve the use of juridical oath-formulae which invoke the Gentile deities. Sometimes, participation in Gentile cults could involve conducting legal transactions at Gentile temples, with the Gentile gods acting as intermediaries. Or it may involve serving as priests of the gods. Or it may involve actual worship of the deities in terms of making offerings for various reasons or setting up shrines and dedicating them to the gods. Some of these might overlap, that is, one aspect of participation such as the priestly service of the gods might at the same time involve the worship of the gods and certainly temple attendance. All these various aspects of participation reflect different ways and degrees in which idolatry at the practical level is practised by Jews, although the Jews involved may not necessarily agree that what they were doing constitutes idolatry. In other words, there remain ambiguities.

a. *Jews' participation in Gentile cults*
Some inscriptions show that Jews visited temples of Gentile deities for various reasons. From a few graffiti which are on the rocks near the Temple of Pan near Apollinopolis Magna/Edfu in Upper Egypt, dated sometime from second century to first century BCE, it is evident that Jews visited the Temple of Pan. There are at least three examples of such visits. The first two show two Jews, one Theodotos who gives praise to god for his safe return from the sea (*CPJ* no. 1537) and the other Ptolemaios who renders praise to god (*CPJ* no. 1538). To be sure, both these inscriptions do not specify the god to whom the praise is directed. Although Theodotos and Ptolemaios' presence at the Temple of Pan could be taken to suggest that they were rendering praise to Pan, there is no reason why they could not give praise to the true God (since θεός is a common designation of God).

Besides, Pan could well mean the 'universal God' to the Jews in question (as the word πᾶν, 'all' shows).[90] Thus, could Theodotos and Ptolemaios consider Pan to be the equivalent of the Jews' God? The open declaration of themselves as Jews raises the question as to why they should make themselves known if they were praising a Gentile god. However, if they intended to praise the true God, the use of the common term θεός without specifying who this θεός was could lead others to confuse the 'true' God with the Gentile god. This means that by mentioning the 'true' God, such confusion could be avoided. Why then did they not mention the 'true' God? Could it be that rendering praise to Pan by Jews was more widespread and common than we think? There is for now no ready answer to this question, although the next inscription might suggest this possibility. What can be concluded is that Theodotos and Ptolemaios, both Jews, visited a Gentile temple.

The next inscription, also found in the Temple of Pan, on the rock facing the east of the temple (Horbury and Noy, no. 123; second or first century BCE), refers to a Jew named Lazaros who visited the Temple of Pan for a third time.[91] This third visit of Lazaros might suggest the possibility that it is much more common for Jews to visit Gentile temples than we think. This may explain why Theodotos and Ptolemaios openly declared themselves to be Jews if they had the Gentile god in mind. If visits to Gentile temples were more common, it might be that some form of participation in the Gentile cult was also relatively common such as giving praise to Pan. In that light, there is little reason for Theodotos and Ptolemaios to conceal their Jewish identity.[92] These are, however, speculations. We cannot be absolutely certain or conclusive about these Jews simply on the basis of what is written on a few inscriptions.[93] What can be certain is that these Jews, that is, Theodotos, Ptolemaios and Lazaros, had all visited a Gentile temple, and one of them (Lazaros) was even there a third time.[94] The above inscriptions show that some Jews did not appear to have difficulty visiting Gentile temples. The reasons and purposes may vary from Jew to Jew. The interesting point to

90. Barclay (1996: 100) raises several questions which render the issue of whether Theodotos and Ptolemaios praised the true God or the Gentile god an uncertain one. My concern here is to illustrate that Jews visited Gentile temples. What their purposes were can be uncertain if no evidence exists.

91. A similar but uncertain inscription in the name of Lazaros is provided in Horbury and Noy (1992: 211–12, no. 124).

92. Thus, in referring to Theodotos and Ptolemaios, Goldenberg (1998: 64) is not convincing in his argument that a Jew thanking his God in a Gentile temple will naturally do so with calculated vagueness, since the declaration of their Jewish identity is not so vague after all.

93. Horbury and Noy (1992: 208) point out that the inscription is written on the rock face west of the temple, inside a frame, without the dedication to Pan Euodos. Taking their cue from A. Bernand's suggestion that the frame is intended to isolate the inscription from the neighbouring text, which is to Pan, they argue that the positioning and the wording of the inscriptions (i.e. no's 121–24) suggest that the God referred to is not Pan. However, there are difficulties with such a theory. First, it would be almost impossible to establish its purpose; and second, if the inscription was not to Pan, an equally difficult question would arise as to how it came to be placed next to those dedicated to Pan. This conclusion of Horbury and Noy is therefore not necessary, nor is it convincing.

94. Horbury and Noy (1992: 211) cite a Dr Thompson as suggesting that τρίτος could also mean that there were 'two others'. But in the absence of such evidence in inscriptions and the single mention of Lazaros, the more likely translation of τρίτον remains 'a third time'.

note is that such visits to Gentile temples suggest the possibility that there were other Jews who also found attendance at or visits to Gentile temples something that did not necessarily render them unfaithful to their Jewish tradition.

b. *Use of Gentile oath-formulae and legal transactions at Gentile temples*
Two inscriptions from Gorgippa (*CIJ* no's. 690, 41 CE; 690a, 67–68 CE), reveal the use of the Gentile oath-formulae by Jews. The formula is a simple line invoking Zeus, Earth and Sun (ὑπὸ Δία, Γῆν, Ἥλιον). Both inscriptions are addressed to God most high (θεῶι ὑψίστωι), which suggests that the persons making the oath were Jews. Of the two, *CIJ* 690 is more uncertain in term of its Jewish origin. Lifshitz, writing in the prolegomenon to Frey's *CIJ*, however, notes that the epithet παντοκράτωρ cannot be pagan while εὐλογητός can only be Jewish.[95] Thus, he is of the opinion that the Jewish origin is beyond question.[96]

Both inscriptions, as may be apparent, show that the Jews concerned at least remained loyal to the 'God most high'. The first in fact reveals that Pathos was dedicating his slave in the prayer-house (ἀνέθηκεν ἐν τῆι προσευχῆι, 8–9). The second shows that the Jew Neokles manumitted his slaves with the order that sought to ensure their safety. They did not seem to view their identity as Jews a reason for avoiding the use of such a Gentile oath-formula.[97]

In an inscription from Delphi (*CIJ* no. 711, 119 BCE), a Jew by the name of Ἰουδαῖος (Ioudaios)[98] made a sale to Apollo of his slave named Ἀμύντας (Amyntas), apparently a will meant to manumit Amyntas should Ioudaios die (Ἐπεὶ δὲ κά τι παθῆ Ἰουδαῖος, ἐλεύθερος ἔστω Ἀμύντας, 5–6). It is not clear whether Amyntas was a Jew; nor is it clear whether Ioudaios was a practising Jew (i.e. law-observing Jew) either. What is clear is that Ioudaios was a Jew who participated in the Gentile cult of Apollo by making a sale of his slave to Apollo. Such a legal transaction usually took place in the Gentile temple, with the deity serving as an intermediary. This is because slaves in the ancient world could not enter into a legal contract with their masters.[99] However, Ioudaios as slave owner had the choice of how he would free his slave but chose the Gentile way, by using the Gentile oath-formula in a Gentile temple, even though this may not square with his ancestral tradition.[100]

95. *CIJ* prol., 67.
96. Cf. Williams (1998: 123) who similarly accepts the Jewish identity of the inscription, and the next (i.e. *CIJ* 690a), on the basis of the divine epithets that appear in them.
97. Such oath-formulae might have gained a reputation of being efficacious among the Gentiles. Further, it might prove a more effective rendering of a manumission which may otherwise not be recognized. Oaths in the ancient world often carry the element of malediction against the transgressors of the oath, particularly imprecations on tombs against those who might rob the graves of the deceased. See Ferguson 1993: 219; Horbury and Noy 1992: 20.
98. According to Williams (1998: 195 n. 48), this name is probably a Hellenized form of Judah.
99. For a more detailed treatment of the rights of slaves with regard to legal contracts with their masters, see Westermann (1955: 34 '39).
100. It is of course possible that Ioudaios has abandoned his Jewish customs. But there is no evidence to suggest that and any such guesses can only be speculative.

Two further examples of the manumission of Jewish slaves may be seen in two inscriptions (*CIJ* no's. 709 and 710; Delphi, mid-second century BCE).[101] The first (*CIJ* no. 709) shows the sale of three Jewish women slaves to the Pythian Apollo (τῶι Ἀπόλλωνι τῶι Πυθίωι). As mentioned earlier, since slaves in the ancient world had no legal rights to enter into any legal contracts with their masters, their manumission could be obtained in a number of ways: by paying for their own freedom; or by being granted freedom by their masters; or by being purchased by another free person who then set the slaves free; or by sacral manumission which was one of the popular forms.[102] This sacral manumission was the form to which the present inscriptions refer. The three women were freed by being sold to Apollo, a sale which they themselves had entrusted to Apollo (καθὼς ἐπίστευσε Ἀντιγόνα καὶ θευδώρα καὶ Δωροθέα τῶι θεῶι τὰν ὠνάν). That the sale took place in the temple of Apollo is beyond doubt since the sacral manumission had to be conducted before the presence of the god. Further, it involved the priest of Apollo Amyntas (ὁ ἱερεὺς τοῦ Ἀπόλωνος Ἀμύντας) as one of the witnesses.

The second inscription is a shorter one but otherwise similar (*CIJ* no. 710). It, too, is about a sacral manumission of a slave by sale to Apollo. The slave named Judaeus who was of Jewish origin (Ἰουδαῖος τὸ γένος Ἰουδαῖον) had similarly entrusted the sale to the god (καθὼς ἐπίστευσε Ἰουδαῖος τῶι θεῶι τὰν ὠναν).

In the above discussions on sacral manumission, freedom of the slaves was obtained after the slaves had entrusted the sale to the god. Πιστεύω is here appropriately translated as 'entrust', while it also carries the meaning of 'commit'. It suggests that the slaves in question were putting themselves and their manumissions in the trust of god by agreeing to the sale. It must be noted, however, that being slaves, they probably had little choice on where and how they were manumitted. What these inscriptions show is that while Jewish slaves had little choice on how and where they were manumitted, the more popular type of manumission, which was the self-purchase through trust sale to the god Apollo, might offer itself to those Jewish slaves who had a choice. The four elements mentioned by Westermann in this type of manumission would be attractive to Jewish slaves.[103] They may be quite prepared to participate in the Gentile cult in order to secure these 'elements' of freedom. It also reveals that some Jews, when they were put in a situation where other alternatives were not forthcoming, were willing to follow the custom of the day, that is, the customs of the surrounding

101. Cf. Feldman 1996: 63. Williams (1998: 5) makes the assumption that these Jewish slaves have been Seleucid prisoners of war who had been enslaved and taken to Greece during the early period of the Maccabean period.

102. According to Westermann (1955: 35–36), the manumission by self-purchase through trust sales to the god Apollo consisted of four elements: status, personal inviolability, right to work as one pleased, and the privilege of going where one pleased. Such Delphic manumissions involve the god Apollo acting as the medium, which is the entrustment sale itself. The more important type in this group are the 'outright' manumissions which represent a complete and immediate separation of the slave from any control by the former owner. This could account for its popularity.

103. See n. 102 above.

Gentile environment, even though they might appear contradictory to their Jewish tradition.

c. *Jews in the service of the gods*

Two high profile Jews appear in literary works as well as some inscriptions, namely Dositheos son of Drimylos and Philo's nephew Tiberius Julius Alexander, which unambiguously show them to be in the service of the gods. Dositheos is recorded in the third book of the Maccabees as a renegade Jew who saved the life of Ptolemy IV Philopator (*3 Macc.* 1.3). The author describes Dositheos as one who had renounced the Law (μεταβαλὼν τὰ νόμιμα) and abandoned his ancestral beliefs (τῶν πατρίων δογμάτων ἀπηλλοτριωμένος) (*3 Macc.* 1.3).[104] Such a description no doubt comes from an author who does not view Dositheos favourably. To the author, Dositheos was unfaithful to the Jewish tradition, but only according to his perception and definition of what constitutes faithfulness.[105] One of the papyri shows that Dositheos had no difficulty in the service of the king, even the priestly service.[106] According to the papyri (*CPJ* no's. 127d and 127e), Dositheos was priest of Alexander and the gods Adelphoi and the gods Euergetai (ἱερέως Δωσιθέου τοῦ Δριμύλου Ἀλεξάνδρου καὶ θεῶν Ἀδελφῶν καὶ θεῶν Εὐεργετῶν) during the reign of Ptolemy III Euergetes I, in 222 BCE. This, according to Tcherikover and Fuks,[107] was the highest priesthood in Hellenistic Egypt.[108] Other inscriptions tell us that Dositheos was ascending in his political career. In 240 BCE Dositheos was one of the heads of the royal secretariat (ὑπομνηματογράφος, *CPJ* no. 127a); while in 225/224 BCE he travelled in Egypt with Ptolemy III (μετὰ τοῦ βασιλέως, *CPJ* no. 127c). The highest priesthood must have come as a further ascent for Dositheos. Although this might indicate that he had abandoned his Jewish tradition and faith, it could well be that Dositheos continued to regard himself as a Jew who saw no contradiction in assuming the priestly office. This is particularly so if the priestly office was viewed more as a political one by Dositheos, in which case it would mean a political promotion. As far as the papyri (i.e. *CPJ* no's. 127d and 127e) are concerned, Dositheos was clearly an active participant in the ruler cult of the pagans. He therefore represents the category of Jews who participated in Gentile cults and gods.

We turn now to Philo's nephew Tiberius Julius Alexander. Literary sources from both Philo and Josephus reveal something about Tiberius. While Philo

104. Barclay (1996: 104) observes that what Dositheos does goes against the Jewish communities in Egypt which avoid recognizing the claimed divinity of the Ptolemaic kings.

105. Barclay (1996: 83–84) observes that the author of *3 Maccabees* 'considered citizen rights, enlistment in the Dionysiac cult, proximity to the king and the abandonment of Jewish food laws as a "package" which Jews either accepted or rejected'. Thus Dositheos is understandably described in an unfavourable light (*3 Macc.* 1.3).

106. The identification of Dositheos in our inscription with that of *3 Maccabees* is proven since *CPJ* no's. 127d and 127e were discovered. For details of discussion, see Tcherikover and Fuks (1957–64: I, 230–31).

107. Tcherikover and Fuks 1957–64: I, 231.

108. For a more detailed treatment of the development of the ruler cult, see Ferguson (1993: 185–97).

mentions little about Tiberius (*Prov.* 1 and 2; *Anim.*),[109] Josephus tells us that he was brought up in a wealthy family (*Ant.* 18.159–60) well connected politically (*Ant.* 19.276–77). He joined the Roman service at a relatively young age,[110] whose ascent up the political ladder was almost unhindered.[111] His first appointment was to the post of epistrategos of the Thebaid in 42 CE. He was next appointed the procurator of Judaea in 46 CE, a post he kept for two years (Josephus, *Ant.* 20.100–203).[112] In 63 CE, Tiberius was a high-ranking military officer. By 66 CE Tiberius had reached the peak of an equestrian career, being appointed by Nero as prefect of Egypt (Josephus, *War* 2.309). In the reign of Vespasian, between 69 CE and 70 CE, Tiberius was made 'prefect of all the army' (πάντων τῶν στρατευμά-των ἐπάρχοντος, Josephus, *War* 6.237). One wonders how as a high-ranking Roman official Tiberius could remain a practising Jew. Josephus tells us that Tiberius did not abide by the customs of his ancestors (τοῖς...πατρίοις οὐκ ἐνέμεινεν...ἔθεσιν, *Ant.* 20.100). Tcherikover and Fuks are not convincing with their view that Josephus is not necessarily referring to any overt act of apostasy.[113] Tiberius' service in the Roman government, taking military oaths and the like meant that he had to conform to the non-Jewish way of life. And Josephus probably has in mind Tiberius' honouring of the Egyptian deities. In *OGIS* 663, Tiberius plays an important role in setting up a relief of Claudius during which he also offers worship to the Egyptian deities Khonson and Seb. Further, in *OGIS* 669, he makes reference to the providence of the gods and to the deity of the emperors.[114] The latter is also seen in *CPJ* no. 418a in which Vespasian is proclaimed as εἷς σωτὴρ καὶ εὐεργέτης (one saviour and benefactor), κύριε σεβαστέ (lord Augustus), Ἄμμωνος υἱός (son of Ammon),[115]

109. In *Prov.* Philo appears to be engaged in a dialogue with Tiberius over the providence of God which Tiberius rejects. In *Anim.* both argue about the rationality of animals. Philo argues against animals having any reason at all and explains that the seemingly rational acts of animals are but due to the order of nature. Tiberius argues that animals do possess reason and that there is a moral and juridical relationship between animals and humanity. Against this reasoning of Tiberius, Philo argues that humanity are privileged with reason while animals are devoid of it. However, it is important to note that Tiberius is not speaking himself but his views are represented here. We may therefore have to take it with a pinch of salt.

110. Tcherikover and Fuks (1957–64, II: 188) inform us that Tiberius' first civil appointment was in 42 CE. If we date Tiberius' birth to sometime between 14 and 16 CE, then he would be only about 26–28 years old at his first civil appointment.

111. There is an intervening period of up to 15 years, i.e. between 48 and 63 CE, during which we have no information about Tiberius. Whether or not he might have been sidelined politically during this period is uncertain, although it is strange that there is complete silence if he was continually ascending, or if he was doing what could eventually bring him further promotion, politically. If he was sidelined during the 'silent period', then his promotion in 63 CE must be due to a change in his political fortunes.

112. See Feldman in the LCL vol. 456, p. 54, note 'c'.

113. Tcherikover and Fuks 1957–64, II.188–89.

114. Both *OGIS* 663 and 669 are cited in Barclay (1996: 106 n. 6).

115. This is clearly a religious title since Ammon is a deity accepted by the Greeks as identical with Zeus (Ferguson 1993: 190). By proclaiming Vespasian as the son of Zeus, Tiberius and the crowds that support him are as good as rendering divine honours to Vespasian. Cf. *OGIS* 383 where the same honour given to Antiochus I of Commagene in the first century BCE with the title 'The Great

and θεὸς Καῖσαρ Οὐεσπασιανός (divine Caesar Vespasian). By making the proclamation, Tiberius makes himself the 'priest' of the cult of Vespasian! It therefore shows that Tiberius, though a Jew, had not only served in the Roman administration, but also participated in both the Egyptian cults and the imperial cult. This raises the question whether Tiberius had totally abandoned his Jewish customs. Even if he had abandoned the Jewish tradition, did he still regard himself a Jew?

Barclay carefully notes that Tiberius' assimilation would require him to abandon most if not all the Jewish customs.[116] While it is highly probable that Tiberius had abandoned most of his Jewish tradition, there are at least some hints that he still regarded himself a Jew, and therefore continued, possibly, to view some elements of the Jewish tradition with at least respect if not reverence. Josephus (*War* 6.236ff) records Tiberius as one of those generals who were against the destruction of the Temple of the Jews. While it could be politically expedient for Tiberius to both agree with Titus' opinion as well as gain the general support of the Jews, it could equally be possible that the Temple still represented an important part of his heritage. Josephus (*Ant.* 20.100) comments that Tiberius' father was known for his religious devotion. Even though Tiberius himself did not seem to adhere to his ancestral tradition, he would quite certainly have been taught the central motifs of the Jewish faith, not least the Temple and its significance. Another hint may be seen in the fact that Josephus never mentions Tiberius' 'unfaithfulness', until much later when he was probably dead. Turner notes the difference in tone between Josephus' *Jewish War* and *Antiquities of the Jews*.[117] He points out that at the time when Josephus published his *Jewish War*, Tiberius was still alive and therefore a patron about whom he 'deliberately abstained' from making offensive remarks. It was around 93 CE when Tiberius was either dead or 'politically null' that Josephus mentioned Tiberius as having abandoned his ancestral customs. But if any reference to Tiberius as 'unfaithful' were offensive to him, it might imply that Tiberius did not regard himself as such.

Further, Tiberius had been generally tolerant of the Jews, leaving them as much as possible to live according to their customs when he was governor of Egypt (Josephus, *War* 2.220). Even though he gave orders to crush the riots in Alexandria, it was not without some efforts on the part of Tiberius to mediate between the warring Jews and Greeks (Josephus, *War* 2.487–94).[118]

King Antiochus, the God, the Righteous One, the Manifest Deity' allows the setting up of the image of Antiochus alongside the great gods and the offering of sacrifices in honour of him also, in addition to the gods (cited in Ferguson 1993: 192 n. 82).

116. Barclay 1996: 106. See further Barclay (1998a: 87–88) where Tiberius is included among the 'apostates'.

117. Turner 1954: 63.

118. Since Josephus views Tiberius as one who 'did not abide by the Laws of his fathers', it is unlikely for Josephus to say anything positive about Tiberius, let alone any hints of Tiberius' possible positive attitude towards the Jews. Anything positive about Tiberius by Josephus would therefore have to be taken seriously.

Thus, Tiberius may still regard himself a Jew, although others would most probably consider him an apostate. His involvement or participation in the worship of Egyptian deities as well as the ruler cult shows him to be disregarding his ancestral tradition of worshipping the one true God of the Jews. At the same time, his declaration of Vespasian by various honorific titles constitutes a setting up of the cult of Vespasian, thus putting himself in the 'priestly service' of the imperial cult. He thus serves as another example of a Jew who participated in Gentile cults and ruler cult.

d. *Jews' worship of the gods*

One of the ways in which Jews had engaged in Gentile cults can be seen in their joint dedication of religious shrines to Gentile gods with other pagans. Three Gentile inscriptions which Horbury and Noy include in their appendix (no. 3) bear Jewish names,[119] indicating the Jews' dedication to Gentile cults. One is dedicated to various gods (Θρίπιδι Κολάνθαι Πανὶ θεοῖς συννάοις τὸ ἱερόν, the shrine to Triphis, Kolanthes, Pan and their fellow gods, Horbury and Noy, no. 154, Ptolemais in 138/7 BCE), while the other two are dedicated to Apollo, Zeus, and the associated gods (Ἀπόλλωνι καὶ Διὶ καὶ τοῖς συνεστίοις θεοῖς τὸ ἱερόν, Horbury and Noy, nos.155 and 156, Hermopolis Magna 80–69 BCE and 78 BCE respectively). Even though they are all Gentile inscriptions set up for the express purpose of dedicating their shrines to the gods, the combined number of Jewish names comes to ten.[120] The first inscription (Horbury and Noy, no. 154) mentions the names of those on the inscription as members of the association (οἱ συνοδίται). It is uncertain as to the nature of the σύνοδος. However, it is likely that religious activities, including worship of the gods, formed part of the routines of the σύνοδος. The second and third inscriptions mention the citizens as founders (οἱ συμπολιτευόμενοι κτίσται) whose names appear on the inscriptions. It is most likely that they were founders of the shrine dedicated to Apollo, Zeus and the gods. Since they were soldiers posted to Hermopolis, they may have little choice as Horbury and Noy have suggested,[121] although it is also possible that they had voluntarily chosen to engage in the dedication. The question of the soldiers' willingness in participating cannot be settled conclusively. What is unambiguous is their participation in a joint dedication with their fellow pagans of religious shrines to Gentile gods.

While we have seen inscriptions concerning manumission of Jewish slaves who entrusted their sale to the gods, another inscription shows a Jew, Moschos, setting up an altar to the gods (*CIJ* I, no. 711b; Amphiareion of Oropos, third

---

119. Horbury and Noy 1992: 246–50.

120. Ἄβραμ Ἀλωσμαθουτος, col. b. l.19 (Horbury and Noy 1992: 246, no. 154); Ὑρκανὸς Πτολεμαίου, col. I. l.19, Χάβας Ἡροφῶντος, col. II. l.121, Ἀπολλόδωρος Ζαββδήλου, col. II. l.124 and Πτολεμαῖος Δωσιθέου, col. II. l.134 (Horbury and Noy 1992: 247, no. 155); Ἀγγίων Χρυσίππου, col. I. l.65, Καινίων Κοσακάβου, col. II. l.88, Χελκίας Διονυσίου, col. II. l.93, Ἀγγίων Συνμάχου, col. II. l.112, Μίλιχος Βαράκου, col. III. l.179 (Horbury and Noy 1992: 249, no. 156).

121. Horbury and Noy 1992: 248.

century BCE).[122] Apparently Moschos had a dream in which he received a command from the gods Amphiaraos and Hygieia (Ἀμφιαράου καὶ τῆς Ὑγιείας)
to record on an inscription the vision he had seen. Subsequently he set up an altar
to the gods at the temple. While it is impossible to control what one dreams
about, Moschos was prepared to believe in the gods of his dream and obey their
command.

The above discussions take us through different ways in which idolatry was
practised by Jews. In these various idolatrous practices, at least four observations
emerge: (1) in almost all the examples cited above, the Jews involved in idolatry
did not appear to have abandoned fully their identity as Jews; (2) in almost all the
examples, the practices do not always fit perfectly our definitions of idolatry set
out in Chapter 2; for example, a visit to the Gentile temple remains ambiguous in
terms of whether it is an idolatrous act; (3) while most of the examples cited
above could be argued as examples of 'divided loyalty', that is, 'unfaithfulness',
to the true God of the Jews, the reverse could be argued, that is, 'divided loyalty'
suggests ambiguity and thus need not be viewed as idolatrous, so long as one
remains 'faithful' to one's ancestral tradition. And (4) idolatry is not as clear-cut
as it may seem at first, that is, while there are clearly defined terms there remain
ambiguities which can be exploited.

The above observations once again raise the question which we raised in the
beginning of this chapter. Could such ambiguities of what constitutes idolatry be
one reason that accounts for the behaviour of the 'strong' in 1 Corinthians 8–10?
And could our examples cited above, both literary and archaeological (inscriptions and papyri), provide helpful parallels to the behaviour of the 'strong' in
1 Corinthians 8–10?

7. Summary and Conclusion

The function of this chapter has been to examine the possible background and
parallels to the behaviour of the 'strong' in 1 Corinthians 8–10.

We examined first of all the LXX ban on reviling other people's gods in Exod.
22.27a and asked whether the 'strong' could have been aware of the ban and that
their restraint from criticizing other gods might be a result of their familiarity
with such a command. We raised a question as to why the 'strong' should visit
Gentile temples and participate in Gentile cults, an act which did not seem to
square with the requirement of the second commandment, and raised the
possibility that the 'strong' may have a different understanding of the true God.

The Letter of Aristeas serves as an example of such a possibility. In this letter,
we see an accommodating Pseudo-Aristeas who, through the courtier Aristeas he
created, equated the God of the Jews with other people's gods, namely Zeus.
This became the central motif around which the entire letter revolves. Such
accommodation is seen in various examples such as the viewing of the king's

---

122. Cf. *CIJ* prol., 82. See Schürer (III, 65) who compares the various manumission inscriptions to
sieve out evidence for Jewish communities in Upper Egypt.

action as pious and also the translators' overall positive description of the king's Gentile religious life. The example of Aristeas' equation of the true God of the Jews with other people's gods suggests that there is a possibility of a conceptual overlap between some Jews and Gentiles over the true God. A brief survey of the use of θεὸς ὕψιστος by both Jews and pagans in literary and inscriptional sources shows that Jews and Gentiles could use a common term to refer to God. It therefore indicates that such a conceptual overlap exists. Could there be a conceptual overlap in terms of the true God in the theology of the 'strong'?

We moved on to consider Artapanus, who serves as an affirmation of Pseudo-Aristeas and of the conceptual overlap between the true God and other gods. But Arptanaus goes beyond Pseudo-Aristeas. For in Artapanus, we see a confluence of two different religious traditions: Jewish and Egyptian. For example, Moses is turned into a 'cultural hero', and a 'military hero', to use Gruen's words, who warded off the Ethiopian invaders. The lack of concern about the use of non-Jewish religious material in Artapanus reveals Artapanus' accommodation to other religious traditions. Artapanus' use of Moses further raises the question of the exploitation of ambiguity in the definitions of idolatry. We asked whether there might be areas of ambiguity for the 'strong' as to what constitutes idolatry.

But Pseudo-Aristeas and Artapanus represent Jewish accommodation to other religious traditions only at the intellectual level. We looked at practical examples of Jews' accommodation and participation in Gentile cults from literary and inscriptional sources and saw that Jews did participate in Gentile cults in varying degrees, even though some of them probably continued to regard themselves as Jews. Although some Jews participated in Gentile cults because of coercion or compulsion, many seem to have done so willingly. But we also made four observations and concluded that while there may appear to be clear-cut definitions of idolatry, there remain ambiguities which can be exploited.

These examples of Jews' accommodation/participation in Gentile cults might throw light on the behaviour of the 'strong' in 1 Corinthians 8–10. Could they serve as parallels to the behaviour of the 'strong' in 1 Corinthians 8–10 where the 'strong' Corinthians, possibly under Jewish influence, might similarly have believed that the God of the Christ-believing people is the same as the god/s of other religious traditions, since there is only one God? Like the various examples of Jews' accommodation/participation in Gentile cults seen in both literary and inscriptional sources, could the 'strong' have attended Gentile temples and participated in religious rituals which included the eating of idol-meat, without believing that their behaviour was idolatrous? In other words, what we are doing here in this chapter may enable us to look at the 'strong' in a different light, that is, from a cognitive level to a practical level the 'strong' could have operated with a rather different understanding of what constitutes idolatry, an understanding different from that of Paul.

Chapter 5

PAUL VERSUS THE 'STRONG' ON IDOLATRY

1. *Introduction*

In this chapter, we turn to Corinth, and to the differences of views there, which may have parallels to the variety we have seen in Chapters 2 to 4. What is the view of the 'strong' concerning other gods? And what are the views of Paul? Are there areas of agreement or disagreement, and if so, what are they? Thus, in the following, we will first look at the 'knowledge/theology' of the 'strong' which forms their basis for attending pagan temples and eating idol-meat. Such a study can only be undertaken by a close examination of the slogans of the 'strong' in 1 Corinthians 8–10 itself; and Paul's argument in 1 Corinthians 10 concerning idolatry: how exactly does Paul view idolatry? And in 1 Cor. 10.20–21, what does Paul mean when he hinges his critique of idolatry on the notion of δαιμόνια?

The discussion of the views of the 'strong' and Paul raises the question of authority, which will be discussed in the next chapter. It may be mentioned briefly at this point that in most cases of idolatry among the Diaspora Jews disciplinary action was meted out in order to preserve and maintain the Jewish identity as a people. The law always constituted the final 'court' of appeal for the Jews in the Diaspora, with regard to 'right' or 'proper' behaviour. However, this cannot be said about the Corinthian church which, though influenced by Judaism/s, was not a Jewish assembly. What then is their 'authority'? And what is Paul's prescription for them?

Thus, this chapter will pave the way for the next (Chapter 6), which will look at the question of authority and the role of 1 Corinthians 9 in the overall argument of Paul.

The above study will enable us to compare the Diaspora Jewish views and practices concerning idolatry (Chapters 3–4) with those of Paul, the 'strong', and the 'weak'. And we should be able to see how our definitions of idolatry set up in Chapter 2 may shed light on such a comparison. By making such a comparison, we will see the parallels between the different Diaspora Jewish positions and those in Corinth. This would then help to explain why the parties in Corinth have different positions and the reasons for the conflict over idolatry.

2. *Idolatry of the 'Strong': A Brief Overview*

What is the practice of the 'strong'? A brief overview of 1 Corinthians 8–10 is necessary in order to understand the behaviour of the 'strong' and how their behaviour might be idolatrous based on our definitions set out in Chapter 2.

In 1 Cor. 8.9 Paul cautions the 'strong' on the use of their liberty. The 'strong' are apparently attending pagan temples and eating idol-meat, as seen in v. 10.[1] This kind of behaviour may be viewed as idolatrous according to our definition of idolatry as 'wrong kinds of worship'. Whether they intend it or not, their consumption of sacrificed food at a pagan temple renders them idolatrous.

Further, in 1 Cor. 10.14, Paul tells the 'strong' to 'flee from the worship of idols'.[2] 1 Corinthians 10.14–21 suggests that the 'strong' not only attend pagan temples and eat idol-meat, but their presence at the pagan temple also involves some form of pagan religious ritual (v. 20) which Paul says is an act of partnership with 'demons',[3] which will lead to divided loyalty (between the Lord and 'demons'). For Paul the 'strong' are 'unfaithful' to God by turning to alien gods, even though they do not recognize the idols that represent them. Further, since vv. 16–17 and 1 Cor. 11.25 refer to the Lord's supper as an expression of God's covenant in Christ, Paul's words in v. 21 suggest a breach of the ancestral tradition of the covenant of God in Christ by the 'strong'. This fits our definition of idolatry as 'unfaithfulness'.

If the 'strong' are indeed idolatrous in their behaviour, we need to ask what is their basis. Or put differently, what causes them to behave in an idolatrous manner? In Chapter 4 above, we saw that there were Jews in the Diaspora who did not see anything wrong with their behaviour when they attended pagan temples or used pagan juridical formulae. We therefore need to examine the 'knowledge' or 'theology' of the 'strong' and ask if there might be parallels between such Diaspora Jews and the 'strong'. Such an examination will have to proceed from the cognitive level to the practical level.

---

1. Hays (1997: 135) rightly comments: 'One key to following Paul's argument is to recognize that he is primarily addressing the problem of sacrificial food consumed *in the temple of the pagan god* (8.10; 10.14, 21). That must have been the primary issue raised by the Corinthians' letter' (italics original). Barrett (1968: 196) points out that Christians could also be attending pagan temples, like their rationalistic Greek counterparts who continued attending such temples for social reasons, even though they saw no religious meaning to such events. Fee (1987: 357–62) takes the view that some of the Corinthians returned to the 'practice of attending pagan meals' after Paul left Corinth. This practice was prohibited by Paul earlier but the Corinthians in their letter to him disagreed. This view has been taken to suggest that the 'strong' are Gentile believers. But there is no evidence to suggest that the 'strong' are Gentiles. And as we argued in Chapter 1, the ethnicity of the parties involved is not clear at all, other than that of Paul. Gooch (1993: 80–83) rightly points out that pagan temple meals in Corinth always involved religious rites. This suggests that the food which the 'strong' ate in the pagan temple was idolatrous food.

2. Cf. Barrett (1968: 230) who sees this as an injunction not only to disapprove but also to avoid occasions that involved feasts that had religious content.

3. Essentially Fee's point (1987: 359–60). See also Fee (1980: 172–97). So also Gooch (1993: 80–83) who argues against Willis (1985a: 8–64), whose view is that most of these temple meals were purely social in nature.

3. The γνῶσις of the 'Strong'

1 Corinthians 8.1, περὶ δὲ τῶν εἰδωλοθύτον, indicates that Paul is responding to a subject raised in the Corinthians' letter to him, and that the issue extends throughout 1 Cor. 8.1–11.1,[4] in which he cites several of the Corinthians' slogans as he responds to them. It is possible to tell from these slogans the belief or theology of the 'strong' which gives rise to their specific practice of attending idol-temples and eating idol-meat. In particular, 1 Cor. 8.1, 4, and 6 are verses which need study. In the following, I will look at these verses and seek to answer the questions: (1) what is the 'knowledge' of the 'strong'? and (2) how does this 'knowledge' give rise to their practice of attending pagan temples and eating idol-meat?

a. *1 Corinthians 8.1 – πάντες γνῶσις ἔχομεν*

That this is a quote of the Corinthians' words can be seen in the repeated οἴδαμεν ὅτι in vv. 1 and 4 and the repeated ὅτι in v. 4 (οἴδαμεν ὅτι...καὶ ὅτι...).[5] And there is general agreement among scholars that πάντες γνῶσιν ἔχομεν is a slogan of the Corinthian 'strong'.[6]

The quote stresses *all* (πάντες), thus indicating that the 'strong' have expected this 'knowledge' to be confined not just to a privileged élite but to be shared by all.[7] But what is this γνῶσις? Schmithals has suggested that the γνῶσις of the Corinthians is in fact 'Gnosticism' the content of which is the 'doctrine of knowledge'.[8] He further argues that γνῶσις is gospel for the Corinthian Gnostics. This suggestion is weak in that Schmithals is reading into the Corinthians' γνῶσις a second-century phenomenon.[9]

Barrett correctly argues that the word γνῶσις is much wider and includes 'speculative theology in general' which focuses on the 'doctrine of God'.[10] This is confirmed by vv. 4 and 6 which are two further slogans of the Corinthians. As Murphy-O'Connor has pointed out, such a γνῶσις, which is shared by all the

---

4.   Thus the question whether there is consistency between 1 Cor. 8.1–13 and 10.23–11.1, and 10.1–22. In the first two sections, it is argued, Paul seems to take a more lenient stance, while in the last section he appears to treat idolatry quite differently. However, a closer examination of 1 Cor. 8.1–13 and 10.23–11.1 would show that Paul is equally strong in his language against eating idol-meat in these sections (see below).

5.   Fee 1987: 365 n. 30; see also Hurd (1983: 120–21).

6.   Giblin (1975: 530) observes that Paul usually employs one ὅτι when expressing his own idea. Hurd (1983: 68) provides a list of scholars in favour of this position. Modern scholars include Conzelmann (1975: 140); Barrett (1968: 189); and Fee (1987: 365), among others.

7.   Pearson (1973: 43) and Murphy-O'Connor (1978b: 545) agree that it is a 'knowledge' which is to be shared by all. Cf. Willis 1985a: 67–70. Héring (1962: 67) argues that Paul makes a digression about γνῶσις because the 'strong' had boasted in 1 Cor. 5.2 that they had a superior knowledge which did away with the scruples about idol-meat.

8.   Schmithals 1971: 143.

9.   See Fee (1987: 365 n. 32) where Fee rejects this suggestion as 'circular reasoning'.

10.   Barrett 1968: 189.

Corinthians, must be basic to the Christian belief.[11] Fee thinks that the Corinthians have believed γνῶσις to be a gift of the Spirit which makes them spiritual and that it is something all believers should have.[12]

R.A. Horsley advocates that this *gnosis*, in view of 8.4, is theological and refers to the 'knowledge of God'.[13] He shows that the language of the Corinthians in 1 Corinthians 1–4, especially that of the 'perfect vs. child', parallels the pneumatikos-psychikos distinction in Philo.[14] The 'perfect' refers to a spiritual status achieved by the Corinthian pneumatikoi, whose achievement is reflected in such self-designations as 'wise', 'powerful', 'nobly born', 'kings', and 'rich'.[15] These self-designations refer to a spiritual élite who have established their status through an intimate relation with Sophia.[16] For the 'strong', the way to the highest spiritual status is the possession of wisdom (Sophia) which will then free them from all earthly influences and bodily passions.[17] The best parallels to these features of the Corinthians' understanding can be found in Philo and Wisdom of Solomon, as Horsley seeks to show.[18]

Horsley links the γνῶσις of 1 Cor. 8.1 with the Sophia of 1 Corinthians 1–4 and argues that the two refer to the same thing. While Horsley is right in referring the γνῶσις of 1 Cor. 8.1 to 'knowledge of God', he is wrong to link it to the Sophia of 1 Corinthians 1–4, as Paul draws a sharp distinction between the γνῶσις of 1 Corinthians 8 and the Sophia of 1 Corinthians 1–4. Paul can agree with the content of the 'knowledge' in 1 Corinthians 8, albeit with some qualification, but not so with the Corinthian Sophia in 1 Corinthians 1–4.[19]

Indeed, the context of 1 Corinthians 8 reveals two considerations: (1) the practical situation of whether or not eating idol-meat is permitted; and (2) the difference in the basis of eating idol-meat on the part of the 'strong' and that on the part of the 'weak' as the root of the situation. This means that the γνῶσις of 1 Cor. 8.1 is more likely to be a form of knowledge that either permits or disallows a person to eat idol-meat. What then is this 'knowledge'? 1 Corinthians 8.4 provides the clue.

b. *1 Corinthians 8.4 – οὐδὲν εἴδωλον ἐν κόσμῳ καὶ οὐδεὶς θεὸς εἰ μὴ εἷς*
There are two parts to this verse: (1) οὐδὲν εἴδωλον ἐν κόσμῳ; and (2) οὐδεὶς θεὸς εἰ μὴ εἷς. The first half of the slogan of the 'strong' would therefore be 'an idol is nothing in the world', that is, it is of no significance to the 'strong'.[20]

11. Murphy-O'Connor 1979: 78.
12. Fee 1987: 366.
13. Horsley 1980: 35.
14. Horsley 1976: 280.
15. Horsley 1976: 281; cf. 1977: 231 and 1980: 43.
16. Horsley 1976: 281; 1979: 46–51.
17. Horsley 1976: 288; cf. 1977: 244; 1979: 48–49.
18. Cf. Pearson 1973: 35–37.
19. Cf. Tomson 1990: 193.
20. Fee (1987: 371) recognizes the ambiguity of οὐδέν as either attributive or predicative but quite correctly states that either case means there is 'no reality to idols'. Cf. Murphy-O'Connor 1978b: 546.

The word εἴδωλον is a Hellenistic Jewish conception whose usage is not found among the Greeks.[21] The term for the cultic objects in pagan Greek is ἄγαλμα, while human statues are normally called ἀνδριάς and εἰκών; although it can be used for images of the gods, shades or apparitions, the cultic object is never called εἴδωλον.[22] We may say, as Horsley does, that this principle of the Corinthian 'strong' has arisen out of a Hellenistic Jewish enlightenment.[23] According to Büchsel, the New Testament usage of εἴδωλον rests on that of the LXX or the Jews,[24] which suggests that the 'strong' have based their idea on the LXX as well as Hellenistic Judaism.[25] This is even more probable if they (the 'strong') had been influenced by the type of Judaism seen in Chapter 4 above, where we discussed Jews' accommodation to idolatry.

In Chapter 3, we saw the critique of idolatry by the Diaspora Jews. One of the emphases there is the rejection of idols and idol-makers, which could be summarized, in the words of Horsley, as the 'antithesis between *ignorance of God* and *knowledge of God*'.[26] This could possibly form another aspect of the content of the γνῶσις of the 'strong'. But it is also possible that the 'strong' hold a belief similar to that found in *The Letter of Aristeas*, that is, a recognition of other people's gods but not the idols that represent them. Such a belief would make it easier for the 'strong' to accommodate themselves to idolatry.

The phrase ἐν κόσμῳ reveals the Corinthians' belief that the world is the realm within which idols in the form of wood or stone and such like are found. However, the κόσμος is but part of the creation of the one God. Hence God is frequently described as 'Begetter', 'Father', 'Maker' or 'Cause' by Philo and Wisdom when discussing knowledge.[27]

Thus the 'strong' are informed by a 'knowledge' that the idols' existence means nothing and they therefore have no power over them. This first half of the slogan, 'idols are nothing in the world' forms the negative aspect of the knowledge. There is a positive aspect of the 'knowledge' which is the second half of the slogan, οὐδεὶς θεὸς εἰ μὴ εἷς.

'There is no God but one' seems to be a clear statement of the monotheistic belief of the Corinthian 'strong'. Murphy-O'Connor says, 'When viewed in the

21.   Büchsel 1964: 377.
22.   Büchsel 1964: 376. *Contra* Conzelmann 1975: 142.
23.   Horsley 1980: 36.
24.   Büchsel 1964: 378.
25.   Horsley (1980: 38–39) observes that within Judaism itself there were two distinct traditions of polemic against idols or false gods: (1) the tradition that contrasts lifeless idols with the one, true, creating and redeeming God; this is seen especially in Hellenistic Judaism; and (2) the tradition that saw in idolatry the service or influence of demons. The Corinthian 'strong' could have held (2) before but have probably modified their view to one that regards idols as totally nothing after their conversion to Christianity. This might suggest that there is a fundamental conflict of idea between Paul and the 'strong'.
26.   Horsley (1980: 39) argues that ignorance of God is in fact the same as thinking that idols are gods and knowledge of God means a knowledge that idols are nothing. Cf. Fee (1980: 180), 'They all have γνῶσις about idols, namely that Jewish-Christian monotheism by its very nature rules out any genuine reality to an idol'.
27.   Cf. Horsley 1980: 40.

perspective of Paul's preaching *oudeis theos ei mê heis* can only mean that one God alone enjoys the prerogative of existence'.[28] However, is this statement about the oneness of God affirmed by the Greeks? Or is it one of Christian mono-theistic belief, or one of Hellenistic Jewish origin so that when the 'strong' use it, it is a modified view of their previous religious belief?

It is more possible that the 'one God' is a basic Jewish confession of God as One,[29] but has been inherited by Christian confession as may be seen in the confession of Christ as Lord in 1 Cor. 8.6[30] in addition to the confession of 'one God'.[31] It must be emphasized that the Christian doctrine of God was still fluid even up to the third century CE,[32] so that what we have in 1 Corinthians 8 is probably a very basic and early confession of God. In other words, it is largely a Jewish confession. What is more important is that both Paul and the 'strong' could share the affirmation and its correlate that 'idols are nothing'; but they differed in what they said and did thereafter.

That 1 Cor. 8.4 is a basic Jewish confession of 'God as one' can also be found in various works of Hellenistic Jewish literature such as Josephus and Philo.[33] It is therefore more likely that the second half of the Corinthian slogan in 1 Cor. 8.4 has originated from Hellenistic Jewish monotheism of the 'one God' to the exclu-sion of all other beings, gods, and idols.[34] The question is: what does the concept of 'one God' really mean to the 'strong'? Is it the type found in *The Letter of Aristeas*, that which allows for a conceptual overlap between the God of the Jews and the god of the pagans? This question is particularly important since the 'strong' do not seem to have difficulty attending pagan temples and eating idol-meat, even though they hold the view that there is no God but one. As discussed in Chapter 4, section 2, c above, if the 'strong' were aware of the LXX command not to revile other people's gods, and if there is a conceptual overlap in their understanding about other people's gods, then it would account for their behaviour. But such a concept would mean the 'strong' have, in Paul's mind, confused the true God with other gods, thus rendering them idolatrous at the cognitive level, as our definition in Chapter 2 would classify them.

From the above, 1 Cor. 8.4 provides us with an insight into the theological understanding of the 'strong' and there are two aspects of it: (1) negatively, it views idols as nothing in the world and therefore as having no power over their lives; and (2) positively, it holds the view that there is only one God, with the possibility of a conceptual overlap about the true God as discussed in Chapter 4. With this γνῶσις of the nothingness or non-reality of idols and the oneness of

---

28. Murphy-O'Connor 1978b: 546.

29. Horsley 1980: 36.

30. Willis (1985a: 84) is of the opinion that the monotheistic confession is inherited from Judaism, a fundamental truth for the 'strong' to conclude that 'idols are nothing in the world'.

31. See Grant (1986: 84–94) for a brief treatment of the 'Christian Doctrines of God'.

32. Grant (1986: 91–94) looks at Origen's work on God and makes such a conclusion.

33. *Ant.* 3.91; *Spec. Leg.* 1.30; *Op. Mund.* 170–72; *Conf. Ling.* 170–71 and *Leg. All.* 3.48, 126. See Horsley (1980: 35) who links the 'strong' with those who seek wisdom in 1 Corinthians 1–4.

34. Cf. Deut. 6.4; Isa. 44.8; 45.5.

God, the 'strong' probably believe that their 'freedom' (ἐλευθερία) and 'right' (ἐξουσία) allow them to freely eat idol-meat, even at the pagan temple.

The above may be an introduction to a more established position on the common confession of 'one God' and 'one Lord' in 1 Cor. 8.6, which may not be easily comprehended by all as Paul points out in v. 7. To have a fuller understanding of the practice of the 'strong' we will now turn to 1 Cor. 8.6.

c. *1 Corinthians 8.6 - the Confession*

The verse begins with the strong adversative, ἀλλ' ἡμῖν, pointing to a credal confession.[35] As 1 Cor. 8.7 points out, this is a 'knowledge' that is not shared by all. In other words, it probably comes from the 'strong' who have worked out this confession in such a way as to be independent of Paul (but the content of which is fully agreed with by Paul) and not easy for the 'weak' to comprehend fully. It is also the confession which is central to the theology of the 'strong' that gives rise to their practice of eating idol-meat.

The confession may be studied in two divisions: (1) εἷς θεὸς ὁ πατὴρ ἐξ οὗ τὰ πάντα καὶ ἡμεῖς εἰς αὐτόν; and (2) εἷς κύριος Ἰησοῦς Χριστὸς δι' οὗ τὰ πάντα καὶ ἡμεῖς δι' αὐτοῦ. The first brings us to the very reality of the 'one God' whom the Corinthian 'strong' confess as their Father, which is a clear reference to the famous Jewish *Shema* in Deut. 6.4 with which the Jewish-influenced Corinthian 'strong' would have been familiar. It speaks of not only the fatherhood of God but the creatorship of God.[36] The expression τὰ πάντα has been a subject of debate. Is it to be understood as referring to the new order of salvation as

---

35. Conzelmann 1975: 145 n. 51; Willis (1985a: 84) observes that the credal character of this verse is in the balanced phraseology of the style; see his n. 70. However, although Fee (1987: 373–74) thinks it is possible for this verse to find its origin in a credal confession, he holds the view that the words were Paul's own. The question is sharpened by Murphy-O'Connor (1978a: 257) who makes a distinction between a declaration and a confession and argues for the former on the basis that a confession is a considered declaration which is theoretical and abstract. Whereas a declaration or acclamation 'is rooted in the wonder inspired by the experience of power'. He goes on to say, 'This dimension of power as experienced confirms the classification of I Cor. VIII, 6 as an acclamation, because this precise aspect is highlighted by the *hêmeis di' autou* which produces the effect *hêmeis eis auton*' (257–58, italics original). This view is similarly held by Giblin (1975: 534). However, if v. 6 is an acclamation due to the dimension of power experienced and that a confessional formula would have been too theoretical and abstract, it would mean that the 'weak' would less likely have any problem understanding it since they too had experienced conversion and thus probably the power that came with it. On the contrary, 1 Cor. 8.7 tells us that ἀλλ' οὐκ ἐν πᾶσιν ἡ γνῶσις, which implies the possibility that vv. 4, 6 and particularly v. 6 could well be a credal confession which is too highbrow for the 'weak'. See Horsley (1978b: 130) who argues that the verse is a credal confession arising from Stoic doxology. It appears that it was a credal confession with which the Corinthians were familiar at their conversion and it could even well be possible that it was recited at their baptism. Murphy-O'Connor (1979: 80) states that it is in fact an acclamation uttered during a baptismal liturgy. This begs the question then as to what the difference between a baptismal-liturgical acclamation and a baptismal credal confession is. Further, the context of 1 Corinthians 8 indicates that v. 6 is probably central to the γνῶσις of the 'strong'.

36. Cf. Horsley 1980: 46. Héring (1962: 69–70) discusses various creation models but settles on the Jewish Kabbalah conception of creation which describes God as creating the universe by taking from himself all the elements of creation.

Murphy-O'Connor has argued?[37] It must be noted that the context of 1 Corinthians 8 is that of eating idol-meat. Even though the confession probably has a much wider meaning for the Corinthians at the time of their conversion – when they turned from the former belief (in this case Judaism for the Jewish Christians, and pagan belief for those Jewish-influenced Gentile Christians)[38] to acknowledge Christ as their Lord and as the agent of all that they have and are – it seems to be applied to this very specific context of idol-meat. Thus τὰ πάντα would more likely be a reference to all creation.

It appears that the 'strong' possess the knowledge that all things come from the one God, which obviously includes food, even idol-meat. And since idols are nothing and insignificant, and since God is the one God who has created all things, it is perfectly all right for the 'strong' to eat idol-meat.

Such a γνῶσις means for the 'strong' a legitimation for their very practice. They are in a spiritual state of 'freedom' and 'power' as they acknowledge God as their Father and creator and their own creatureliness, thus their dependence on and existence for him.[39] Eating idol-meat is therefore not wrong at all, but a way of expressing one's belief. Yet, this behaviour is viewed by Paul as sharing in the table of demons and which, according to our definitions, would be seen as a form of rebellion against the true God and a wrong kind of worship even if their intention is not. But the 'strong' need not view this as Paul does. For them, the definitions of idolatry may be different.

That the one God is not only the creator but also the Father to the 'strong' means that they now have to live for him, that is, ἡμεῖς εἰς αὐτον. But living for God would also imply a conscious and deliberate effort in rejecting idols and all that they stand for. They are therefore not to be held back by any thought that idols have power over them. This would have given rise to their 'freedom' in eating idol-meat. Indeed, such concept and practice are not without parallels. Artapanus could hold a positive view of Moses and Judaism while at the same time attribute to Moses all the Egyptian religious traditions (see Chapter 4, section 5 above). Further, it is highly possible for the 'strong' to view the true God as the 'most high God', just as Philo does. But the 'strong' differ in their application of this knowledge of God as the highest (see Chapter 4, section 4 above). And as in Chapter 4, section 4 above, it is possible that there is a conceptual overlap between the understanding of the 'strong' regarding the true God

37. Murphy-O'Connor 1978a: 263–65.

38. By this, I am not making a statement as to who are Jewish or Gentile Christians. The point is that even if all the Corinthians have this belief at the point of their conversion, the practical implications for different individuals or groups may still differ.

39. Fee (1987: 374–75) lists three realities about God in this verse: (1) that God is now to be understood to be the Father; (2) that God is the source and creator of all things; and (3) that Christians now exist for his purpose. And Barrett (1968: 192) rightly states, 'He is therefore described as **the Father** (primarily of his only Son, Jesus Christ; secondarily also of those who through Christ have a derivative relationship), **from whom come all things** (that is, he is the Creator) **and to whom our own being leads** (literally, *and we unto him*; that is, we exist in order to serve him, and our destiny is to be found in him)...' (emphasis original).

and other people's understanding, since the cult of Ζεὺς Ὕψιστος was officially recognized in Corinth.

In the second part, the word κύριος has several meanings.[40] However, it must be seen in conjunction with what follows: δι' οὗ τὰ πάντα καὶ ἡμεῖς δι' αὐτοῦ. This phrase is a parallel to the one before and speaks about the relationship of Jesus Christ to God in creation and redemption. The 'strong' would probably acknowledge Jesus Christ as κύριος, the agent of creation and redemption (hence διά). This, according to Barrett, means that Jesus Christ 'stands in close relation, but is not identical, with God'.[41] Thus the 'strong' believe Jesus Christ is the agent of creation and, in terms of redemption, the intermediary between God and humanity. And the context of 1 Corinthians 8 shows they know they have been redeemed into 'freedom', because idols are nothing in the face of Christ the Lord; and they now belong to God the Father.

Horsley has pointed out that in Hellenistic Judaism, 'a sense of one's inability to sin can be rooted in the possession of *sophia* and *gnosis*'.[42] However, while Jesus Christ could be seen as the *sophia* which is the instrument of God's creation in Jewish Wisdom literature,[43] Horsley's view that the 'strong' have attained a spiritual status of 'wisdom', 'power' and 'perfection' is possible but cannot be confirmed from the text.[44]

Armed with this confession as their γνῶσις, the 'strong' are able to say, 'we all possess knowledge', 'idols are nothing in the world' and 'there is no God but one'. This γνῶσις thus gives them the 'right' or 'freedom' to attend pagan temples and eat idol-meat. How this 'right' or 'freedom' is appropriated by the 'strong' will need to be examined, particularly because the concept is also seen in Josephus' citation of the Numbers 25 incident.

d. *The* ἐξουσία *of the 'strong'*
In 1 Cor. 8.9, Paul cautions the 'strong' on the use of their ἐξουσία, as he does not want their exercise of ἐξουσία to become a stumbling-block to the 'weak'. In 1 Cor. 10.23 Paul cites yet another slogan of the 'strong' in their justification for eating idol-meat: πάντα ἔξεστιν, which is also seen in 1 Cor. 6.12.[45] What is this ἐξουσία? Does it imply that the 'strong' are turning to themselves and their γνῶσις as their 'authority'?

The word ἔξεστιν is defined as 'it is permitted', 'it is possible', and 'proper' by BAGD. In the light of the participation of the 'strong' in eating idol-meat, the

---

40. See Quell and Foerster (1965: 1039–95) for these studies.
41. Barrett 1968: 193.
42. Horsley 1980: 47 (emphasis original).
43. See Héring 1962: 71.
44. Horsley 1976.281; cf. 1977: 231 and 1980: 43; see also 1979: 46–51. See further his commentary (1998: 144–45) where Horsley recognizes the various slogans to be the theological knowledge of the 'strong'.
45. Fee (1987: 384 n. 46) rightly observes that the words ἐξουσία and ἐλεύθερος/ἐλευθερία are 'nearly synonymous' in Paul's argument. On 1 Cor. 6.12, Fee is of the opinion that it is a crisis of the abuse of freedom 'to act as they (the "strong") pleased' (1987: 252). Barrett (1968: 144) thinks that the slogan receives a qualified agreement from Paul who draws a different conclusion.

'permission' or 'possibility' could be understood as a claim of 'freedom'.[46] And according to BAGD, ἐξουσία carries the meaning of 'freedom of choice', 'right to act, decide', among others.[47]

Thus, the 'strong' appear to believe that eating sacrificial food is part of their ἐξουσία. Further, their present knowledge (γνῶσις) serves as the foundation for that ἐξουσία. And their slogan, πάντα ἔξεστιν, expresses their ἐξουσία to eat idol-meat.

There are at least two ways to explain 'freedom'. Firstly, 'freedom' could be viewed as the Christian claim of being 'freed' from the Mosaic Law, after their conversion to Christianity. Such 'freedom' represents a kind of liberation from something burdensome and oppressive, that is, the burdens of the Law. The participation of the 'strong' in pagan temple meals which involves eating sacrificial food could be seen as an effort to claim this 'freedom' in a practical way. The second is the claim of the intrinsic value of humanity, that is, human 'freedom'. This perspective sees 'freedom' as deeply rooted in the 'one God' who gives all people the 'freedom' to be what they are and live according to the γνῶσις that is derived from this 'one God'. In this sense, the 'strong' can claim their γνῶσις of the 'one God' and the 'non-entity of idols' and thus their 'freedom' to live according to this knowledge. Such a claim is not without parallel.

In Josephus' account of the Midianite women's seduction of the Israelite youths, a parallel to the claim of the 'strong' to their 'rights' and 'freedom' may be seen. In *Ant.* 4.131-154, the Israelite youths are described as having fallen in love with the Midianite women and, after these women demanded that the Israelites conform to their (Midianite) belief system and follow their customs and worship their gods, giving in to the women's demand (*Ant.* 4.137). *Antiquities* 4.139 tells us that the youths accepted the belief in a plurality of gods and were certain about sacrificing to the Midianite women's gods according to their (i.e. the Midianites') established rites. What follows is that Moses tried to reason with the youths (*Ant.* 4.141-44), only to receive a robust response from the chief of the tribe of Simeon, Zambrias, who argued that Moses was a tyrant who secured the Israelites' obedience to the law by compulsion (*Ant.* 4.145-46). Zambrias' accusation against Moses of 'robbing us of life's sweets and of that liberty of action' (τὸν βίον αὐτεξούσιον) may be seen as an expression of a belief that went beyond a mere giving in to the Midianite women's seduction.[48] The αὐτεξούσιος, which means 'free power' or 'self-determination', points to the meaning we have

46. Conzelmann (1975: 108-109) carefully takes the term, ἔξεστιν, to mean 'it is permitted' and that it is linked to the 'knowledge' of the 'strong'. As mentioned in section 3, a, b, and c, the 'knowledge' of the 'strong' forms their theology which 'permits' them to behave in an idolatrous manner.

47. Hays (1997: 101) refers to this as a 'philosophically-informed autonomy', which means that the 'strong' are free to do anything as they please. However, Hays' suggestion that the 'strong' could have drawn on the kind of philosophical tradition found in Epictetus has not taken into consideration the nature of the 'knowledge' or 'theology' of the 'strong', which we have shown to be Jewish. And if we can find Jewish parallel to such a claim to 'freedom', our case that the behaviour of the 'strong' is Jewish would be considerably strengthened (see further below).

48. Cf. Borgen 1996: 19.

mentioned earlier, that is, the 'freedom' given to all humanity.[49] Further, Zambrias' insistence that such 'freedom' belonged to 'free people' (τῶν ἐλευθέρων) who 'have no master' (δεσπότην οὐκ ἐχόντων) (*Ant.* 4.146) shows his belief that he, and indeed all those who joined the Midianite women, were 'free people' and that they therefore ought to exercise their αὐτεξούσιον. Such an appeal to 'free power' and to 'freedom' (ἐλευθερία) shows that Zambrias was feeling oppressed and that he could not access the truth because of Moses' tyranny (*Ant.* 4.149).

If Josephus' reworked story of the Midianite women is a reflection of the situation of the Graeco-Roman world of attractions, and thus 'temptations', to the Jews in the Diaspora, and if Josephus wrote this to address the issue of the dangers posed by Gentile cultural religious values on Judaism,[50] then it is possible that such a claim on one's 'self-determination' might be quite widespread. And this serves as a parallel to the claim of the 'strong' that 'all things are lawful' (πάντα ἔξεστιν, 1 Cor. 10.23; cf. 1 Cor. 6.12).

Although Paul recognizes the ἐξουσία of the 'strong', he does not agree with the way they exercise their ἐξουσία, that is, by attendance at pagan temples and consumption of idol-meat (...ἡ ἐξουσία ὑμῶν αὕτη... 1 Cor. 8.9).[51] For such actions are idolatrous and can lead to their destruction. And in the process, the 'weak' are also stumbled. Instead, he urges the 'strong' to imitate his willingness not to use his own 'rights' as an apostle, thus reiterating his opposition to the way the 'strong' are exercising their 'rights' (1 Cor. 9.1; see Chapter 6 below for further discussion of Paul's renunciation of his rights).

e. *Conclusion*

The above examination of the slogans of the 'strong' and their 'freedom' shows that they have taken a liberal stand over idol-meat. They hold the belief that idols are nothing in the world and that there is no God but one. Their knowledge of the 'one God' could possibly be paralleled by the conceptual overlap found in *The Letter of Aristeas*, Artapanus and such like: the one God is universally worshipped, even though different people call him by different names. But their knowledge was further modified when they became Christians, and this γνῶσις is further seen in their credal confession quoted by Paul in which the 'strong' acknowledge God as creator and father. Consequently they feel free to eat what God has created, which is an exercise of their γνῶσις.

Further they acknowledge Jesus Christ as Lord, to whom their existence and redemption are due. Even though they hold similar views of the 'one God' as

49. Cf. Borgen 1996: 19; Horbury 1998: 119.
50. Van Unnik 1974: 261. Feldman (2000: 378 n. 391) observes that Num. 25.1–2 speaks quite differently from Josephus' description. He is also right to point out the fact that while Josephus is addressing his work primarily to non-Jews, he is also directing his work at Jews as well, as seen in various indications such as the present incident of Israelites' worship of Baal-Peor here in Numbers 25 and Samson's relations with foreign women (Judg. 14.1–16.31; *Ant.* 5.286–317) (see Feldman 2000: 378 n. 392).
51. Fee (1987: 384–85) rightly points out that this 'freedom' of the 'strong' is close to 'freedom to act as they please without restraint'. Cf. Horsley (1998: 145) who reiterates that the 'strong' possess 'absolute authority' out of their knowledge.

Philo does (see Philo, *Leg. All.* 3.82, discussed in Chapter 4, section 4 above), they differ over the practical application of this belief. While Philo's view meant a total abstinence from and condemnation of idolatry, their γνῶσις gives them the ἐξουσία to behave in an idolatrous manner according to their own preference, with little regard for the 'weak'. Such behaviour is not without parallel, as we have seen in Chapter 4, section 6, above the various aspects of idolatrous behaviour of some Diaspora Jews.

Several definitions of idolatry spelt out in Chapter 2 are operative here. First of all, the 'strong' could be considered idolatrous for being 'unfaithful' to God through their participation in the ritual eating in the pagan temple. The category of 'unfaithfulness' shows they disregarded ancestral tradition/customs. In the light of the tradition which Paul had passed on to them (the Lord's Supper), their behaviour is considered as contrary to the gospel (see below). Second, the 'strong' could be considered idolatrous in terms of the wrong acts of worship. While they may hold a right view of God (there is no God but one), their attendance at pagan temples and eating idol-meat there is inappropriate to the worship of the true God, although they may not intend to worship the idols. Third, the 'strong' could be considered idolatrous because of the cognitive error of confusing or mixing God with δαιμόνια.

Paul, however, does not approve the behaviour of the 'strong'. For him, the behaviour of the 'strong' constitutes idolatry because eating at a pagan temple before the pagan idols is an act of sharing the table with δαιμόνια. He rejects such behaviour and warns that the 'strong' run the risk of being condemned by the true God. This whole saga or conflict over idolatry seems to boil down to the question of definitions. Paul seems to have a different view of what constitutes idolatry. To enable us to have a better understanding of Paul's position, we will now look at some of the terms which he uses in his argument against the behaviour of the 'strong'.

4. *The Use of* δαιμόνιον

Does Paul think that the consumption of idol meat is a matter of indifference? Does he, like the 'strong', believe that idols are nothing? In what way does he differ from the 'strong' in opinion? He apparently rejects the practice of the 'strong'. What are his reasons? In 1 Cor. 10.20, Paul makes a connection between idols and δαιμόνια. What does Paul mean when he quotes from Deut. 32.17? To understand Paul's view, the meaning of δαιμόνιον and its significance in Paul's argument, I will first look at its use in the Septuagint. While the Septuagint does not use the term in a widespread manner, those places where the term is used are significant in that they are related to the idolatrous behaviour of Israel. An examination of this term should also lead us to Paul's use of the term elsewhere.

a. *Δαιμόνιον in the Septuagint*

Paul's use of the word δαιμόνιον is found within a quotation of Deut. 32.17, suggesting that his understanding of the term is most likely influenced by the very passage itself. 1 Cor. 10.20 reads, ἀλλ' ὅτι ἃ θύουσιν, δαιμονίοις καὶ οὐ θεῷ θύουσιν. The LXX Deut. 32.17 reads, ...ἔθυσαν δαιμονίοις καὶ οὐ θεῷ. In this passage, the term is used to refer to the gods whom the Israelites worshipped. However, in Deuteronomy 32 itself, the objects of the Israelites' idolatrous worship are variouly called: 'no-gods' (vv. 17, 21), 'strange gods' and 'gods' (vv. 16, 17), 'new gods' (v. 17), and 'idols' (v. 21). Do all these terms mean the same thing and are they together also taken to refer to 'demons' in v. 17? Does Paul make any distinction between idols and 'demons'? What is important is that by our definition in Chapter 2 the worship of the 'no-gods', 'strange gods', 'new gods' and 'idols', other than the true God is idolatrous.[52] If idols and pagan gods are no-gods, a view which the 'strong' in Corinth also hold, what then does the term δαιμόνια mean? The text in Deuteronomy 32 seems to suggest that the δαιμόνια are a reference to the gods of the nations, represented by their idols. Other Septuagintal texts may shed more light.

In Ps. 95.5, the psalmist refers to the gods of the Gentiles as demons (δαιμόνια),[53] in contrast to Yahweh who is the creator. In Ps. 90.6, the term δαιμόνιον seems to carry the idea of 'evil spirit' (δαιμονίου μεσημβρινοῦ), while the term μεσημβρινοῦ indicates that the psalmist has in view the realm of the spirits.[54] Meanwhile, Ps. 105.36–38 (LXX) employs the terms δαιμόνια and idols interchangeably.[55] The idols of v. 36, though not mentioned in v. 37, are again mentioned in v. 38, both of which refer to the objects of the Israelites' sacrifice of their children. Verse 37 comes in between and explains that the child sacrifice is to 'demons' (τοῖς δαιμονίοις).[56] However, since in the majority of Jewish texts, 'idols' are ridiculed as being dumb and stupid, lacking any power or efficacy, the δαιμόνια could well be a reference to the spirits behind, or represented by, the idols.[57]

The use of the term in Isaiah may be seen in three ways. In Isa. 13.21, calamity is promised to Israel's enemies. Babylon, which is the nation that takes Israel into captivity, is described as a place for wild beasts, and where 'demons' will make merry (δαιμόνια ἐκεῖ ὀρχήσονται).[58] A similar description about the nations in

52. A breach of the covenant, so Craigie (1976: 382); *pace* von Rad (1966: 198) who sees here a subordination of history to theology.

53. This is the translation of the Hebrew אלילים, which Anderson (1972: 683) thinks is a term of contempt. Dahood (1968: 358) translates it as 'rags', linking it to the teraphim to denote 'old rags'.

54. Cf. Anderson 1972: 658. The idea here is that the realm of evil spirits is destructive, hence indicating that the translators view 'demons' as such.

55. Allen (1983: 53–56) sees the psalm as a penitential prayer which recalls the sins of Israel, which suggests a connection between vv. 36–38 and vv. 28–31 (on the worship of Baal of Peor). This would mean that the psalmist views 'idols' and 'demons' to be the same.

56. See Dahood 1970: 74–75.

57. Anderson (1972: 746) observes that the Hebrew term שדים is found only here and Deut. 32.17. שדים according to Anderson, are always connected with the Akkadian שד, which refers to certain subordinate spirits which have been invested with power to do good or evil. The LXX translators would have been aware of the significance of the term and their choice of δαιμόνια to translate שדים suggests that they thought 'demons' to be some kind of subordinate spirits. Since the context of the psalm concerns evil deeds, the 'demons' here would rightly refer to some evil spirits.

58. This is later echoed in the New Testament, Rev. 18.2, where Babylon is similarly depicted as

general is also given in Isa. 34.14 where the wrath of God upon the nations is represented by the desolation of the Gentile lands, with all the princely glory coming to naught (v. 12). Animals which are not normally very welcome are present, such as the hawk, the porcupine, the owl and the raven (v. 11), the jackals and ostriches (v. 13), and the hyenas (v. 14). The presence of these animals indicates a land that is wild, uninhabited and desolate.[59] It may be symbolic of a spiritual state of desolation. The description of the Gentile lands in the LXX, of δαιμόνια calling out to their fellow satyrs (ὀνοκενταύροις: small 'demons' that resemble tailless apes that haunt wild places), further suggests that there is a spiritual realm in which the evil spirits dwell. The mention of the animals parallels that of the 'demonic', thus giving the impression that the Gentile nations would be completely devastated.

The second use of the term is found in Isa. 65.3 in which δαιμόνια are described as Israel's object of worship (θυμιῶσιν ἐπὶ ταῖς πλίνθοις τοῖς δαιμονίοις).[60] However, these 'demons' are described as ἃ οὐκ ἔστιν. In this second usage, the 'demons' appear to be viewed in a similar fashion as the 'idols' (cf. Chapters 2 and 3 above), that is, they are hand-made, dumb and powerless blocks of wood, or silver or gold. In short, they are insignificant.

The third use of the term is in Isa. 65.11, where Israel's idolatry is manifested in the people's setting up a table for δαιμόνια (ἑτοιμάζοντες τῷ δαιμονίῳ τράπεζαν). It is not clear whether a literal 'table' is meant here; nor what the 'table' actually looks like if a literal one is meant. It could refer to a raised platform on which sacrifices are placed, such as bricks (e.g. Isa. 65.3), or to a symbolic 'table' such as the mountain on which worship takes place (e.g. Isa. 65.7). Whatever it is, what is important for our purpose is that the setting up of some form of 'altar' for worshipping and offering sacrifices to 'demons' is not without precedent. And Paul's description of the behaviour of the 'strong' in 1 Cor. 10.21 could well be an allusion to the setting up of a table for the δαιμόνια in Isa. 65.11.[61] Such a setting up of a table for δαιμόνια will lead to a destiny of destruction (Isa. 65.12). The δαιμόνια here clearly refer to the objects of worship which are contradictory to Yahweh, the true God.

---

an erstwhile place of might which has become a 'dwelling place of demons' (κατοικητήριον δαιμονίων), 'a haunt of every foul spirit' (φυλακὴ παντὸς ὀρνέου ἀκαθάρτου), and 'a haunt of every foul and hateful bird' (φυλακὴ παντὸς θηρίου ἀκαθάρτου καὶ μεμισημένου). In this passage, Babylon is negatively portrayed as a place where such 'evil' and 'distasteful' beings dwell. Thus, what is used to describe Babylon can also be said to be 'evil', since Babylon in the Jewish tradition is always an 'evil' place. See further Watts (1985: 199) who describes the conquered Babylon as 'a virtual ghost-town'.

59. Watts (1987: 13) rightly points out that the line between the wild animals and the various demons, phantoms and ghosts is hard to draw. Such difficulty suggests the wildness and desolation of the place, and therefore the evil nature of those that dwell there.

60. See Watts (1987: 343) who observes that such worship includes the rites of pagan worship.

61. In the context of Isaiah 65, the setting up of a table for δαιμόνια is an act that directly contradicts the worship of Yahweh, that is, it is an idolatrous act that rebelled against Yahweh and abandoned the ancestral tradition, as defined in Chapter 2 above.

In Bar. 4.7, the author speaks of Israel's idolatry as sacrificing to 'demons and not to God'. This is also a possible allusion to Deut. 32.17. In v. 35, the author, like Isaiah 13, describes the nations that exiled Israel as those places that were inhabited by 'demons' (κατοικηθήσεται ὑπὸ δαιμονίων τὸν πλείονα χρόνον). This suggests that the author has a negative understanding of δαιμόνια, and since he uses δαιμόνια in a contrasting manner to God who is good, he probably understands δαιμόνια as evil spirits. Thus, 'demons' in Baruch appear to be antithetical to God, who represents what is good (2.27), righteous (1.15; 2.6, 9; 5.9), and merciful (3.2; 4.22; 5.9), who provides salvation (4.24).

The most explicit reference to δαιμόνια as evil spirits is found in the Book of Tobit. The Book tells the story of a woman named Sara who failed to marry her fiancé because each time before she was married, her prospective husband would be killed by an evil spirit called Asmodeus (Ἀσμοδαῖος τὸ πονηρὸν δαιμόνιον, 3.8).[62] This happened seven times.[63] For Asmodeus was in love with Sara (δαιμόνιον φιλεῖ αὐτήν, 6.14). In the story, Tobit is praying for his son Tobias; while Sara is praying for deliverance. Their prayers are answered by God, who sends his angel Raphael to heal Sara and Tobit (3.17; 5.4). In this story, the δαιμόνιον is an evil spirit that troubles humans. And this is precisely what Asmodeus will do to Tobias to whom God has willed Sara to be married. But the angel Raphael instructs Tobias on how he may relieve himself of the demonic trouble.[64] A certain elaborate ritual of smoking a fish heart and liver is carefully detailed to Tobias (6.7–9, 17).[65] Tobias' fears of the evil spirit are allayed by the angel, who tells him to view the evil spirit as nothing (τοῦ δαιμονίου μηδένα λόγον ἔχε, 6.16). Instead, Tobias is to pray to God, who is merciful (6.17).[66] In the end, the evil spirit Asmodeus tries to harm Tobias, but the latter, acting on the instruction of the angel, does exactly what he has been instructed. The evil spirit flees, upon smelling the smoke from the heart and liver of the fish (8.3). Although this story is fictional,[67] it indicates the understanding of the author, and possibly the understanding of the times, regarding δαιμόνια,[68] which may serve as the background to Paul's understanding when he quotes Deut. 32.17.[69] And as

62. See Schürer (III, 222–23), Zimmermann (1958: 2–5), and Nowell (1999: 978–85) for a summary of the story. For a short but succinct exposition, see Nickelsburg (1984: 40–46).

63. See Zimmermann (1958: 62) for the use of the number 'seven'.

64. Zimmermann (1958: 66) comments that Asmodeus is a 'formidable adversary' and requires an agent of God to overcome him. Such an act of sending an angel on the part of God shows that the author understands Asmodeus to be real and powerful.

65. 'Smoking' itself has been known to be used to ward off attacks of evil spirits; see *ERE*, vol. 4, 724a, 727a.

66. It is interesting to read the address of Tobias to the angel Raphael, Ἀζαρία ἄδελφε, of which Ἀζαρια means 'God helps' (see Dan. 1.6–7). Tobias' address shows the power of Asmodeus as Tobias clearly needs the help and mercy of God. On the theme of God's mercy, see Nickelsburg (1984: 42).

67. For the character and genre of the Book of Tobit, see Zimmermann (1958). For a more up to date work, see Nowell (1999: 978–85).

68. Cf. Zimmermann 1958: 27–32.

69. Even a cursory reading of the story shows that the author is heavily influenced by the biblical writings. On this, see Zimmermann (1958: 12–15); for the sources of the plot, see Nowell (1999: 979–82).

the above discussion shows, most of the authors of the above LXX passages seem to have been influenced by Deut. 32.17, which might also suggest that their views are shared by Paul as well, when he quotes the same text to argue his point.

b. *Paul's use of the term δαιμόνιον and related concepts*
Paul's use of the term is found only in 1 Cor. 10.20–21 among the undisputed Pauline letters.[70] On the basis of our examination of the term's use in the LXX, we may detect Paul's understanding of δαιμόνιον in his frequent mention of the unseen spirit-world, not least in 1 Corinthians. In other words, since there is a general tendency towards treating δαιμόνια as evil spirits in the LXX passages which use the term, it is possible that Paul might have viewed δαιμόνια in the same manner. This may further suggest that Paul has in mind the evil spirits, which he believes lie behind the idols, when he uses the term δαιμόνια in 1 Corinthians 10. We will turn first to 1 Corinthians, and thereafter the other letters of Paul.

In 1 Cor. 2.4, Paul speaks about his preaching and his message as a demonstration of the spirit and of power. While he does not specify what 'spirit' (πνεῦμα) he has in mind, it is clear that he is referring to the Spirit and power of God.[71] Hence in 2.5, he argues that the purpose of such preaching and its message is that the faith of the Corinthians might rest on the power of God (ἐν δυνάμει θεοῦ). He then sets out the argument that he still speaks wisdom, but not of 'this age' (οὐ τοῦ αἰῶνος τούτου) nor of the 'rulers of this age' (τῶν ἀρχόντων τοῦ αἰῶνος τούτου) (v. 6). While 'this age' (ὁ αἰων αὐτός) could well refer to this 'world' in which the Corinthians live, and the 'rulers of this age' a reference to the political and religious leaders of this world (e.g. v. 8), as Robertson and Plummer maintain,[72] it is very likely that Paul has in mind a double meaning, that is, the 'rulers of this age' are the spirits of the spirit world whose cause is advocated by the religious and political 'rulers of this age'.[73] Cullmann is right in assuming that the 'invisible angelic powers' stand behind the earthly rulers.[74] But

---

70.   They are: the Epistle to the Romans, First and Second Epistles to the Corinthians, the Epistle to the Galatians, the Epistle to the Philippians, the First Epistle to the Thessalonians, and the Epistle to Philemon.

71.   Cf. Barrett (1968: 65) takes the two as a hendiadys. Clearly Paul is here referring to the work of the Holy Spirit. See also Hays (1997: 36) and Fee (1987: 95 n. 28).

72.   Robertson and Plummer (1911: 36–37) maintain that the 'rulers of this age' are primarily the Jewish leaders, and any reference to the 'spirits' is incompatible with v. 8.

73.   Against Witherington III (1995: 127) who understands ἄρχοντες τοῦ αἰῶνος τούτου as the earthly rulers, and Hays (1997: 44) who sees no reference in this verse and its context to the demonic powers.

74.   Cullmann 1951: 191–93. See further Lietzmann (1931: 11–12); Héring (1962: 16–17); Barrett (1968: 70); Conzelmann (1975: 61); among others. But Fee (1987: 103–104, and also nn. 22–24) argues strongly against such an interpretation. His reasons are not necessarily persuasive. First, there is no reason why there should be a link between 1 Cor. 2.6 and Col. 1.16 and Eph. 6.12. It depends on whether one takes these latter epistles to be from Paul. In the light of the disputed Pauline authorship of these two epistles, any comparison with them would be presumptuous. Second, even though he finds no evidence for the use of the term for demon, there is no reason why Paul cannot mean more than just earthly rulers. Third, while Paul uses the term to refer to earthly rulers elsewhere (Rom. 13.3),

this does not mean that earthly rulers always act on behalf of the spirit world, since Paul elsewhere exhorts believers to submit to earthly authorities (cf. Rom. 13.1–12). What Paul is saying is that the 'earthly rulers' may indirectly advocate the cause of the demonic powers, whether intentionally or unintentionally. Thus, in 1 Cor. 2.12, Paul explicitly points out that he himself and the Corinthians have not received the 'spirit of the world' (τὸ πνεῦμα τοῦ κόσμου), but the 'Spirit which is from God' (τὸ πνεῦμα τὸ ἐκ τοῦ θεοῦ).[75] While it is entirely possible for Paul to have in mind the one Spirit which believers have received,[76] it is likely that Paul wants to differentiate between those who have received his gospel and those who seek after the wisdom of the world. This indicates Paul's belief that there are two kinds of πνεῦμα which are diametrically opposed to each other: the Spirit of God and the spirit of the world.[77] The Spirit of God enables believers in their understanding of God's truths (2.10, 12–13);[78] but the spirit of the world is associated with folly (3.18–19). And such folly is rightly the result of the work of the 'God of this age' (see discussion on 2 Cor. 4.4 below).

In 1 Cor. 5.5, in rebuking the Corinthians for doing nothing to sanction the person who committed the act of sexual immorality, Paul announces his judgment and tells the Corinthians to remove such a person by handing him over to Satan (τῷ σατανᾷ) for the destruction of the flesh (εἰς ὄλεθρον τῆς σαρκός).[79] The point Paul is making is the expulsion of the incestuous person from the community of believers.[80] The region into which the person is expelled would be the world where Satan dwells and rules.[81] Here Satan is associated with 'destruction', which, in the context of Paul's argument (i.e. the purpose of such destruction is that the culprit might be saved eschatologically),[82] is further linked to 'sin' and therefore to what is evil. This is further seen, for example, in 1 Cor. 7.5, where Paul advises the married couples not to deprive each other of their conjugal rights save for the purpose of prayer. He attributes any sexual unfaithfulness resulting

the overall context of 1 Corinthians in fact favours inclusion of the meaning of the spirit world. See Barrett 1968: 69–70 and Horsley 1998: 58.

75. Hays (1997: 45–47) notes that Paul in 1 Cor. 2.10–13 has a simple point: 'The hidden wisdom of God (Christ crucified) is revealed to us by the Spirit of God'.

76. Adams 2000: 116–17.

77. Barrett (1968: 75) states that Paul did believe in a 'spiritual force opposed to God'. Against Fee (1987: 113), who thinks that Paul is saying something about the Holy Spirit, and Robertson and Plummer (1911: 45) who prefer this to mean 'the spirit of human wisdom, of the world as alienated from God'.

78. Thus Hays 1997: 45–47; Barrett 1968: 74–76; Fee 1987: 109–15.

79. I.e. 'sinful lusts', so Robertson and Plummer (1911: 99). Satan is used here as a tool, so Barrett (1968: 124–27).

80. Fee (1987: 208–14) states that outside the church is the sphere of the Spirit, the domain of Satan. For an interpretation based on 'boundaries observance', see Furnish (1999: 50–54).

81. It is possible that a traditional understanding is in view here, as seen in Jn. 12.31; 16.11, where Satan seems to be alluded to as the ruler of this world (ἄρχων τοῦ κόσμου τούτου). Robertson and Plummer (1911: 99) take this to refer to a region outside the commonwealth and covenant where Satan rules. Barrett (1968: 126) notes that 1 Cor. 5.5 means the exclusion of the person from the sphere of Christ's work.

82. Gundry-Volf 1990: 113–14,

from such sexual abstinence to the work of Satan. While the lack of self-control is the result of sexual abstinence, Satan is depicted as an evil being who takes advantage of a situation to 'tempt' believers into what is considered as 'immoral' (τὰς πορνείας, 1 Cor. 7.2).[83] Such a negative depiction of 'Satan' is also seen in 2 Cor. 11.13–15, where Paul describes the false apostles as 'deceitful workers' (ἐργάται δόλιοι) who disguise themselves as Christ's apostles (2 Cor. 11.13). The false apostles' 'deception' is then attributed to 'Satan' who 'disguises himself as an angel of light' (v. 14).[84] In v. 15, Paul puts the false apostles and Satan together by accusing the former of being the 'servants' of the latter (διάκονοι αὐτοῦ), thus making Satan the origin of falsehood. The word μετασχηματίζω is used in Phil. 3.21 to indicate the glorious body into which the human, lowly body of the believer would be transformed.[85] In other words, it connotes a 'change' from the previous appearance. The word is used here in 2 Cor. 11.14 to describe the transformed appearance of Satan, thus indicating the nature of the 'deception' of Satan,[86] of which the 'change' or 'transformation' is meant to hide the true 'nature' of Satan.

Apart from the above, 'Satan' is also described as a 'harasser'. In 2 Cor. 12.7, Paul attributes his physical ailment to 'Satan', whom God uses to keep him from excessive elation over his apparent ecstatic experience. And the antidote to the suffering is the 'grace' of God.[87] Thus Paul views 'Satan' as a spiritual being that does evil, albeit with limitations.[88] This 'evil' is probably what he has in mind when he describes the eschatological judgement of God on 'every rule and every authority and power' (1 Cor. 15.24). In 1 Cor. 15.25, these elements are described as the 'enemies' (τοὺς ἐχθρούς),[89] who will eventually be 'crushed' (cf. Rom. 16.20).

83.   Barrett (1968: 157) notes that Satan will tempt the sexually unsatisfied married partners to seek satisfaction in fornication. Fornication is seen as an act of disobedience to God's command to be pure, and therefore an 'evil' act. Thus, Satan is evil. Cf. 1 Thess. 2.18, where Paul speaks about his desire to visit the Thessalonians but is hindered by Satan. Apparently, Paul's desire to visit the Thessalonians is so that he may strengthen them in their faith (1 Thess. 3.2–3); the 'hindering' by Satan is therefore seen as the work of the 'evil' one who seeks to frustrate God's work and upset the faith of the believers, as he will say later that he fears that the 'tempter' (a reference to Satan) might tempt the Thessalonians into giving up their faith (1 Thess. 3.5).

84.   Martin (1986: 351) is mistaken in singling out the middle term σχῆμα and using its meaning to refer to the transformation as evil. See Barrett (1973: 286) who sees the thought in this verse as connected with the deception of Eve, which is seen also in 1 Cor. 11.3. Thus, Barrett comments: 'Paul regarded the opposition to his work as of Satanic origin, that is, he considered it to be directly opposed to God'.

85.   Cf. *4 Macc.* 9.22 where the eldest of the Jewish youths who suffer under the torture of Antiochus is described as being as though 'transformed' (μετασχηματιζόμενος) by fire into immortality.

86.   The interesting observation to be made here is that Paul refers to the 'masquerading' in both instances, using μετασχηματίζειν and μετασχηματίζεται to refer to the 'false apostles' and 'Satan' respectively. The meaning is simply 'to disguise'; see Schneider (1971: 957–58).

87.   Martin (1986: 412–16) provides a full discussion of Paul's 'thorn in the flesh'. Cf. Barrett 1973: 314–16.

88.   Barrett (1973: 316) notes that the 'messenger of Satan' was sent by God. So Satan is limited in terms of what he can do, for God is in control.

89.   Cf. 2 Cor. 2.11, where Paul urges the Corinthians to forgive one of their number whom they

The above notion of 'evil spirits' and 'Satan' seems to fit the common understanding of the world of δαιμόνια.[90]

In 2 Cor. 4.4, Paul attributes the spiritual blindness of those who do not accept his gospel to the 'god of this age' (ὁ θεὸς τοῦ αἰῶνος τούτου) who is not the true God, but Satan/devil,[91] whose work is to keep people from seeing the light of the gospel, which is the glory of Christ (τῆς δόξης τοῦ Χριστοῦ).[92] The 'god of this age' is therefore the antithesis of this glory.[93] By his 'darkness' he has blinded people from the gospel, and therefore the glory, of Christ. The above discussion indicates that Paul uses the three categories, 'rulers of this age', 'god of this age', and 'Satan', interchangeably because he understands them to be the same spiritual force.

The above understanding seems to be the most explicit in 1 Cor. 8.5. The verse is read, καὶ γὰρ εἴπερ εἰσὶν λεγόμενοι θεοὶ εἴτε ἐν οὐρανῷ εἴτε ἐπὶ γῆς, ὥσπερ εἰσὶν θεοὶ πολλοὶ καὶ κύριοι πολλοί. Two points may be noted. First, Paul understands the entire cosmos as comprising two realms of heaven and earth, the former being that of the spirits, and the latter that of the physical world.[94] Second, Paul understands that there are 'gods' and 'lords'.[95] Willis

---

have apparently punished, in order that 'Satan' may be kept from taking advantage over the situation. What this situation really is we are not totally certain. What is certain is that Paul does not want the Corinthians to withhold forgiveness for too long as he seems to hold the view that it could serve as an opportunity for Satan, who has his own 'designs' (τὰ νοήματα).

90.   In Origen's *Contra Celsum*, Celcus asks a question which might reflect the position of the 'strong': 'If these idols are nothing, what harm will there be in taking part in the feast?' (8.24). Origen's response is that idol-meat is sacrificed to demons and that anyone eating it becomes a partaker of demons (8.30). While Celsus argues that there are many 'demons' from whom one receives all the natural endowments such as air, food, water, and the like, Origen's tactic is to cast demons in a wholly negative light. Paul seems to do the same, that is, to paint idols in a negative light to show that they are evil spirits that in fact cause the 'strong' to breach the covenant of Christ. See Cheung 1999: 229–32, 267–71. Cf. *Epistle of Barnabas* 16.7; Tertullian, *De Spectaculis* 13; Clement of Alexandria, *Paedogogus* 2.1.8–10. See Cheung (1999) who discusses in whole or in part the above early Christian authors.

91.   Against Young and Ford (1987: 115–18). The context of 2 Corinthians 4 indicates thus, and scholarly opinion favours the interpretation that the 'god of this age' is a reference to Satan, or devil; see Plummer (1915: 114–15), Héring (1967: 30), Barrett (1973: 130), Martin (1986: 78–79), Thrall (1994: 305–308) and Witherington III (1995: 386).

92.   Segal (1990: 60–62) notes that Paul's prophetic calling is to proclaim the face of Christ which is the glory of God. He further argues that Christ is identified with God at the believer's baptism (based on his [Segal's] understanding of Phil. 2.6–11). This way of looking at Christ's glory strengthens the idea that the work of the 'god of this age' is to thwart the work of proclaiming the gospel of salvation.

93.   Cf. 2 Cor. 6.14–7.1, where a series of parallelism is set out: righteousness and iniquity; Christ and Belial; believer and unbeliever; the temple of God and idols; by which Paul seeks to argue for a community of believers that are separated from the world, that is, not to become 'partners' with unbelievers. Cf. Barrett (1973: 130–32) who persuasively argues that this is a bold reference to devil/Satan.

94.   Conzelmann (1975: 142–43) interprets 'in heaven and on earth' as being within creation. Fee (1987: 372–73) maintains that Paul does not think the 'gods' exist objectively but subjectively, i.e. in the sense that they are believed in by those who worship them. He bases his argument on Paul's use

maintains that 8.4-6 sets forth the Corinthians' defence while v. 5b, ὥσπερ εἰσὶν θεοὶ πολλοὶ καὶ κύριοι, is Paul's own qualification.[96] Thus, from these two points, it is not unreasonable to make the following observations. Paul's concept of the spiritual realm is that there are 'gods' and 'lords' who are in fact 'rulers of this age', spirits which are diametrically opposed to the true God. The realm in which these 'spirits' dwell is denoted by the word οὐρανός, which refers to a realm that is above the earth.[97] However, these 'spirits' are represented on earth through physical objects erected by human beings,[98] even though God rules the heavens and the earth. Thus, when Paul says that the sacrifices pagans make to idols, they in fact make to 'demons' and not to God, he is most probably referring to the 'evil spirits' which the idols represent. Thus, while Paul agrees with the 'strong' that idols are physically nothing, he does not agree with their conclusion that they can therefore freely eat idol-meat.

of the word λεγόμενοι 'so-called': 'They are "so-called" because they do not have existence in the form their worshippers believe them to have'. However, this makes light of 1 Cor. 8.5b where Paul explicitly says there are many gods and many lords. Cf. Gal. 4.8 where Paul seems to believe in the reality of the gods which he refers to as 'beings'. Cf. Barrett (1968: 192–94, 236–38) who ably argues that Paul does not think that the 'beings' are the true God but demons which are subordinate and yet powerful; similarly Robertson and Plummer (1911: 167). Cf. 1 Cor. 10.20–21; see below for further discussion. Thus Adams (2000: 140–43) is right in observing that the 'strong' probably understand κόσμος according to standard Greek usage: order, unity, beauty, and such like, and therefore are able to find legitimation for their idolatrous behaviour since only God is good and so is his world. But Paul disagrees with such an understanding and believes that there are real spiritual powers. For a thorough treatment of κόσμος in its linguistic and historical backgrounds, see Adams (2000: 41–77).

95. There is unlikely any distinction between 'gods' and 'lords' intended here. See Robertson and Plummer (1911: 167) who do not see any distinction between 'gods' and 'lords'; Barrett (1968: 192) notes that the use of 'gods' and 'lords' is in view of the double statement which follows about God the Father and the Lord Jesus Christ; Conzelmann (1975: 143) cautions against taking the distinction too strictly. Fee (1987: 373) and Hays (1997: 139) take the 'gods' to be the traditional Graeco-Roman deities while 'lords' to be the figures venerated in mystery cults. In view of Paul's emphasis that what the pagans worship are not gods, it seems that Conzelmann's caution is worth our attention. See also Klauck (2000: 28–29) for a discussion of the gods.

96. Willis 1985a: 86.

97. The basic Greek idea of οὐρανός has a double reference (*TDNT* 5.497ff), which refers to heaven as the firmament over the earth, and as encompassing all things in an absolute sense. In LXX, the usage is meant to add vividness and concreteness to what is 'above', and to express the transcendence of God. Although there seems to be a plurality of heavens in Judaism, the concept has never been separated from the concept of a realm above the physical earth, except in some quarters of Hellenistic Judaism (e.g. *1 En.* 71.5–10). But in the New Testament, its use with the earth (γῆ) often comes from the Old Testament and corresponds to the LXX. Traub (*TDNT* 5.518) argues that the concept in Pauline usage means that the saving event in Jesus Christ results in God's rule over all, i.e. heaven and earth. Cf. Rom. 8.38–39.

98. Dio Chrysostom's mouthpiece Pheidias gives a vivid picture of how humans yearned for the gods like children who had been separated from their parents yearned for the latter (see Dio Chrysostom, *Or.* 60–61). This shows how humans came to venerate the gods through worshipping the idols, with which they represent the gods. Thus Klauck (2000: 27) correctly concludes that the god is never absorbed into his image, nor is he fully identical to it.

5. *Paul's Use of* εἴδωλον[99]

Although the term εἴδωλον is rarely used as a reference to the image of a divine person or being by the Greeks, its meaning as 'phantom', 'image', 'form' or 'shadow'[100] could have constituted part of the conception among Jews. Philo, for example, uses εἴδωλον to refer to what is unreal or deceptive.[101] The Jewish usage of the term is primarily pejorative, as demonstrated in Chapters 2 and 3.[102]

In Chapter 3, we have demonstrated the hostile attitude of Diaspora Jews towards idolatry and their negative description of idols, and how such attitude fits our definitions of idolatry in Chapter 2. While we have seen Jewish parallels to the 'strong' in Chapter 4, how does Paul's position compare with the Jewish attitudes in the Diaspora? This question requires us to look into Paul's view of idols.

There are seven occurrences of the term in the undisputed letters. It is found once each in Romans, 2 Corinthians, and 1 Thessalonians, while the rest in 1 Corinthians. Of those found in 1 Corinthians three are in 1 Corinthians 8–10. It is worth looking at these uses.

Romans 2.22 consists of two questions which are among a series Paul poses to Jews concerning the law.[103] And Paul's second question (βδελυσσόμενος τὰ εἴδωλα ἱεροσυλεῖς; v. 22b) implies that the Jews abhor idols.[104] The word βδελύσσεσθαι, whose only other occurrence in the New Testament is in Rev. 21.8, means not only 'abhorring' but also 'detesting' something that is 'abominable'.[105] The word was also found in a papyrus to refer to hatred for the Jews

---

99.   In this section, I will confine myself to Paul's view of εἴδωλον without looking at the use of the term in the LXX, as I have already demonstrated in Chapter 2 the definitions and patterns of idolatry in the LXX. Here, it is sufficient to state that the term is used in the LXX to translate as many as 18 Hebrew words that refer to different forms of idolatry and idols (this does not include other LXX texts outside of the Hebrew Bible). These terms are אל, אלוה, אלה, אליל, במה, בעל, גלולים, הבל, המן, מפלצת, עצב, עצב, פסילים, לסף, צלם, שעיר, שקוץ, תרפים, of which עצב appears in two different forms (taken from Hatch and Redpath [1998: 376]; see Büchsel [1964: 377]). Although Newton (1998: 128–31) has carried out a very helpful survey of the term's pre-Christian usage, he rightly observes that the use of the term as a reference to divinity is rare (130, 131). The use of the term in the LXX seems overwhelmingly negative in all the cases when the term is used.

100.   BAGD 221.

101.   E.g. *Conf. Ling.* 69, 71, 74; *Omn. Prob. Lib.* 146; *Praem. Poen.* 19.

102.   Büchsel (1964: 377–78) observes that the Greeks 'have no comprehensive expression for what the Jews call εἴδωλον. The language of the LXX is biblical or Jewish Greek in this respect. Jewish religion has coined a new expression out of an existing term' (377).

103.   This is particularly explicit in v. 17: εἰ δὲ σὺ Ἰουδαῖος ἐπονομάζῃ καὶ ἐπαναπαύῃ νόμῳ καὶ καυχᾶσαι ἐν θεῷ (but if you call yourself a Jew and rely on the law and boast in God); and v. 24 where Isa. 52.5 is quoted as saying that the name of God is being blasphemed among the Gentiles 'because of you' (δι᾽ ὑμᾶς).

104.   We have already seen such Jewish attitude in Chapter 3 above. However, Barrett's (1991: 54) statement that 'the Jew regards an idol with horror because it claims a devotion to which only the true God is entitled' is too simplistic, as we have shown in Chapter 4 that Jews may not always view an idol with horror. And as the 'strong' also demonstrate, idols are not always viewed with horror.

105.   BAGD 138. Cf. Josephus, *War* 6.172; *Ant.* 14.45. Moo (1996: 163 n. 32) suggests that this word, i.e. βδελύσσεσθαι is used in the LXX with reference to idols. Cranfield (1975: 169 n. 4),

(*CPJ* I, no. 141). Paul's use here reflects the Jews' attitude which he certainly approves. But his question suggests that he equates the 'condemnable-ness' of the Jews with that of the idols, which indicates he views both negatively.[106] And his attitude towards the idols is pejorative.[107] Paul's use of the term εἴδωλον in 1 Thess. 1.9 would illuminate more on this attitude.

In 1 Thess. 1.9, Paul simply states that the Thessalonians have turned to God from idols (ἐπεστρέψατε πρὸς τὸν θεὸν ἀπὸ τῶν εἰδώλων) to serve a 'living and true God' (θεῷ ζῶντι καὶ ἀληθινῷ).[108] While nothing is said about the 'idols', the description of the Thessalonians' 'turning', involving the two words, πρός and ἀπό,[109] and of God as 'living and true', shows that the 'idols' are 'non-living and untrue'. Thus, Best is right in saying that '(I)n contradistinction to false and non-existent idols, God is described as **real** and **living**' (emphasis original).[110] The reverse is true; that is, in saying that they have turned to the 'living and true' God, Paul is saying that the idols are neither 'living' nor 'true'.[111] What it means, therefore, is that the idols have no life, and therefore cannot produce truth. Any claim about the truth that purportedly comes from the idols is therefore falsehood. This idea is also reflected in 2 Cor. 6.16, where Paul juxtaposes the temple of God and the idols and insists there should be no relation between the two.[112] Plummer argues that the opposition is between God's temple and the images of false gods.[113] The point of this comparison is the term

however, rightly cautions against such a notion. Dunn (1988: 114) brings our attention to the fact that βδέλυγμα which means 'abomination' is often a reference to idolatry; see e.g. Isa. 2.8, 20; Dan. 11.31.

106. Cranfield (1975: 169) posits that Paul is saying the Jews are not free from idolatry's taint and that they use the stolen articles because they think there is no longer idolatry in Israel; cf. Strack-Billerbeck (III, 111–13), cited in Cranfield (1975: 169); see also his n. 5.

107. Cf. Josephus, *Ant.* 4.207b. Philo, *Conf. Ling.* 163, equates theft, adultery, and robbing temples. See Chapter 3, section 3, c and d on Philo and Josephus, respectively.

108. Best (1972: 85–87) is of the view that 1 Thess. 1.9b, 10 contain a pre-Pauline statement of the church's faith, on the basis that several words are used which either are not normally used or are used in an unusual way (e.g. 'turned', 'real', 'to serve', 'out of heaven', 'wait', the use of the article in the formula 'raised from the dead', etc.). The only Pauline favourite term is εἴδωλον. Further, Paul always makes the cross the content of the Christian faith, but not so here. Cf. Bruce 1982: 17–18).

109. BDF §239 and §180 respectively. The combined use of πρός and ἀπό is significant in that an antithesis is not only made very clear but also forceful.

110. Best 1972: 82.

111. Thus Frame (1912: 87) refers to them as dead and false, 'not being what they purport to be'.

112. Martin (1986: 201) says that Paul sees idolatry as suggesting 'the element of the licentious and immoral behaviour that accompanied the sin of worshipping false deities'. Whether or not Paul has in mind a temple of idols is not clear. In the first-century Graeco-Roman world there certainly were many pagan temples. But Martin's (1986: 201–202) point is valid that Paul has applied the concept of the physical Temple in Jerusalem to the understanding of the believers as the spiritual temple of God. Thus, 'the introduction of an "idol" causes the temple to be defiled and so rendered unworthy of God' (202).

113. Plummer 1915: 208. Could this be an allusion to 2 Kgs 21.7 and 23.6 where Manasseh had put a graven image of Ashera in the temple of the Lord, which Josiah later removed and burnt? There is no evidence to suggest that Paul is alluding to this particular event. However, he certainly has in mind the believers' status as God's people and possibly their association with or participation in idolatry.

συγκατάθεσις, which, though it is a *hapax* in the New Testament, is found in
Hellenistic writers such as Philo (e.g. *Poster. C.* 175; *Vit. Mos.* 2.228). And it
means 'union', 'agreement'.[114] The reason Paul is making this point is that the
believers are the temple of the 'living God',[115] suggesting again that idols are
non-living things. Hence, there can be no συγκατάθεσις between the two.

In the occurrences of the term in 1 Corinthians, Paul clearly views idols as
nothing. In 1 Cor. 8.4, he agrees with the Corinthians about an idol's insignificance
(see section 3 above); and in 12.2, he says they were formerly led astray by 'dumb
idols' (τὰ εἴδωλα τὰ ἄφωνα),[116] thus revealing his views on idols as similar to
those of the Diaspora Jews discussed in Chapter 3. And in 1 Cor. 10.20 Paul
disagrees with the 'strong', by arguing that there is a difference between idols and
the actual object the pagans worship. This subtle distinction that Paul is making
between δαιμόνια and εἴδωλα can be further seen in his understanding of the
gods and lords in heaven and on earth and his use of the Deuteronomy passage.[117]

6. *The Distinction between εἴδωλα and δαιμόνια in Paul*

Thus far our discussion reveals that Paul and the 'strong' may share the same
opinion about the idols but differ over the application of this knowledge. For the
'strong', it means they could do what they liked because idols were nothing. For
Paul, because idols are nothing, one must not have anything to do with them.

We have also raised the possibility that Paul understands there is more to idols
than their physical insignificance. Our discussion above indicates that Paul
believes there are evil spirits behind the idols the pagans worship, and he seems
to draw a distinction between εἰδώλα and δαιμόνια. Further, Paul's reference to
many gods and many lords ἐπὶ γῆς (and ἐν οὐρανῷ) indicates his full
awareness of the religious pluralism in the Graeco-Roman world, not least in
Corinth. Among the pagan gods are cults with shrines and temples built in their
name. For example, the shrine of Athena (Minerva); the shrine of Hera (Juno)
near the Fountain of Glauke; various sanctuaries of Apollo (including the

114. BAGD 773.

115. Although there is a textual variant here over the words ἡμεῖς and ναός, it is the word ζῶντος
that is more relevant here.

116. Thiselton (2000: 911–12) ably defends a translation of 'you used to be carried away to idols
that were incapable of speech'; similarly, Fee (1987: 576–77). This is similar to 1 Thess. 1.9. See,
however, the implausible idea of Conzelmann (1975: 205), and also his n. 13, that this could mean
'demons'. See also Robertson and Plummer (1911: 259–60) and Barrett (1968: 278–79) who argue
that with regard to the idols Paul's point is they are dumb and have no answers to questions.

117. Cf. Epistle of Jeremiah, whose author encourages the Jews not to fear the pagan idols because
they are no gods, by pouring scorn on the pagan idols. Throughout, the refrain that the pagan idols are
no gods (οὐκ εἰσὶ θεοί) is repeatedly emphasized (vv. 16, 23, 29, 49, 51, 56, 65, 69, 72). The author
draws a distinction between the idols, which he scornfully ridicules, and the 'gods' whom the exiled
Israelites might fear. The author's point in the letter, therefore, is to allay the fear among the people
by exposing the idols of Babylon as οὐκ εἰσὶ θεοί. In other words, there is the implication that there
are 'gods' in the world. And this could well be a parallel to Paul's statement in 1 Cor. 8.5 that there
are many gods and many lords.

Peribolos of Apollo and the Temple of Apollo); the temple of Aphrodite-Tyche (Venus-Fortune); a temple of all the gods; a temple of Heracles; a temple of Poseidon; the sanctuary of Asklepios and Aphrodite and the like.[118] Sawyer observes that on the ascent to the Acrocorinth, there were many small temples of foreign cults, such as the Egyptian Isis and Sarapis.[119] Could Paul have made a distinction between the idols of these gods and the 'spirits' behind them?[120] We now turn to look at Paul's quotation of the Deuteronomy passage, which will shed more light on this.

Paul's use of the Deuteronomy passage and the original passage in the LXX bear little difference except that, in his use of the LXX passage he contemporizes the Israelites of Deuteronomy 32 and applies the sense to the pagans of the Graeco-Roman world.[121] In Deut. 32.17, the Israelites probably thought they were worshipping the true God (cf. Chapter 3). And if Deuteronomy 32 is a reference to the golden calf incident, then the possibility of this idea that the Israelites thought they were worshipping the true God is further strengthened. Scholars continue to disagree over what οὐ θεῷ means. Does it mean 'to a no-god', as Robertson and Plummer have argued,[122] or 'not to a god', as Grosheide has so posited,[123] or 'not to God',[124] which NIV, RSV and NRSV render, or 'to that which is not God', as REB translates it? Or is it to be rendered 'to demons who are not God' according to NJB? The way to resolve this exegetical difficulty is by looking at the meaning of each rendering and comparing it with the most probable meaning which the context of 1 Cor. 10.14–22 allows.

Robertson and Plummer's rendering, 'no-god', refers to an object of the sacrifices but denies it has any divinity. REB's rendering appears similar to that of

118. Pausanias, in his description of Corinth (2.2.6–2.5.4), provides a very helpful list of gods and goddesses, which sheds light on the religiously pluralistic environment of the Corinthian church. See also Sawyer (1968: 76–77). See Newton (1998: 91–114) for an updated discussion of the archaeological evidence for the Corinthian cults.

119. Pausanias 2.4.6; cf. Sawyer 1968: 77. See Gooch (1993: 2–5) for his discussion on the archaeological findings on Demeter and Kore.

120. Cf. Fee (1987: 473) where he takes the view that these gods such as Sarapis and Isis are 'demons'.

121. In Deut. 32.17, it is part of the Song of Moses in which Moses is recorded to recount the idolatrous acts of the Israelites in worshipping other gods and strange gods, whom their ancestors never worshipped. In 1 Cor. 10.20, Paul uses this to apply to the pagans, since the idols represent the pagan gods, and since it is the pagan temples which the Corinthian 'strong' visit and where they eat idol-meat. This does modify the LXX text of Deut. 32.17. However, such an application also suggests that Paul retains the meaning of the term δαιμόνια.

122. Robertson and Plummer (1911: 216) have based their position on Deut. 32.21 which, in the LXX, reads αὐτοὶ παρεζήλωσάν με ἐπ᾽ οὐ θεῷ...κἀγὼ παραζηλώσω αὐτοὺς ἐπ᾽ οὐκ ἔθνει ('they have made me jealous with a no-god...and I will make them jealous with a no-people').

123. Grosheide (1953: 235) thinks that the οὐ θεῷ refers to 'not to a god' on the basis that Gentiles did not bring their sacrifices to the true God. However, Gentiles would not agree; and the Corinthians might still think that the pagan sacrifices were meant for the true God, as it is entirely possible that the believers themselves have thought otherwise about the gods of the pagans.

124. This makes the assumption that the worshippers and those who witness their worship think the sacrifices are meant for the true God. The rendering is therefore meant to contrast between 'demons' and the true God.

Robertson and Plummer.[125] Both of these renderings would almost equate the object as a mere εἴδωλον, which neither the context of Deut. 32.17 nor that of 1 Cor. 10.14–22 allow, as the use of the term δαιμόνια suggests more is meant.[126] Grosheide's rendering recognizes the existence of 'a god' as a divinity, but denies the sacrifices are made to him. Such a rendering has the potential of confusion over the distinction between 'a god' and 'demons'. NJB's translation, unfortunately, is right in what it says but wrong in what it does not say. 'Demons' are indeed not God; and the sacrifices are indeed made to them, as Paul clearly argues. But the idea of οὐ θεῷ is not brought out at all.

The context of 1 Cor. 10.14–22, particularly Paul's contrast of the table of δαιμόνια with that of the Lord, suggests the rendering 'not to God' to be more likely, of which the 'God' is a reference to the true God.[127] This is particularly clear in vv. 21–22, where Paul argues that the 'strong' cannot be partners of 'demons' and the Lord at the same time. Further, if the 'strong' think that the object of the pagans' sacrifice is the true God, a point already made earlier, hence their free and accommodating attitude towards pagan temples and idol-meat, then it is not surprising that Paul should press the point that the object of the pagan sacrifices is 'not to God'. Such an attitude is not without parallels. In Chapter 4 above we have seen the parallels of such an identification of the true God with other gods in *The Letter of Aristeas* as well as the conceptual overlap in both Jewish and pagan uses of Theos Hypsistos revealed by inscriptional sources. Paul's statement could well be meant to draw out the distinction between the true God and the dead and dumb idols which represent the δαιμόνια. And in 1 Cor. 10.14, Paul continues his warning to the 'strong' to 'flee from idolatry' (φεύγετε ἀπὸ τῆς εἰδωλολατρίας), after his explication of the danger of idolatry. This is followed by the juxtaposition of the table of the Lord and the table of δαιμόνια. For Paul, the table of the Lord represents the Christian tradition which recalls the suffering of Christ for the believers (cf. 1 Cor. 8.11).[128] Therefore, drinking the cup and eating the bread at the Lord's table is a 'sharing' (κοινωνία, 1 Cor. 10.16)

125. Although REB's rendering seems similar to that of NJB's, the former emphasizes the fact that the object is not God, while the latter emphasizes that the objects of the sacrifices are demons with a qualification that they are not God.

126. Even if the Deut. 32.17 can be shown to mean no more than merely 'to a no-god', Paul's idea of δαιμόνια would suggest that he has injected a new idea into an Old Testament concept. Conzelmann (1975: 172) believes that Paul is here contradicting himself: the 'gods' are non-existent, but yet Paul regards them as real, that is, demons. But see Barrett (1968: 237) who thinks that Paul does not believe the idols are anything in the world, but still believes in the 'reality of an unseen spirit-world'.

127. *Pace* Fee (1987: 472 n. 47) who finds 'not to God' irrelevant as he argues that Paul does not intend to say that pagans are not sacrificing to God. Thus, Fee takes this to mean 'not to a god' or 'to demons, even to one who is no-god'. However, Fee's idea of Paul's intention is based on the assumption that the Corinthians have a neatly thought out conception of God. If the 'strong' were to think otherwise, i.e. that the pagans also worship the true God but by another name (just as pseudo-Aristeas shows us), then Paul would more likely be saying to the 'strong' that they are mistaken and that the pagans in fact sacrifice to 'demons' and not to God.

128. Cf. Mitchell (1991: 254–56) who argues that Paul is appealing to cultic ties to unite (or reconcile) the divided Corinthians again.

in Christ's blood and body, that is, his suffering.[129] Von Soden has theorized that the 'strong' (whom he refers to as Corinthian Gnostics) have the misconception that their initiation into Christ through the sacraments has gained them the spiritual security against all 'charm'.[130] But there is no evidence to suggest this.[131] The reasons for the behaviour of the 'strong' are most likely their γνῶσις[132] and 'freedom'. Paul's mention of the Lord's Supper need not be because he wants to counter a 'super-sacramental' view of the Lord's Supper.[133] What he wants to do, more likely, is to stress the status of the 'strong', that is, they are 'partners' of the body of Christ, and therefore must be faithful to Christ. But it is with the Christian tradition of the Eucharist that Paul puts forward the argument that those Israelites who ate the sacrifices in fact became 'partners' (κοινωνοί) of the altar (1 Cor. 10.18; cf. Exod. 32.4–6),[134] a possible allusion to Isa. 65.11 where the Israelites are said to have forsaken the Lord and set up a 'table' for Fortune. In that passage, the sins of the Israelites are twofold: the forsaking of Yahweh and the setting up of a table and filling up of the cups with wine. This constitutes the Israelites' 'unfaithfulness' to Yahweh as they disregarded their ancestral tradition and turned to worship an alien cult.[135] The worship of the alien cult by the Israelites is described as 'preparing a table for the demon' (ετοιμάζοντες τῷ

129. Robertson and Plummer (1911: 212–13) forcefully argue that Paul's point is that by eating idol-meat before the pagan idols is to 'become a sharer in the Sacrificial Act, and all that that involves'. Thus, Paul is making a clear distinction between the idols which he agrees with the 'strong' are nothing (which he reiterates in 1 Cor. 10.19), and the 'demons' which he believes are spiritual forces; see also Thiselton (2000: 775–76).

130. Von Soden 1972: 257–68; similarly, Barrett 1968: 220–29; Conzelmann 1975: 167; Fee 1987: 443; Yeo 1995: 160, 176; Witherington III 1995: 220; Oropeza 2000: 110–11.

131. The statement closest to such a suggestion is v. 12, where Paul warns against those who think they stand lest they fall. But it still does not show that the 'strong' think they have secured their salvation through the sacraments. Mitchell (1991: 139, 251–52) stresses that Paul is not countering such a sacramental view, because, she maintains, Paul is merely sketching out the analogy with the Corinthians.

132. Gardner (1994: 141–43) argues that the Corinthians probably regarded themselves as having the gifts of the Spirit, particularly γνῶσις. However, he does not discuss the aspect of ἐξουσία of the 'strong'.

133. Against Oropeza (2000: 109), who objects to Gardner's argument against the 'sacramental' interpretation' (see Gardner 1994: 141–43) on the basis of Paul's mention of the Lord's Supper in 1 Cor. 10.16–22 and 11.17–34. But the mention of the Lord's Supper in 1 Cor. 10.16–22 could well be Paul's basis for rejecting the idolatrous behaviour of the 'strong', as he argues that he does not want the 'strong' to be partners of both the table of demons and of the Lord; whereas the detailed discussion of the Lord's Supper in 1 Cor. 11.17–34 has a rather different context.

134. Fee (1987: 470–71) takes this to be a reference to the meals prescribed in Deut. 14.22–27. However, the use of the designation τὸν Ἰσραὴλ κατὰ σάρκα (Israel according to the flesh) in 1 Cor. 10.18 could suggest that Paul has in mind the idolatrous Israel during the wilderness experience. And just as Fee (1987: 470 n. 38) says that κατὰ σάρκα seems to imply that there is another Israel κατὰ πνεῦμα, the Israel κατὰ σάρκα may well be a reference to Israel that acted in the way of the flesh, that is, in idolatry.

135. See Chapter 2 above for our definition of idolatry. Yeo (1995: 173) comments: '…the use of the Lord's Supper in the argument is meant to imply that exclusive loyalty to God (thus prohibition against idolatry) should derive from the Corinthians' κοινωνία (sharing) of God's love. In other words, idolatry is the practice of communion with demons, which is infidelity.'

δαιμονίῳ τράπεζαν) and 'filling up the drink offering to Fortune' (πληροῦντες τῇ τύχῃ κέρασμα). The word τύχη is a rendering of the Hebrew גד, which is a god's name meaning Fortune.[136] Another god's name, מני, is found in the Hebrew but not translated in the Greek. It means a 'god of destiny'. It appears that the translators of the LXX did not see a great difference between these deities. As far as they were concerned, the table the Israelites had set up was basically set up for the 'demon', and, together with the 'filling of the cup', they both refer to 'cultic meals eaten in honor of these deities'.[137] Thus the Israelites in Isa. 65.11 are guilty of being partners of 'demons'. And if Paul has in mind Isa. 65.11 when he mentions the table of demons, then he must have regarded the eating of idol-meat by the 'strong' a 'partnership' with demons and therefore an act of unfaithfulness against Christ. The repeated use of the phrase, 'as some of them were/did', in vv. 6-10 indicates that Paul views the act of eating idol-meat to be similar to the idolatrous acts of the Israelites in the wilderness.[138]

Paul's statement in vv. 20b and 21b suggests that the 'strong' have participated in some form of pagan sacrifices.[139] And Fee rightly points out that the language of the Christian meal[140] points to the 'vertical dimension' of the 'binding covenantal relationship' the Corinthians have with Christ.[141] The 'strong' cannot be simultaneously 'partners' of the Lord's table (cf. 1 Cor. 10.17) and that of the 'demons' (1 Cor. 10.21).[142] However, like the 'unfaithful' Israelites who disregarded the ancestral tradition, the 'strong' have breached the covenant with Christ. Thus Paul rhetorically asks whether the 'strong' are trying to 'provoke' the Lord to jealousy (v. 22), an allusion to Deut. 32.16. He is here evoking, intertextually,[143] all the three passages, Deuteronomy 32, Psalm 95, and Isaiah 65,

---

136. See Liddell and Scott (1940: 1839). A closely related concept of τύχη is 'providence'. It is possible that the Israelites were offering to a 'god' identified as Fortune on a more cognitive level. The relation to 'Destiny' or the 'god of destiny' might suggest such a possibility.

137. Watts 1987: 345.

138. The phrases may differ, but they all refer to what the Israelites 'did': καθὼς κἀκεῖνοι ἐπεθύμησαν (v. 6); καθὼς τινες αὐτῶν (vv. 7, 8, 9); καθάπερ τινὲς αὐτῶν (v. 10). Robertson and Plummer (1911: 203) argue that this phrase 'assumes that the Corinthians have done what they are here charged not to do'. This does not explain the phrase well, as it means that prior to the writing of 1 Corinthians Paul had, in the same way that he is now warning them, charged them not to participate in idolatry. Fee (1987: 452) puts it differently: 'Paul does not want what happened to Israel to be repeated in their (the Corinthians') case; the danger lies in their repetition of Israel's sins (vv. 7–10), which if persisted in will then lead to similar judgment'. Similarly Hays (1997: 162). See Thiselton (2000: 731–32) and Gardner (1994: 150–52) for a thorough discussion.

139. See Cheung (1999: 114, 118) who implausibly hints that the 'strong' have brought the idol food from the pagan temple to the church for consumption during worship in the church but agrees that this is not altogether certain.

140. Cf. Conzelmann (1975: 174) who says that this is an allusion to 'competition' between the pagan meals and the Christian Lord's Supper.

141. Fee 1987: 473.

142. Cf. 2 Cor. 6.16 where, building upon his argument in 1 Cor. 10.21, Paul argues that the temple of God (i.e. the Corinthian church) has nothing in common with idols as the former is the living God.

143. See Hays (1989), who proposes intertextuality as a model for interpreting Paul's use of the Old Testament. He explicates the phenomenon of intertextuality as 'the imbedding of fragments of an earlier text within a later one' (14). Thus, when it comes to Paul, Hays sees Paul as viewing himself

taking elements from each and interweaving them to bring home the point that the 'strong', by eating idol-meat in the pagan temple, are in fact committing acts of idolatry which turn them into partners with 'demons'.[144] For the 'strong', it is their ἐξουσία to attend pagan temples and eat idol-meat. Their 'knowledge' informs them that idols are nothing, and eating idol-meat is therefore a matter of indifference. But Paul is saying to them that it is not a matter of indifference, nor of 'freedom' to choose as they wish, but it is a matter of resisting 'temptation' (πειρασμός, 1 Cor. 10.13) and therefore of one's faithfulness to the Lord Jesus.[145] Such idolatrous behaviour also dishonours the true God by mixing him with δαι-μόνια. The 'strong' are therefore treading on highly dangerous grounds – they must beware, lest they fall (1 Cor. 10.12).

However, if the idols are not the primary concern for the 'strong', then there should be other reasons why they (the 'strong') think pagans still offer sacrifices to their idols. Just as the Israelites had gathered around their golden calves and proclaimed, 'These are your gods, O Israel, who brought you up out of the land of Egypt', the 'strong' could well think that even though idols are nothing, the pagans could be offering sacrifices to the true God. Thus, for the 'strong', the word εἴδωλον probably carries no pejorative meaning;[146] but for Paul, while idols in the sense of the physical object are nothing there are indeed gods and lords who are 'evil spirits' represented by the idols. Therefore, when the pagans sacrifice to their idols, they are in fact sacrificing to these 'evil spirits' whom Paul calls 'demons'.

7. *The Danger of Idolatry*

Paul urges the Corinthians to feel from τῆς εἰδωλολατρίας (1 Cor. 10.14). Thiselton argues that the covenant theme links 10.1–13 and 10.14–22. The

as a prophetic figure who proclaimed the Word of God as all the other prophets and sages had always done, but in a way that 'reactivated past revelation under new conditions' (14). For Hays, 'Paul's citations of Scripture often function…as tropes: they generate new meanings by linking the earlier text (Scripture) to the later (Paul's discourse) in such a way as to produce unexpected correspondences, correspondences that suggest more than they assert' (24).

144. Mitchell (1991: 255–56) mistakenly argues that by bringing in the question of 'partnership with demons', Paul is making a compromise position that allows him to urge the 'strong' to avoid cultic associations. Gundry-Volf (1990: 129–30) rightly says that Paul is wanting the 'strong' to adhere to Christ by having κοινωνία with Christ and by refusing to have any association with demons through cultic meals.

145. See Barrett (1968: 229) who views Paul's words in 1 Cor. 10.13 as implying that more severe trials are expected. Fee (1987: 460) argues for a double function. On the one hand, Paul is reassuring the Corinthians that they would not fall in the ordinary trials of life as there is always divine aid. On the other hand, they are therefore to flee from idolatry because there is no divine aid 'when one is "testing" Christ' through idolatry. Conzelmann (1975: 169) suggests the point here to be comfort for all, both the 'strong' and the 'weak', and that Paul is here referring to 'eschatological salvation'. This, however, misses the context of Paul's argument in 1 Corinthians 10. Hays (1997: 166) rightly points out that Paul is here contrasting the 'testing' that God allows and the dangers of 'testing' the Lord.

146. Although Philo (*Somn.* 2.133–35) views εἴδωλον as unreal phantoms, he draws a different conclusion, i.e. the idols are therefore dead and dumb. But the 'strong' do not express such negative views at all.

mention of the Lord's Supper and Paul's warning against becoming partners with demons lends weight to Thiselton's point. And if the covenant theme is present here, then it strengthens our case that what the 'strong' are doing in the presence of the idols is a breach of the covenant with Christ, and thus is an idolatrous sin.[147] For Paul, the 'strong' are 'idolatrous' by their eating in an idol's presence (1 Cor. 10.21).[148] And there is real danger if they continue in it. This is stated throughout 8.1–11.1. For example, 8.12 states that it is in fact a 'sinning' against Christ (εἰς Χριστὸς ἁμαρτάνετε). 9.27 subtly implies that the 'strong' can become 'disqualified' if they are not careful. In 10.9 Paul tells the 'strong' not to put Christ to the test, linking it to 8.12. The inclusion of Christ in his argument suggests that Paul intends to show the 'strong' that they do have a spiritual relationship with Christ which is, however, being tested by idolatry. Thus, in 10.12, a warning is given to those who think they stand, as they may fall if they are not careful.[149] And in 10.22, there is the warning that idolatrous behaviour of the 'strong' can arouse the Lord's jealousy (παραζηλοῦμεν τὸν κύριον;).[150] μὴ ἰσχυρότεροι αὐτοῦ ἐσμεν; Paul is therefore suggesting to the 'strong' that their idolatrous behaviour is a contest of strength against the Lord's.[151] And they will not stand because the Lord is stronger. The danger of idolatry is explicitly focused upon in 1 Cor. 9.24–10.12, where Paul uses first the analogy of the (Isthmian) games, before moving on to draw the conclusion on the basis of Old Testament.

a. *Indiscipline and disqualification*
1 Corinthians 9.24–27 brings out this reality very forcefully. For if the 'strong' were to persist in their unscrupulous eating of idol-meat, then they are running a race for which they might lose their prize.[152] Paul likens the Christian life to running a race (i.e. Isthmian games),[153] for which discipline is indispensable. In

147. Thiselton 2000: 750. See also Yeo (1995: 172), who rightly argues that 10.14–22 is a climax of 10.1–22.

148. Fee (1987: 441 n. 1) observes that the failure of many interpreters in recognizing this reality is the reason why many of them have great difficulty with either vv. 1–13 or vv. 14–22 or both. Gardner (1994: 169–70) suggests that Paul is here trying to stress the issue of worshipping the one true God. This way of looking at the attendance of the 'strong' in an idol's temple raises the issue of obedience to the first and second commandments, which defines the behaviour of the 'strong' as idolatrous. See Chapter 2 for our definition of idolatry and the discussion of the first and second commandments. See also section 2 above for our brief overview of the idolatry of the 'strong'.

149. The basic theme of falling and its cause have been the basis for scholarly works on the 'perseverence' of Christians, of which the recent more notable ones are Gundry-Volf (1990) and Oropeza (2000).

150. Cf. Gardner 1994: 171.

151. See Oropeza (2000: 156) who thinks that Paul probably has in mind Israel's wilderness 'testing' of Yahweh.

152. Gardner (1994: 106) argues that Paul's emphasis here is on the completion of the race, hence the 'prize'. If the 'strong' fail to complete the 'race' by giving up their rights to eat idol-meat, they would then forfeit their 'imperishable' prize, which is eschatological (Fee 1987: 437). Paul's point is that the 'strong' 'must let the goal determine their present behaviour' (Gundry-Volf 1990: 237)

153. According to Murphy-O'Connor (1983: 14–16), the (Isthmian) games were initiated in the early-sixth century BCE but passed on to the neighbouring town of Sicyon after Corinth was sacked in

such a race, self-control (ἐγκρατεύεται, v. 25)[154] is of utmost importance as part of the preparation for the contest.[155] And the 'strong' are aware of this. Paul wants to emphasize that discipline determines victory in the games.[156] But by engaging in idolatry, the 'strong' will lose the race and become 'disqualified' (ἀδόκιμοι);[157] the reverse is the prize (an imperishable wreath)[158] – the eschatological salvation. Like Paul, they should avoid 'disqualification' (ἀδόκιμος, v. 27).[159] In other words, what the 'strong' do in the present has implications for the future. And they will either win or lose the race, with no option 'in between'. The question is neither that of indifference nor 'rights' or 'freedom', it is about succumbing to temptations (πειρασμός),[160] and about idolatry – how they relate to 'idols'/'phantoms'/demons. Paul therefore views their behaviour as 'unfaithful', and their conceptions about God wrong. And regardless of their intentions, their idolatrous involvement in the temple would have been acts of worship. In other words, some of those definitions as set out in Chapter 2 are operative in Paul.

Paul is therefore raising the stakes here. The 'strong' face the danger of eschatological 'destruction', despite their present spiritual 'status' of being Christians who are baptized into Christ and are partakers of the Lord's Supper.[161] The

---

146 BCE. The (Isthmian) games were held every two years; Corinth recovered the administration of the games sometime between 7 BCE and 3 CE, after it was established as a Roman colony.

154. The word ἐγκρατεύομαι carries the meanings of 'controlling oneself', 'abstaining from something'; BAGD 216. Cf. 1 Cor. 7.9.

155. Cf. Philo, *Omn. Prob. Lib.* 26, and *Prov.* 2.58.

156. Fee 1987: 433 n. 1; *contra* Conzelmann (1975: 162 n. 31) who does not think there is any connection between what Paul says and the games, even though he acknowledges that the games were widespread then.

157. Although Paul uses the word ἀδόκιμος to refer to himself, the context shows that he is implying the possible 'disqualification' of the 'strong' if they do not exercise their ἐξουσία carefully but allow it to cause others to fall and thus put a hindrance in the way of the gospel. See BAGD 18. *Contra* Thiselton (2000: 717). Cf. Gardner (1994: 107) who argues otherwise.

158. Barrett (1968: 216–17) argues that this means the 'share' in the gospel, which refers to the 'benefits' of the gospel in 1 Cor. 9.23. However, he does not explain what these benefits are. Fee (1987: 437) interprets this to be the eschatological victory, which is the 'final salvation' (1987: 459).

159. The 'prize' is the antonym of ἀδόκιμος. Since in 1 Cor. 10.5, Paul speaks about the destruction of the Israelites in the wilderness, the 'prize' here would most likely be referring to 'salvation'. And in speaking of his own discipline, Barrett (1968: 218) argues that Paul wants his body to be brought out of the obedience to sin into the service of God. Thus, *contra* Thiselton (2000: 717), Paul seems to be saying that even his own salvation is not guaranteed by his conversion and other spiritual experiences. Gundry-Volf (1990: 120–25) argues forcefully that Paul's warning here includes both physical punishment and the loss of salvation.

160. Conzelmann (1975: 169) points out that this is not just a mere possibility but a reality in Corinth.

161. But this does not necessarily mean that the 'strong' adopt a magical view of the sacraments. Von Soden's (1972) theory that the 'strong' adopted a magical view of the sacraments, that is, they were protected from any harm by hostile spiritual powers, may be attractive. Fee (1980: 180, and 1987: 443) makes a similar point. However, given Paul's reminder to them in 1 Corinthians 11 to take a more serious approach to the Lord's Supper, it is not clear whether the Corinthians really have a high view of the sacraments. Further, there is no compelling evidence for the 'magical' view.

'eschatological salvation' of the 'strong' will depend on their 'discipline', which he further elaborates in 1 Cor. 10.1–12, using the Old Testament examples.

b. *Disqualification of Israel and its lessons*
In 1 Cor. 10.1–11, Paul uses five different Old Testament examples to show the reason why God punished the Israelites. But these are preceded by the introductory statement of the status of Israel in the wilderness (vv. 1–4) and the fact that God was displeased with most of them (v. 5). Verses 6–11 then set out five main examples of the Israelites' idolatrous behaviour.[162] These are: (1) the 'craving' for evil; (2) the idolatry of Israel in the wilderness (v. 7); (3) sexual immorality (v. 8); (4) testing the Lord (v. 9); and (5) murmuring against the Lord (v. 10). The warning in vv. 1–12 concerning the danger of idolatry comprises three parts. The first is the statement of Israel's status. The second is the various idolatrous acts of Israel. And the third is the summary statement of the warning of the possible fall. What is the status of Israel, how does Paul view it, and what is its relation to Paul's overall argument against the idolatry of the 'strong'?

In vv. 1–5, Paul argues that the ancestors of Israel supposedly fulfilled their 'ritualistic' requirements. In v. 2, he expounds the experiences of the Israelites in the wilderness in terms of the Christian rites of baptism and Eucharist.[163] However, as Conzelmann maintains, Paul does not seek a point-for-point correspondence, but to find a correspondence in the overall 'exodus' from Egypt to the overall Christian 'conversion' in the Corinthian church.[164] The Corinthians' conversion is signified by their baptism in Christ and their participation in the Lord's Supper.[165] In his use of explicit figurations, as Hays points out, Paul seeks to drive home the point that just as the Israelites thought they had escaped from Egypt under Moses and were therefore safe when they were not, so the 'strong' ought not to think that their 'conversion' from the 'dumb idols' (cf. 1 Cor. 12.2) to Christ would grant them immunity from punishment.[166] This thought is conveyed in v. 5, Ἀλλ’ οὐκ ἐν τοῖς πλείοσιν αὐτῶν εὐδόκησεν ὁ θεός. The term ἀλλά emphasizes the contrasting thought that even though the Israelites had followed Moses, God could still be displeased with them.[167] Thus following Moses is ruled

---

162. Even though some of these acts may not appear to be directly related to idolatry, our definition in Chapter 2 above does classify the five acts under idolatry. The following discussion will make clear this argument. See also Hays (1997: 164) who shows that in every of the examples food is the issue.

163. Cf. Fee (1987: 444) who views this as a prefiguring of the Corinthians, that is, the Old Testament examples are the 'types' of what the Corinthians (i.e. the 'strong') are experiencing; similarly, Héring (1962: 84). Conzelmann (1975: 165) argues that Paul is here looking at the church (i.e. the true Israel) in the light of a transformed understanding of the Israelites' wilderness experience. Cf. Hays 1989: 210 n. 18.

164. Conzelmann 1975: 165–66.

165. Thus Fee (1987: 443 n. 10) rightly and cautiously states that Paul's statement here is a mixture of 'type and 'analogy'; and by 'type', Fee means that Paul sees 'a correspondence between earlier biblical events and the present situation.

166. Hays 1989: 91.

167. See Thiselton (2000: 730) for the translation of ἀλλά here as an emphatic 'nevertheless'. Cf. Gardner 1994: 148.

out as a guarantee of God's favour. Subsequent behaviour with regard to the Israelites' faithfulness to the covenant God was instrumental to their continued blessing from God. Paul is therefore drawing parallels between the Israelites' experiences and the 'presumed spiritual security' of the 'strong' (based on their γνῶσις), and then deriving lessons from those experiences. Thus, in v. 6, he says, ταῦτα δὲ τύποι ἡμῶν ἐγενήθησαν.[168] We may tabulate the above in the following.

The Israelites' experiences	Paul's interpretation	Lesson for 'us'
ὑπὸ τὴν νεφέλην ἦσαν καὶ...διὰ τῆς θαλάσσης διῆλθον (1 Cor. 10.1; Exod. 13.21; 14.22).	εἰς τὸν Μωϋσῆν ἐβαπτίσθησαν ἐν τῇ νεφέλ καὶ ἐν τῇ θαλάσσῃ (1 Cor. 10.2).	Like us, i.e. the Corinthians who have received the baptism in Jesus' name, the Israelites had also been baptized, but into Moses.
...πάντες τὸ αὐτὸ πνευματικὸν βρῶμα ἔφαγον...πάντες τὸ αὐτὸ πνευματικὸν ἔπιον πόμα (1 Cor. 10.3–4a; Exod. 17.6).	ἔπιον γὰρ ἐκ πνευματικῆς ἀκολουθούσης πέτρας, ἡ πέτρα δὲ ἦν ὁ Χριστός (1 Cor. 10.4a).	While the Israelites appeared to be eating from the manna which came from heaven and drinking from the rock from which water flowed, the rock in fact accompanied them and it was Christ himself! We too, eat the same meal and drink the same drink.
Ἀλλ᾽ οὐκ ἐν τοῖς πλείοσιν αὐτῶν εὐδόκησεν ὁ θεός (1 Cor. 10.5a).	κατεστρώθησαν γὰρ ἐν τῇ ἐρήμῳ (1 Cor. 10.5b). Ταῦτα δὲ τύποι ἡμῶν ἐγενήθησαν...(1 Cor. 10.6a; cf. Num. 11.4–15, 31–35; 14.1–16).	Still, God was not pleased with most of them and he demonstrated his displeasure with the Israelites by destroying them. Similarly, since these are written down for our instructions, we too run the risk of facing God's wrath and 'destruction', if we are not faithful to his covenant.

As seen above, Paul seems to re-interpret the event of the wilderness wandering of the Israelites as a form of baptism. The idea of the people being baptised εἰς τὸν Μωϋσῆν is not mentioned in the Old Testament, nor can it be found in Jewish literature.[169] In trying to re-interpret the Israelites' experiences in the wilderness as examples and instructions for the 'strong' in Corinth, Paul would need to find the link that ties that two situations. The Christian formula 'into Christ'

168. Thus, Paul can say to them that if they think they know, they in fact do not really know (1 Cor. 8.2). He also implies that they do not really love God, and therefore are not known by God (1 Cor. 8.3). See Fee (1987: 368) and Thiselton (2000: 624–27) who recognize a clear connection between knowledge and love. Yeo (1995: 187) views Paul's words as a correction of the knowledge of the 'strong'. See also Willis 1985a: 81.

169. Cf. Barrett (1968: 221) explains that 'into Moses' has no Jewish parallel and that is was presumably made up by Paul on the basis of the Christian formula, 'into Christ'; similarly, Héring (1962: 86).

serves as a very important and useful category by which a link with the Israelites' experiences may be made. The reason is that it is the category of 'into Christ' that makes the 'conversion' of the Corinthian Christians meaningful and different. This is seen in, for example, Rom. 6.3 where Paul tells the Christians at Rome that their baptism into Christ Jesus (ἐβαπτίσθημεν εἰς Χριστὸν Ἰησοῦν) is equivalent to baptism into his death (εἰς τὸν θάνατον αὐτοῦ ἐβαπτίσθημεν).[170] Since the 'strong' have cited the *Shema*, the non-reality of idols, and their ἐξουσία as their justification for eating idol-meat, as we have seen in section 3 above, Paul's use of Old Testament examples is most apt. For it draws the parallels between the Israelites' presumed 'salvation' and that of the 'strong', and the Israelites' punishment and the same possible danger the 'strong' face by eating idol-meat.

Thus, the Israelites' experiences are not 'kinds of sacraments'. Rather, Paul is re-interpreting them in terms of the Christian sacraments.[171] The important point is his use of the word πνευματικός to describe the 'food' and 'drink' of the Israelites, which may be linked to his description of the Corinthians as not being πνευματικοί but ψυχικοί and σαρκικοί (1 Cor. 2.14; 3.1–4).[172] For if some of the Corinthians have claimed to be πνευματικοί (cf. 1 Cor. 14.37), then Paul's use of the word precisely points to the reality that even if they appear to be spiritual by virtue of their supposed participation in 'spiritual' acts, they are not thereby free from God's wrath. And when they, as partakers of the table of the Lord, also become partakers of the table of 'demons', they become precisely like the Israelites in the wilderness who become idolatrous and immoral.

Paul further says that the 'rock' from which water flowed was Christ,[173] thus giving a new spiritual understanding of the faithful God who provided the water through Christ.[174] A few key points concerning the function of 1 Corinthians 8–10 suggest that the issue of idolatry governs Paul's entire argument throughout the section, and thus his identification of the 'rock' as Christ, and vice versa is meant to make his parallels work. For example, in 8.1, Paul begins with περὶ δὲ τῶν εἰδωλοθύτων; in 9.1–23, he puts up a defence of his apostolic authority and sets himself as an example to the 'strong'; in 9.24–10.13, he then warns the 'strong' against idolatry, from which he urges them to flee in 10.14; and in 10.15–21, he continues his argument and points out the incompatibility of the

170. Although εἰς τὸν Χριστόν Ἰησοῦν is different from ἐν Χριστῷ, the former certainly makes the latter possible. And it is in this sense that the Corinthians' baptism 'into Christ' enables them to be 'in Christ'.

171. See our discussion in section 6 above, particularly n. 133.

172. Although 1 Cor. 3.1–4 is related to division in the church, 1 Corinthians 9, which we will discuss in the next chapter, is precisely about Paul's defence of his apostolic authority, which suggests that both chapters are related. Thus, it is possible that some of the 'strong' in 1 Corinthians 8–10 are among those whom Paul accuses of being of the flesh in 1 Corinthians 3.

173. Cf. Thiselton 2000: 727–30. On this as the pre-existent Christ, see Lietzmann (1931: 44–45), Conzelmann (1975: 166–67) and Fee (1987: 449). Others such as Hanson (1959: 79 [cited in Willis 1985a: 138 n. 65]), Robertson and Plummer (1911: 201) view the rock as the literal Christ. Barrett (1968: 222) sees this identification as a parallel to the Corinthians' experience.

174. Gardner 1994: 148. Thiselton 2000: 730. Cf. Hays 1989: 91.

Lord's table and the table of δαιμόνια. In other words, the issue throughout is idolatry, and Paul's use of the various examples is governed by this overarching issue. However, while Paul's view of idolatry is similar to those of the Diaspora authors discussed in Chapter 3 above, his concerns and questions take on a different stance in the light of Christ. For Paul, 'Christ' is the one with whom the Corinthians have entered into a covenant (cf. 1 Cor. 11.25).[175] And by identifying the 'rock' with Christ, Paul is stretching his language in order to show the parallels between the Israelites in the wilderness and the 'strong'. This allows him to establish the framework for determining what should be the proper behaviour for the 'strong', that is, the Old Testament examples of idolatry.[176] Thus, he can show that the Israelites' unfaithfulness to Yahweh parallels the unfaithfulness of the 'strong' to Christ.[177]

Further, Paul considers their idolatrous eating before the presence of the idols as 'partnership with demons' (1 Cor. 10.20–21),[178] whether they intend it or not. In Chapter 2, section 1, a, I have set out one of the definitions of idolatry as 'wrong kinds of worship', not only in terms of actions, but also intentions. In the case of the 'strong', they may not intend to be partners with 'demons', but their action renders them as such. Another definition of idolatry is that of mixing God with demons. And by being partners with 'demons', the 'strong' are also idolatrous by this definition of mixing God with 'demons'. Their action, moreover, renders them 'unfaithful'. Like the Israelites, the 'strong' have no guarantee of freedom from punishment for their idolatrous behaviour.

c. *The 'strong' crave for evil*
1 Corinthians 10.6 spells out Paul's view of the Old Testament events: they are written down for our instruction (ταῦτα δὲ τύποι ἡμῶν ἐγενήθησαν). But what kind of instruction, and what is the purpose of the instruction? Paul says it is for the purpose that believers may not 'crave evil'. There are at least two issues involved here. First is the word τύποι. It means 'types', or, as some translations have it, 'examples'.[179] Fee argues that Paul probably intends a meaning between

175. Thus, any act or behaviour that violates the covenant with Christ constitutes idolatry, just as unfaithfulness to the covenant with Yahweh renders the Israelites idolatrous, as the definitions of idolatry in Chapter 2 show.

176. Hays 1997: 159–60. See also Hays (1989: 92) who argues from intertextuality that the metaphor of the story of the Israelites in the wilderness creates a framework within which Paul judges the 'strong' and shows them what is the proper ethical response to their idolatrous behaviour.

177. See Oropeza (2000: 155–57), who connects Paul's caution against testing Christ with the question about provoking the Lord to jealousy in 10.22. While there is a possible link between the two, Paul clearly uses two very different words, i.e. ἐκπειράζω and παραζηλόω. It would be more correct to say that the former leads to the latter. That is to say, the behaviour of the 'strong' in eating idol-meat is an act of testing Christ which, if it is not stopped, will lead to the provocation of the Lord's 'zeal'.

178. Robertson and Plummer (1911: 217) unnecessarily conclude that the article suggests 'the demons' are regarded as a *society*. Rather, Fee (1987: 472–73) rightly states that it is simply idolatry that involves the worship of demons. Barrett (1968: 237) draws a difference between the personal relation and the eating.

179. Cf. Gardner (1994: 112–15), who prefers 'typology' to refer to 'an *attitude* or approach to

'these things have been made our examples' and 'these things have happened as types of us'.[180] The important point, however, is that Paul seems to be saying that the Israelites shared similar 'spiritual' experiences as the 'strong', and vice versa.[181] By inference, their fall or destruction would most likely happen to the 'strong' if the latter also do what they (i.e. the Israelites) did. And Paul is precisely concerned to make sure that what had happened to the Israelites never happens to the 'strong'. Hence, this leads to the second issue, which is the word ἡμῶν. Although the nature of the genitive is difficult to determine,[182] the genitive in the clause τύποι ἡμῶν indicates that it is 'us' for whom the τύποι are intended.[183] Further, the genitive ἡμῶν also links the Israelites' experiences to the situation in Corinth.[184] By using the genitive ἡμῶν, Paul creates an inseparable relation between what happened to Israel in the wilderness and what could possibly happen to the 'strong' in the present. There are five Old Testament examples.[185]

The first, 10.6, is a possible reference to Num. 11.4–34 which details the Israelites' craving for meat. Paul describes them as people who crave 'evil' (ἐπι-θυμητὰς κακῶν).[186] The Israelites did not accept what God had given them but 'craved' for meat and the abundant fish in Egypt. This parallels the Corinthian situation: the eating of idol-meat by the 'strong' may also be a craving after evil. And Paul could well view the eating of idol-meat by the 'strong' as an indication of their dissatisfaction with what they have (non-idolatrous food) and are (status without the freedom to freely eat idol-meat); and so view any such dissatisfaction with what God has given to be a form of 'rebellion'.[187] The second thing Paul

Scripture than to any particular *application* of Scripture' (italics original). After examining the use of the term 'midrash', Gardner chooses the phrase 'typological midrash' to describe 1 Cor. 10.1–13.

180. Fee 1987: 452.

181. It is clear that Paul views believers in Christ, whether they are Gentiles or Jews, as part of the new people of God through the new covenant in Christ. For example, in Rom. 11.17–24, Paul points out that Gentile believers are in fact branches grafted on to Israel. Hays (1989: 96–97) is right that the division between Jews and Gentiles is removed to the extent that Paul sees in the church a 'fundamental continuity' with Israel and its story. This would mean the story of Israel has a place in the ethical life of the new people of God.

182. Fee 1987: 451 n. 7; cf. Robertson and Plummer 1911: 203; Barrett (1968: 223–24) says the use of the word ἡμῶν indicates that Paul is including himself in the warning.

183. See Conzelmann (1975: 167) who translates this as 'examples for us'.

184. This further proves that Paul is here 'calling the shots', i.e. he is the authoritative apostle, the father of the Corinthians in Christ (1 Cor. 4.15b), who decides the framework for what constitutes idolatry, and how the framework is to be interpreted. On the authority of Paul, see Chapter 6 below.

185. Willis (1985a: 143) and Fee (1987: 453) see four examples. See, however, Héring (1962: 90–91); and particularly, Meeks (1995: 129), who illustrates more convincingly that there are five examples.

186. Cf. Barrett 1968: 224; Hays 1997: 162–63. Fee (1987: 452 n. 9) notes that the word ἐπιθυμία could have positive meanings, but is pejorative in this case and the two occurrences in the LXX (Num. 11.34; Prov. 1.22). Cf. Thiselton 2000: 733. See also the discussion of this word by Willis (1985a: 143–46). Cf. Num. 11.4, καὶ ὁ ἐπίμικτος ὁ ἐν αὐτοῖς ἐπεθύμησαν ἐπιθυμίαν, which is most likely behind Paul's thought (Meeks 1995: 129).

187. Numbers 11.15 shows that Moses wished to die rather than continue leading the people. The kind of 'craving' among the Israelites represented by their 'cries' are not a simple complaint. It is

might have in mind is the fact that the 'craving' of the Israelites suggests their desire for their former way of life in Egypt. When Paul uses this example of Israel as a way to warn the 'strong', it is highly possible that he is suggesting that by freely eating idol-meat and thus committing the sin of idolatry, the 'strong' are expressing their desire for their former way of life.[188] And if the 'strong' were to persist in eating idol-meat, then they are betraying God by disregarding their covenant with God, the covenant expressed in the sacraments of the church. As we have discussed in Chapter 2, section 1 above, such acts are clearly idolatrous.

A second and more explicit example is found in v. 7 which cites the LXX text of Exod. 32.6 verbatim. It reads, ἐκάθισεν ὁ λαὸς φαγεῖν καὶ πεῖν καὶ ἀνέστησαν παίζειν ('The people sat down to eat and to drink and rose up to play'). Scholars disagree over the meaning of the citation. Wayne Meeks, for example, argues that this is a midrash which Paul inserts into a homily (i.e. 10.1–13), and that the word παίζειν here is meant to include the list of all the five sins.[189] Fee argues that the exact citation gives the content of the 'evil things' mentioned in v. 6,[190] and is intentional so as to point out to the 'strong' that the Israelites '*ate* in the presence of the golden calf'.[191] Philo views the golden calf incident as an imitation of the Egyptian animal worship.[192] The LXX, however, explains this as an attempt by the Israelites to define for themselves their own religious belief when they declared, οὗτοι οἱ θεοί σου, Ἰσραηλ, οἵτινες ἀνεβίβασάν σε ἐκ γῆς Αἰγύπτου ('these are your gods, O Israel, who brought you out of the land of Egypt', Exod. 32.4).[193] It is, of course, entirely reasonable for Philo to suggest that this is an imitation of their former land. The important point about the citation is that it seems to be the climax of the idolatrous acts of Israel. Philo's description of the people's behaviour as 'revelling and carousing the livelong night, and unwary of the future', and as being 'wedded to their pleasant vices' suggests an understanding of the event as widespread rebellious behaviour resulting from the worship of the calf. Although this could involve not

possible that they might even border on 'rebellion' against Moses and stage a 'return' to Egypt. Cf. Num. 14.3, where the people were wanting to return to Egypt as a result of the uncertainties ahead.

188. By this, I am not suggesting that the 'strong' are either Gentiles, or Jews. What is important is that whether one is a Jew or a Gentile, it is possible for a Christian to desire the former way of life. In the case of idolatry, the former way of life for a Jew could well be conceptual idolatry (see Chapter 2, section 2, Chapter 4, sections 3 and 4), although it could also involve actual idol-worship or temple attendance (cf. Chapter 5, section 4). For a Gentile, it could of course be a return to actual idol worship. What is important for our purpose is that the 'strong', the 'weak' and Paul have all had Jewish influence (see Chapter 1, section 3, a to c, and f).

189. Meeks 1995: 124–36. Cf. Fee (1987: 454 n. 20) who views this as a 'dubious' suggestion. Barrett (1968: 225) and Conzelmann (1975: 167) rightly link the citation to idolatry. Cf. Hurd (1983: 143), who argues that Paul's condemnation of idolatry in 10.1-22 is hypothetical as he (Paul) has not heard of anything idolatrous in Corinth. This is trivialising the matter to which Paul has painstakingly devoted three chapters for discussion.

190. Fee 1987: 454. Thus, Fee views vv. 6–13 as comprising four, rather than five, sins.

191. Fee 1987: 454. See also Yeo 1995: 170. Cf. Conzelmann 1975: 167 n. 33.

192. *Vit. Mos.* 2.162; *Spec. Leg.* 3.125.

193. The difference is subtle, but the point is that the golden calf is proclaimed as '*your* gods', not the gods of the Egyptians.

only idolatrous worship of the golden calf, but also sexual play, as the word παίζειν in the context of Exodus 32 might suggest[194] – and as Fee argues this is further borne out by the various descriptions of the Israelites in Exod. 32.25 as 'breaking loose' and 'running wild' – it is not altogether certain since Exodus 32 is relatively quiet about the sexual play.[195] The point of Exodus 32 is meant as an explicit demonstration of the wrath of God against the people who worship the golden calf (cf. Exod. 32.35). Paul therefore quotes it to demonstrate the displeasure of God with idolatry.[196]

The third Old Testament example is the immorality of the Israelites in the wilderness (v. 8). This verse is often regarded as a reference to Num. 25.1–18. The connection of idolatry in v. 7 to sexual immorality in v. 8 may well reflect Paul's intention to draw the parallel between the Israelites' idolatrous and sexually immoral behaviour and that of the Corinthians, whom Paul rebukes for their sexual licence in 1 Cor. 5.1–5, 10–11; and 6.9–10, 12–20 (apart from their idolatry in our current discussion). The question is whether Paul, in warning against idolatry here, also intends a warning against sexual immorality. And if so, why? Does it imply that sexual immorality leads to idolatry, or idolatry leads to sexual immorality? If 1 Corinthians 8–10 is about the issue of idolatry, why does Paul mention sexual immorality unless it has to do with idolatry? In the case of Numbers 25, the two issues are inseparable. In his commentary on Numbers 25, Josephus expands on the story and describes the unfortunate event as resulting from a strategy of Balaam which he advised King Balak of Midian to adopt (*Ant.* 4.126–30). As we have discussed in Chapter 3, section 4, b above, the strategy was to use the Midianite women to tempt the Israelite youths, till they became 'overmastered by their passions' (*Ant.* 4.130); the women should then withdraw from them and require them to abandon their ancestral laws and their God and demand that they worship the gods of the Midianites and Moabites. In other words, Josephus sees a link between sexual immorality and idolatry. And this could be because in Num. 25.1–3 the Midianite women have invited the Israelite youths to join them in the worship of their gods (ἐκάλεσαν αὐτοὺς ἐπὶ ταῖς θυσίαις τῶν εἰδώλων αὐτῶν... Num. 25.2). The link between sexual immorality and idolatry is very clearly demonstrated by Halbertal and Margalit. Marriage as a metaphor, as we have seen in Chapter 2 above, helps to explain the conception of the relationship between Israel's God and her. The metaphor suggests that Israel is the wife of

194. See Thiselton's discussion of 1 Cor. 10.7 (2000: 734–37) and his translation of παίζειν as 'virtual orgy'. Cf. Schrage 1995: 398.

195. Fee (1987: 454–55) views that this 'certainly carries overtones of sexual play'. Cf. Meeks (1995: 131–32) who demonstrates that the word means 'to joke, mock, make fun of'. And Meeks further shows that the word as used by Philo means 'dance' (1995: 132 n. 22). Thus, the situation could be a pure riotous celebration of deliverance from Egypt. Further, in Exod. 32.31, Moses is recorded to have confessed to God the sin of the Israelites as that of making for themselves gods of gold. No hint of sexual play is made in that confession.

196. Hays (1989: 94) comments: '...because Jews as well as Gentiles stand under God's just sentence of universal condemnation; there is no distinction. Because there is no distinction, the golden calf story becomes a parable of the human condition apart from the gospel, a condition of self-destructive idolatry.'

Yahweh. Any idolatry is therefore a sexual sin.[197] That there is sexual immorality in the church in Corinth is clear (cf. 1 Cor. 5.1–5). Fee is of the opinion that the feasting in the temple in Corinth might at times also involve sexual play. He adduces four reasons for the possibility: (1) Numbers 25 alluded to here links together sexual play and the eating of sacrificial food before the Baal of Peor; (2) 1 Cor. 10.7, which alludes to Exod. 32.6, also joins idolatry with sexual play;[198] (3) in 1 Cor. 6.12–20, Paul re-applies the concept of the 'temple' in 3.16–17 to the Christian who has visited prostitutes; this could be an allusion to the connection of sexual immorality with pagan temples; and (4) every other mention of idol food in the New Testament is accompanied by a reference to sexual immorality. Of the four reasons, the first has validity. However, Paul's mention of sexual immorality could be because he thinks it leads to idolatry.[199] But that does not necessarily mean that temple prostitution is the issue in these three chapters of the epistle.[200] The lack of any mention by Paul throughout 1 Corinthians 8–10 except here shows that feasting involving sexual play may not be present at all.[201] The second reason is less persuasive, as explained in n. 195. The third is at most remotely plausible (as an argument). Still, it need not mean that feasting in the temple involves sexual play.[202] It would be quite uncharacteristic of Paul to be silent in these chapters until now, and to only mention it by way of allusion to an Old Testament example. The fourth reason, while it may suggest such an understanding, does not lend weight to the theory that the feasting in a Corinthian pagan temple involves sexual play. Fee cites two texts, namely, Acts 15.29 and Rev. 2.14, 20. In the case of Acts, it is the Apostolic Decree that is in view. However, being the Apostolic Decree, it is only natural for the apostles to include sexual immorality in their list of forbidden things, particularly so in the Graeco-Roman world where sexual immorality is rampant. But that does not mean the Corinthians attend pagan temple feasting that is followed by or involves sexual play.[203] The cases of Rev. 2.14 and 2.15 are a specific reference to Numbers 25 and Ahab's idolatry through Jezebel in 1 Kings and 2 Kings. Although the former explicitly mentions sexual immorality, it is what leads to idolatry, not the other way round. And in the case of Ahab and Jezebel sexual immorality is

197. Halbertal and Margalit 1992: 11–20. See Chapter 2, section 2 above.

198. In this case, Fee takes the word 'play' (παίζειν) as connoting 'sexual play' (1987: 454–55); see n. 194 above.

199. *Contra* Robertson and Plummer (1911: 204) who do not think that immoral intercourse preceded the Moabite women's invitation. Cf. Hays 1997: 163–64.

200. Gardner 1994: 151.

201. Cf. Josephus's *Ant.* 18.65–80, where Josephus recounts the story of how Paulina was deceived into sexual intercourse with Mundus, under the pretext that the sexual intercourse was to be with the god Anubis. Although the activity took place in a temple, it is quite different from the idolatry in 1 Corinthians 8–10. The former was a straightforward deception; the latter is about idolatrous behaviour in terms of eating idol-meat and engaging in the worship of demons.

202. Against Thiselton (2000: 738–39), whose argument is based on various archaeological findings of temple prostitution; and Yeo (1995: 107–109) who argues on similar basis.

203. See Hurd (1983: 253) who posits that sexual sin here could be used figuratively to mean idolatry, but concludes, quite implausibly, that Paul attempted to enforce the decree (260).

not specifically mentioned in 1 Kings and 2 Kings. And it is only one case about which little information is given or known. What is telling is that in 1 Cor. 5.11 Paul seems to view those who are sexually immoral and the idolaters to be separate groups. This is seen in the use of the word ἤ, which is a 'disjunctive' conjunction.[204] The most satisfactory explanation of this Old Testament allusion is thus that Paul is telling the Corinthians not to be like the Israelites in their sexual immorality because sexual liaison with pagans can lead to idolatry, which was the case in Numbers 25.[205]

The fourth Old Testament example is couched in an interesting manner: μηδὲ ἐκπειράζωμεν τὸν Χριστόν, καθώς τινες αὐτῶν ἐπείρασαν... ('let us not put Christ to the test, just as some of them tested...' v. 9). Some manuscripts do not have Χριστόν but κύριον.[206] Others have θεόν instead of either Χριστόν or κύριον.[207] But the reading Χριστόν has good textual support.[208] The fact that Paul has identified the 'rock' in v. 4 with Christ and warns the 'strong' not to provoke the Lord (τὸν κύριον) to jealousy (10.22) suggests that he is using these terms interchangeably to refer to the same object of the offence of idolatry committed by the 'strong'.[209] What is important is Paul's description of the Israelites: (καθώς) τινες αὐτῶν ἐπείρασαν... Although it is not clear to what Old Testament text Paul is alluding, it is most probably Num. 21.4–7 where the specific mention of 'snakes' is made.[210] The Numbers 21 incident is cited probably because there the people complained and murmured against Moses for the lack of the kind of food they had while they were in Egypt. This harks back to the 'craving for evil' in v. 6. It again relates to food, and is probably why Paul views it as a testing of the Lord. The word ἐκπειράζωμεν or its cognate does not appear in the LXX Numbers 21, but does in Ps. 78.18 (LXX Ps. 77.18). It is possible that Paul could have been influenced by the Psalm.[211] And his reason for urging the Corinthians

---

204. Cf. BDF §446.

205. Cf. Halbertal and Margalit (1992: 23–25) where they rightly point out that there are two levels: (1) people worship idols in order to be sexually promiscuous; and (2) the initial attachment to idols because of the desire to be sexually promiscuous eventually leads to actual belief in the idols. While it could be possible that some of the 'strong' might have visited the pagan temples and eaten idol-meat because of their desire for sexual services, no evidence from the text of 1 Corinthians 8–10 suggests this. Paul is unlikely to be so reticent on this had this been the case.

206. ℵ B C P 33. 104. 326. 365. 1175. 2464 *pc* sy^hmg. Robertson and Plummer (1911: 205–206) prefer τὸν κύριον.

207. A 81 *pc*.

208. P⁴⁶ D F G Y 1739. 1881 M latt sy co; Ir^lat Or^1739mg. Barrett (1968: 225) and Fee (1987: 457), and also Fee's n. 34 argue that the original is most certainly τὸν Χριστόν. See also Conzelmann 1975: 164; Schrage 1995: 400–401. See further Thiselton (2000: 740).

209. Cf. 1 Cor. 8.6, where Paul seems to view the one Lord as the same Jesus Christ (εἷς κύριος Ἰησοῦς Χριστός).

210. Willis (1985a: 151) does not think that Paul has any specific Old Testament text in mind. However, Fee (1987: 456 n. 31) rightly refutes Willis' point; cf. Conzelmann 1975: 168. Barrett (1968: 225) thinks that Ps. 78.18 is a summary of Num. 21.4–7.

211. Fee (1987: 456–57) argues that vv. 20–21 show that the challenge of the 'strong' to Paul's prohibition against cultic meals is tantamount to 'putting Christ to the test'. Conzelmann (1975: 168) maintains that the warning is 'purposely couched in general terms'; this point is taken up by Willis

not to 'put Christ to the test' is that to his mind, the Israelites did exactly the same, that is, testing Christ, and a huge number of them died. And by implication, they would equally face 'destruction'. What does Paul mean by 'testing' Christ? In what way do the 'strong' put Christ to the test? In the Numbers 21 incident, the people rebelled against Moses and against God. Paul is not here making an allegorical interpretation, which is confirmed by the lack of an interpretation of the 'snakes' in 1 Cor. 10.9.[212] What Paul is telling the 'strong' is that by insisting on their right to eat idol-meat and persisting in such behaviour they are in fact 'testing' Christ. Barrett argues that what Paul has in mind is that the 'strong' are trying and testing the Lord by 'seeing "how far they could go" in idolatry'.[213] Robertson and Plummer think that Paul does not have any specific thing in mind other than the 'general frailty and faultiness' of the Corinthians.[214] But there seems to be a pattern, that is, Paul has a specific purpose in mind when he cites or alludes to the various Old Testament examples. And Paul did not cite these examples at random, but he probably selected them with careful consideration, to ensure that they fit his purpose. What seems clear is that Paul views the participation of the 'strong' in the pagan cultic meals as 'putting' Christ to the 'test'.[215]

The final Old Testament example is in v. 10. It is recognized among scholars that the verse could be an allusion to either Num. 14.1–38 or Num. 16.41.[216] The former is about the people's 'grumbling' against Moses after they heard about the reports of the ten spies. It is interesting that the people's grumbling is described, among other things, as 'testing' the Lord (ἐπείρασάν με... Num. 14.22). The latter passage is about the people's rebellion against Moses over the killing of Korah and his company. In both cases, there is no mention of a destroyer. Which story is Paul alluding to in v. 10? Conzelmann does not think there is any clear distinction between 'grumbling' in v. 10 and 'tempting' in the previous verse.[217] Barrett theorizes that Paul is driven by the momentum of the Old Testament material and that there is no evidence that 'grumbling' is a particular failing of the Corinthians.[218] Robertson and Plummer and Fee, however, see the failing of the

---

(1985a: 152), who briefly surveys a range of views and concludes that Paul is here influenced by rhetorical style and 'perhaps spurred on by recalling the example of Israel in the wilderness'.

212. See Barrett 1968: 226.

213. Barrett 1968: 225–26. But Barrett also concedes that it is reasonable to say that there is 'an irritable refusal' on the part of both the Israelites and the Corinthians to accept the conditions which God has laid down for them. Cf. Yeo (1995: 170–71) who views 'testing Christ' as the 'vulgar display of pride in their participation in the cultic meal...' Cf. Newton 1998: 329.

214. Robertson and Plummer 1911: 205. Cf. Conzelmann 1975: 168; and Willis 1985a: 152.

215. Hays 1997: 165.

216. See Hays 1997: 165. Thiselton (2000: 742) cites Hays on this point.

217. Conzelmann 1975: 168.

218. Barrett 1968: 226. Cf. Willis (1985a: 152–53) who finds it impossible to determine who is being referred to as the 'destroyer', even though its similar expressions can be found in such texts as 2 Sam. 24.16; 1 Chron. 21.15; Exod. 12.23; Wis. 18.20–25. He concludes that 'Just as no concrete Old Testament passage is being used, so too it is possible that no specific occasion at Corinth is being corrected. There is no reason to think Paul is addressing the grumbling (past or expected) of the strong except in a most general way'.

Corinthians in their murmuring against Paul.[219] Robertson and Plummer go a step
further by suggesting that Paul is warning against those who might be murmuring
against him for his punishment of the incestuous man in 1 Corinthians 5 and for
his severe rebukes in 1 Corinthians.[220] But why would Paul speak against the
incestuous man in 1 Corinthians 5 and only defend his proposed punishment of
the man here in 1 Corinthians 10, with only a verse that is not altogether explicit?
And there is no reason for Paul to be so veiled in his warning against such
Corinthians, if he could be so strong in speaking up against the incestuous man in
1 Corinthians 5. It therefore has to mean otherwise. Hurd has argued that 10.1–22
is 'a second and somewhat stronger attempt' by Paul to persuade the 'strong' not
to eat idol-meat.[221] And if Paul is writing to make clarifications on what he had
written or instructed earlier concerning idol-meat, and since 1 Cor. 8.1 suggests
that the Corinthians had raised the matter in their letter to him, then it is possible
that he has encountered some criticism of his position on idolatry, and very
possibly his apostleship. In 1 Corinthians 9, as we will argue in the next chapter,
Paul defends his apostolic authority and sets himself as an example to the
'strong'. This would suggest that the 'grumbling' in 10.10 may be related to their
criticism of Paul's apostolic authority and the judgment they pronounce against
him.[222] As a result, he is now telling them that he remains the apostle with
authority, and that he is an example to them. And if Paul thinks he is an imitator
of Christ (1 Cor. 11.1), then any criticism against him would be a criticism
against Christ. This would similarly constitute 'putting Christ to the test' and
'murmuring' against Christ. It is also possible that the 'strong' have 'grumbled'
over the prospects of losing business clientele or risking their social networks if
they do not attend pagan cultic meals.[223] And by alluding to the 'grumbling' of
the Israelites, Paul may have in mind such possible 'grumbling' of the 'strong'.[224]

The danger of such murmuring is that of destruction. While there is no mention of the 'destroyer' (ὁ ὀλοθρευτής) in the Numbers passages alluded to above
in the LXX,[225] Paul certainly believes in such an agent,[226] and very possibly understands the 'destroyer' to be an agent of God who is sent out to execute God's

219. Robertson and Plummer 1911: 206; Fee (1987: 458) says that it is very likely that the
Corinthians' 'grumbling' against Paul probably also involves 'grumbling' against God. And this, he
says, is why Paul includes this Old Testament example as a warning of the coming judgment.
220. Robertson and Plummer 1911: 206. See Willis (1985a: 153 n. 133) for his criticism of this
position.
221. Hurd 1983: 142.
222. Thus the second person plural imperative γογγύζετε might well be deliberate, that is, to
exclude himself. See Fee 1987: 457 nn. 36–37.
223. This has been a hypothesis of Chow (1992), especially 83–166, and Clarke (1993). However,
Meggitt (1998) has viewed otherwise, even though his counter-argument is not without problems. See
Chapter 1, section 3 for our survey of the various scholars.
224. Fee 1987: 457–58; and Hays 1997: 165.
225. One other possible passage is Num. 17.1–11 where the Israelites are warned against
complaining through the sprouting staff of Aaron.
226. Robertson and Plummer 1911: 206, 'The Apostle assumes that there was such an agent, as in
the slaying of the firstborn (τὸν ὀλεθρεύοντα, Exod. xii.23), and in the plague that punished David
(…) and in the destruction of the Assyrians (…)'; Barrett 1968: 226. Cf. Fee 1987: 457 n. 38.

punishment. This is indicated in v. 22, where Paul rhetorically asks whether the 'strong' are provoking the Lord to jealousy. The question of 'destruction' in the Numbers passages is the physical destruction of the complainants, so that they would not enter into the promised land. In the Corinthians' case, Paul seems to be referring to an eschatological destruction, that is, the loss of one's salvation. This is seen in v. 11, where Paul summarizes the Israelites' examples by setting forth the purpose for which these events were recorded: πρὸς νουθεσίαν ἡμῶν ('for our warning'). The word πρός indicates the purpose. And in the next clause εἰς οὓς τὰ τέλη τῶν αἰώνων κατήντηκεν ('on whom the ends of the ages have arrived'), Paul sets his argument in an eschatological perspective, that is, the Israelites' wilderness behaviour and its subsequent destruction have been written down for the present generation (ταῦτα δὲ τυπικῶς συνέβαινεν ἐκείνοις...), so that they would be warned and so behave in a way that does not provoke God to jealousy (cf. 10.22). In the case of the Corinthians, the prospects they face are eschatological because the ends of the ages have arrived on them.[227]

Paul's use of the various Old Testament examples reveals a pattern, which may be described in the following. By heaping up all the Old Testament examples, Paul shows that the Israelites faced destruction because their idolatrous behaviour had aroused the wrath of God. This may be tabulated as follows.

What Israel was and did (1 Cor. 10.1–10)	*The result of the Israelites' behaviour*
Our ancestors 'enjoyed salvation' (vv. 1–4);	God was not pleased with most of them and they were struck down in the desert (v. 5);
They craved evil (καθὼς κἀκεῖνοι ἐπεθύμησαν, v. 6);	God's anger was aroused against them and he sent a plague among them which killed many (cf. Num. 11.34);
They worshipped the golden calf (v. 7);	The Lord was angry with them and sent a plague among them (cf. Exod. 32.35);
They engaged in sexual immorality (v. 8a);	Twenty-three thousand fell in a single day (v. 8b; cf. Num. 25);
They tested Christ (v. 9a);	They were destroyed by snakes (v. 9b);
They grumbled (v. 10a);	They were destroyed by the destroyer (v. 10b).

What the above table clearly shows is that in every case, death is the result. Even where Paul does not mention death as the penalty, their Old Testament references would explicitly state it. That such a result or penalty seems to be in Paul's mind is explicit in v. 12, which reads, ὥστε ὁ δοκῶν ἑστάναι βλεπέτω

---

227. The exact nuance is not clear. See Robertson and Plummer (1911: 207) who interpret 'ages' as the successive periods of human history and the sum-total of its end has come to us. Barrett (1968: 227) posits that Paul believes he and the Corinthians are living in the 'last days' of world history, before the coming of the messianic age. Fee (1987: 459) offers a view closer to that of Barrett that the present 'age' is the 'new age' begun by Jesus Christ through his death and resurrection. Hence, the new people of God are the people of the 'End' times. Cf. Wright 1992: 447.

μὴ πέσῃ ('So then, let the one who thinks he/she is standing watch out lest he/she fall').[228] This warning summarizes the story of Israel in the wilderness and serves as a direct application of the Israelites' experiences to the situation of the Corinthians. It seems that the 'strong' think that they are spiritually secure, and they therefore do not have to fear any consequences of their behaviour. They think idols are nothing and that there is only one God the Father and one Lord Jesus Christ. However, Paul is now telling them to watch out. For the Israelites had fallen in the desert, even though they seemed to be doing well. The 'strong' therefore will fall, if they persist in their idolatry. What they face at present is in fact a testing of their faithfulness to God. The solution to or the way out of the current problem is by enslaving oneself to the gospel of Jesus Christ, a theme which will be discussed in the next chapter. The 'strong' will do well by giving up their rights to freely and unscrupulously eat idol-meat in the pagan temples. Verse 13 is therefore addressed to both the 'strong' and the 'weak'. To the 'strong', visits to the pagan temples and eating idol-meat before the pagan gods constitute a partnership with 'demons'. It is an act of 'unfaithfulness' to the true God; and it dishonours the true God by confusing or mixing God with other gods/demons. Further, since the 'strong' have been baptised into Christ Jesus and are participants in the Lord's Supper, by becoming 'partners' with 'demons', they in fact break the covenant with God through Jesus Christ, through whom all things and the 'strong' come into existence (cf. 1 Cor. 8.6b). They therefore are treading on highly dangerous ground. The address to the 'weak' is that what they face, that is, their struggle with their 'damaged conscience' is a test from which God will provide a way out.[229] In other words, God will provide a 'way out' to both the 'weak' and the 'strong'.[230] The important point for both groups is the exhortation in v. 14: φεύγετε ἀπὸ τῆς εἰδωλολατρίας ('flee from idolatry').[231] Both the 'strong' and the 'weak' must resist idolatry by fleeing from it;[232] failing which they will face God's divine punishment.

Verse 22 explains what this divine punishment is all about. By engaging in idolatrous behaviour, Paul argues, the 'strong' run the risk of incurring the jealousy or zeal (ζῆλος) of God. The word παραζηλόω means 'provoke to

228. Gardner (1994: 152–53) argues that Paul is here speaking in covenant language and that Paul's use of the term ἵστημι meant that he believed the 'strong' thought they really 'had complete covenant security'. See also Gundry-Volf (1990: 120–30) for a discussion of v. 12. Gundry-Volf argues that the 'fall' refers to the loss of the appearance of salvation. However, 1 Corinthians 8–10 consistently shows that the 'strong' have salvation, and as 10.9 suggests the 'strong' in fact had Christ and tested him.

229. Gundry-Volf 1990: 128–29.

230. Conzelmann (1975: 169) takes this as the reference to the eschatological manifestation and liberation, that is, the one eschatological salvation. However, v. 14 makes this interpretation unlikely.

231. Barrett (1968: 91): '…God will never allow it to become impossible for him to resist. He (the Christian) must resist, and he must not put his trust in false securities…' Cf. Willis 1985a: 157–59; and Fee 1987: 460–63.

232. Fee (1987: 464) thinks that 'the way out' does not include the 'headlong pursuit of idolatry'; Robertson and Plummer 1911: 211, however, take this 'flight' as the sure ἔκβασις. Cf. Barrett 1968: 230.

jealousy'.[233] It refers to actions that arouse God's zeal (ζῆλος). Paul is reminding the Corinthian Christians that God's 'zeal' for the faithfulness of his 'new people' can mean that he will mete out the 'death' penalty by withholding from the Corinthians the eschatological salvation.[234] And if the 'strong' want a trial of 'strength', then let them beware that the Lord is stronger (1 Cor. 10.22). Thus, by setting out the Israelites' wilderness experiences of idolatry and subsequent destruction by God, Paul brings before the 'strong' the danger of idolatry.

The danger of the final 'disqualification' and God's destruction constitutes two aspects. On the one hand, the idolatrous behaviour of the 'strong' is 'sinning' against Christ when they cause the 'weak' to stumble by 'sharing' in the table of δαιμόνια. By sinning against Christ, the 'strong' are putting a hindrance in the way of the gospel, which has implications for their eschatological salvation. By 'sharing' in the table of δαιμόνια they have betrayed God by breaking and disregarding the new covenant in Christ; they have dishonoured the true God by mixing him with other gods/δαιμόνια. They therefore incur the wrath or arouse the 'zeal' of God. On the other hand, the Israelites' own idolatry and subsequent destruction are an indication that God's jealousy, which was provoked by the Israelites, can still be provoked and he can still mete out the same justice to the idolatrous Corinthians: destruction. This 'destruction' is now seen or interpreted by Paul within an eschatological perspective. Thus, the framework for defining and interpreting idolatry is the Old Testament examples, not the γνῶσις of the 'strong'.

8. *Summary and Conclusion*

The function of this chapter has been to examine the differences of views between Paul and the 'strong'. We have looked at the slogans of the 'strong' and concluded that the 'strong' hold the view that 'idols are nothing' and that there is only 'one God'; this knowledge was modified by their Christian belief as seen in their confession (cf. section 3, c, above). Their γνῶσις then gives rise to their claim to ἐξουσία which forms the basis for their behaviour of attending pagan temples and eating idol-meat there. Conceptually, their thought on the 'one God' parallels the conceptual overlap concerning the true God found in *The Letter of Aristeas* (Chapter 4, section 3) and Artapanus (Chapter 4, section 6). Their attendance at pagan temples parallels the examples seen in Chapter 4, section 6.

We also looked at Paul's view of δαιμόνια and his use of the concept elsewhere. We then moved on to look at his position on idolatry. We have examined the use of the term δαιμόνια in the Septuagint and other Pauline epistles. The overall indication of these texts is that there are gods and lords in

---

233. BAGD 616. It is not referring to the general idea of being provoked to anger.

234. Cf. Barrett (1968: 228) who comments, 'Moment by moment, the Christian life is lived by faith only, without any human guarantee. As the Israelites were lured by the Moabite women into fornication, idolatry, and so into destruction, so the idolatry, which apparently the Corinthians, secure in their sacramental life, thought they could safely trifle with, could lead them into fornication and destruction.'

heaven and on earth, and these deities are probably understood to be similar to spiritual beings in the spirit realm. The Book of Tobit provides the most explicit illustration of this hypothesis. Further, we have also seen that Paul's use of the term is not found anywhere else in his epistles. However, he does reflect an understanding of the spirit world through his reference to Satan, the realms of the flesh and the spirit, and his suggestion that the 'strong' are in fact entering into 'partnership' with δαιμόνια when they eat idol-meat in the presence of the pagan gods. He can agree with the 'strong' over the doctrine of the 'one God' and the fact that 'idols are nothing', but he differs from the 'strong' over their application of such knowledge.

While Paul may hold a belief in the existence of δαιμόνια he seems to make a distinction between idols (εἰδώλα) and 'demons' (δαιμόνια). We have argued that Paul's view of idols follows the traditional Jewish position on idols. For him, idols are dead, without life, and insignificant – they are nothing! But because of the fact that the idols in fact represent the gods or evil spirits behind the idols, there are dangers in eating idol-meat in the pagan temple or before the pagan gods. Paul therefore sets out the danger of idolatry by showing that their idolatrous behaviour, when it causes fellow believers to fall, is tantamount to 'sinning' against Christ because they have by their behaviour put a hindrance in the way of the gospel. What this means is that Paul is now setting before the 'strong' a new paradigm, which is Christ. Simultaneously, Paul also intertextually alludes to the Israelites' idolatrous examples and shows the 'strong' that the Israelites were punished for their idolatrous behaviour, even though they appeared to be doing well. The 'strong' therefore have no guarantee against God's just punishment, if they persist in idolatrous behaviour. Their baptism and participation in the Lord's Supper do not exclude them from God's jealousy, and therefore punishment. Thus, Paul establishes the Old Testament examples as the framework for defining and interpreting the idolatrous behaviour of the 'strong'.

Several definitions of idolatry appear to be operative in Paul's thought: (1) worship of other gods/alien cult through 'unfaithfulness' to the true God and breach of the covenant; (2) dishonouring the true God through the cognitive error of mixing or confusing God with other gods/δαιμόνια; wrong kinds of worship/intention (by eating in an idol's presence).

What this chapter shows is that Paul, the 'strong' and the 'weak' do agree on some areas of belief, but they also differ over how they apply their knowledge. All three parties clearly agree that there is 'one God' and idols are nothing in the world. This particular area of agreement parallels Chapters 2 and 3, where we saw the widespread condemnation of idolatry in both the LXX and some Diaspora Jews. Throughout, the first two commandments appear prominent. The pattern in the LXX reveals the subtle differentiation between misrepresenting Yahweh and the worship of alien cults, while the Diaspora Jews (Chapter 3) reveal that very strict definitions are adopted for condemning idols and idol-makers. Paul and the 'weak' clearly parallel those examples found in Chapters 2 and 3, although Paul goes further in his belief that δαιμόνια are real. The 'strong' differ from the two in that while they believe in 'one God' and that 'idols are nothing', they consider their action harmless. There is only 'one God' and they are 'free' in Christ. Thus, they clearly do not adopt those definitions operating in Paul and the 'weak'. Instead, they parallel such Diaspora Jews like Pseudo-Aristeas, Artapanus, and the like. Further, their non-condemning attitude might reflect a possible awareness of the LXX ban on reviling other people's gods in Exod. 22.27a.

These three parties show that the definitions set out in Chapter 2 do not always operate as a package. And different Jews can adopt different definitions of idolatry. The above raises the question of who is to decide what is the right or appropriate behaviour with regard to idolatry. In other words, it is a question of authority. Another question Paul's argument raises is that of 'freedom' in Christ. How should the 'strong' exercise their right (ἐξουσία) since they are 'free' in Christ.[235] 1 Corinthians 9 is set between 1 Corinthians 8 and 10 for this important purpose: Paul's defence of his apostolic authority so as to set himself as the authoritative example to the 'strong'. This is the subject of the next chapter.

---

235. Cf. 1 Cor. 10.23, where Paul seems to echo the repeated use of πάντα ἔξεστιν by the 'strong'. This same claim is also seen in 6.12, πάντα μοι ἔξεστιν.

Chapter 6

PAUL'S APOSTOLIC AUTHORITY AND EXAMPLE

1. *Introduction*

In Chapter 5, we have looked at Paul's view of idolatry and his position on the behaviour of the 'strong' with regard to idol-meat. We have also demonstrated how the definitions of idolatry set up in Chapter 2 apply to the two positions. Our analysis shows that Paul adopts a strict 'modified' Jewish stance on idolatry: idolatry can lead to the loss of one's eschatological salvation. But the same cannot be said about the 'strong', whose knowledge serves as the basis for their 'freedom' to attend pagan temples, eat idol-meat, and even engage in idolatrous rituals. And while the 'strong' appeal to the Jewish *Shema*, Paul appeals to 're-interpreted' biblical history as the framework for judging such a conflict. Having compared both Paul's position on idolatry and that of the 'strong', one matter remains: what then is the function of 1 Corinthians 9? Is Paul's authority in any way related to what he is arguing in 1 Corinthians 8 and 10? This calls for an examination of Paul's authority, which is the primary issue of 1 Corinthians 9.

If Paul's authority is an issue in 1 Corinthians 9, does it then suggest that the battle over idolatry hinges on who has the final 'say' on what constitutes idolatry? And if the definitions of idolatry depend on who makes the final decision, does 1 Corinthians 9 not also serve as a way in which Paul seeks to re-affirm his apostolic authority? In other words, is 1 Corinthians 9 a defence of Paul's authority as an apostle? But is Paul's apostolic authority being challenged in Corinth?[1] This will require an examination of not only 1 Corinthians 9, but also 1 Corinthians 1–4. In 1 Cor. 11.1, Paul urges the Corinthians to be imitators of him. What does 1 Corinthians 9 have to say about this? In other words, is Paul presenting himself as an example to the 'strong'? And if so, what sort of example is he trying to set for the 'strong'?

Although the unity of 1 Corinthians 8–10 has posed a challenge, once the question of the function of 1 Corinthians 9 is settled, its place in 1 Corinthians 8–10 would become apparent. It is sufficient at this juncture to say that the scholarly

---

1. As the criticism of or challenge to Paul's authority is an issue in 1 Corinthians, such a challenge could serve as a foundation for later or further challenge to Paul's authority. However, although it could be valuable to look at 2 Corinthians 10–13 to see how this might be the case, I will not look at this question as 2 Corinthians 10–13 probably represents a later, and most likely, different development as a result of the false apostles' attack on Paul.

view which takes 1 Corinthians 9 as a digression or excursus[2] is now less accepted and that recent scholarship tends to accept the unity of these chapters.[3]

2. *Is 1 Corinthians 9 Paul's Defence of his Apostolic Authority?*

There are basically two views on 1 Corinthians 9. The first regards 1 Corinthians 9 as Paul's defence of his apostolic authority (henceforth 'defence'). The second argues that Paul is setting himself as an example to the 'strong' to give up their rights to eat idol-meat, by showing that he has himself given up his rights to material support (henceforth 'example').[4]

Willis has proposed that in 1 Cor. 9.1–14 Paul is not arguing for his 'rights', but *from* it, to set himself as an example to the Corinthians.[5] Citing Weiss, Willis argues that verses 1 and 2 are too brief for an actual defence.[6] Since the rhetorical questions in these verses assume a positive response, and since Paul has stated that the Corinthians are the seal of his apostleship, the ἀπολογία cannot be a defence.[7] Further, Willis takes the participle τοῖς ἀνακρίνουσιν in 1 Cor. 9.3 to be future, so that the statement is rendered 'my defence to those who *would* examine me'. Thus, 'Paul is *anticipating* criticism rather than *answering* a previous complaint'. Willis argues that Paul's rights have already been strongly established so that he is able to make something of his renunciation of them. 1 Cor. 9.4–14 is not meant to establish Paul's right to support, but to remind his readers of the established fact of his authority.[8] It is therefore not a defence of his authority but meant to allow him to show that he has given up his rights and so set himself as an example to the Corinthians.[9]

2.   E.g. Weiss 1910: xliii, 231; Robertson and Plummer 1914: xxiv; Barrett 1968: 219; Héring 1962: xiii-xiv; and Schmithals 1971: 93. Schmithals splits 1 Corinthians 9 up into two with 9.1–23 belonging to Epistle B, while 9.24–27 belongs to Epistle A.
3.   See, for example, the arguments for the unity of these chapters by Hurd (1965: 131–42), Conzelmann (1975: 137), and Fee (1987: 357–63). Cf. Willis (1985b: 33–48) who bases his argument about the function of 1 Corinthians 9 on the unity of chs. 8–10; and Mitchell (1991: 249–50) who takes 1 Corinthians 9 as a digression in terms of it making a comparison or amplifying a given point in the argument, but prefers to term it 'an exemplary argument'. However, not all recent scholars have accepted the unity of these chapters; cf. Yeo (1995: 73–83) who represents recent scholarship which continues to prefer the partition theory. Yeo has tried to develop his own by suggesting that there are letters A, B, C, D, E, and F. For him, 1 Cor. 9.24–10.22 belongs to letter B; 1 Cor. 8.1–13, 9.19–23, 10.23–11.1 belong to letter C, while 1 Cor. 9.1–18 belongs to letter E. The rest of the epistle is variously contained in these letters.
4.   Few scholars hold the view that both purposes are present in 1 Corinthians 9; cf. Martin (1990: 83) who accepts that 1 Corinthians 9 is both a defence and an example, but takes the position that it is a fictitious defence against fictitious opponents. Horrell (1996: 205) is probably the only modern scholar who takes both purposes seriously. See further below on the double purpose.
5.   Willis 1985b: 40. Willis' work, clearly, provided support to Mitchell's more elaborated hypothesis.
6.   Willis 1985b: 34; Weiss 1910: 233.
7.   Willis 1985b: 34.
8.   Willis 1985b: 35.
9.   This is somewhat similar, though not exactly identical, to Mitchell's argument that Paul calls his argument a 'defence' in order to justify using himself as an example for the Corinthians (see below).

Although Willis is right that in 1 Cor. 9.9–23 Paul is setting himself as an
example to the Corinthians, he seems to suggest at several points that Paul is establishing his rights so as to show that he has renounced them.[10] But why should Paul
establish his rights if they are not called into question?[11] Further, Willis' treatment of the two words, ἀπολογία and ἀνακρίνω, is inadequate in that he does
not take into account the larger context of the letter as a whole.[12]

Willis' view is taken up by Mitchell who, in her book, *Paul and the Rhetoric
of Reconciliation*, argues that attempts to see 1 Corinthians 9 as true defence had
failed.[13] For her, 1 Corinthians 9 constitutes a 'mock defense speech' in which
Paul presents himself as the 'example of the proper non-divisive, conciliatory
behavior' for the Corinthians to follow.[14] She argues that the term ἀπολογία in
9.3 has received a somewhat mistaken forensic focus, whose advocates have
failed to analyse 1 Corinthians 9 as a true defence against real charges.[15] The only
possible charge which anyone reading 1 Corinthians 9 can reconstruct is 'an historically implausible one: *that Paul did not take the Corinthians' money*' (emphasis original).[16] This is because she views this reconstruction to be 'scarcely
possible' and that even if it was historically feasible, the argument of 1 Corinthians 9 does not constitute an 'appropriate rhetorical defense' against such a
charge. Mitchell concludes that in 1 Corinthians 9 Paul calls his rhetorical response
a 'defence' in order to justify his use of himself as an example to the Corinthians.[17]
The double purpose advocated by some scholars, that is, 1 Corinthians 9 as both a
defence and Paul's example to the Corinthians, is dubbed the 'dubious "kill two
birds with one stone"' by her.[18] In a lengthy footnote,[19] she argues that her own
attempts to analyse 1 Corinthians 9 as a true defence have yielded no convincing
proof in that the 'charge and issue of the case tend to disappear'.[20]

A slightly different view is held by Martin who argues that 1 Corinthians 9 is
a poor defence, if it is a defence at all.[21] For he finds reading 1 Corinthians 9 as a
defence makes it difficult to fit in with the issue of idol-meat in chs. 8 and 10.

10.   For example, 'Paul has established his rights so strongly so that …' (35), and towards the end
of the essay, '…Paul establishes at length an ἐξουσία which he will not use,…' (40). Thus, Horrell
(1996: 204) understands Willis to be saying that 'Paul establishes his rights (ἐξουσία) as an apostle in
order to emphasise the fact that he has given them up, so as not to place any hindrance (ἐγκοπή) in
the way of the gospel'.
11.   Barrett (1968: 200) observes, 'It is also true that Paul would hardly have spent so long on the
question of apostolic rights if his own apostolic status had not been questioned in Corinth'.
12.   So Fee 1987: 393. Fee 1987: 394 n. 10. Cf. Conzelmann (1975: 152–53) who implausibly
argues that the form of expression in 1 Cor. 9.3 shows that in 1 Corinthians 9 Paul is defending himself against opponents from outside the Corinthian community.
13.   Mitchell 1991: 244 n. 330.
14.   Mitchell 1991: 130. Her position is being followed by Witherington III (1995: 203).
15.   Mitchell 1991: 244.
16.   Mitchell 1991: 246
17.   Mitchell 1991: 246.
18.   Mitchell 1991: 244.
19.   Mitchell 1991: 244 n. 330.
20.   Mitchell 1991: 245.
21.   Martin 1990: 77.

Rather, it functions basically as an example, not a defence of Paul's apostleship, and is a digression in the form of a defence.[22] Using the metaphor of slavery, Martin argues that Paul is introducing an alternative way of looking at his work, that is, he is a manual labourer who works under compulsion and unwillingly and therefore does not expect any wages because Christ has given him the trust of a steward.[23] It is Paul himself who raised the subject of his refusal of material support; since he knows that his refusal would be unacceptable to the Corinthians, he puts the chapter as a defence. In other words, he is defending himself proleptically against possible accusations against him.[24] Thus, in 1 Corinthians 9 Paul is putting up a 'fictitious', 'rhetorical', defence of himself for refusing to live like the other apostles and for rejecting the church's material support. By demonstrating his own status as one who has given up his rights to material support and as a leader who works as a manual labourer, Paul is showing that 'conventional status indicators are overturned in Christian form of leadership'.[25] For Martin, 1 Corinthians 9 is both a defence and an example, but the defence is a fictitious one. The opponents are themselves fictitious, created for Paul's own rhetorical purposes.[26] Fee has noted that in vv. 1–12 one rhetorical question after another are being issued, with a total of 16 in all.[27] Further, the tone of Paul's argument is too vigorous for Martin's fictitious theory to be possible. And Chow's thesis is valid that the Corinthians could possibly have been offended by Paul's refusal to accept material support from them, as they view the reception of material support as one of the marks of a true apostle, hence their questioning of Paul's apostleship.[28] Therefore Paul's defence would be real.

We will now turn to re-consider the evidence in 1 Corinthians 9. In 9.1, Paul poses several questions: 'Am I not free? Am I not an apostle? Have I not seen Jesus our Lord? Are you not my work in the Lord? These questions all begin with οὐκ or οὐχί, which shows that Paul expects the answers to be in the affirmative,[29] which indicates his own belief that he is 'free', an 'apostle', that he has indeed seen the risen Lord, and that the existence of the Corinthian Christian community is the result of his work. But why should Paul be asking these questions if there is no challenge to his 'freedom', 'apostleship', the claim that he has seen the risen Lord, and even his ministry in Corinth? In 1 Cor. 8.13, Paul has stated that he would never eat meat again if food is a reason for a fellow

---

22. Martin 1990: 77.
23. Martin 1990: 72.
24. Martin 1990: 78.
25. Martin 1990: 80.
26. Martin 1990: 83.
27. Fee 1987: 392 n. 1.
28. Chow 1992: 107–10; Chow's thesis suggests that the opponents are real and therefore Paul's defence is equally real. However, it is not necessary for us to accept that those Corinthians who have been offended by Paul are rich and powerful patrons in Corinth.
29. This does not mean that the Corinthians would necessarily respond in the positive, i.e. Paul could be rhetorically manipulating them into a 'yes' response. And this is where Willis (1985b: 34) misunderstands the function of the word οὐ, which merely tells us that the question expects a positive answer, but does not tell us that the respondent believes the answer to be so.

Christian to stumble. Later, in 1 Cor. 9.19, he says that he is willing to allow himself to be a slave to all, even though he is 'free' with regard to all. This might suggest that he has practised this principle of not eating meat before, a practice which has possibly caused some Corinthians to question his 'freedom', which also has implications for his 'apostleship' since he has taken up manual labour, an act which makes him appear less than free, as an apostle should be free from earning his own living. In his *Social Context of Paul's Ministry*, R.F. Hock identifies four possible means of support which a philosopher in Paul's day could draw on. They are charging fees, entering a household of the socially able and influential, begging, and working.[30] Of these, Paul has clearly adopted one, that is, working. Being their apostle, Paul not only refuses financial support from the Corinthians, but also takes on manual labour (cf. 1 Cor. 4.12; 9.12b, 15a), an act which might give the impression that the Corinthians cannot afford to support their apostle,[31] or that Paul has rejected them[32] (hence disrespecting them).[33] Thus, Paul's behaviour constitutes an offence to the Corinthians, leading to the questioning of his apostleship. Paul's statement that he and Barnabas are entitled not to work for a living serves as an argument against such a perception of his apostolic authority. In 1 Cor. 4.9–13, all the weaknesses and social lowliness mentioned seem to be the results of Paul's manual labour mentioned in v. 12.[34] And we are told in 1 Thess. 2.9 that he worked night and day in order not to be a burden to the believers.[35] This has led to an attack on his apostleship. Thus, Paul begins 1 Corinthians 9 with questions about his status.[36] And the specific rhetorical questions rule out Mitchell and Martin's suggestion that the chapter is a 'mock' or 'fictitious' defence. Why does Paul think that his authority might be questioned, if what he has done in 1 Corinthians 8 is only to suggest to the Corinthians, when they eat idol-meat, to consider those whose conscience is weak? Why does he not pose questions or make statements along the line of love, such as he has done in 1 Corinthians 13? Barrett describes the style of Paul as 'counter-attacks in the vigorous debating style of the diatribe'.[37] Indeed, the questions suggest this; the larger context of the letter proves it very likely an actual questioning of Paul's apostolic authority is present. Since being an eye-witness of the earthly Jesus is one of the

30. Hock 1980: 52–59.
31. Martin 1990: 70; Horrell 1996: 214–15.
32. Marshall 1987: 165–258; cf. Chow 1992: 108–109.
33. Holmberg 1978: 95. Holmberg also states that Paul's reluctance to receive support from the Corinthian church led to deeper mistrust which eventually broke out in open conflict (e.g. 2 Cor. 10–13).
34. Horrell 1996: 203. See also further discussion in Thiselton (2000: 363–64).
35. Cf. Holmberg 1978: 89–93.
36. Barrett (1968: 199–200) points out that what Paul says in 8.13 might invite the Corinthians to question his authority as an apostle, particularly when 'spiritual liberty' was their catchword. Although this makes the defence appear more like an anticipatory one, Barrett is of the opinion that Paul's own status as an apostle had been questioned.
37. Barrett 1968: 200; cf. Epictetus 3.22.38 where freedom is the characteristic theme of the wandering Cynic preacher who asks, 'Am I not free from sorrow? Am I not free from fear? Am I not free?'

criteria of an apostle,[38] the question, 'have I not seen Jesus our Lord?' becomes necessary. The specificity of the questions in fact betrays the possibility that the opponents of Paul have cast doubts on his apostleship by questioning his claim of having seen the Lord. And Paul has gone a step further by arguing that the Corinthians themselves are a proof of his apostolic work. 'Are you not my work in the Lord?' is rhetorically posed since Paul knows there is only one answer, and that is also the only answer the Corinthians can give.[39] And the double answer in v. 2 makes these questions even more crucial. And such questions would be redundant if his apostolic authority has not been questioned.[40]

Verse 2 further indicates that Paul's authority is being questioned. Mitchell and others, beyond saying that Paul is simply calling his argument a defence in order to justify using himself as an example for the Corinthians, have not adequately dealt with this particular statement: εἰ ἄλλοις οὐκ εἰμὶ ἀπόστολος. For we get the impression that there are some who do not accept Paul's apostleship, hence Paul's immediate following statement, ἀλλά γε ὑμῖν εἰμι (but to you I am).[41] And the further statement that the Corinthians are the seal (ἡ σφραγίς) of his apostleship in the Lord would be equally strange and unnecessary, if Paul's apostolic authority has not been questioned. The rephrasing of the statement that the Corinthians are his work in the Lord in 9.2 not only reflects Paul's emphasis on his apostolic work among the Corinthians; but more importantly, it suggests that those who question Paul's authority also call into question his work. Hence, the stronger emphasis from 'yes, you are my work in the Lord' to 'you are the

---

38.   Cf. Acts 1.21–22; Bruce (1986: 50) comments that the two essential qualifications of an apostle are being the companion of the Lord during his earthly ministry and being an eye-witness of his resurrection. See, however, Best (1995: 14–16) who demonstrates that the definition of an apostle is unclear. Dunn (1998: 571) observes that Paul began insisting on his being an apostle from Galatians onwards, but does not explain why he has only done so after Galatians and not before. But cf. Héring 1962: 75. Cf. 1 Cor. 15.1–10 which is crucial for Paul's understanding of his own apostleship.

39.   Earlier, Paul points out that he is the founding apostle in the sense that he planted (ἐγὼ ἐφύτευσα, 1 Cor. 3.6), laid the foundation (θεμέλιον ἔθηκα, 1 Cor. 3.10) for the Corinthian church, and became the Corinthians' father through the preaching of the gospel (ἐν γὰρ Χριστῷ Ἰησοῦ διὰ τοῦ εὐαγγελίου ἐγὼ ὑμᾶς ἐγέννησα, 1 Cor. 4.15).

40.   Dunn (1998: 571) has rightly pointed out that whether the Jerusalem apostles recognize Paul's claim that his commissioning experience is equivalent to having seen the Lord is a question we cannot fully answer, and it does seem probable that Paul's claim may not convince all the leaders. This has already shown up in a rather subtle way in Gal. 2.11–12, where Peter, whom Paul understood to have been entrusted with the gospel for the circumcized (2.9), appeared in a mixed, though predominantly Gentile church founded by Paul.

41.   On the face of the verse, it is possible that these people or opponents might have come from outside the Corinthian community; however, it is entirely possible that Paul is referring to some among the Corinthians who cast doubts on his apostleship, whom he therefore calls 'others' (ἄλλοι). The former would suggest that these opponents are leaders from Jerusalem, an unlikely scenario as there is a complete lack of such hostility against them as is evidenced in Galatians; the latter would mean that Paul is addressing some, not all, the Corinthians in the epistle. As there is no evidence to suggest that the 'others' come from outside the Corinthian community, it is more likely that Paul has in mind some of the Corinthians, i.e. they are ἄλλοι compared to you.

seal of my apostleship in the Lord' (cf. 2 Cor. 10.12–18).[42] In other words, while not everyone who witnessed the resurrection of the Lord was an apostle,[43] Paul's apostleship is confirmed by the existence of the Corinthian Christian community itself.[44] In both 9.1b and 2b, Paul uses the phrase ἐν κυρίῳ, which suggests that he regards his ministry to the Corinthians as the result not only of his having seen the risen Lord but also his being commissioned by him (cf. 1 Cor. 15.8–10; ἀπόστολος Χριστοῦ Ἰησοῦ, 1 Cor. 1.1).[45]

Further, Paul categorically states in v. 3 that he is making his defence (ἀπολο-γία) against those who judge him (τοῖς ἀνακρίνουσίν με). There are three words that we need to examine: ἀπολογία, τοῖς ἀνακρίνουσιν, and αὕτη. The first can simply refer to a speech of defence one gives in response to one's opponents (cf. Josephus, *Apion* 2.147; Acts 22.1); or it can be a forensic term which denotes a courtroom style of debate in which one puts up a defence against one's accusers (cf. Josephus, *War* 1.621); or it can at times refer to one's eagerness in defending oneself (cf. 2 Cor. 7.11; Phil. 1.7, 11).[46] Philo uses the term in largely the same sense as a 'real defence' against accusations or in the sense of a plea against charges brought against a person.[47] All the above uses never refer to a 'mock' defence or a 'fictitious defence'. They may differ in degree such as an ἀπολογία may be in the form of a plea against a charge. And there is no reason for Paul to use the term to mean otherwise.

The second term further lends weight to the view that Paul's defence is against real opposition. The phrase τοῖς ἀνακρίνουσιν may be a description of those who question Paul's authority. Willis has misunderstood ἀνακρίνουσιν as a future participle. But ἀνακρίνουσιν is rightly understood as a present, active, participle.[48]

42.   The 'seal' (σφραγίς), i.e. the Corinthians themselves, authenticates his apostleship. Conzelmann (1975: 152 n. 11) says the 'seal' means it is a 'legally valid attestation'; Barrett (1968: 201) comments: 'It is a visible token of something that already exists; thus the Corinthian church does not make Paul an apostle, and his apostleship does not depend on it…but its existence is a visible sign of his apostleship'.

43.   Cf. 1 Cor. 15.6; see also Best (1995: 15–16) who points out that not everyone who carried out missionary work would have been called an apostle.

44.   Thus, Héring (1962: 75–76) is right when he points out that if others wished to contest Paul's apostolic authority, 'there was the missionary work accomplished at Corinth by Paul'.

45.   Out of the seven undisputed letters of Paul, Paul claims to be an apostle in only four of these, namely, Romans, 1 and 2 Corinthians, and Galatians. This suggests that the claim may be related to the possibility of his apostleship being questioned. Indeed, apart from Romans, the other three letters have all had this particular element. The mention of his apostleship in Romans may be considered 'understandable' since the Christians there in all probability did not know him personally, with perhaps the exception of a few (Romans 16), if ch. 16 may be taken as a clue to the people who personally knew Paul. Cf. Best 1995: 19–23.

46.   BAGD 96.

47.   E.g. *Leg. All.* 3.65, 66, 68, 75; *Agr.* 92; *Jos.* 52, 80, 222; *Vit. Mos.* 1.286, 303; *Spec. Leg.* 2.95; 3.142; 4.24; *Virt.* 197; *Flacc.* 7, 126; *Leg. Gai.* 38, 67, 350.

48.   This has antecedent in 1 Cor. 4.3 where Paul says that he is being judged (using the same term ἀνακρίνω) by the Corinthians and possibly their assembly of opposing leaders (ἀνθρωπίνης ἡμέρας). Ἀνθρωπίνης ἡμέρας has been noted by scholars, e.g. Barrett (1968: 101) and Fee (1987: 161), to refer to the Corinthians trying to set up a court to mimic the Day of the Lord's judgment. On Willis' position, see Fee (1987: 401 n. 24).

The 'judges' of Paul's apostolic office would naturally look at other aspects of Paul's teaching and practice, including manual labour, his position on idol-meat, and such like.

The third word to be examined is αὕτη. Does it refer to what precedes (i.e. vv. 1–2),[49] or to what follows (i.e. vv. 3–27)?[50] The placement of αὕτη at the end of the sentence, that is 'my defence…is this', rather than at the beginning, that is 'this is…my defence…', shows that vv. 1–2 serve as Paul's statements of his identity as an apostle by way of questions; and vv. 3–18 elaborate his statements in vv. 1–2. In other words, αὕτη need not be a reference to either what precedes or what follows, but it should be seen as a reference to Paul's overall defence which extends all the way to v. 18. Paul is showing that while he holds the same concept as his critics on what constitutes an apostle in the area of material support, he does not hold the same conviction on its practice. A long and sustained piece of rhetorical defence here clearly suggests that Paul has a 'real attack' in view. And the questions Paul puts forward in vv. 4–6, which seem to be different from those in vv. 7–18, classify the rights under three main headings: the right to food and drink; the right to a believing wife; and the right not to work. The defence shows that Paul himself has these rights, particularly the right to material support.[51]

Apart from the evidence in 1 Cor. 9.1-6, we may find evidence elsewhere in the letter which shows that Paul's authority in Corinth is being questioned.

3. Evidence from 1 Corinthians 1–4

There are verbal links between 1 Corinthians 9 and 1 Corinthians 1–4 which point to the possible thematic links between the passages in question, and therefore to the question of Paul's authority in Corinth. In 1 Cor. 9.1 Paul begins with several questions which are followed by the argument that the Corinthians are the work of his apostolic labours in the Lord. This work (τὸ ἔργον, 3.14) is repeated in 9.2, which is further linked to the subject of work in 3.9–15, where Paul speaks about the work in architectural terms. It is the work of the builder (3.13). The builders are co-workers of God (θεοῦ…συνεργοί, 3.9) who include the Corinthians. And it is here that Paul says he is the skilled master builder (σοφὸς ἀρχιτέκτων) who laid a foundation (θεμέλιον ἔθηκα) (3.10). Now in 1 Cor. 9.1b–2, he says that the Corinthians are his work (τὸ ἔργον) in the Lord.

In 1 Cor. 9.3, Paul speaks about making his defence, which is linked back to 4.3. In both instances, the word ἀνακρίνω is used to describe his critics' action.[52]

---

49. Robertson and Plummer 1911: 179.

50. Conzelmann 1975: 152 n. 13; Fee 1987: 401; Collins 1999: 335. Conzelmann further cites 2 Cor. 1.12 as evidence for his argument. Barrett (1968: 202) recognizes that either way is possible.

51. The principles of marriage have been set out in 1 Corinthians 7 and Paul does not need to elaborate on them again here. Further, the problem the Corinthians have with Paul is really that of his manual labour and not accepting material support from them.

52. Other examples of judgment of the areas against Paul are 'food and drink' (1 Cor. 9.4; 4.11), 'manual labour' (1 Cor. 9.6–14; 4.12).

The next verbal link can be seen in the matter of spiritual food. Paul argues that he has sown spiritual good among the Corinthians (εἰ ἡμεῖς ὑμῖν τὰ πνευματικὰ ἐσπείραμεν...9.11). This closely parallels the 'planting' of 3.6.[53]

In 1 Cor. 9.15, Paul mentions his ground for boasting. The word used here is καυχημά, whose verb καυχάομαι, in two different forms,[54] is used in 1 Cor. 1.29, 31b. Although 1 Cor. 1.31b is a quotation from Jer. 9.23–24, the use of the word in both passages suggests that Paul thinks he is applying the Jeremiah quotation to himself in 9.15.[55] Most likely Paul believes that his boasting is about what he has done for the gospel (1 Cor. 9.12).

The even more important verbal link between 1 Corinthians 9 and 1 Corinthians 1–4 is that of proclaiming the gospel. In 9.16–18, Paul emphasizes that proclaiming the gospel is an 'obligation' (ἀνάγκη) for him, an οἰκονομία entrusted to him (1 Cor. 9.17). This echoes the οἰκονόμοι of 4.1–2 (cf. 1.17). Further the same proclamation is said to have its reward (μισθός), which is mentioned in both 3.8,[56] and 9.18, thus linking the two passages.

One final link may be seen between 9.23 and 4.10. In 9.23, Paul says that he is all things to all people 'for the sake of the gospel' (διὰ τὸ εὐαγγέλιον). In 4.10, he speaks of himself and his fellow workers as fools 'for the sake of Christ' (διὰ Χριστόν). Certainly, in refusing material support and by taking up manual labour 'for the sake of Christ', Paul faces many uncertainties, hunger and thirst, and physical dangers (4.11–13). And in his efforts to be 'all things' to 'all people', he similarly faces problems, including attacks on his apostolic authority. But in both instances, he claims it is all for the sake of Christ (1 Cor. 2.2).[57]

The verbal links demonstrated above between 1 Corinthians 9 and 1 Corinthians 1–4 justify our search for evidence in 1 Corinthians 1–4 about the challenge to Paul's authority. If indeed 1 Corinthians 1–4 can confirm such a challenge, then it is likely that Paul's argument in 1 Corinthians 9 may be a genuine defence of his authority.

What evidence is there in 1 Corinthians 1–4 that proves the challenge to Paul's authority? To begin with, the first sign of problems in the Corinthian church is party division in relation to certain personalities (1 Cor. 1.10, 12; 3.4), and it implies that not all the Corinthians accept Paul as their apostle, since some of them recognize such figures as Cephas and Apollos as their preferred leaders.[58] There

53. Fee (1987: 125, 409) argues that 'spiritual food' is the gospel, i.e. both 'milk' and 'solid food'.
54. Ὁ καυχώμενος ἐν κυρίῳ καυχάσθω (1 Cor. 1.31).
55. Cf. 2 Cor. 10.17 where the Jeremiah quotation is used in a context similar to that of 1 Cor. 9.1–2.
56. τὸ ἔργον has been mentioned in 9.1–2; and again in 3.14 to refer to the work of building the Corinthian church.
57. Fee (1987: 432) strangely states that Paul is not referring to the content of the gospel, but to the 'progress' of its proclamation. But it is difficult to see how the 'gospel' here could refer to its 'progress' without reference to its 'content'.
58. Munck (1959: 135–67) does not think there are factions in Corinth. Dahl (1967: 313) argues that the slogans do not mean that there are four parties, but that Paul is more probably addressing the Corinthian church as a whole in chs. 1–4.

are certainly quarrels among the Corinthians.[59] Paul mentions some possible causes: the attractions of the baptizers to their own following (1.14–17); the issue of 'wisdom' (σοφία, 1.18–31); and the boast about the perceived greatness of the leaders (3.21–22). Munck maintains that 1 Cor. 11.19 is meant to be taken eschatologically, and that factions are meant to bring out the genuine Christians.[60] Both αἵρεσις and σχίσμα, used interchangeably, appear to be the cause of the quarrels,[61] which may lead to the possibility of Paul's apostolic authority being questioned.

Dahl rightly observes that the issue of unity and the quarrels in Corinth are related to the function of the apostles and Christian leaders, and the esteem in which they are being held.[62] Further, the theme of Paul's relations to the church, according to Dahl, 'comes in at all important points of transition'. Dahl argues that Paul is therefore always pointing to the 'special ministry' entrusted to him as the basis that he should not be judged by anyone; and having his own ministry and suffering in mind. All this leads up to Paul's conclusion that he is the Corinthians' father in Christ Jesus through the gospel (4.15). Dahl concludes that all this is to '*re-establish his authority as apostle and spiritual father of the church at Corinth*' (emphasis mine).[63]

Dahl's observations are helpful. For in 1 Cor. 1.17–25, Paul points out that he is sent to do just one thing: to proclaim the gospel. And his proclamation is not according to worldly ways of wisdom (2.1, 4), but in weakness, fear, and trembling (2.3), with a demonstration of the Spirit and of power (2.4). However, Paul's status is being undermined because he does not speak in superior words or wisdom,[64] by which the Corinthians are judging his apostleship.[65] But how does Paul's style of public speaking relate to the kind of defence Paul puts up in 1 Corinthians 9? What can be said is that 1 Corinthians 1–4 demonstrates that Paul's authority is being questioned on grounds of his speech; while in 1 Corinthians 9, his defence shows that his rejection of the Corinthians' offer of material support is yet another ground. And Dahl is right to say that the party slogans 'are all to be understood as declarations of independence from Paul'.[66] What is clear at this point is that Paul's authority in Corinth is not altogether firm. Other signs also testify to this hypothesis.

59. Dahl 1967: 318.
60. Munck 1959: 136–37.
61. *Pace* Munck (1959: 139); Welborn (1987: 86) calls this 'church politics'.
62. Dahl 1967: 320.
63. Dahl 1967: 321.
64. Two references may shed light on this point: the first is 2 Cor. 10.10 where Paul's opponents criticize his speech as 'contemptible' (ὁ λόγος ἐξουθενημένος); the second is 2 Cor. 11.6 where Paul admits that he is untrained in speech (ἰδιώτης τῷ λόγῳ); cf. Litfin 1994: 154–55, and also his n. 16.
65. Litfin (1994: 151–52) states that 'Paul's ministry was singularly focused upon his role as a public speaker'. He cites the verbs which dominate Paul's references to his ministry, namely, εὐαγγελίζω, κηρύσσω, καταγγέλλω, λαλέω, παρακαλέω, and μαρτυρέω. His detailed listing of these verbs in the Corinthian correspondence alone amounts to 24. See 1994: 152 n. 14.
66. Dahl 1967: 322; cf. Litfin 1994: 183–85.

In 1 Cor. 3.6, 10; 4.15, Paul implies that the Corinthians are questioning his apostolic authority, because they do not duely recognize him as the founder of their church. Indeed, Apollos poses no threat to Paul's authority since he views himself and Apollos as co-workers of God (1 Cor. 3.5, 9) among the Corinthians (1 Cor. 3.5). What Paul is arguing against is the divisions within the church. Litfin is right that there are only two groups: those for Paul; and those against Paul.[67] This disunity is what drives him to be as 'critical of those who aligned themselves with Christ and with himself as he was of the others',[68] although Paul would likely be more pleased had all the Corinthians aligned themselves with him. 1 Corinthians 3 shows that while Paul believes he and the other workers are equal, he also wants the Corinthians to recognize him as founder of the church and accept his authority. Any other contestants will be unreliable, and their work will be perishable (1 Cor. 3.13; cf. 3.16–17).

1 Corinthians 4.15 reveals that Paul does not forbid the Corinthians from having παιδαγωγοί; but they must have only one 'father' in Christ. The παιδαγωγοί[69] may assist the Corinthians in their understanding of Christian behaviour,[70] but Paul remains the one they are to imitate. This is seen most clearly in use of the word οὖν (therefore) in 4.16. Why does Paul repeat what he has already emphasised in 3.6–10? There are three possible reasons.

First, there is disunity among the Corinthians which Paul strongly disapproves. Secondly, the Corinthians have begun to recognize the leadership of other people at the expense of Paul. The third reason lies in the possibility that the Corinthians have somehow 'devalued' Paul's status as their founding father and therefore no longer follow his ways. Thus, in 4.17, Paul says he is sending Timothy to 'remind' them of 'my ways in Christ Jesus'. To do this, Paul has to restore or re-establish his authority as founding apostle of the Corinthian church.[71] He 'begot' them ἐν Χριστῷ Ἰησοῦ διὰ τοῦ εὐαγγελίου.[72] Thus the lack of recognition of his status as founding father shows his authority is being questioned.

In addition to the above, 1 Cor. 4.1-5 also suggests that Paul is being 'judged' by the Corinthians. In v. 1, he states how the apostles are to be viewed: servants of Christ and stewards of God's mysteries (οὕτως ἡμᾶς...ὡς ὑπηρέτας

---

67. Litfin 1994: 184.
68. Litfin 1994: 181; Barrett (1968: 86–87) says Paul is aware that someone else may build upon his foundation.
69. The preceding word μυρίους, meaning 'ten thousand', cannot be literal. It should mean 'innumerable, countless', as Fee (1987: 185 n. 16) rightly renders it. Cf. BAGD 529.
70. Barrett (1968: 115) suggests that the 'tutors' might teach the Corinthians 'wisdom'. Fee (1987: 185) explains that παιδαγωγός as a 'guardian' was an ordinary but trusted slave to whom a father handed his children (usually sons) to be overseen by the slave.
71. Dahl (1967: 329) states that re-establishing his apostolic authority, as founder and spiritual father of the Corinthian church as a whole, is necessary for Paul before he could go on to answer the questions raised by the Corinthians.
72. He is therefore deliberate when he refers to Timothy as his 'beloved and faithful child in the Lord' (4.17), pointing out to them that they are not his only children in the Lord; there are others. And Fee (1987: 185) says that Paul's unique relationship to the Corinthians gives him 'a special authority over and responsibility toward them'.

Χριστοῦ καὶ οἰκονόμους μυστηρίων θεοῦ).[73] They are therefore accountable to God alone,[74] and the Corinthians are in no position to judge them (vv. 2–5). What Paul is therefore saying is that apostles carry the authority of Christ, and therefore of God, to do their work. What is required (ζητεῖται)[75] of them is faithfulness (i.e. πιστός τις εὑρεθῇ, 4.2). The Corinthians have questioned Paul's apostolic authority because they do not regard him as 'wise' in speech, nor fully recognize his founding contributions, nor his status as their 'father' in Christ. Further, they probably regard his manual labour demeaning of an apostle (cf. 1 Cor. 4.9–13), and his refusal to accept material support from them a sign that he is not an apostle. In 1 Cor. 4.9–13, Paul explicitly says he has grown weary from the work of his hands, and again here in 1 Corinthians 9 that he has given up his rights to material support. But the criterion which Paul is setting up here is faithfulness, which only the Lord can judge (1 Cor. 4.4), a principle that is either not known to the Corinthians or deliberately ignored by them.[76] The words ἀνακρίνω and κρίνω, and the attention on Paul himself, all point to some form of judgement against Paul, which calls for a brief discussion.

Paul's reference to a 'human court' (ἀνθρωπίνη ἡμέρα) in v. 3 and the mention of 'before the time' (πρὸ καιροῦ) in v. 5 suggest that the Corinthians have set themselves up like a grand jury against Paul, as if they were acting on the eschatological 'Day' of God.[77] But the Corinthians must not pronounce judgement before the 'Day' of the Lord, for it is the judgement of God on the 'Day' of the Lord that counts. Thus Paul contrasts the 'human day' against 'the Lord's Day', exposing the insignificance of the former.[78] Because the judgement of God would expose the 'purposes of the heart', Paul may be issuing a thinly veiled threat to the Corinthians that the 'purposes' of their heart will eventually be

73.   The use of ἡμᾶς instead of μέ should be seen in connection with 3.22–23 where Paul says he belongs to the Corinthians and the Corinthians belong to Christ and Christ to God. Paul is the one who 'planted', i.e. the one who preached the gospel to the Corinthians, thereby bringing into existence the Corinthian church. Thus, while the use of ἡμᾶς includes other apostles, Paul is primarily referring to himself. Thus, in v. 3, Paul very quickly moves back to the singular ἐγώ and says that he is a victim of the Corinthians' judgement. Cf. Conzelmann 1975: 83.

74.   Fee 1987: 158.

75.   ζητεῖται is supported by B Ψ 0289 M latt sy co, and is preferred over ζητεῖτε as the context seems to support the reading, even though the latter has relatively significant support from several manuscripts: P[46] ℵ(*) A C D F G P 6. 33. 104. 365. 1505. 1739. 1881. 2464 *al.* Fee (1987: 157) and Barrett (1968: 101) think ζητεῖτε is probably secondary. Héring (1962: 27) thinks that there is no reason against ζητεῖτε provided it is used as an imperative. His translation of 4.2 as 'Hence, moreover, seek nothing else of administrators than that they are faithful', though quite literal, does not seem appropriate to the context.

76.   Fee (1987: 160) prefers a narrower meaning of 'faithfulness' here which he takes to mean 'absolute fidelity to the gospel as he received it and preached it'. The overall context of 1 Corinthians, however, indicates a much broader meaning.

77.   The phrase πρὸ καιροῦ which means 'before the time' is defined by ἕως ἂν ἔλθῃ ὁ κύριος (until the Lord comes), thus referring to the eschatological 'Judgement Day' of the Lord. Cf. Fee 1987: 163 nn. 30–31; see also BAGD 334.

78.   Certainly the 'judgement' of the Corinthians must have meant much to Paul, as may be seen in his reference to it here and in 9.3, and his efforts in defending himself.

exposed,[79] which will serve as the basis for either reward or punishment from God. These are not simple explanations of the eschatological judgement day of God. They are serious arguments set within a larger context of a tense relationship between Paul and the Corinthians in which his apostolic authority is being questioned.

Finally in 1 Cor. 4.16–21, Paul urges the Corinthians to be imitators of him (μιμηταί μου γίνεσθε , 4.16), which assumes awareness of Paul's teachings on the part of the Corinthians (cf. 1 Cor. 4.17). However, to ensure the Corinthians' imitation, Paul sends them Timothy to 'remind' (ἀναμνήσει) them of his 'ways in Christ Jesus' (τὰς ὁδούς μου τὰς ἐν Χριστῷ Ἰησοῦ),[80] which precisely model those of the earthly Jesus (cf. 4.9–13), and include manual labour and the refusal of material support. But the Corinthians' criteria differ from what Paul considers to be God's perspective.[81] Hence, Paul must carry the authority in order to be imitated! Meeks is therefore right in saying that the conflicts between Paul and the Corinthians are 'directly *about* authority; they are questions about who makes decisions and who has to obey, and why'.[82]

This leads to Paul's warning that if the Lord wills, he will come and find out what 'power' (τὴν δύναμιν, 4.19) is behind these 'arrogant people'; for the kingdom of God is not dependent upon 'speech' (ἐν λογῷ), but on 'power' (ἐν δύναμει, 4.20; cf. 1 Cor. 2.4–5). Thus, the power-challenge here is who has the δύναμις to determine how people behave in Corinth. And Paul may have to resort to something more drastic in order to safeguard his authority (v. 21). If the Corinthians change their attitudes and accept Paul's ways in Christ, then the consequence would be 'love'; the alternative is 'discipline'.

Although the above statements of Paul in 1 Corinthians 1–4 may not individually reveal that Paul's apostolic authority is being questioned at Corinth, taken as a whole, they strongly suggest that Paul's apostolic authority is not altogether a settled issue. The party divisions indicate that not all Corinthians are loyal to Paul; some have probably given his status as an apostle less recognition than Paul would have liked it to be. His arguments that he is the one who 'planted', the

79.   Cf. 1 Cor. 3.13–15 where a close parallel has been set up in which Paul uses the metaphor of testing materials by fire to describe the eschatological judgement of God.

80.   Chow (1992: 98) compares the sending of Timothy to the Corinthians and the sending to the Thessalonians (1 Thess. 2.17–3.13) and the Philippians (Phil. 2.19–24) and observes that both the Thessalonians and the Philippians seem quite positive about Paul and vice versa. Further, the language of warmth and such like, which is present in 1 Thess. 2.17–3.13, is absent from 1 Cor. 4.14–21. Another observation also points to the fact that Paul and the Corinthians are having problems. Unlike the Thessalonian and Philippian passages, in 1 Cor. 4.14–21, Paul actually explains the sending of Timothy. And in 1 Cor. 16.10–11, he seems to be concerned about Timothy's reception. The explanation in 1 Cor. 4.14–21, coupled with 16.10–11, suggests that if the Corinthians are 'examining' and questioning Paul's authority, they may pose a challenging threat to Timothy and even possibly despise him; see Fee 1987: 188–89.

81.   Cf. Fee 1987: 186–87; see also Litfin 1994: 226–33.

82.   Meeks 1983: 117. Paul's absence from Corinth might have also contributed to the difficulty with his authority (cf. 1 Cor. 4.8, 19); see Barrett (1968: 117). Fee (1987: 190) says that Paul's failure to return to Corinth after some years, his lack of wisdom and eloquence combine to give the gospel and himself a poor showing. This therefore leads to the Corinthians' attitude towards him.

'skilled master-builder' who laid the foundation, point to the same suggestion that his apostolic position is less than firm. Some of the Corinthians have probably looked to other leaders, instead of Paul. This has implications for Paul and his preaching. The grounds for calling into question Paul's authority are various: his inability to speak 'wisdom', his manual labour, his lifestyle, and his refusal to accept material support (cf. 1 Corinthians 9). Paul, however, argues that the Corinthians have perceived apostles wrongly, that is, from a worldly perspective. God's perspective is that they are servants and only God can judge them. Further, Paul's ways are the ways in Christ Jesus which he has taught in every church, including the Corinthian church. As their founding father, he wants them to model their lives after his. He will visit them to execute disciplinary action against those who are 'arrogant', but will display love should they alter their attitudes and behaviour. Thus, Paul's authority as an apostle at Corinth is very much under challenge.

4. *The Double Purpose of 1 Corinthians 9: Authority and Example*

If Paul's authority as an apostle is challenged in Corinth, and 1 Corinthians 9 constitutes his defence, we would then need to ask how he defends his authority. Further, why does Paul speak of enslaving himself to others in 1 Cor. 9.19–23, when he has just sought to re-establish or defend his authority in 9.1–18? In what follows, I would argue that Paul has a double purpose in 1 Corinthians 9: defence of his apostolic authority and example to the 'strong' on idolatrous behaviour. The example includes discipline with regard to idolatry and its eschatological benefits (1 Cor. 9.24–27).

In 1 Cor. 9.1–18, Paul re-establishes his authority by putting forward 17 questions, which reveal the answers he is expecting. And these answers further indicate what the Corinthians would have understood Paul to be doing – the defence of his authority. The first few verses show that Paul believes that he is not only an apostle, but a 'free apostle', in the sense that he is free to accept or to reject the support to which he is entitled. The importance of ἐξουσία, following 1 Cor. 8.9, is played out in Paul's argument throughout. Being 'free', being an 'apostle', and having seen the Lord are all one and the same thing for Paul.[83] For it was precisely during his seeing the Lord that he was set free by the gospel, made an apostle and commissioned to preach to the Gentiles (Gal. 1.11–12, 15; cf. 1 Cor. 15.8–10).

According to Paul, apostleship comes with several entitlements: food and drink (9.4), a wife (9.5), freedom from work (9.6), and rewards from spiritual work (9.7–12a); which are coupled with a 'command' of the Lord (ὁ κύριος διέταξεν... vv. 13–14). Paul's argument involves three stages: (1) illustrations from everyday life (9.4–11); (2) scripture, the cultic tradition, a command of the Lord (9.13–14); and (3) actual practice – the giving up of his 'right' – and his reasons (9.12b, 15–23).

---

83.   Malherbe 1994: 239.

In the first stage Paul argues that he is entitled to basic food and drink, which is directly related to the eating of meat in ch. 8. In 1 Cor. 8.13, Paul says he will never eat meat if it causes fellow Christians to fall. And it highlights the nature of 'freedom' and 'right', that is, they are intertwined in the sense that Paul has ἐξουσία to be 'free' (ἐλεύθερος), and has the 'freedom' to choose how his ἐξουσία is to be exercised. This idea of having the 'right' to food and drink there-fore anticipates what he will say in 9.19–23.[84]

The entitlement to a believing wife, however, is problematic. It is possible that Paul's unmarried status (cf. 1 Cor. 7.8) has been judged by the Corinthians to be an indication of the inauthenticity of his apostleship,[85] on the basis that most other apostles[86] are accompanied by their spouses.[87] The reference to the other apostles indicates that the Corinthians have compared Paul to them.[88] Thus, the mention of spousal company becomes necessary in Paul's effort in establishing his apostolic authority.

The right to basic necessities is expanded in two further questions with two different metaphors, one military and the other agricultural (v. 7). Both are meant to elicit a negative answer. The point of the questions is that whatever one may be, one expects to be sustained by one's 'produce' or 'flock', it is one's right.[89] Paul is saying he is similarly entitled to the 'produce' of his 'work' – the Corinthians (cf. vv. 1–2; 11–12).[90] Thus, he sets aside their questioning of his authority on the basis of his refusal of material support.

In the second stage of the three-stage argument Paul moves from everyday life analogies to a more authoritative basis, for his case does not rest on mere human

84.   Fee (1987: 402) thinks this analysis is difficult to sustain. For he argues that 8.1–13 is not just about eating idol food, but about eating it in idol temples. Besides, other passages such as 9.19–23, 10.29b–30, and 10.31, show that Paul does not always abstain from such food. He is correct in arguing that Paul has a right to the support of 'food and drink' from the Corinthians. However, Paul has refused such support and is therefore being judged. Thus, the 'food and drink' here has to do with not only his right to the Corinthians' material support, but also his giving up of the support and his reasons for it, which Paul has already briefly mentioned in 8.13. Those passages Fee cites in fact precisely argue that Paul will do whatever he has to do in order to advance the gospel, including abstaining from idol-meat. Cf. Barrett 1968: 202; Conzelmann 1975: 153.

85.   Fee 1987: 403.

86.   οἱ λοιποὶ ἀπόστολοι (the rest of the apostles) could be a reference to the Twelve. However, from 1 Corinthians 15, we know Paul has a broader definition of an apostle.

87.   Barrett (1968: 203) observes that it is not only an apostolic theory but also an apostolic practice that apostles have the right to have their wives maintained by the communities in which they work. Conzelmann (1975: 153) questions whether we should add 'at the expense of the community' to ἀδελφὴν γυναῖκα περιάγειν, although he does not discuss the issue.

88.   Fee (1987: 403), 'Even his fellow tentmakers are a married couple (Acts 18.3). How is it, the Corinthians wonder, given what all others do, that he and his companions are not accompanied by wives? Does this also say something about the authenticity of his apostleship?'

89.   Fee 1987: 405; Barrett (1968: 204–205) makes these statements: '… A soldier on service expects to be maintained; why not an apostle?… A vinedresser expects to be nourished from that on which he bestows his labour; why not an apostle?… A herdsman reaps advantage from the flock he cares for; why not an apostle?…'

90.   Fee (1987: 405), 'He (Paul) should expect to be sustained from his "produce" or "flock" – the church that owes its existence to him'.

reasoning but on 'written' authority (ἐν γὰρ τῷ Μωϋσέως νόμῳ γέγραπται...
1 Cor. 9.9)[91] – the scripture – which constitutes an appeal to God's authority,
since the Law is none other than the Word of God. This is a powerful use of the
Jewish source of authority, particularly if the 'strong' have had Jewish influence
(cf. Chapter 5). The citation is from Deut. 25.4, οὐ κημώσεις βοῦν ἀλοῶντα
(1 Cor. 9.9).[92] The powerful argument from this particular citation is that Paul
hints that by calling into question his apostolic authority, the Corinthians are in
fact trying to apply a muzzle on him, that is, to control him.[93] However, like a
labouring ox, he is not to be 'muzzled', for he is entitled to the 'grain'. Presumably, if a law has been laid down to 'protect' animals,[94] certainly human
labourers ought to be even more protected, indeed, rewarded.[95] Therefore, Paul
maintains that those who labour for spiritual reasons ought to reap even more
physical rewards (1 Cor. 9.11–12a). And by comparing himself to others who
have laid claim on the Corinthians (εἰ ἄλλοι τῆς ὑμῶν ἐξουσίας μετέχουσιν),[96]
Paul is saying that if others who did not found the Corinthian church receive support from them, then as the founding apostle he has an even greater right to their
support (οὐ μᾶλλον ἡμεῖς;) (9.12a)![97] The difference is that Paul has not made
use of this apostolic right, for the gospel determines all his actions (v. 12b).[98]

In 1 Cor. 9.13, Paul moves to the example from the cultic tradition. Those who
are employed at the temple as well as those who serve at the altar both get their
food from the temple and the altar, respectively. It is possible that they are an
allusion to Lev. 6.16 and Deut. 18.1, where Aaron and his sons, and the levitical

91. The series of questions from v. 9 all the way to v. 12a assume on the part of the Corinthians a
knowledge of the scripture, which strongly suggests the Jewish background of some of the Corinthians. This further strengthens our case that the Corinthians have in one way or the other been influenced by Jewish culture, in whatever form.

92. This is a slightly different quotation from the LXX which reads: Οὐ φιμώσεις βοῦν ἀλοῶντα.
Both κημόω and φιμόω basically mean quite the same thing, i.e. to put a 'muzzle' on the animal.

93. Horrell (1996: 215) rightly argues that Paul refuses the Corinthians' material support so as not
to be obligated to them.

94. The command not to muzzle an ox while it is treading out the grain has to be taken to serve as
a 'protection' of the animal from being deprived, rather than as a 'reward', since for an ox to eat from
the grain while treading it appears to be a convenience. By re-interpreting the command and applying
to himself, Paul effectively alters the concept of 'protection' of the command to that of 'reward'.

95. Héring (1962: 78) views this as a Rabbinic argument *a minori ad maius*, from lesser to
greater. Weiss (1910: 237), 'Wie Pflüger und Drescher arbeiten müssen auf Hoffnung, auf Lohn und
Anteil an der Ernte, so ist auch P. als Missionar angewiesen auf einen Lohn seiner Arbeit'. Certainly,
the logic Paul is operating on is similar to that of the Synoptic tradition, '...are you not of more value
than they (i.e. birds of the air)?' (Mt. 6.26).

96. Who exactly these ἄλλοι are is uncertain. Héring (1962: 78) suggests that the way Paul
speaks of the Judaizing apostles in 2 Cor. 11.20 makes the ἄλλοι appear to be the apostles and
evangelists from Judaea, although he also concedes that there is no way of confirming this. Fee
(1987: 409–10) thinks it more likely refers to Apollos and Peter. It is possible that Paul has in mind
those he mentions in 9.5.

97. BAGD 514, on τῆς ὑμῶν ἐξουσίας μετέχουσιν: enjoy authority over you. Thus, Paul's
'right' to the Corinthians' support is directly related to his apostolic authority over them.

98. Fee 1987: 410–11; Thiselton (2000: 691) argues that ἐγκοπή suggests 'avoiding roughening
the path for the gospel'. See further Barrett (1968: 207).

priests are instructed to eat from what has been sacrificed, as they are the Lord's 'workers'. Hence, Deut. 18.2 says that the levitical priests will have no inheritance because the Lord is their 'inheritance' (LXX: κλῆρος, 'allotment of land'; the Hebrew יהוה הוא נחלתו literally means 'the Lord is their possession'). Although Fee argues that the background is unimportant as both Jewish as well as pagan temples would have had the same principle,[99] the Jewish background of the 'strong', particularly their knowledge that idols are nothing in the world and that there is no God but one, is likely to remind them of the scripture.[100] Moreover, since Paul has just mentioned Deut. 25.4, it is probable that he has in mind the general principles of the Torah on this matter. This is further confirmed by 9.14, 'In the same way, the Lord commanded…' (οὕτως καὶ ὁ κύριος διέταξεν…). It seems unlikely that Paul would allow any possible link between the Synoptic tradition and the pagan temples, and it seems equally unlikely that he would allow such an implication, since he is relatively hostile to idolatry, as we have shown in the previous chapter. If this constitutes yet another reminder of the general principles of the Torah, then Paul has ably led his readers to the point where he has the scriptural backing and the cultic tradition to prove that he has the right to the Corinthians' support.

The next most precise of Paul's arguments is the command of the Lord, which most likely is a reference to Mt. 10.10 and Lk. 10.7 where Jesus teaches the disciples two basic principles when preaching: (1) remain in the house that welcomes them, eating and drinking from what the household has provided, for the labourers are worthy of their wages;[101] and (2) do not move from house to house. Of these, Paul seems to be making use of the point concerning the labourers' worthiness for a wage and interpreting it as a command of the Lord. There are two implications which follow Paul's re-interpretation of this instruction: (1) the apostle has a right to live by the material support of the Corinthians; and (2) since Paul has given up the right to the Corinthians' support, his refusal to accept support would constitute an act of disobedience to the Lord's command. While (1) helps to affirm Paul's right, (2) creates a problem. Murphy-O'Connor asks by what authority Paul re-classified an obligation into a right, and argues that Paul's practice is that he did not consider Jesus' precepts binding all the time, but only as guidelines to be applied critically.[102] Similarly, Witherington takes this as

99. Fee 1987: 412 n. 82. Barrett (1968: 207–208) notes that the customs were widespread in antiquity. But it would be trivializing Paul's argument if, having argued from Deut. 25.4 Paul should now turn to an analogy whose background is unimportant. The background, contrary to Fee, is important because the pagan practice would be considered rather irrelevant to Paul's right as an apostle. Whereas the Jewish scripture is more directly related and relevant to the belief of Paul and the knowledge of the 'strong'.

100. Héring (1962: 79) observes that there may be a parallelism between the priesthood of the Old Covenant and the ministry of the apostles. He further observes that the same analogy is attested in Rom. 15.16. In any case, the phrase οὐκ οἴδατε suggests that the Corinthians are aware of this cultic tradition.

101. The same is also mentioned in 1 Tim. 5.18 where Deut. 25.4 is also part of the teaching on how those who labour in preaching and teaching ought to be treated.

102. Murphy-O'Connor 1979: 87.

Paul's thinking that such a rule is not binding because it was given for his benefit, not as something he has to do to be a true apostle.[103] Fee argues that this word of Jesus is not a 'command' but a proverb which Jesus applied to his instruction to the 72 when he sent them out to preach; and it is meant for the missionaries' benefits.[104] Paul views it as a 'command' of the Lord 'because it has the net effect of the tradition'.[105] And Paul intends to impress upon his readers that his right to their material support is an undisputed fact enshrined in the Lord's command.[106] The Corinthians know best whether Paul is a 'proclaimer' of the gospel; and they know best whether Paul ought to live by the gospel.

Paul moves into the third stage with an obvious question now facing him: if he has so vigorously argued for his apostolic authority and thus his right to material support, why does he refuse the very support to which he has a right? In vv. 12b and 15, Paul says he has not used the right for the reason that he does not want to put any hindrance (ἐγκοπή) in the way of the gospel. The giving up of his right is something in which he can glory; it is his boast (καύχημα) which he will not give up. Thus, his reason and purpose in refusing material support are precisely to fulfil his apostolic function of proclaiming the gospel.

Käsemann argues that Paul's reward is in preaching the gospel without financial reimbursement; this accounts for his refusal of material support, for it would mean losing his boast and his reward. Further, Käsemann says that the ἀνάγκη in 9.16 acts on Paul with 'a force like that of a destiny' so that he is not a free agent; however, he is blessed in his action.[107] Scholars have adduced several reasons for Paul's refusal of financial support, which serve to explain the meaning of the term ἐγκοπή. First, if Paul were to insist on accepting financial support, then the poor among the Gentiles might hesitate about accepting the gospel.[108] This, however, is not the case as Paul did accept support from the Macedonians even though he knew they had experienced extreme poverty (cf. 2 Cor. 8.2).[109] Similarly, Theissen's and Marshall's argument that Paul tries to make the pioneering mission as effective as possible during *the initial stage* by not becoming a financial burden is weak,[110] since Paul in 2 Cor. 11.9 and 12.14 says that he would never burden the Corinthians *at any time*. Second, by refusing financial support, Barrett

103. Witherington III 1995: 210.
104. Fee 1987: 413, see also his n. 96.
105. Fee 1987: 413; Barrett (1968: 208) states that Paul seldom quotes Jesus' words, but does so here in order to build up a particularly strong case for a practice he himself does not apply.
106. Fee (1987: 413 n. 91) notes the use of the word καταγγέλλω instead of εὐαγγελίζομαι to be rare. It is possible that Paul meant it to be a word play, where εὐαγγέλιον and καταγγέλλω both share the cognate of ἄγγελος, so as to emphasize the nature of the 'preaching'.
107. Käsemann 1969: 233. The point is further emphasized: 'Its burden is, that he who loves can and must renounce his rights, however well-founded they may be, if he is to go on really loving and serving effectively'.
108. Barrett 1968: 207; Holmberg 1978: 92; similarly Murphy-O'Connor (1979: 88) adduces the same reason for Paul's refusal of financial support.
109. Thus, the argument of Dungan (1971: 15) that Paul's policy is not to be a burden to the poorer churches does not hold water either.
110. Theissen 1982: 40; and Marshall 1987: 176.

argues, Paul is trying to avoid the misunderstanding that he preaches the gospel for gain, which may also jeopardize the collection mentioned in 16.1.[111] This is possible but unlikely since the two seem to be quite different matters, although they are about money.[112] The third reason has been given by Holmberg and others, that is, Paul would accept financial support from a church only after he has left it.[113] This does not explain Paul's decision not to accept financial support, as he has already left Corinth at the time of writing 1 Corinthians. And the same problem remains an issue even in 2 Corinthians, when Paul has long left Corinth. A fourth explanation is that Paul's behaviour is meant to model the love and self-sacrifice of Jesus,[114] a possible reason as Paul later calls upon the Corinthians to be 'imitators' of him as he is an 'imitator' of Christ (1 Cor. 11.1; cf. 4.16). In other words, by refusing material support, Paul is doing two things. On the one hand, he wishes to imitate Jesus' love and self-sacrifice; on the other hand, he wishes that others too might imitate his attitude and behaviour, the absence of which (a result of his accepting support) would serve as a hindrance to the gospel, that is, the kind of ethical behaviour that should rightly come from one's acceptance of the gospel would be thwarted! This concept of not putting a hindrance to the gospel by imitating Christ is elaborated later in vv. 19–23, where, by making a link between giving up one's right and the proclamation of the gospel, Paul seeks to demonstrate how the 'strong' behave with regard to idol-meat has implications for whether the gospel is advanced or hampered (cf. 1 Cor. 8.10–12). Thus, in vv. 15b–18 Paul spells out the rationale behind his giving up of his right, and so sets himself as an example to the 'strong'.

In v. 12b, Paul states that he would 'endure' (στέγομεν) anything (πάντα) rather than put an obstacle in the way of the gospel. In v. 15b, this refusal to put an obstacle serves as his ground for boasting (τὸ καύχημά μου οὐδεὶς κενώσει),[115] which he would not surrender. The abrupt break that comes after the clause καλὸν γάρ μοι μᾶλλον ἀποθανεῖν ἤ is difficult to explain. Fee rightly says that it is not certain as to how Paul would have intended the sentence to end; but goes on to say that the broken clause has its own power and that Paul probably intended the interrupting sentence.[116] Conzelmann argues that Paul's boast lies precisely in

111. Barrett 1968: 207; Holmberg (1978: 93) further says that the ingrained mistrust in the non-Jewish world of sophists who lived at the expense of others is another possible reason for the common practice that the missionaries work for their own living.

112. If Paul can succeed in arguing for his right to financial support and in showing and persuading the Corinthians that his giving up of the right serves as an example to them, it might even help the collection, that is, like Paul who gives up his right to material support, the Corinthians ought also to demonstrate the sacrificial attitude of Christ, which Paul imitates, by giving generously and sacrificially for the needy Jerusalem church (cf. 2 Cor. 9.6–7).

113. Holmberg 1978: 94; Murphy-O'Connor 1979: 88.

114. Barrett 1968: 207; Holmberg 1978: 93.

115. οὐδεὶς κενώσει has impressive support: P⁴⁶ ℵ* B Dᐟ·ᶜ 33. 1739. 1881 *pc* b; Tert Ambst Pel. Other readings are ἵνα τις κενώσῃ and οὐθεὶς μὴ κενώσει, both of which have weaker support compared to the reading οὐδεὶς κενώσει. See also Thiselton 2000: 693.

116. Fee 1987: 417; Barrett (1968: 208) thinks this is characteristically Pauline as he cites other Pauline passages.

his renunciation of his rights, whose sense is plain in the verses that follow.[117] But he does not explain why, in one moment, Paul says his renunciation is ground for boasting, and in another, seems to contradict himself by saying that if he preaches the gospel it is not a boast for him (ἐὰν γὰρ εὐαγγελίζωμαι, οὐκ ἔστιν μοι καύχημα, 9.16a). His view that the sentence breaks down unless we read ἤ as ἦ, 'truly', may have some merit.[118] In other words, the sentence would have read, 'For it is good for me rather to die; truly no one shall empty me of my boast'. This means in the first part of the clause, Paul rejects the notion of the previous clause that he might be setting out his rights in order to claim them. And in the second part, he argues that no one, indeed no Corinthian, will be able to convince him to change his mind about refusing support. For this is his boast.

The seemingly contradictory clause in 9.16a is in fact exactly what Paul is saying: preaching the gospel is not his boast because he was called to do so,[119] but the preaching *for free* is!

This is the point of v. 17. Paul's use of the words ἑκών and ἄκων indicates that he understands 'reward' (μισθός) as the result of a voluntary act. Thus, if his preaching of the gospel was 'willing' (ἑκών), he would receive a 'reward' (μισθὸν ἔχω); if not, then what he is doing is a 'stewardship' entrusted to him (οἰκονομίαν πεπίστευμαι). This point is further developed by Martin who analyses 1 Corinthians 9 on the basis of the concept of slavery in the context of moral philosophy and concludes that when Paul uses ἑκών, ἄκων and ἀνάγκη, he is implying that he is a slave of Christ – free people act willingly, but slaves act unwillingly.[120] Martin then argues that Paul's action would produce two kinds of reaction. One reaction would be from the educated, trained people who were familiar with the moral philosophical discourse, which is one of shock as they would view Paul's admission that he is preaching under 'compulsion' as an indication that he is not a free, wise and true philosopher. The other reaction would be from the ordinary people unfamiliar with the moral philosophical discourse and would therefore view Paul's language positively, as having a high status-by-association form of slavery, that is, slave of Christ.[121] This argument, though attractive, is not without problems. For example, how does one decide if the Corinthian church is made up of these two classes of people?[122] Further, it is not clear whether the Corinthians are aware of and intellectually, though perhaps less consciously, applying such moral philosophical discourse. In 1 Corinthians 9, Paul is simply establishing his

117. Conzelmann 1975: 157.
118. Conzelmann 1975: 156 n. 6; 157 n. 22.
119. Käsemann (1969: 228) rightly says that the 'compulsion' arises out of Paul's commission to preach the gospel. Conzelmann (1975: 157), 'He has not chosen his own calling. He was called and accordingly stands under constraint'.
120. Martin 1990: 74–76. Malherbe (1994: 238–51) analyses Paul's language in the light of Cynics' and Stoics' concepts of determinism and free will. He states: 'Although he has necessity laid upon him to preach the gospel, he does so willingly and has a reward. Were he to preach unwillingly, he would nevertheless have to preach, for he has been entrusted with an οἰκονομία.'
121. Martin 1990: 76–77, 117–18.
122. Meggitt (1998: 102–107) rightly calls into question such division of the Corinthians along social lines.

apostolic authority and setting himself as an example to the 'strong',[123] by showing that he has voluntarily given up his 'right' to support. Barrett's interpretation that because Paul is a slave hired out by God to do his (God's) work, he cannot lay claim to pay,[124] seems more plausible.[125] But what is Paul's reward if his preaching is involuntary?

In 1 Cor. 9.18 Paul paradoxically says that his 'reward' for preaching the gospel is to preach it without 'reward'. This is because his single-minded intention is the proclamation of the gospel from which he derives much joy (Phil. 1.18; 1 Cor. 2.2). Thus, he does not wish the exercise of his right to be an ἐγκοπή to the gospel. Fee therefore correctly argues that Paul's 'pay' and 'boast' refer to the same reality of 'preaching the gospel without accepting support so as to put no hindrance before the gospel'.[126] This serves as his example to the 'strong': as an apostle he has given up his rights; the 'strong' therefore ought also to give up their right to freely eat idol-meat. The corollary is that the 'strong', too, can find their 'reward' in such sacrificial behaviour. The next section is probably the most crucial in Paul's overall argument in 1 Corinthians 9, where he sets out the most important principle that guides his practice of refusing material support and of taking up manual labour.

1 Corinthians 9.19–23 continues from what precedes,[127] and paints various scenarios in which Paul willingly gives up his right by becoming like his audience. Verse 19 picks up the theme of 9.1 again, Ἐλεύθερος γὰρ ὢν ἐκ πάντων... (For though I am free from all...), which speaks about Paul's freedom (ἐλευθερία) as an apostle, to either accept or refuse material support. In 9.19, Paul refers to another aspect of this 'freedom', that is, 'freedom' in respect of others. In other words, he *is* free from how others think he should behave. Yet, he has enslaved himself to all (πᾶσιν ἐμαυτὸν ἐδούλωσα). Here lies the paradox of Paul's argument: on the one hand, he insists on his freedom and authority; on the other hand, he willingly allows the status of others to decide how he should behave. But, he is precisely free to do what he likes, including enslaving himself to others!

The governing principle that determines how he would exercise his 'freedom' appears to be the single-minded desire to win others to the Lord. The phrase ἵνα τοὺς πλείονας κερδήσω indicates the particular goal to which Paul will do all

123. Horrell (1996: 206) observes that the key words 'right' (ἐξουσία) and 'offence' (πρόσκομμα, 8.9; ἐγκοπή, 9.12), and the related words (ἀπρόσκοπος, 10.32; and κερδαίνω, 9.19–23) show that the example is meant for the 'strong'.

124. Fee (1987: 419–20, and also n. 33) points out that the contrast between ἑκών and ἄκων is a clear reference to 'free' and 'slave'.

125. Barrett 1968: 209–10.

126. Fee 1987: 421. Barrett (1968: 210) comments: '...the preaching without charge (...) is itself the reward, because it means that he is putting no stumbling-block in the way of the gospel (v. 12), and thus has a better chance of seeing the Gospel flourish than would otherwise be possible'. Cf. Käsemann 1968: 223; Héring 1962: 81.

127. Horrell 1996: 208. Cf. Conzelmann (1975: 158) who finds the paradox appropriate; see also his nn. 27, 29 where he takes issue with Weiss for taking v. 17 as a gloss and arguing that v. 18 is a conclusion from v. 17 is pointless.

to subject his 'freedom'. The word κερδαίνω appears five times in vv. 19–23 with σώζω appearing once. Κερδαίνω carries the meaning of 'winning' and 'gaining'. In our text the term means leading people to salvation in Christ (vv. 22–23), which includes the kind of behaviour that should rightly issue from the gospel and its maintenance.[128] In terms of idolatry, Paul's goal is to 'win' people to the point of maintaining faithfulness to God (cf. v. 18). And he sets out four groups of people among whom he has allowed himself to be a member, in order to meet this goal (vv. 20–23). They are: the Jews (Ἰουδαῖοι), those under Law (οἱ ὑπὸ νόμον), those without Law (οἱ ἄνομοι), and the 'weak' (οἱ ἀσθενεῖς).[129]

To the Jews, Paul says he becomes 'like' (ὡς)[130] a Jew. However, he does not say anything about the Law, which may suggest that there are Jews who, though they may be Jews, do not adhere strictly to the Law (see Chapter 4 above). The second group, those under the Law, could refer to the Jews who may be described as strict Jews with regard to their strict adherence to the Law of Moses. Thus, Paul could well have such Jews in mind.[131] But it could be possible that Gentile God-worshippers as well as the proselytes to Judaism who have unilaterally subjected themselves to the Law, might have also been in Paul's mind. The third group, those without the Law, is a clear reference to Gentiles. The fourth group, the 'weak', may still constitute a proper group that cuts across all ethnic boundaries to include strict Jews, Gentile converts, Gentile God-worshippers, all of whom have scruples regarding eating food that has been sacrificed to idols. To the 'weak', Paul does not say he becomes 'like' (ὡς)[132] the 'weak', but he becomes 'weak' (ἐγενόμην τοῖς ἀσθενέσιν ἀσθενής, 9.22). But what does Paul mean when he says he 'became' like all these groups of people?

128. Cf. Murphy-O'Connor (1979: 91) who suggests that Paul views conversion as a process which will culminate only on the day of the Lord, therefore 'each individual has to be continually "re-won" for Christ'.

129. Murphy-O'Connor (1979: 89–90) maintains that there are three groups. A closer examination will show otherwise.

130. ὡς was omitted by F G* 6*. 326. 1739 *pc*; Cl Or[1739mg], perhaps, as Fee (1987: 422 n. 2) suggests, because of their feeling the dissonance of a Jew saying that he became like a Jew. Paul's use of ὡς could mean that he recognizes his status in relation to God no longer as a Jew, but as a Christ worshipper and an apostle of Christ. Cf. 2 Cor. 5.17, 'Therefore if a person is in Christ, he/she is a new creation; the old has passed away, behold, the new has come'.

131. Barrett (1968: 211) cites Moulten's view that Paul might be referring to a particular occasion, possibly that of Timothy's circumcision.

132. The only clause without ὡς in the series is ἐγενόμην τοῖς ἀσθενέσιν ἀσθενής, ἵνα τοὺς ἀσθενεῖς κερδήσω ('to the weak I became weak, in order that I might win the weak', 9.22). Fee (1987: 422 n. 5, and 431), Conzelmann (1975: 161 n. 28) and Gardner (1994: 103) have all noted its absence. Barrett (1968: 215) cautions against pressing too much significance out of this. It is to be noted, however, that ὡς is attested by א² C D F G Ψ and made the majority text reading. Horrell (1996: 208 n. 54) is right in saying that the insertion is more easily explained than an omission. The omission, however, is supported by P⁴⁶ א A B 1739 *pc* lat; Cyp. The significance lies in the fact that in 1 Cor. 8.10–13, Paul urges the 'strong' to consider the 'weak', for whom Christ died, who may fall as a result of the exercise of their 'right' to eat idol-meat by the 'strong'. Now that Paul mentions the various groups whom he would become 'like', but appears to deliberately leave out the word 'like' to show the 'strong' his becoming one of the 'weak', his example for them therefore is much more powerful.

To begin with, Paul unambiguously states that he enslaved himself to everyone. At the end of v. 22, he says that he 'became all things to all people in order
that he might save some' (τοῖς πᾶσιν γέγονα πάντα, ἵνα πάντως τινὰς
σώσω). This is the fundamental principle of Paul: enslavement of himself to all
for the sake of the gospel, for the chief aim of 'saving' the members of the
groups. Thus, to the Jews, Paul becomes like a Jew so as to win the Jews. Does
this mean that Paul would revert back to the practices of the Jews, just to win
them? Fee argues that Paul is free from all the Jewish peculiarities such as circumcision, food laws, and special observances.[133] At the same time, Paul probably has no difficulty with Jews continuing their practices, as long as they are not
made the requirement for a right relationship with God.[134] Thus, Paul is willing to
adapt his style in such a way as to win the Jews, that is, he could still practise
Jewish customs when appropriate. The word ὡς thus provides the qualification –
he does not become a Jew, but *like* a Jew.

This is the same principle which governs the second group. Paul is careful to
state that while he becomes like those under the Law, he is himself not 'under the
Law' (v. 20b). Similarly, when he becomes like those 'without the Law', he is
nevertheless not outside God's law but 'under Christ's law' (ἔννομος Χριστοῦ,
v. 21).[135] The qualifications in both instances seem to be a safeguard against
possible misunderstanding or misinterpretation on the part of the Corinthians
over what Paul might have meant. Paul is no longer under the Law because he is
a free man in Christ, whose law is an expression of the law of God. What is the
law of Christ? According to Gal. 6.2, ἀγάπη appears to be Paul's concept of the
law of Christ, which seeks to bear one another's burdens.[136] Thus for Paul exercising ἀγάπη is the law of Christ expressed, hence the law of God. But to the
'weak', Paul becomes weak (v. 22). The context of Paul's defence and example to
the 'strong' suggests that the 'weak' here probably refers to the 'weak' in 1 Corinthians 8.[137] And the word κερδαίνω could also mean 'keeping' the 'weak'.
Barrett is right in saying that this would mean '*keep* them for the church, instead

133. Fee 1987: 428.
134. Fee 1987: 428; cf. Conzelmann (1975: 160), 'He (Paul) is able as a Jew to practice Jewish
customs, without teaching that the Law is a way of salvation. And he does not have to deliver the
Jews from their practice of the Law, but from their 'confidence' in the Law as a way of salvation
(Phil. 3.2ff)'.
135. Hollander 1998: 125. This is a difficult clause with regard to whether it should be objective
genitive or subjective genitive. Fee (1987: 429 n. 43) argues for the objective genitive for ἄνομος
θεοῦ, i.e. Paul is not lawless 'towards God'. However, cf. Barrett (1968: 212–13) who suggests that
this could be done by emphasizing the genitives 'in relation to the implied law' and so render 'not
subject to the law *of God*', 'under obligation to the law *of Christ*'. The context suggests that a
subjective genitive for both ἄνομος θεοῦ and ἔννομος Χριστοῦ makes more sense. See further Blass
and Debrunner §182 on genitive with adjectives.
136. Barclay 1988: 158–59. Longenecker (1990: 275–76) argues that ὁ νόμος τοῦ Χριστοῦ here
stands for the prescriptive principles stemming from the heart of the gospel, 'which are meant to be
applied to specific situations by the direction and enablement of the Holy Spirit, being always motivated and conditioned by love'. Murphy-O'Connor (1979: 90), '…for all practical purposes, Paul is
guided by 'the law which is in Christ', and whose single demand is love'. Cf. 1 Corinthians 13.
137. Willis 1985b: 37.

of driving them out by wounding their consciences'.[138] In the light of 8.13, Paul is saying that when he seeks to keep the 'weak' from falling into idolatry, he is in fact 'winning' them. And it is Paul's example to the 'strong'.

The last clause, 'I have become all things to all people, in order that I might save some' sums up Paul's basic principle in 'winning' and 'keeping' others for the Lord.[139] Paul models this principle after the life of Jesus and the cross, by doing manual labour and facing persecutions, always carrying in his body the 'death of Christ' (2 Cor. 4.10). In 2 Cor. 8.9, Paul uses the generosity of Jesus to encourage the Corinthians to be generous towards the Christians at Jerusalem. This seems to be the *modus operandi* of Paul's attitude towards the preaching of the gospel: he gives up his right to material support and becomes like his audience, in order to 'win' them to the Lord. Thus, in 1 Cor. 11.1 he tells the Corinthians to imitate him, just as he imitates Christ.

Martin uses the concept of humiliation-exaltation in Phil. 2.6–11 to explain Paul's self-enslavement,[140] which forms the framework of Paul's soteriology and ethics. This means that when Paul enslaves himself to all, he is not giving up power but merely shifting the power to a lower status.[141] The use of Phil. 2.6–11 explains Paul's imitation of Christ. Martin is right in saying that lying behind Paul's reasoning in 1 Corinthians 9 is his theology of the cross.[142] For it is the self-sacrifice of Jesus on which Paul's own principle is based. We are told in the Christ-hymn that Christ lowered himself and became a human person, even though he was equal with God, being obedient even to death. This motif seems to be behind Paul's own self-enslavement. Even though he is an apostle who has authority and complete freedom,[143] Paul puts the gospel at the centre of his decisions and behaviour, demonstrating to the 'strong' the need and importance of living and behaving in a manner that would advance the gospel. 1 Corinthians 9.23 neatly summarizes his example, 'I do all this for the sake of the gospel' (πάντα δὲ ποιῶ διὰ τὸ εὐαγγέλιον). The key word on such behaviour and attitude seems to be 'discipline', which is governed by the principles Paul will set out in 9.24–27 (see Chapter 5, section 7, a, above).

We have shown that 1 Corinthians 9 constitutes Paul's defence of his apostolic authority. We have also looked at how Paul establishes his authority by arguing from daily experiences, the Jewish scripture, and cultic tradition, that he has apostolic rights to material support. But by establishing his right to material support, Paul seeks to show that he has given up his right, so as to set himself an example to the 'strong'. In 1 Cor. 10.31–11.1, Paul rounds up his argument of 1

---

138. Barrett 1968: 215

139. Fee's argument that the word σώσω means that κερδήσω in the five instances before must mean 'win'. However, the broader meaning of κερδαίνω need not exclude itself from σώζω, which, if taken as a process, would certainly include the work of κερδαίνω.

140. Martin 1990: 129–30.

141. Martin 1990: 134.

142. Martin 1990: 135.

143. Horrell (1996: 207) points out that Paul 'asserts his freedom (v. 1) only to show that he has enslaved himself to all (v. 9)'. This self-enslavement may be seen as an act of discipline, resulting from his own imitation of Christ's self-lowering.

Corinthians 8–10 by outlining four imperatives which the 'strong' ought to be doing: (1) glorify God in whatever they do; (2) avoid giving offence to all; (3) please all with the view of saving them (a clear echo of 9.19–23, which argues against the 'partition' theories); and (4) become imitators of Paul.

In 10.23, Paul corrects the claim of the 'strong', 'all things are lawful', by pointing out that not all things build up. The 'strong' ought to know this since their participation in idolatrous acts is causing the 'weak' considerable unease and concern. Hence in v. 24, he says to them not to seek their own advantage, but that of the others. Seeking the advantage of others is not indiscriminate; it must be governed by the first imperative: glorify God. Further, do visits to pagan temples, eating idol-meat, participating in pagan religious rituals, and the like, hinder the gospel? Even if the 'strong' have the right to do any of these things, should they not give up their right, just as Paul gives up his right to material support, in order to save others and not to cause offence to the 'weak'? All these imperatives have the capability of glorifying God, which picks up the 'thanks-giving' in v. 30. It suggests that what one does must be capable of being a 'praise', or a means of 'praise' to God.[144] The 'strong' must consider how the exercise of their freedom in eating idol-meat is capable of causing others to render praise, honour and the like, to God, or whether it is causing others to fall. The concern to glorify God is then to be translated into one's behaviour in relation to others. The second imperative is 'give no offence to all' (v. 32). Three groups are mentioned here: Jews, Greeks and the church of God. Perhaps the 'weak', as we have suggested earlier, comprise both Jews and Gentiles whose Jewish influence concerning idolatry has caused them to be scrupulous about the behaviour of the 'strong'. Thus, the exercise of the freedom by the 'strong' in attending pagan temples, eating idol-meat, and even possibly participating in pagan religious rituals, is causing offence to such ones. In the end, the church of God will be scandalized. Barrett comments, 'I do not act to the glory of God if I give to an idol some of the honour due to God alone; nor if I cause scandal or ill-feeling in the church, or cause a fellow-Christian to fall from his faith'.[145] Similarly, the third imperative for the 'strong', which is to please everyone, is to be seen in conjunction of the first two imperatives. Paul has already argued for and demonstrated his own giving up of his right to material support, so as not to put an obstacle in the way of the gospel, but to become a slave to all. Paul's voluntary surrender of his right to material support and willing self-enslavement are described here by himself as πάντα πᾶσιν ἀρέσκω μὴ ζητῶν τὸ ἐμαυτοῦ σύμφορον ἀλλὰ τὸ τῶν πολλῶν, ἵνα σωθῶσιν. This parallels 9.22b, where Paul describes his enslavement to the various groups as τοῖς πᾶσιν γέγονα πάντα, ἵνα πάντως τινὰς σώσω. In 9.22b, Paul says he has become all things to all people; in 10.33, he says he pleases everyone in everything. In both

---

144. BAGD 204, 'to the praise of God'. Cf. Aalen (1976: 46), where meanings include 'honour', 'fame', 'repute'. In 1 Cor. 10.31, Aalen takes it to be 'to the glory of God'.

145. Barrett 1968: 244. Héring (1962: 99) argues that it is addressed to the 'strong' as much as it is to the 'weak', whose 'over-scrupulousness' might be a shock to pagans whom the gospel is meant to win. But this is stretching Paul's point and missing the context of 1 Corinthians 8–10.

instances, Paul's purpose is expressed in the ἵνα clause, both of which aim at 'salvation'. There is yet another difference between the two verses: in 10.33, Paul adds a qualifying clause that he does not seek his own benefits but that of others; whereas this is absent in 9.22. And it should mean the same thing, that he seeks to become like others that they may be saved. The third imperative is therefore to be seen as a recapitulation of Paul's example in 1 Cor. 9.19–23.[146] Having spelt out the first three imperatives, Paul then issues the final imperative: be imitators of me, as I am of Christ (11.1). And the summary confirms 9.1–23 is about imitation of Paul as well.

Is Paul being arrogant when he asks the Corinthians to imitate him? The qualification Paul makes is instructive, καθὼς κἀγὼ Χριστοῦ (just as I also am of Christ). While Paul is telling them to imitate his example, he also tells them that his example is the result of imitating Christ. And as we have discussed earlier, Paul's enslavement is modelled after the life and the cross of Christ; his imperative to the 'strong', and indeed, to all the Corinthians, is to imitate the self-sacrificial life of Christ, which is expressed on the cross. The very closing imperative interestingly acts like a declaration of Paul's authority as the founding apostle of the Corinthian church. Thus Paul once again asserts his position and status as the founding apostle who has authority over the Corinthian church, and so echos his statement in 4.16.

5. *The Centre of Authority: Who is to Decide?*

The above discussion of 1 Corinthians 9 raises a further question: who is to decide what is the right or appropriate behaviour with regard to idolatry? In the case of the situation described in 1 Cor. 8.1–11.1, the answer appears uncertain. For the 'strong' do not seem to agree with Paul's position, and have even called into question his authority. Meanwhile, the 'weak' do not seem to agree with the behaviour of the 'strong' and are recipients of Paul's sympathy. In Chapter 5, we have set out the theology of the 'strong' which serves as the basis for their idolatrous behaviour. In Chapter 4, we have also shown the possible conceptual overlap between the understanding of the 'strong' concerning the true God and that of other people who do not worship Yahweh or believe in Jesus; and the possibility that the 'strong' may be aware of the LXX (Exod. 22.27a) ban on reviling other people's gods. Paul therefore argues in 1 Corinthians 10 that the objects of the pagan sacrifices are in fact demons, destroying the basis of the 'strong' and therefore their 'authority'. In 1 Corinthians 9, he seeks to show them the authority on which decisions for the Corinthian community may be based.

The Jewish community in the Diaspora had their own leadership structure whereby decisions for the community were made.[147] Moreover, the Law served as the basis for the communities' life, both within and outside.[148] Philo tells us that

146. Barrett 1968: 245.
147. See, for example, Applebaum (1974: 464–503); see further Gallas (1990: 178–91) for his treatment of Paul's reception of the 39 lashes from the synagogue.
148. Cf. Goodenough 1968.

198 *Idolatry and Authority*

the people gathered together on the Sabbath to listen intently and in quiet alert-
ness learn 'what is best and profitable and capable of improving the quality of the
whole of life' (*Spec. Leg.* 2.62). Josephus tells us that the Jews managed their
affairs and settled their differences in accordance with their native laws (*Ant.*
14.235). Further, the Jewish assemblies were centres of authority for decision-
making over such matters as religious (cf. Acts 23.1–3), social (*CPJ* I no. 138)[149]
and legal affairs (cf. Philo, *Leg. Gai.* 156–57; Josephus, *Ant.* 16.167–68) for individual local communities. In other words, for most of the matters pertaining to
the Jewish communities in the Diaspora, the leaders of the Jewish assemblies and
the Law provided the leadership.

The question arising from this conclusion is, 'what happens when deviant
behaviour takes place?' In *3 Macc.* 2.30–31, it is recorded that a minority of
Jews, having seen and experienced the sufferings they had to undergo as a result
of strictly following their religious tradition, took up the offer of Ptolemy IV
Philopater's to worship Dionysus which came with the reward of Alexandrian
citizenship. But the great majority of the Jews 'resisted' (ἐνίσχυσαν) and 'did
not abandon their religion' (οὐ διέστησαν τῆς εὐσεβείας) (*3 Macc.* 2.32). The
behaviour of the minority who 'gave in' to the king may be described as 'deviant', that is, departing from the majority 'behaviour' which was considered the
norm.[150] And the author of *3 Maccabees* suggests that the norm from which the
minority departed was the 'holy God and his Law' (τὸν ἅγιον θεόν...τοῦ θεοῦ
τὸν νόμον...). The result for the minority deviant behaviour was punishment by
death (*3 Macc.* 7.10-12, 14-16).[151]

While *3 Maccabees* seems to paint a rather negative picture of the minority of
Jews who departed from the religious tradition of the Jews, the author appears to
be inclined towards giving a positive picture of the Jews and the kind of good
fortune that went with one's faithfulness to the 'holy God and his Law'. What is
important is that within the Jewish community there seemed to be an established
norm which defined what was appropriate behaviour in general, and with regard
to idolatry in particular. Further, the 'zeal' for the Law was held up as the basis
for violent actions against deviants, when the Law cannot be imposed.[152] Thus, the
Law and 'zeal' for the Law seem to be what the author has in mind as the norm;
and the Law is held as the final authority to which appeals are made.

The issue of authority in the Diaspora Jewish community serves as a contrast
to the situation in 1 Corinthians 9, particularly the question of Paul's authority.
Like the majority Jews in *3 Maccabees*, the 'weak' in Corinth hold to a particular
'norm' with regard to idolatry. Their position finds parallels in Chapter 3 where a
hostile and negative attitude towards idolatry can be seen in Jewish literature like
Philo, Wisdom of Solomon, Sibylline Oracles, and so on. However, the 'strong'

149. This seems to be the only surviving record, a papyrus from Egypt, dated possibly in the first
century BCE, of an actual meeting in a Diaspora assembly held by members of a Jewish burial club.
150. Cf. Barclay 1995: 114–27.
151. See Seland (1995) for an interesting study of lynching, and how this is in fact not against
the Law.
152. Cf. Hengel 1989.

adopt a more accommodating stance towards idolatry. They have no scruples in visiting pagan temples, eating idol-meat, and even possibly participating in idolatrous rituals. What they have done would be viewed as 'deviant' behaviour, based on the perception of the 'weak'. Thus, the problem between these two parties, the 'strong' and the 'weak', arises.

However, unlike the Jews in *3 Maccabees*, the Corinthians do not seem to have a final court of appeal available. But this is where Paul's authority as the founding father plays a most crucial role. It is not clear who decides what is the right or appropriate behaviour with regard to idolatry in the Corinthian church. Just as the Jews in the Diaspora turned to the assembly and possibly leadership for settling their disputes and managing their affairs, Paul is seeking to turn the Corinthians to himself for settling their dispute over idolatrous behaviour. Even though some Corinthians may have questioned his apostolic authority, Paul sees himself as the one who preaches to them the gospel and to whom the Corinthian church owes its existence. What can be certain is that Paul, in establishing his authority among the Corinthians, seeks to make himself the 'final court of appeal' where he rules on the issue of idolatry, on the basis of the gospel.

6. *Summary and Conclusion*

The above discussion focuses on the function of 1 Corinthians 9 and argues that in this particular chapter, Paul puts up a defence of his apostolic authority because it has been called into question by some Corinthians. His defence consists of the establishment of his right to material support from the Corinthians, thus, proving his apostleship and authority. In defending his authority, Paul is not seeking to lay claim to the material support to which he has a right; he is in fact wanting to demonstrate that he has given up his right to material support, thus offering himself as an example to the 'strong' with regard to their accommodating behaviour in freely eating idol-meat. Because the behaviour of the 'strong' has caused some unease among the 'weak' Corinthians, Paul tells them to imitate him by also giving up their right to eat idol-meat, so as not to cause any of the 'weak' members to fall.

Paul argues from various scenarios and shows that preaching the gospel is a necessity laid upon him for which he has no claim of reward. Thus, his preaching is involuntary; however, his giving up of the right to material support is voluntary. He has done so because of his desire not to put any hindrance in the way of the gospel. Further, he finds his reward in preaching the gospel 'free of charge'. This he does by taking up manual labour and by 'becoming all things to all people', so that he might bring as many as he can to the Lord.

Such a concept is modelled after the life and the cross of Christ. Paul acknowledges that he is free from all; but he is free precisely to become a slave to all. This is the action he takes in order to imitate Christ. Ultimately, his exhortation to the 'strong' to imitate him is based on the principle that he imitates Christ. Thus, his exhortation to imitate him is to be viewed as an exhortation to imitate Christ.

By defending his apostolic authority and setting himself as an example to the 'strong', Paul is able to turn the Corinthians to his gospel and the biblical history as interpreted by him as the 'final court of appeal' whereby he, as the founding father of the Corinthian church, rules on the issue of idolatry. For the gospel has now taken over the place of the Law, and the biblical history is reinterpreted in the light of the gospel. Thus, Paul, Christ, gospel, and salvation are all aligned with each other and serve as a new standard of authority. And such an authority is able to carry out discipline by excluding the 'deviants' (i.e. those who fail to live up to its standards) from the eschatological salvation.

Chapter 7

CONCLUSIONS

1. *Summary*

The main function of this study has been to establish Jewish parallels to the positions of the three parties on idolatry in 1 Corinthians 8–10, namely the 'strong', the 'weak', and Paul. This helpfully enables us to situate the positions of the three parties in the world of the Corinthian church. In carrying out this task, I have looked at the various interpretations put forward by various scholars over the past two decades or so, together with F.C. Baur. Baur had advocated a theory that saw a conflict between Paul and the Jerusalem apostles, and that Paul's opponents used a different tactic in the church at Corinth from that used in Galatia. Others had posited different theories. The survey reveals a gap in the history of scholarship in the interpretation of 1 Cor. 8.1–11.1. Much attention has focused on the consistency and meaning of the text between 1 Corinthians 8 and 10.[1] Some have tried to study the section by looking at the Graeco-Roman religions and the practices of eating.[2] However, none of the scholarly works has attempted a full-scale definition of idolatry; all simply assume its definition. As part of the thesis, I have established a critical tool that carefully defines idolatry in a multifaceted way, based on the work of Halbertal and Margalit, by which the various selected Jewish texts in the Jewish Diaspora during the Second Temple period were examined, beginning with the Septuagint, followed by the Jewish authors, various inscriptions and papyri, and finally the New Testament passage in question. These studies reveal that while Jews in general abhorred idolatry, there were Jews in the Diaspora who were not altogether free from idolatrous behaviour and/or intention.[3] Their idolatry took various forms: actual idolatrous behaviour in visiting pagan temples and invoking pagan gods; cognitive error in terms of confusing the true God with nature or the gods; misrepresenting Yahweh with an object; and open abandonment of the Jewish ancestral tradition.

My examination of the various Jewish practices with respect to idolatry reveals an interesting pattern, that is, although all the definitions of idolatry appear to combine in defining idolatry, they do not necessarily operate as a package. And different Jews could adopt different definitions and so carve out spaces for

---

1. See the survey of Gardner (1994: 2–10).
2. E.g. Willis 1985a; Gooch 1993: 1–46; Witherington III 1995: 191–95; Newton 1999.
3. This is seen in Chapter 4 above. See, however, Cheung (1999), whose thesis is based on a mistaken view that Jews *always* abhorred idols and abstained from idolatrous practices.

themselves.[4] In other words, a person may appear idolatrous to another person, when in fact that 'idolatrous' person may not consider his or her behaviour idolatrous at all because of the different definitions adopted. And the different practices need not mean a difference in belief. In fact, most Jews would accept the monotheistic belief of the 'one God', just as Paul and the 'strong' do. But this is the crucial point of departure: how they apply that belief in their practical life may be very different, as the Jewish authors mentioned in both Chapters 3 and 4 show.

It is a recognized fact that the Torah had been the basis for the Jews with regard to their behaviour vis-à-vis the Gentile environment. And in most cases of dispute within the Jewish community the 'Law' constituted the 'final' court of appeal. In other words, there remained some form of authority, and hence discipline, for the Diaspora Jewich communities. But this is not so for a community like the Corinthian assembly, in which no solution or resolution concerning idol-meat seems to be in sight. In order to resolve the issue, Paul's authority/leadership is of crucial importance: who is to decide what constitutes idolatry? We see that Paul not only re-affirms his apostolic authority, but also uses his own sacrifice as an example to the 'strong' to give up their right to freely eat idol-meat. He further appeals to the biblical history of Israel to drive home the need for and basis of discipline with regard to idol-meat (cf. 1 Cor. 10.1–11). This question of leadership and discipline followed our discussion of Paul's position on idolatry: idolatry is an act contrary to the biblical ancestral tradition and a participation in the table of δαιμόνια. The idolatrous acts of Israel in the wilderness brought about their destruction, despite their seemingly spiritual security under the leadership of Moses. Thus, Paul's warning to the 'strong' is that if they think they stand (cf. 1 Cor. 10.12), they ought to be careful lest they fall. The implication is that by freely eating idol-meat and participating in the worship of the Gentile gods, the 'strong' incur the wrath of God and so run the risk of being destroyed as well, despite their seemingly secure position in Christ.[5] His solution to the entire saga is offered in the example of Christ, who is embodied in his own apostolic practice of self-sacrifice and self-abasement. Thus, he urges the 'strong': be imitators of me as I am of Christ (1 Cor. 11.1).

2. *The Answers to our Questions*

This thesis began with a list of questions, whose answers are complex but not necessarily insuperable. First of all, we may compare the positions of the three parties, namely, the 'strong', the 'weak', and Paul, with the Diaspora positions on idolatry. In Chapter 4, we have seen that some Jews were idolatrous on the

---

4. See, for example, Halbertal (1998: 159–72).
5. Thus, the argument that 1 Corinthians 8 and 10 deal with different issues is weak. Paul's caution that the presence of the 'strong' might serve as an encouragement to the 'weak' to eat idol-meat implies that the presence of the 'strong' in an idol temple, even if they do not actually participate in the worship of the gods, was most probably seen as idolatrous or viewed as having involved some form of idolatrous practice.

cognitive level, as represented by Artapanus and Pseudo-Aristeas. Further, evidence from inscriptions and papyri shows that there were Jews who did not seem to view accommodation to idolatry as something objectionable, even though it is evident that they continued to regard themselves as Jews and remember their Jewish heritage. The 'strong' in 1 Corinthians 8–10 seem to reflect a somewhat similar attitude or behaviour. For example, their slogans in 1 Cor. 8.4 that idols are nothing in the world, and that there is no God but one, seem to compare well with the attitude of many of the Jews surveyed in Chapter 3.[6] And the conceptual overlap in the minds of the Diaspora Jews concerning other peoples' gods, as evidenced in *The Letter of Aristeas* (as discussed in Chapter 4, section 3), seems to parallel the thoughts of the 'strong' as their slogan 'there is no God but one' suggests a conceptual overlap. Thus, while the 'strong' share the same concept about that 'one God' as Philo, they have an entirely different practice (see Chapter 4, section 4 above). Their temple attendance is therefore not of any particular concern to them, just like those Jews surveyed in Chapter 4, section 6, a. Hence, we have suggested in Chapter 4 that they could have been aware of the LXX ban in Exod. 22.27a (see Chapter 4, section 2, c). The term εἴδωλον is therefore not used pejoratively by the 'strong'. The parallel between the examples of Diaspora Jews' accommodation to idolatry and that of the 'strong' appears clear.

The position of the 'weak' seems to be more scrupulous. For Paul tells us that they were accustomed to idols, and given the fact that Paul is constantly making reference to them, it is reasonable to assume that they abhor idols. They would probably view any acts of idolatry as objectionable and their past association to idolatry would provide them with the reason for rejecting idols. In Chapter 3, we have examined the reactions of Diaspora Jews to idolatry and found them to be wholly negative and condemning; they tended to ridicule, reject, and pour scorn on idols and idol makers. While there is no explicit mention of how the 'weak' react to idolatry, their scruples and objections may be seen as paralleled to those of the Diaspora Jews in Chapter 3. In other words, while their past association with idols is causing them to be wary of idols and idol-meat,[7] Jewish influence concerning idols could have generated in them a scruple that did not permit them to eat idol-meat. And their conversion to Christ had most likely caused them to adopt a more stringent Jewish stance like that of the Diaspora Jews discussed in Chapter 3. Besides, they could be simply following Paul's instructions in his previous letter (cf. 1 Cor. 5.9–11).

Paul's position seems to be somewhat complicated. For Paul was a Jew, and probably held a position that was informed by the Diaspora Jewish reactions against idolatry. However, he has become a believer and an apostle of Jesus Christ. Even though he continues to abhor idols, the reasons are no longer the same as those of the Diaspora Jews. He does not think that the idols are nothing, unlike the 'strong'. Nor does he simply condemn the idolatrous behaviour of the

---

6. The use of the term εἴδωλον also suggests Jewish influence, which could well explain the background to this particular slogan (see the γνῶσις of the 'strong' in Chapter 5, section 3 above).

7. Their ethnicity is not the question here, as I have already demonstrated in Chapter 4 that Jews could still be idolatrous even though they may regard themselves as Jews.

'strong' as wrong and contrary to the Law. Paul represents a new position. He recognizes that there are gods and lords both in heaven and on earth (cf. 1 Cor. 8.5) while holding to the monotheistic confession of the one God (cf. 1 Cor. 8.6). But it is also here that he differs from the 'strong' over the one God. In 1 Cor. 8.6, he appeals to the confession of the 'strong' and reminds them that Jesus Christ is the purpose and agent of creation (Chapter 5, section 3, c). Further, his concerns are twofold: (1) the idolatrous behaviour of the 'strong' may become a stumbling block to the 'weak', leading them to idolatry, and so putting a hindrance to the gospel of Jesus Christ;[8] and (2) the idolatrous behaviour of the 'strong' will result in their incurring the wrath of God and cause them to run the risk of losing their eschatological salvation. Paul's concerns for the eschatological salvation of the 'strong', and the advancement (or hindrance) of the gospel, are then interwoven into an argument that involves his defence or re-affirmation of his apostolic authority on the one hand, and on the other hand, the willing surrender of his apostolic right to material support as an example to the 'strong'. His argument for his apostolic authority situates him in a position of leadership again, that is, he is the founding father of the Corinthian assembly and one who imitates Christ; he therefore has the final authority to define what constitutes idolatry and what is proper Christian behaviour. In other words, as the founding apostle of the Corinthian church, Paul sees himself as responsible for carrying out discipline with regard to idolatry in that church. For the 'strong', their 'knowledge' and 'freedom' allow them to eat idol-meat without scruples. While this shows that they (the 'strong') have a self-understanding as Christ-believers, for Paul, their behaviour is idolatrous, besides lacking in love and consideration for others (cf. 1 Cor. 8.1–3). Their attendance at pagan temples, consumption of idol-meat there, and their possible participation in pagan rituals render them idolatrous on several fronts. Conceptually the 'strong' are idolatrous in the sense that they have thought the true God to be the same as the god/s pagans worship. Further, by accusing them of sharing in the table of δαιμόνια, Paul accuses the 'strong' of confusing the true God with 'demons'. And in terms of the re-interpreted biblical history, the 'strong' have abandoned ancestral tradition and breached the new covenant of Christ.

Throughout, Paul's position takes a different twist from the Jewish tradition: Christ and his gospel are the ultimate determinant of how the 'strong' should behave with regard to their 'freedom' as Christians. And even if the 'strong' were to have a right self-understanding, they still face judgment and destruction if they behave improperly, that is, accommodating to idolatry by freely eating idol-meat and causing the 'weak' to fall, and so putting a hindrance to the gospel of Jesus Christ. This argument of Paul is put forward with an intertextual allusion to the biblical texts which are interwoven here. The implication is strong: the Corinthian 'strong' appeal to the Jewish monotheistic confession of the one God and other slogans for their behaviour, Paul appeals to a reinterpreted biblical history to show the important role the centrality of Christ and his gospel plays in

---

8. Thus, 1 Cor. 9.12 should be read in the light of what Paul says in 1 Cor. 8.13, and his willing subjection of his freedom to the status of others in 1 Cor. 9.19–23.

the issue of idolatry, authority and Christian discipline (i.e. with regard to Christian 'freedom'). The 'freedom' and 'knowledge' of the 'strong' are being countered by Paul's imperative to imitate him as he is an imitator of Christ. This leads to the next question of what constitutes the foundation of ethical behaviour for Paul.

3. *A Possible Fresh Approach to Understanding Paul's Ethics?*

The above discussion of 1 Corinthians 8–10 concludes that Paul views idolatry as an act that is contrary to the biblical ancestral tradition, a rebellious act that involves partnership with δαιμόνια and breaks partnership with the Lord, an unloving act that can possibly cause a 'weaker' fellow believer to fall, an act that reflects spiritual indiscipline that invites God's wrath and the possible loss of eschatological salvation. For Paul, Christian 'freedom' and 'knowledge' of the one God and the insignificance of idols must be balanced by a life that is modelled or imitated after that of Christ by imitating Paul's.[9] And such a life involves acts or patterns of behaviour that willingly subject one's 'rights' to the consideration of those who are 'weak' in their 'knowledge' and 'freedom'.[10] Thus, in 1 Corinthians 9, Paul sets himself as an example by explaining to the Corinthians his principles for living: allow the status of others to determine how one should behave, with the ultimate purpose of winning them to the gospel. This ethical principle of Paul means that the 'Law' is no longer to be the basis for ethical behaviour, but rather the advancement of the gospel of Jesus Christ. Thus, the new paradigm for action is Christ/gospel/salvation/Paul. This raises the question as to whether there is continuity or discontinuity between Paul and the 'Law'. Scholarship has of late focused on the continuity between Paul and the Law. P.J. Tomson, for example, argues that in 1 Corinthians 9 Paul expounds his rights as an apostle in connection with a halakhic saying of Jesus. For him, Paul's citation of Deut. 25.4 constitutes an appeal to the Law and Paul's paraphrasing of various Old Testament stories is directly related to Jewish targumic and midrashic tradition.[11] Similarly, though not entirely from the same approach, Brian Rosner says that when Paul argues against the Law, it is only the legal requirements for salvation that he is opposing. Apart from that, Paul does not repudiate the Law.[12] Eckhard J. Schnabel maintains that when Paul exhorts the Galatians to love one another, he is saying that love as the law is in its entirety the expression of the will of God.[13] While many parts of the Torah have no factual validity, Schnabel argues, 'the Torah remains the revelation of God's will in its new relation to Jesus Christ'.[14] The Christian is therefore not 'absolved' from fulfilling the Torah

---

9.   Cf. Hays 1996: 41–43.
10.   Their 'conscience', in this case, would be sensitive to what the 'strong' do and how they live.
11.   Tomson 1990: 77–78.
12.   Rosner 1995: 7; cf. Hotz 1995: 51–57.
13.   Schnabel 1995: 272.
14.   Schnabel 1995: 273.

as the 'law of Christ'.[15] The argument of Paul in 1 Cor. 8.1–11.1 is therefore theocentric. This has implications for our understanding of Paul's ethics.

Are Paul's ethics based on the Law, so that his instructions for Christian conduct are but lessons from the Jewish scriptures? Or are they fundamentally different from the Law? To put it another way, is there continuity between Paul and the Law? If there is continuity, how then does Paul determine ethical Christian behaviour? David Horrell has recently argued that Paul accepts the legitimacy of the right of the 'strong' to eat idol-meat and does not rule out participating in pagan temple activities.[16] What Paul offers is his own example of giving up his legitimate rights in the interest of others, an act that is modelled after the Christ-like pattern. While Paul agrees with the theological principles of the 'strong' in eating idol-meat, he argues for a different ethical conduct that is founded upon a 'christological praxis', a pattern of action shaped by the self-giving of Christ. Although Horrell points out an important paradigm which Paul is shaping, he has not taken into consideration the fact that Paul seems to view the behaviour of the 'strong' as constituting idolatry (1 Cor. 10.14), and his frequent correction of the theological basis of the 'strong'.

Our study suggests that there may be a fresh approach towards understanding Paul's basis for ethical behaviour: while Paul applies aspects of the Old Testament at various points in his argument, he seems to reinterpret them. Could it be that Paul, having converted to the gospel, is now appealing to biblical history only when it serves to highlight the ethical Christian behaviour? This could be seen in his insistence that he is no longer under God's 'Law', meaning the Torah, but under Christ's 'law' (1 Cor. 9.21), meaning the 'law' of love which he expounds elsewhere (cf. Gal. 5.13; 6.2). And if we were to view Paul's use of the Old Testament as primarily the scripture of God for life, to be interpreted and understood in terms of the Christ-event and his love, then there is little justification to posit that there is continuity between Paul and the 'Law'.[17] Although 1 Corinthians 8–10 does not raise the question of the Law exhaustively or extensively, the point Paul makes seems to hang on the gospel, and the expression of the gospel of Christ in the life of the Christian community in Corinth. Thus, we may begin to re-examine Paul's ethics in the light of the fact that Paul *reinterprets* the Jewish scripture to advance the gospel, not so much to continue the Torah-requirements.[18] In other words, Paul has carefully moved the basis for action from Law to Christ, thus defining for the Corinthian church what is distinctively Christian action. And it is in this sense that the present proposal for understanding 1 Corinthians 9 may make a fresh contribution to understanding the ethics of Paul in general, and in 1 Corinthians in particular.

This may be illustrated through a brief reflection on 1 Cor. 10.23–11.1, where it is certain that ignorance of the religious history of the meat frees a person from

15. Schnabel 1995: 272.

16. Horrell 1997: 83–114.

17. Even if we pick out all the statements in Paul's letters that show a positive attitude to the 'law', in almost every case, Christ and his gospel seem to be the main subject, not the 'law'.

18. Westerholm 1988: 198–209; see the contrasting essays in Rosner (1995).

any religious responsibility (cf. 10.25). For a Christ-believer, guilt of idolatry is absent so long as there is no religious history involved in the meat being consumed. This is probably why Paul allows consumption of meats in non-religious contexts: markets or homes, where idolatry and its definitions may not be relevant. However, vv. 27–28 point out another scenario, when one is invited to a meal, presumably at a private home of an unbeliever. While a private unbeliever's home may not carry religious connotations as strongly as a Gentile temple, once the religious history of the meat is made known, the definitions of idolatry would come into operation. Paul seems concerned about the 'conscience' of the unbeliever present, when the religious history of the meat is made known to the believer. This suggests a concern similar to that in 1 Cor. 8.10, where a 'strong' believer's consumption of idol-meat in a Gentile temple may cause a 'weak' believer to fall. In 1 Cor. 10.23–11.1, the consumption of the sacrificial meat in the presence of the unbeliever may lead the latter into deeper idolatry, making the believer party to the unbeliever's idolatrous sin. The ethics of Paul then is the fulfilment of Christ's law, which is love serving as the basis for the believer's abstinence. This may encourage the unbeliever to consider Christ's gospel; at the same time Paul believes it will glorify God. Hence Paul ends this section of the letter with a call to imitate him (1 Cor. 11.1).[19]

4. *Historical Reconstruction: Ancient Judaism and Early Christianity*

Our study above has other implications, namely, our understanding of ancient Judaism and early Christianity as they relate to idolatry. Our survey in Chapter 1 indicates that most scholars seem to take for granted that idolatry was abhorred by all Jews, and therefore most would regard the 'weak' as primarily Gentile believers on the basis of Paul's statement that they were 'accustomed' to idols (1 Cor. 8.7). There seems to be a connection between idolatry and ethnicity: *all* Jews reject idols; *all* Gentiles are idolatrous. While the latter clause may appear representative of most Gentiles, the former cannot be true, as our discussions in Chapters 2 and 4 have shown. The reason for the generalized conclusion of most scholars is the fact that there is little effort in discovering what constitutes idolatry for the Jews.[20] And the fact of the matter is that there were different definitions of idolatry for different Jews. And there are varying degrees of idolatry, as may be seen in the way Israelites variously define for themselves what is true worship and how different Jews could justify practices for themselves.[21] But this is not particular to ancient Judaism alone. In fact, there is an equally ambiguous understanding of what constitutes idolatry in early Christianity, of which our

19. See Stanley 1959: 859–77; Watson (1989: 301–18) considers this section in the light of Graeco-Roman rhetoric. See also our discussion in Chapter 6, section 4.

20. See, for example, Dunn (1991: 19–21) who argues that in the post-exilic period Jewish monotheism became a fundamental dogma of Judaism. But monotheism per se is not necessarily the opposing side of idolatry. For a monotheist could view all other gods as expressions of the 'one deity', as Hengel (1974: 1.261–67) has ably demonstrated.

21. See, for example, Halbertal (1998: 159–72).

study of 1 Cor. 8.1–11.1 is a powerful piece of evidence. And it also suggests that whatever Jewish influence the Corinthians might have had, it was not as clear as we might want it to be. And in this regard, it would be beneficial for a clear separation between Judaism and ethnicity to be made, whenever the former is discussed. Our study also demonstrates that the composition of Jews and Gentiles in the Corinthian assembly must remain at least fluid and, at most tentative.

Our investigations further indicate that our understanding of how ancient Judaism and early Christianity viewed idolatry cannot be easily absolutized. Nor can our view of the two religions be based on a generalized notion that all Jews and Christians in the Diaspora abhorred and rejected idolatry. Ancient Judaism and early Christianity are, after all, not as settled and stable as most scholars have made them out to be. We may speak of 'Judaism/s', and early 'believers' in Christ. And 'monotheistic' Jews and Christians need not be free from 'idolatry', depending on our and their definitions of these terms. The implication seems to be that it would be wise to avoid an 'absolutized' opinion, and to adopt a more 'fluid' idea of what constitutes idolatry. And in the light of our discussions of 1 Corinthians 9, it appears that what constitutes idolatry is to a great extent dependent upon who has the authority to decide what constitutes idolatrous behaviour.

BIBLIOGRAPHY

Aalen, S.
    1976   'Glory', in *NIDNTT* IV: 44–48.

Adams, Edward
    2000   *Constructing the World: A Study in Paul's Cosmological Language* (SNTW; Edinburgh: T&T Clark).

Albeck, S.
    1990   'The Ten Commandments and the Essence of Religious Faith', in Gershon 1990: 261–89.

Albertz, Rainer
    1994   *A History of Israelite Religion in the Old Testament Period*. I. *From the Beginnings to the End of the Monarchy* (OTL; trans. John Bowden; Louisville, KY: Westminster/John Knox).

Allen, Leslie C.
    1983   *Psalm 101–150* (WBC, 21; Dallas, TX: Word Books).

Anderson, A.A.
    1972   *Psalm (73–150)* (NCB; Grand Rapids: Eerdmans).

Applebaum, S.
    1974   'The Organization of the Jewish Communities in the Diaspora', in S. Safrai and M. Stern (eds.), *The Jewish People in the First Century* (CRINT; Assen: Van Gorcum): I, 464–503.

Attridge, Harold W.
    1984   'Josephus and his Works', in Stone 1984: 185–232.

Bar-Kochva, B.
    1996   'An Ass in the Jerusalem Temple – the Origins and Development of the Slander', in Feldman and Levison 1996: 310–26.

Barclay, J.M.G.
    1988   *Obeying the Truth: A Study of Paul's Ethics in Galatians* (SNTW; Edinburgh: T&T Clark).
    1995   'Deviance and Apostasy: Some Applications of Deviance Theory to First-Century Judaism and Christianity', in P.F. Esler (ed.), *Modelling Early Christianity: Social-Scientific Studies of the New Testament in its Context* (London: Routledge): 114–27.
    1996   *Jews in the Mediterranean Diaspora, From Alexander to Trajan (323BCE-117CE)* (Edinburgh: T&T Clark).
    1998a   'Who Was Considered an Apostate in the Jewish Diaspora?', in G.N. Stanton and G.G. Stroumsa (eds.), *Tolerance and Intolerance in Early Judaism and Christianity* (Cambridge: Cambridge University Press): 80–98.
    1998b   'Josephus v. Apion: Analysis of an Argument', in Mason 1998: 194–221.

Barrett, C.K.
    1968   *A Commentary on the First Epistle to the Corinthians* (BNTC; London: Adam and Charles Black).

1973   *A Commentary on the Second Epistle to the Corinthians* (BNTC; London: Adam and Charles Black).

1982   *Essays on Paul* (Philadelphia: Westminster Press).

1991   *The Epistle to the Romans* (BNTC; Peabody, MA: Hendrickson, rev. edn).

Bartlett, J.R.

1985   *Jews in the Hellenistic World: Josephus, Aristeas, the Sibylline Oracles, Eupolemus* (Cambridge: Cambridge University Press).

Batnitzky, Leora

2000   *Idolatry and Representation: The Philosophy of Franz Rosenzweig Reconsidered* (Princeton, NJ: Princeton University Press).

Baur, F.C.

1876   *Paul the Apostle of Jesus Christ, his Life and Work, his Epistles and his Doctrine* (London: Williams and Norgate, 2nd edn).

1878   *The Church History of the First Three Centuries* (2 vols; London: Williams and Norgate, 3rd edn).

Bertram, G.

1972   'ὕψος, κ.τ.λ.', in *TDNT* VIII: 602–20.

Best, E.

1972   *The First and Second Epistles to the Thessalonians* (London: Adam & Charles Black).

1995   'Paul's Apostolic Authority?', in S.E. Porter and C.A. Evans (eds.), *The Pauline Writings* (Sheffield: Sheffield Academic Press): 13–34. (originally published in 1986 under *JSNT* 27: 3–25).

Bickermann, E.

1930   'Zur Datierung des Pseudo-Aristeas', *ZNW* 29: 280–98.

Bilde, P.

1988   *Flavius Josephus between Jerusalem and Rome* (Sheffield: *JSOT* Press).

Boccaccini, G.

1991   *Middle Judaism, Jewish Thought 300 BCE to 200 CE* (Philadelphia: Fortress Press).

Borgen, P.

1984   'Philo of Alexandria', in Stone 1984: 233–82.

1996   *Early Christianity and Hellenistic Judaism* (Edinburgh: T&T Clark).

1997   *Philo of Alexandria: An Exegete for his Time* (Leiden: E.J. Brill).

Brownlee, W.H.

1986   *Ezekiel 1–19* (WBC, 28; Waco, TX: Word Books).

Bruce, F.F.

1982   *1 and 2 Thessalonians* (WBC, 45; Waco, TX: Word Books).

Büchsel, F.

1964   'εἴδωλον', in *TDNT* II: 375-79.

Burchard, C.

1965   *Untersuchungen zu Joseph und Aseneth* (Tübingen: J.C. Mohr [Paul Siebeck]).

1985   'Joseph and Aseneth', in *OTP* II: 177–247.

Carroll, R.P.

1986   *Jeremiah* (OTL; London: SCM Press).

Charlesworth, J.H. (ed.)

1983   *The Old Testament Pseudepigrapha*, I (2 vols; London: Darton, Longman and Todd).

1985   *The Old Testament Pseudepigrapha*, II (2 vols; London: Darton, Longman and Todd).

Chesnutt, R.
    1995   *From Death to Life: Conversion in Joseph and Aseneth* (Sheffield: Sheffield Academic Press).
Cheung, Alex T.
    1999   *Idol Food in Corinth: Jewish Background and Pauline Legacy* (JSNTSup, 176; Sheffield: Sheffield Academic Press).
Childs, Brevard S.
    1974   *Exodus* (OTL; London: SCM Press).
Chow, John K.
    1992   *Patronage and Power: A Study of Social Networks in Corinth* (JSNTSup, 75; Sheffield: Sheffield Academic Press).
Clarke, A.D.
    1993   *Secular and Christian Leadership in Corinth: A Socio-Historical and Exegetical Study of 1 Corinthians 1–6* (Leiden: E.J. Brill).
Clark, Ernest G.
    1973   *The Wisdom of Solomon* (CBC; Cambridge: Cambridge University Press).
Collins, J.J.
    1974   *The Sibylline Oracles of Egyptian Judaism* (Missoula: Society of Biblical Literature).
    1983   'Sibylline Oracles', in *OTP*, I: 317–472.
    1984   'The Sibylline Oracles', in Stone 1984: 357–81.
    1985   'Artapanus', in *OTP*, II: 889–903.
    1997   *Jewish Wisdom in the Hellenistic Age* (Edinburgh: T&T Clark).
    2000   *Between Athens and Jerusalem: Jewish Identities in the Hellenistic Diaspora.* (New York: Crossroad, rev. edn).
Collins, R.F.
    1999   *First Corinthians* (SP, 7; Collegeville, MN: Glazier).
Conzelmann, H.
    1975   *1 Corinthians* (Hermeneia; Philadelphia: Fortress).
Cook, A.B.
    1925   *Zeus: A Study in Ancient Religion* (Cambridge: Cambridge University Press).
Craigie, Peter C.
    1976   *Deuteronomy* (NICOT; Grand Rapids: Eerdmans).
Cranfield, C.E.B.
    1975   *A Critical and Exegetical Commentary on the Epistle to the Romans* (ICC; Edinburgh: T&T Clark).
Cullmann, Oscar
    1951   *Christ and Time: the Primitive Christian Conception of Time and History.* (London: SCM Press).
Dahl, N.A.
    1967   *Studies in Paul: Theology for the Early Christian Mission* (Minneapolis: Augsburg).
Dahood, M.
    1968   *Psalms II, 51–100* (AB, 17; Garden City, NY: Doubleday).
    1970   *Psalm III, 101–150* (AB, 17A; Garden City, NY: Doubleday).
Davies, E.W.
    1995   *Numbers* (NCB; Grand Rapids: Eerdmans).
Davies, G.H.
    1962   'Ephod', in *IDB* IV: 118–19.
Davies, G.I.
    1992   *Hosea* (NCB; Grand Rapids: Eerdmans).

Davies, Meg
    1994   'Review of "Michael Goulder, *A Tale of Two Missions* (London: SCM, 1994)"', *ExpTim* 106: 26–27.
De Vries, S.J.
    1985   *1 Kings* (WBC, 12; Waco, TX: Word Books).
Downing, F. Gerald
    1994   'Review of "Michael Goulder, *A Tale of Two Missions* (London: SCM Press, 1994)"', *Theology* 97: 465–66.
Dungan, David L.
    1971   *The Sayings of Jesus in the Churches of Paul* (Philadelphia: Fortress Press).
Dunn, James D.G.
    1988   *Romans 1-8* (WBC, 38A; Waco, TX: Word Books).
    1991   *The Partings of the Ways: Between Christianity and Judaism and their Significance for the Character of Christianity* (London: SCM Press; Philadelphia: Trinity Press).
    1998   *The Theology of Paul the Apostle* (Edinburgh: T&T Clark).
Durham, John I.
    1987   *Exodus* (WBC, 3; Waco, TX: Word Books).
Ehrhardt, A.
    1964   *The Framework of the New Testament Stories* (Manchester: Manchester University Press).
Fee, G.D.
    1980   'Εἰδωλόθυτα Once Again: An Investigation of 1 Corinthians 8-10', *Bib* 61: 172–97.
    1987   *The First Epistle to the Corinthians* (NICNT; Grand Rapids: Eerdmans).
Feldman, Louis H.
    1984   'Flavius Josephus Revisited: the Man, his Writings, and his Significance', in *ANRW* II.21.2: 763–862.
    1993   *Jew and Gentile in the Ancient Word: Attitudes and Interactions from Alexander to Justinian* (Princeton, NJ: Princeton University Press).
    1996   *Studies in Hellenistic Judaism* (Leiden: E.J. Brill).
    2000   *Flavious Josephus, Tradition and Commentary*. III. *Judean Antiquities 1-4* (Leiden: E.J. Brill)
Feldman, L.H. and J.R. Levison (eds.)
    1996   *Josephus' Contra Apionem: Studies in its Character and Context with a Latin Concordance to the Portion Missing in Greek* (Leiden: E.J. Brill).
Ferguson, E.
    1993   *Backgrounds of Early Christianity* (Grand Rapids: Eerdmans, 2nd edn).
Finn, T.M.
    1985   'The God-Fearers Reconsidered', *CBQ* 47: 75–84.
Frame, J. Everett
    1912   *A Critical and Exegetical Commentary on the Epistle of St. Paul to the Thessalonians* (ICC; Edinburgh: T&T Clark).
Fraser, P.M.
    1972   *Ptolemaic Alexandria* (3 vols; Oxford: Clarendon Press).
Freudenthal, J.
    1875   *Alexander Polyhistor und die von ihm erhaltenen Reste judäischer und samaritanischer Geschichtswerke* (Hellenistlische Studien 1-2; Breslau: H. Skutsch).
Frey, J.-B.
    1975   *Corpus Inscriptionum Iudaicarum* (Rome: Pontifical Institute of Biblical

Archaeology. Vol. 1 revised with a prologue by B. Lifshitz, New York: Ktav [1936, 1952]).

Furnish, V.P.
1999   *The Theology of the First Letter to the Corinthians* (NTT; Cambridge: Cambridge University Press).

Gager, J.G.
1972   *Moses in Greco-Roman Paganism* (SBLMS, 16; Nashville: Abingdon Press).

Gallas, Sven
1990   ' "Fünfmal vierzig weniger einen..." Die an Paulus vollzogenen Synagogalstrafen nach 2 Kor 11.24', *ZNW* 81: 178–91.

Gardner, P.D.
1994   *The Gifts of God and the Authentication of a Christian: An Exegetical Study of 1 Corinthians 8-11.1* (Lanham, MD: University Press of America).

Gershon, L. (ed.)
1990   *The Ten Commandments in History and Tradition* (Jerusalem: The Magnes Press, Hebrew University of Jerusalem).

Giblin, C.H.
1975   'Three Monotheistic Texts in Paul', *CBQ* 37: 527–47.

Gnuse, R.K.
1997   *No Other Gods: Emergent Monotheism in Israel* (Sheffield: Sheffield Academic Press).

Goldenberg, R.
1997   'The Septuagint Ban on Cursing the Gods', *JSJ* 28: 1–9.
1998   *The Nations that Know Thee Not: Ancient Jewish Attitudes towards Other Religions* (New York: New York University Press).

Gooch, P.D.
1993   *Dangerous Food: 1 Corinthians 8-10 in its Context* (Waterloo, Ontario: Wilfrid Laurier University Press).

Goodenough, E.R.
1968   *The Jurisprudence of the Jewish Courts in Egypt: Legal Administration by the Jews under the Early Roman Empire as Described* (Amsterdam: Philo Press).

Goulder, M.
1991   'Σοφία in 1 Corinthians', *NTS* 37: 516–34.
1994   *A Tale of Two Missions* (London: SCM Press).

Grabbe, L.L.
1992   *Judaism from Cyrus to Hadrian* (London: SCM Press).
1997   *Wisdom of Solomon* (GAP; Sheffield: Sheffield Academic Press).

Grant, R.
1986   *Gods and the One God: Christian Theology in the Graeco-Roman World* (London: SPCK).

Gray, J.
1962   'Tammuz', in *IDB*, IV: 516.

Greenberg, M.
1990   'The Decalogue Tradition Critically Examined', in Gershon 1990: 83–119.

Grosheide, F.W.
1953   *Commentary on the First Epistle to the Corinthians* (NICNT; Grand Rapids: Eerdmans).

Gruen, Erich S.
1998   *Heritage and Hellenism: The Reinvention of Jewish Tradition* (Berkeley, CA: University of California Press).

Guenther, Heinz O.
　　1993　'Gnosticism in Corinth?', in Bradley H. McLean (ed.), *Origins and Method: Towards a New Understanding of Judaism and Christianity*, essays in Honour of John C. Hurd (JSNTSup, 86; Sheffield: *JSOT* Press): 44–81.

Gundry-Volf, Judith M.
　　1990　*Paul and Perseverance: Staying In and Falling Away* (WUNT 2, Reihe 37; Tübingen: J.C.B. Mohr [Paul Siebeck]).

Halbertal, M.
　　1998　'Coexisting with the Enemy: Jews and Pagans in the Mishnah', in G.N. Stanton and G.G. Stroumsa (eds), *Tolerance and Intolerance in Early Judaism and Christianity* (Cambridge: Cambridge University Press): 159–72.

Halbertal, M., and A. Margalit
　　1992　*Idolatry* (trans. Naomi Goldblum; Cambridge, MA: Harvard University Press).

Harrison, R.K.
　　1982　'Ephod', in *ISBE* II: 117–18.

Hatch, Edwin and Redpath, Henry A.
　　1998　*A Concordance to the Septuagint and the Other Greek Versions of the Old Testament (Including the Apocryphal Books)* (Grand Rapids: Baker Books, 2nd edn).

Hays, R.B.
　　1989　*Echoes of Scripture in the Letters of Paul* (New Haven: Yale University Press).
　　1997　*1 Corinthians* (Interpretation; Louisville: John Knox).

Hengel, M.
　　1974　*Judaism and Hellenism* (2 vols.; translated from 2nd German edition; London: SCM Press).
　　1989　*The Zealots: Investigations into the Jewish Freedom Movement in the Period from Herod I until 70 AD* (Edinburgh: T&T Clark).

Héring, J.
　　1962　*The First Epistle of St Paul to the Corinthians* (London: Epworth Press).

Hobbs, T.R.
　　1985　*2 Kings* (WBC, 13; Waco, TX: Word Books).

Hock, R.F.
　　1980　*The Social Context of Paul's Ministry: Tentmaking and Apostleship* (Philadelphia: Fortress).

Holladay, Carl R.
　　1983　*Fragments from Hellenistic Jewish Authors*, I (SBL Texts and Translations, 20; Pseudepigrapha Series, 10; Chico, CA: Scholars Press).

Hollander, H.W.
　　1998　'The Meaning of the Term "Law" (ΝΟΜΟΣ) in 1 Corinthians', *NovT* 11: 117–35.

Holmberg, Bengt
　　1978　*Paul and Power: the Structure of Authority in the Primitive Church as Reflected in the Pauline Epistles* (Lund: CWK Gleerup).

Horbury, W.
　　1998　*Jews and Christians: In Contact and Controversy* (Edinburgh: T&T Clark).

Horbury, W. and D. Noy
　　1992　*Jewish Inscriptions of Graeco-Roman Egypt* (Cambridge: Cambridge University Press).

Horrell, David G.
　　1996　*The Social Ethos of the Corinthian Correspondence: Interests and Ideology from 1 Corinthians to 1 Clement* (SNTW; Edinburgh: T&T Clark).

1997 'Theological Principle or Christological Praxis? Pauline Ethics in 1 Corinthians 8.1-11.1', *JSNT* 67: 83–114.

Horsley, R.A.

1976 'Pneumatikos vs. Psychikos: Distinctions of Spiritual Status among the Corinthians', *HTR* 69: 269–88.

1977 'Wisdom of Word and Words of Wisdom in Corinth', *CBQ* 39: 224–39.

1978a 'Consciousness and Freedom Among the Corinthians: 1 Corinthians 8-10', *CBQ* 40: 574–89.

1978b 'The Background of the Confessional Formula in 1 Kor 8.6', *ZNW* 69: 130–35.

1979 'Spiritual Marriage with Sophia', *VC* 33: 30–54.

1980 'Gnosis in Corinth: 1 Corinthians 8.1-6', *NTS* 27: 32–51.

1998 *1 Corinthians* (Nashville: Abingdon).

Hotz, T.

1995 'The Question of the Content of Paul's Instructions (1981)', in Rosner 1995: 51–71.

Houtman, C.

2000 *Exodus*, Historical Commentary on the Old Testament, III (Belgium, Leuven: Peeters).

Hurd, J.C.

1983 *The Origin of 1 Corinthians* (Macon, GA: Mercer University Press).

Hurtado, L.W.

1998 'First-Century Jewish Monotheism', *JSNT* 71: 3–26.

Jones, D.R.

1992 *Jeremiah* (NCB; Grand Rapids: Eerdmans).

Käsemann, E.

1969 *New Testament Questions of Today* (London: SCM Press).

Kasher, A.

1996 'Polemic and Apologetic Methods of Writing in *Contra Apionem*', in Feldman and Levison 1996: 143–86.

Klauk, Hans-Josef

2000 *The Religious Context of Early Christianity: A Guide to Graeco-Roman Religions* (SNTW; Edinburgh: T&T Clark).

Koester, H.

1982 *History, Culture, and Religion of the Hellenistic Age*, I (Philadelphia: Fortress Press).

Kolarcik, M.F.

1999 'Universalism and Justice in the Wisdom of Solomon', in N. Calduch-Benages and J. Vermeylen (eds), *Treasures of Wisdom, Studies in Ben Sira and the Book of Wisdom* (Uitgeverij Peeters, Leuven: Leuven University Press): 289–301.

Kraabel, A.T.

1981 'The Disappearance of the God-Fearers', *Numen* 28: 113–26.

Kraemer, Ross S.

1998 *When Aseneth Met Joseph: A Late Antique Tale of the Biblical Patriarch and his Egyptian Wife, Revisited* (Oxford: Oxford University Press).

1999 'Recycling Aseneth', in Athalya Brenner and Jan W. van Henten (eds). *Recycling Biblical Figures* (Papers read at a NOSTER colloquium in Amsterdam 12–13 May 1997; Leiden: Deo): 234–65.

Kümmel, W.G.

1972 *The New Testament: The History of the Investigation of its Problems* (trans. S. Mclean Gilmour and Howard C. Kee; Nashville: Abingdon Press).

Levinskaya, I.
1996   *The Book of Acts in its Diaspora Setting* (Grand Rapids: Eerdmans).
Liddell, H.G., and Robert Scott
1940   *An Intermediate Greek-English Lexicon* (Oxford: Oxford University Press, 9th edn with a revised supplement edited in 1996).
Lietzmann, H.
1931   *An die Korinther I, II* (Handbuch zum Neuer Testament, 9; Tübingen: Mohr Siebeck).
Litfin, D.
1994   *St. Paul's Theology of Proclamation: 1 Corinthians 1-4 and Greco-Roman Rhetoric* (SNTSMS, 79; Cambridge: Cambridge University Press).
Longenecker, R.N.
1990   *Galatians* (WBC, 41; Texas, Dallas: Word Books).
MacMullen, R.
1981   *Paganism in the Roman Empire* (New Haven: Yale University Press).
Malherbe, A. J.
1994   'Determinism and Free Will in Paul: the Argument of 1 Corinthians 8 and 9', in Troels Engberg-Pedersen (ed.), *Paul in his Hellenistic Context* (Edinburgh: T&T Clark): 231–55.
Manson, T.W.
1962   *Studies in the Gospels and Epistles* (Manchester: Manchester University Press).
Marshall, P.
1987   *Enmity in Corinth: Social Conventions in Paul's Relations with the Corinthians* (Tübingen: J.C.B. Mohr).
Martin, D.B.
1990   *Slavery as Salvation: The Metaphor of Slavery in Pauline Christianity* (New Haven/London: Yale University Press).
1995   *The Corinthian Body* (New Haven; London: Yale University Press).
2001   'Review Essay: Justin J. Meggitt, *Paul, Poverty and Survival*', *JSNT* 84: 51–64.
Martin, R.P.
1986   *2 Corinthians* (WBC, 40; Waco, TX: Word Books).
Mason, S.
1996   'The *Contra Apionem* in Social and Literary Context: An Invitation to Judean Philosophy', in Feldman and Levison 1996: 187–228.
Mason, S. (ed.)
1998   *Understanding Josephus: Seven Perspectives* (Sheffield: Sheffield Academic Press): 64–103.
Meeks, W.A.
1983   *The First Urban Christians: The Social World of the Apostle Paul* (New Haven: Yale University Press).
1995   'And Rose Up to Play: Midrash and Paraenesis in 1 Corinthians 10.22', in Stanley E. Porter and Craig A. Evans (eds), *The Pauline Writings* (Sheffield: Sheffield Academic Press): 124Mason, S.36 (Originally published in 1982, under *JSNT* 16: 64Mason, S.78).
Meggitt, J.J.
1998   *Paul, Poverty and Survival* (SNTW; Edinburgh: T&T Clark).
Metzger, Bruce M.
1971   *A Textual Commentary on the Greek New Testament* (Stuttgart, Germany: United Bible Societies, 2nd edn).
Mitchell, M.M.
1991   *Paul and the Rhetoric of Reconciliation: An Exegetical Investigation of the*

Language and Composition of 1 Corinthians (HUT, 28; Tübingen: Mohr–
Siebeck).

Moo, Douglas
1996   *Romans* (NICNT; Grand Rapids: Eerdmans).

Muir, Steven C.
2000   'Review of "Michael Goulder, *A Tale of Two Missions* (London: SCM, 1994)"'.
(http://www.bookreviews.org/).

Munck, J.
1959   *Paul and the Salvation of Mankind* (London: SCM Press).

Murphy-O'Connor, J.
1978a   '1 Cor 8.6: Cosmology or Soteriology?', *RB* 85: 253–67.
1978b   'Freedom or the Ghetto (1 Cor viii, 1-13; x, 23-xi, 1)', *RB* 85: 543–74.
1978c   'Corinthian Slogans in 1 Cor 6.12-20', *CBQ* 40: 391–96.
1979   *1 Corinthians* (Wilmington: Michael Glazier).
1983   *St Paul's Corinth: Texts and Archaeology* (Wilmington: Michael Glazier).

Newton, D.
1998   *Deity and Diet, the Dilemma of Sacrificial Food at Corinth* (JSNTSup, 169;
Sheffield: Sheffield Academic Press).

Neyrey, Jerome H.
1997   'Review of "Ben Witherington III, *Conflict and Community in Corinth: A Socio-
Rhetorical Commentary on 1 and 2 Corinthians* (Grand Rapids: Eerdmans,
1995)"', *CBQ* 59:182–83.

Nickelsburg, George W.E.
1984   'Stories of Biblical and Early Post-Biblical Times', in Stone 1984: 33–87.

Nilsson, M.P.
1963   'The High God and the Mediator', *HTR* 56: 101–20.

Nock, A.D., C. Roberts and T.C. Skeat
1936   'The Guild of Zeus Hypsistos', *HTR* 29: 39–88.

Nowell, Irene
1999   'The Book of Tobit', in *NIB* (Nashville: Abingdon Press), III: 973–1071.

Oropeza, B.J.
2000   *Paul and Apostasy: Eschatology, Perseverance, and Falling Away in the
Corinthian Congregation* (WUNT, 2, Reihe 115; Tübingen: Mohr–Siebeck).

Overman, J.A.
1988   'The God-Fearers: Some Neglected Features', *JSNT* 32: 17–26, reprinted in
C.A. Evans and S.E. Porter (eds.), *New Testament Background* (Sheffield:
Sheffield Academic Press, 1997): 253–62.

Pascuzzi, M.
2000   'Review of "Richard A. Horsley, *1 Corinthians* (Abingdon New Testament
Commentaries; Nashville: Abingdon, 1998)"', *CBQ* 62: 143–45.

Pearson, B.A.
1973   *The Pneumatikos-Psychikos Terminology in 1 Corinthians: A Study in the
Theology of the Corinthian Opponents of Paul and its Relation to Gnosticism*
(Missoula, MT: SBL for the Nag Hammadi Seminar).

Plummer, A.
1915   *A Critical and Exegetical Commentary on the Second Epistle of St Paul to the
Corinthians* (ICC; Edinburgh: T&T Clark).

Price, Simon
1999   *Religions of the Ancient Greeks* (Key Themes in Ancient History, ed. P.A.
Cartledge and P.D.A. Garnsey; Cambridge: Cambridge University Press).

218 *Idolatry and Authority*

Quell, G., and W. Foerster
    1965   'κύριος, κ.τ.λ.', *TDNT* 3: 1039–1098.
Reider, J.
    1957   *The Book of Wisdom* (New York: Harper).
Robertson, A., and A. Plummer
    1911   *A Critical and Exegetical Commentary on the First Epistle of St. Paul to the Corinthians* (ICC; Edinburgh: T&T Clark, 2nd edn).
Rosner, B. (ed.)
    1995   *Understanding Paul's Ethics: Twentieth-Century Approaches* (Grand Rapids: Eerdmans).
Sandmel, S.
    1979   *Philo of Alexandria: An Introduction* (Oxford: Oxford University Press).
    1984   'Philo Judaeus: An Introduction to the Man, his Writings, and his Significance', *ANRW* II.21.1, 3–46.
Sawyer, W.T.
    1968   *The Problem of Meat Sacrificed to Idols in the Corinthian Church* (Unpublished ThD dissertation, Southern Baptist Theological Seminary).
Schmithals, W.
    1971   *Gnosticism in Corinth: An Investigation of the Letters to the Corinthians* (Nashville: Abingdon Press).
Schnabel, E.J.
    1995   'How Paul Developed his Ethics (1992)', in Rosner 1995: 267–97.
Schneider, J.
    1971   'σχῆμα, μετασχηματίζω', *TDNT* VII:954–58.
Schrage, W.
    1995   *Der erste Brief an die Korinther, II. 1 Kor 6,12-11,6* (EKKNT, 7.2; Zürich: Benziger Verlag).
Schürer, E.
    1973–87   *The History of the Jewish People in the Age of Jesus Christ (175 BC - AD 135)* (3 vols.; rev. and ed. G. Vermes, F. Millar, M. Black and M. Goodman; Edinburgh: T&T Clark).
Seland, Torrey
    1995   *Establishment Violence in Philo and Luke: A Study of Non-Conformity to the Torah and Jewish Vigilante Reactions* (BIS, 15; Leiden: E.J. Brill).
Segal, A.F.
    1990   *Paul the Convert: The Apostolate and Apostasy of Saul the Pharisee* (New Haven: Yale University Press).
Shutt, R.J.H.
    1985   'Letter of Aristeas', in *OTP* II: 7–34.
Spilsbury, P.
    1998   'God and Israel in Josephus: A Patron-Client Relationship', in Mason 1998: 172-91.
Stambaugh, J.E., and D.L. Balch
    1986   *The New Testament in its Social Environment* (Library of Early Christianity; Philadelphia: Westminster Press).
Stanley, D.M.
    1959   '"Become Imitators of Me": The Pauline Conception of Apostolic Tradition', *Bib* 40: 859–77.
Stone, M.E. (ed.)
    1984   *Jewish Writings of the Second Temple Period* (CRINT, 2.2; Assen: Van Gorcum).

Stinespring, W.F.
    1962   'Temples, Jerusalem', in *IDB* IV: 534–60.
Stuart, Douglas
    1987   *Hosea-Jonah* (WBC, 31; Waco, TX: Word Books).
Swete, H.B.
    1914   *An Introduction to the Old Testament in Greek* (Cambridge: Cambridge University Press).
Tcherikover, V., and A. Fuks
    1957–64 *Corpus Papyrorum Judaicarum* (3 vols, 1957, 1960, 1963 [3rd vol with M. Stern and D.M. Lewis]; Jerusalem: Magnes Press).
Theissen, G.
    1982   *The Social Setting of Pauline Christianity* (ed. and trans. John H. Schütz; Edinburgh: T&T Clark).
    2001   'The Social Structure of Pauline Communities: Some Critical Remarks on J.J. Meggitt, *Paul, Poverty and Survival*', *JSNT* 84: 65–84.
Thiselton, A.C.
    2000   *The First Epistle to the Corinthians* (NIGTC; Grand Rapids: Eerdmans).
Thompson, J.A.
    1977   'Israel's Lovers', *VT* 27: 475–81.
Thrall, Margaret E.
    1994   *A Critical and Exegetical Commentary on the Second Epistle to the Corinthians* (ICC; Edinburgh: T&T Clark).
Tomson, P.J.
    1990   *Paul and the Jewish Law: Halakha in the Letters of the Apostle to the Gentiles* (Minneapolis: Fortress Press).
Traub, v. Rad
    1967   'οὐρανός, κ.τ.λ.', *TDNT* V: 497–543.
Trebilco, Paul R.
    1991   *Jewish Communities in Asia Minor* (SNTSMS, 60; Cambridge: Cambridge University Press).
Tromp, J.
    1999   'Response to Ross Kraemer: On the Jewish Origin of Joseph and Aseneth', in Athalya Brenner and Jan W. van Henten (eds.), *Recycling Biblical Figures* (Papers read at a NOSTER colloquium in Amsterdam 12–13 May 1997 (Leiden: Deo): 266–71.
Tuckett, C.M.
    1994   'Jewish Christian Wisdom in 1 Corinthians', in Stanley E. Porter *et al.* (eds.), *Crossing the Boundaries, Essays in Biblical Interpretation in Honour of Michael D. Goulder* (Leiden: E.J. Brill): 201-19.
Turner, E.G.
    1954   'Tiberius Julius Alexander', *JRS* 44: 54–64.
Urbach, E.E.
    1990   'The Role of the Ten Commandments in Jewish Worship', in Gershon 1990: 161–89.
Van der Horst, P.W.
    1994   ' "Thou Shalt Not Revile the Gods": the LXX Translation of Ex 22.28 (27), its Background and Influence', in *idem* (ed.), *Hellenism, Judaism, Christianity, Essays on their Interaction* (Kampen: Kok Pharos): 112–21.
Van Unnik, W.C.
    1974   'Josephus' Account of the Story of Israel's Sin with Alien Women in the

Country of Midian (Num. 25.1ff)', in M.S.H.G. Heerma von Voss (ed.), *Travels in the World of the Old Testament: Studies Presented to Professor M. A. Beek* (Assen: Van Gorcum): 241–61.

Von Rad, G.
    1966   *Deuteronomy* (OTL; London: SCM Press).

Von Soden, H.F.
    1972   'Sacrament and Ethics in Paul', in Wayne Meeks (ed.), *The Writings of St Paul* (New York: W.W. Norton): 257–68.

Watson, D.F.
    1989   '1 Cor. 10.23-11.1 in the Light of Graeco-Roman Rhetoric: The Role of Rhetorical Questions', *JBL* 108: 301–18.

Watts, John D.W.
    1985   *Isaiah 1–33* (WBC, 24; Waco, TX: Word Books).
    1987   *Isaiah 34–66* (WBC, 25; Waco, TX: Word Books).

Weinfeld, M.
    1990   'The Uniqueness of the Decalogue and its Place in Jewish Tradition', in Gershon 1990: 1–44.

Weiss, J.
    1910   *Der erste Korintherbrief* (Göttingen: Dandenhoed and Ruprecht).

Welborn, L.L.
    1987   'On the Discord in Corinth: 1 Corinthians 1–4 and Ancient Politics', *JBL* 106: 85–111.

Westerholm, S.
    1988   *Israel's Law and the Church's Faith, Paul and his Recent Interpreters* (Grand Rapids: Eerdmans).

Westermann, W.L.
    1955   *The Slave Systems of Greek and Roman Antiquity* (Philadelphia: The American Philosophical Society).

Wilcox, M.
    1981   'The "God-Fearers" in Acts: A Reconsideration', *JSNT* 13: 102–22.

Williams, M.H.
    1998   *The Jews among the Greeks and Romans: A Diasporan Sourcebook* (London: Duckworth).

Willis, W.L.
    1985a   *Idol Meat in Corinth: The Pauline Argument in 1 Corinthians 8 and 10* (SBLDS, 68; Chico, CA: Scholars Press).
    1985b   'An Apostolic Apologia: the Form and Function of 1 Corinthians 9', *JSNT* 24: 33–48.

Wilson, R.McL.
    1972   'How Gnostic Were the Corinthians?', *NTS* 19: 65–74.

Winston, D.
    1979   *Wisdom of Solomon* (AB; Garden City, New York: Doubleday).
    1992   'Solomon, Wisdom of', in *ABD* VI: 120–27.

Witherington III, B.
    1993   'Not So Idle Thoughts About *Eidolothuton*', *TynBul* 44: 237–54.
    1995   *Conflict and Community in Corinth: A Socio-Rhetorical Commentary on 1 and 2 Corinthians* (Grand Rapids/Carlisle: Eerdmans/Paternoster).

Wolfson, H.A.
    1948   *Philo: Foundations of Religious Philosophy in Judaism, Christianity and Islam* (2 vols; Cambridge, MA: Harvard University Press).

Wright, N.T.
  1992   *The New Testament and the People of God* (Philadelphia: Fortress Press).
Yeo, Khiok-Khng
  1995   *Rhetorical Interaction in 1 Corinthians 8 and 10: A Formal Analysis with Preliminary Suggestions for a Chinese, Cross-Cultural Hermeneutic* (BIS; Leiden: E.J. Brill).
Young F. and D.F. Ford
  1987   *Meaning and Truth in 2 Corinthians* (Grand Rapids: Eerdmans).
Zimmerli, W.
  1983   *Ezekiel 2* (Hermeneia; Philadelphia: Fortress Press).
Zimmermann, Frank
  1958   *The Book of Tobit, An English Translation with Introduction and Commentary* (JAL; New York: Harper and Brothers).

INDEXES

INDEX OF REFERENCES

Old Testament/Septuagint

Genesis

1.26	55
2.7	14, 56
2.17a	55
3.1–7	55
14.18	105
28.16–22	43
35.1–4	43
41.45	77
41.50–52	77
46.20	77

Exodus

1.11	112
10.18	151
12.23	165–66
13.21	157
14.22	157
17.6	157
17.15	108
20.2	36, 92
20.3	42, 47, 92
20.3–4	31
20.4	37
20.25	69
22.27a	91–95, 124, 171, 197, 203
23.32	92
32	34, 44, 162
32.1–15	43
32.1	43
32.4	38, 43, 47, 161
32.6	163
32.25	162
32.31	162
32.35	162, 167,
34	55

34.6	55, 161
34.15	47
34.17	55

Leviticus

6.16	187
19.4	63
24.15–16	93

Numbers

11.4	160
11.4–15	157
11.4–34	160
11.15	160
11.34	160, 167
14.1–16	157
14.1–38	165
14.3	161
14.22	165
16.41	165
17.1–11	166
21	164–65
21.4–7	164
24.16	105
25	30, 36, 68, 70, 71, 72, 76, 89, 134, 136, 162–64, 167
25.1	38
25.1–2	70, 136
25.1–3	162
25.1–9	38
25.1–18	162
25.2	162
25.3	38
25.10–13	72
33.49	38

Deuteronomy

4.4	64
4.19	62
6.4	5, 131–32
9.15–21	43
9.29	55
14.22–27	151
18.1	187
18.2	188
25.4	187–88, 205
32	138, 149, 152
32.1–43	46
32.8	105
32.16	46, 138, 152
32.16–17	42, 45
32.17	42, 46, 137–38, 140–41, 149–50
32.21	138, 149

Joshua

24.15	42

Judges

2.11–13	42
5.8	42
8.22	47
8.22–28	47
8.23	47
8.27	44, 47
14.1–16.31	136
17.1–13	44
17.4	44
17.5	44
17.6	44
17.7–8	44

17.13	44	9.10	108	40.18–26	84
18.27–31	43	17.3	108	40.19–20	48
		18.14	105	41	52
LXX 1 Kgdms (1 Samuel)		21.8	105	41.7	48
8.6	33	46.5	105	41.21–29	46
8.7–8	33	50.14	105	41.23	46
8.8	33	73.11	105	41.24	46
		77.11	105	41.25	46
LXX 2 Kgdms (2 Samuel)		77:18	164	41.26	46
22.14	105	78.17	105	41.27	46
24.16	165	78.18	164	41.29	46
		83.19	105	43.22–44.28	46
LXX 3 Kgdms (1 Kings)		87.5	105	44	52
2.28	44	90.6	138	44.8	131
11	71	91.1	105	44.9–17	75
12.25–33	43	91.9	105	44.9–20	46, 48, 52,
12.26–30	44	92.2	105		61, 65, 86,
12.27	43	95	152		90
12.28	43	95.5	138	44.15a	47
12.28–30	41	105.28–31	138	44.15b	47
14.3	44	105.36	138	44.15c	47
14.9	43	105.36–38	138	44.15d	47
14.16	43	105.37	138	44.16	47
14.21–24	43	106.37–8	46	44.17	47
14.22	43	105.38	138	44.17a	47
15.1–8	43	107.11	105	44.18	47
15.34	43	115.4–7	56	44.19b	47
16.7	43	115.5–8	61	44.20	47
16.19	43	115.8	61	44.22	46
16.25	43	143.2	108	45.5	131
16.30	43			46	52
21.7	147	*Proverbs*		46.1–2	40
22.18	44	1.7	85	46.1–13	40, 90
22.51–53	43	1.22	160	46.3–4	40
23.6	147			46.5–7	40
		Ecclesiastes		46.7	53
LXX 4 Kgdms (2 Kings)		12.13	85	52.5	146
16.1–20	45			65	139, 152
16.7	45	*Isaiah*		65.3	139
16.9	45	1.3	56	65.7	139
16.10	45	2.8	147	65.11	139, 151–
16.10–18	45	2.20	147		52
16.12–16	45	13	140	65.12	139
16.17–18a	45	13.21	138	65.17	45
16.18b	45	14.14	105		
		34.11	139	*Jeremiah*	
1 Chronicles		34.12	139	2.1–23	90
21.15	165	34.13	139	2.16	41
		34.14	139	2.18	41
Psalms		40	52	2.26–29	47
9.3	105	40.1–44.23	46	3.1–2	38

3.1–23	38	7.20	40	8	41
3.6	39	8	47	8.1	42
3.8–9	39	8.11	40	8.2–6	41, 44
3.11–14	39	8.12	40	8.4	44
3.13	39	8.14	40	9.10	41
3.16	45	11.12	42	10.1–6	41
3.19–20	39	12.2	39	11.1–2	41
3.20	39	12.2–9	39	13.1–6	41
7.8	41	12.3	39		
7.9	54	12.9	39	*Amos*	
7.18	41	12.25	39	2.4	42
7.31	45	14.3–7	45	2.7	41
8.19	47	14.3	45	5.7	41
9.23–24	180	14.4	45	5.25–26	41
10.1–15	47	14.5	45	5.26	41
10.1–16	48, 65	14.6	45	10–12	41
10.6–9	48	16	39	10–15	41
10.7	48	16.15–18	39		
10.10	48	16.18	39	*Habakuk*	
10.12	48	16.24–25	39	2.18–19	44, 84
10.16	48	16.59	39		
11.10	42	20.1–31	40	*Zephaniah*	
16.11	42	20.4–39	42	1.2–6	41
16.19	108	20.19	42	1.5	47
17.2	39	20.23	39		
18.15	47	20.24	42	*Malachi*	
19.4–5	42	20.32	45	2.10	42
19.5	45	23.1–39	40	3.7	42
22.9	42	36.17–18	39		
32.33	45	36.19	39	**New Testament**	
44.1–19	41	37.23	39	*Matthew*	
44.1–29	42	38.10	45	6.26	187
44.16–17	41	43.7–9	39	16.18	8
44.19	41	44.6–14	40		
				Mark	
Lamentations		*Daniel*		10.10	188
3.35	105	1.6–7	140		
3.38	105	11.31	147	*Luke*	
				10.7	188
Ezekiel		*Hosea*			
2.3–7	39, 90	1.2	30,	*John*	
2.5	40	2.1–13	39	12.31	142
2.6	40	2.4	39	16.11	142
2.7	40	2.8	39		
5.5–12	40	2.9–11	30	*Acts*	
5.6	42	2.13	39	1.21–22	177
5.9	40	2.14–15	30	15.20	9
5.11	40	4.2	42, 54	15.28–29	9
6.3–13	40	4.12–19	41, 42	15.29	163
6.9	40	6.7	42	18.3	186
6.13	40	7.13	42	22.1	178

23.1–3   198

Romans
2.17   146
2.22   146
2.22b   146
2.24   146
6.3   158
8.38–39   145
11.17–24   160
13.1–12   142
13.3   141
14.1–15.7   3
15.16   188
16   178
16.20   143

1 Corinthians
1–4   2, 15, 129, 131, 172, 179–81, 184
1.1   178
1.1–9   8
1.10   180
1.12   180
1.14–17   181
1.17   180
1.17–25   181
1.18–31   181
1.19–20   11
1.25   2
1.26   21
1.26–27   2
1.27   22
1.29   180
1.31   180
1.31b   180
2.1   181
2.2   180, 192
2.3   181
2.4   141, 181
2.4–5   184
2.5   11, 141
2.6   141
2.8   141
2.10   142
2.10–13   142
2.12   142
2.12–13   142
2.13   11

2.14   158
3   182
3.1–4   158
3.4   180
3.5   182
3.6   177, 180, 182
3.6–10   182
3.8   180
3.9   179, 182
3.9–15   179
3.10   177, 179, 182
3.10–17   8
3.13   179, 182
3.13–15   184
3.14   179–80
3.16–17   163, 182
3.18–19   142
3.21–22   181
3.22–23   183
4.1   182
4.1–2   180
4.1–5   182
4.2   183
4.2–5   183
4.3   178–79, 183
4.4   183
4.5   183
4.8   184
4.9–13   176, 183–84
4.10   2, 180,
4.11   179
3.11–13   180
4.12   176, 179
4.14–21   184
4.15   177, 181–82
4.15b   160
4.16   182, 184, 190, 197
4.16–21   184
4.17   182, 184
4.19   184
4.20   184
4.21   184
5   8, 166
5.1–5   162–63
5.2   128

5.5   142
5.9–11   9, 203
5.9–13   24
5.10–11   162
5.11   164
6.9–10   162
6.12   6, 15, 134, 136, 171
6.12–20   162–63
6.12b   6
6.13   10
7   179
7.2   143
7.5   142
7.8   186
7.9   155
8   2, 3, 4, 13, 19, 24, 25, 129, 131–34, 172, 174, 176, 186, 194, 201
8–10   5–8, 10–27, 34–35, 49–50, 91–92, 103, 105, 110–11, 124–25, 126–27, 146, 158, 162–64, 168, 171–73, 196, 201–03, 205–06
8.1   2, 3, 13, 18, 128–29, 158, 166
8.1–2   9
8.1–3   204
8.1–6   2
8.1–13   2, 128, 173, 186
8.1–9.23   12
8.1–11.1   1, 11, 29, 128, 154, 197, 201, 206, 208

1 Corinthians (cont.)

8.1a	5	197–99,	9.15b	190
8.2	157	205–06,	9.15b–18	190
8.3	157	208	9.16	189
8.4	2, 5, 6, 9,	9.1	136, 173,	9.16–18	180
	14, 17, 18,		175, 179,	9.16a	191
	19, 24, 96,		192, 195	9.17	180, 191–
	105, 128–	9.1–2	179–80,		92
	29, 131–		186	9.18	179–80,
	32, 148,	9.1–6	179		192–93
	203	9.1–12	175	9.19	176, 192
8.4–6	145	9.1–14	173	9.19–23	13, 173,
8.5	5, 50, 144,	9.1–18	173, 185		185–86,
	148, 204	9.1–23	158, 173,		190, 192–
8.5–6	5		197		93, 196–
8.5b	145	9.1b	178		97, 204
8.6	5, 18, 19,	9.1b–2	179	9.20–23	193
	128, 131–	9.2	173, 177,	9.20b	194
	32, 164,		179,	9.21	194, 206
	204	9.2b	178	9.22	2, 193–94,
8.6b	168	9.3	173–74,		197
8.7	2, 3, 4, 5,		178–79,	9.22b	196
	9, 12, 13,		183	9.22–23	193
	26, 132,	9.3–18	179	9.23	13, 155,
	207	9.3–27	179		180, 195
8.7–13	2	9.4	179, 185	9.24	13
8.7a	3, 5	9.4–6	179	9.24–27	154, 173,
8.7b	3	9.4–11	185		185, 195
8.8	18	9.4–14	173	9.24–10.12	154
8.9	2, 3, 127,	9.5	185, 187	9.24–10.13	158
	134, 136,	9.6	185	9.24–10.22	12, 13, 173
	185, 192	9.6–14	179	9.25	155
8.9–13	3, 4, 13	9.7	186	9.27	154–55
8.10	2, 3, 23,	9.7–12a	185	10	9, 17, 19,
	109, 127,	9.7–18	179		126, 141,
	207	9.9	187, 195		153, 166,
8.10–12	190	9.9–23	174		172, 174,
8.10–13	193	9.11	180		197, 201–
8.10b	3	9.11–12	186		02
8.11	2, 3, 4, 150	9.11–12a	187	10.1	157
8.12	4, 154	9.12	180, 192,	10.1–4	156, 167
8.13	2, 9, 175–		204	10.1–5	156
	76, 186,	9.12a	187	10.1–10	167
	195, 204	9.12b	176, 185,	10.1–11	156, 202
9	10, 24, 27,		187, 189–	10.1–12	156
	28, 126,		90	10.1–13	19, 153–
	166, 171–	9.13	187		54, 160–61
	76, 179–	9.13–14	185	10.1–22	24, 128,
	81, 183,	9.14	188		154, 161,
	185, 191–	9.15	180, 189		166
	92, 195,	9.15–23	185	10.2	156–57
		9.15a	176	10.3–4a	157

10.4	164		38, 148–49	15.44–50	14
10.4a	157	10.20–21	109, 126,	16.1	190
10.5	155–56,		141, 145,	16.10–11	184
	167		159, 164		
10.5a	157	10.20b	152	*2 Corinthians*	
10.5b	157	10.21	127, 139,	1.12	179
10.6	152, 157,		152, 154	2.11	143
	159–61,	10.21–22	150	4	144
	164, 167	10.21b	152	4.4	142, 144
10.6–10	152	10.22	38, 152,	4.10	195
10.6–11	156		154, 159,	5.17	193
10.6–13	161		164, 167–	6.14–7.1	144
10.6a	157		69	6.16	147, 152
10.7	152, 156,	10.23	6, 15, 134,	7.11	178
	161–63,		136, 171,	8.2	189
	167		196	8.9	195
10.7–10	152	10.23–11.1	12, 13, 24,	9.6–7	190
10.8	152, 156,		25, 128,	10–13	172, 176
	162		206–07	10.10	181
10.8a	167	10.24	196	10.12–18	178
10.8b	167	10.25	3, 207	10.17	180
10.9	152, 154,	10.27	3	11.9	189
	156, 164–	10.27–28	207	11.13	143
	65, 168	10.28	2, 4	11.13–15	143
10.9a	167	10.29b–30	186	11.14	143
10.9b	167	10.30	196	11.15	143
10.10	152, 156,	10.31	186, 196	11.16	181
	165–66	10.31–11.1	195	11.20	187
10.10a	167	10.32	192, 196	11.22	12
10.10b	167	10.33	196–97	12.7	143
10.11	167	11	155	12.14	189
10.12	151, 153–	11.1	166, 172,		
	54, 167–		190, 195,	*Galatians*	
	68, 202		197, 202,	1.11–12	185
10.13	153, 168		207	1.15	185
10.14	109, 127,	11.3	143	2.9	177
	150, 153,	11.17–34	151	2.11–12	177
	158, 168,	11.18–22	2	4.8	145
	206	11.19	181	5.13	206
10.14–21	16, 127	11.25	127, 159	6.2	194, 206
10.14–22	13, 149–	11.33–34	2		
	50, 153–54	12	15	*Ephesians*	
10.15–21	158	12.2	4, 148, 156	6.12	141
10.16	150	13	176, 194		
10.16–17	127	14.37	158	*Philippians*	
10.16–22	151	15	15, 186	1.7	178
10.17	152	15.1–10	177	1.11	178
10.18	151	15.6	178	1.18	192
10.19	151	15.8–10	178, 185	2.6–11	144, 195
10.20	109, 111,	15.24	143	2.9–11	15
	127, 137–	15.25	143	2.19–24	184

Philippians (cont.)
3.2ff   194
3.21   143

Colossians
1.16   141

1 Thessalonians
1.9   147–48
1.9–10   4
1.9b   147
1.10   147
2.9   176
2.17–3.13   184
2.18   143
3.2–3   143
3.5   143

1 Timothy
5.18   188

Revelation
2.14   163
2.15   163
2.20   163
18.2   138
21.8   145

Apocrypha
Baruch
1.15   140
2.6   140
2.9   140
2.27   140
3.2   140
4.7   140
4.22   140
4.24   140
4.35   140
5.9   140

Epistle of Jeremiah
16   148
23   148
27   53
29   148
49   148
51   148
56   148
65   148
69   148

72   148

Tobit
3.8   140
3.17   140
5.4   140
6.7–9   140
6.14   140
6.16   140
6.17   140
8.3   140

Wisdom of Solomon
2.23–24   55
7–10   14
10–19   53
13   52
13–15   51, 52, 64,
            65, 75
13.1   52
13.1–9   51, 52, 59,
            66
13.1–15.19 66
13.2   52
13.2–3   52
13.4   52
13.4b   52
13.5   52
13.6   52
13.6–7   60
13.10   51, 52
13.10–16   52
13.10–18   54
13.10–19   52, 66, 84
13.10–15.19 51, 52
13.11–14.2 51
13.13   52
13.14   52
13.16   52, 53
13.17   52
13.18   52
14.1–7   53, 66
14.1–11   53
14.3–6   51
14.3   53
14.4   53
14.7–11   51
14.8–11   53
14.8   53, 54
14.9   53
14.10   53

14.11   53
14.12–21   54, 66
14.12–31   51
14.12   53
14.14   54
14.15   54
14.15–21   65
14.16   54
14.17   54
14.20   54
14.21   54
14.22–29   84
14.22–31   54, 55
14.23   54
14.24–27   54
14.24–28   53
14.27   54, 84
14.28   54
15   55
15–18   78
15.1–6   55
15.1–3   51
15.1   55
15.2   55
15.3   55, 56, 57
15.4–6   51, 55
15.7–13   51, 56
15.7–17   66
15.8   56
15.9   56
15.10   56
15.11   56
15.13   56
15.14–19   51, 56
15.14   56
15.15   56
15.16   56
15.17   56
15.18   56, 57
15.18–19   66, 73, 86
15.19   57
18.20–25   165

Pseudepigrapha
1 Enoch
71.5–10   145

3 Maccabees
1.3   120
2.30–31   198
2.32   198

7.10–12	198	11.8	82	186	101
7.14–16	198	11.8a	81	199	101
		11.8b	81	209	102
4 Maccabees		11.9	81	227	103
9.22	143	11.16	81	232	102
		12.4	81	232–33	102
Artapanus		12.4–5	81	233	102
23.4	112	12.5	81	255	102
27.4	112–14	12.8	81	267	102
27.6	114	13.11	82	270	102
27.9	114	14.1–15	78	271–72	102
27.12	113	14.7	106	274	102
27.21	114	15.2b–6	78	276	102
27.21–22	114	15.6–8	106	280	102
27.22	114–15	15.7	78	281	102
27.25–26	114	15.9–10	78	283	102
27.32	114	15.13	106	287	102
27.37	115	16.7–8	106	290	102
		16.16	78	292	102
Ezek. Trag.		19.2	106		
Exagoge		19.4–11	78	*Orphica*	
239	105	21.13	82	24	104
		21.13–14	82		
Joseph and Aseneth		22.5	106	*Philo the Epic Poet*	
1.4	77	23.10	106	*Frag.* 3	105
2.1	77				
2.2	78	*Letter of Aristeas*		*Sibylline Oracles*	
3.1–3	77	12–14	98	2	83
3.6	79	14	97	2.59	84
4.7–8	77	15	98, 100	2.96	84
4.9–11	77	15–16	96, 98,	3	83, 84, 87
5.1–2	78		103, 108,	3.1–92	83
7.2	78		110	3.1–96	83, 84
8.5	78, 80, 81,	16	98, 99,	3.8	83
	82		100, 102	3.9	84
8.5–7	79, 81	19	99	3.10	84
8.7	79	27	97	3.11	83
8.8–9	78	31	97	3.11–15	88
8.9	80	37	99	3.12	83
8.10	106	40	100	3.13–14	84
9.2	80	42	99, 102	3.15	84
10–13	78	46	101	3.29	84, 88
10.1–13.14	81	121	101	3.29–32	86
10.12–13	81	134–38	100, 103	3.29–39	83
10.13	81, 106	139	97, 100	3.32	84
10.13b	81	139–40	97	3.33	84
11.1	106	140	100	3.34–35	84
11.3	81	144	97	3.36–38	84
11.3b–14	81	177	101	3.39–40	84
11.7	81	181–84	97	3.46–59	84
11.7–9	81	182	101	3.57–59	84

Sibylline Oracles (cont.)

3.59	84
3.75–92	83
3.93–96	84
3.155–61	83
3.193	83
3.221–33	85
3.275–76	85, 88
3.275–79	85
3.276–77	85
3.278	85
3.279	85
3.282–94	85
3.318	83
3.517	105
3.545–54	85
3.547–48	85
3.548	85
3.554	85
3.573–600	86
3.574	105
3.575	85
3.576–79	85
3.580–84	85
3.586–89	85
3.591–94	85
3.595–600	85
3.601–05	85
3.608	83
3.611	83
3.669–709	86
3.702–31	85
3.718–19	87
3.719	105
3.721	88
3.776	83
4	83
5	83, 86, 87
5.52–110	83
5.75	86
5.75–85	86
5.77	86
5.78–79	86
5.80	86
5.81–82	86
5.83	86
5.84	86
5.179–285	83
5.238–85	86
5.256–59	83
5.264–65	87

5.274–85	87
5.278–80	86
5.352	86
5.353	86
5.354	86
5.356	86
5.360	86
5.398–401	83
5.484	87
5.486	87
5.488	87
5.491	87
5.493–504	83
5.494	87
5.495–96	87
5.497	87
5.512–53	83

Philo

Abr.

20–25	57
85–87	57
98	61
255–76	14
267	58, 60
268	60

Aet. Mund.

10	58

Agr.

92	178

Conf. Ling.

12	54
69	146
71	146
74	146
163	147
168–73	62
170–71	131

Congr.

15	58, 59, 64

Dec.

12	36
52	59
52–56	60
52–57	67
52–65	59, 65, 66

52–80	75
52–81	58, 59, 64, 65, 66, 94, 106
53	58, 59
53–58	59
55	59
58	59
61	59
62	59
65	60
66	60
66–76a	60, 65, 66
67	60
68	60
70–71	60
72	60
73–74	61
75	61
76–79	78, 86
76–80	73
76a	61
76b–81	61, 65, 66
77	61
80	62
93	93
156	58

Det. Pot. Ins.

125	60, 64

Flacc.

7	178
46	105
126	178

Fug.

56	64
121	59
180	58, 59

Jos.

52	178
80	178
222	178

Her.

247–83	14

Leg. All.

1.43	59

3.48	131	47–52	58	1.23	63
3.65	178	89–128	58	1.23–27	62, 63, 66
3.66	178	170	58	1.24	63, 64
3.68	178	170–71	67	1.25	64
3.75	178	170–72	58, 131	1.28–31	62, 63, 64,
3.82	105, 137	171	58, 62		65, 66
3.126	131	172	58	1.30	64, 131
				1.53	69, 93
Leg. Gai		*Plant.*		1.54	60, 67
22–65	66	55–60	61	1.56	58
38	178			1.67	67
67	178	*Poster. C.*		1.79	59, 62
75	67	2	58	1.314	57
75–80	66	124–29	14	1.345	64
77	67	165	58, 61	2.62	198
81	66	175	148	2.95	178
93–97	66			2.164	64
98–113	66	*Praem. Poen.*		2.165	106
114	66	19	146	3.1–6	57
115	66	162	58	3.125	60, 161
117–18	66			3.142	178
118	67	*Prov.*		4.24	178
120	95	1	121		
120–36	66	2	121	*Virt.*	
156–57	198	2.58	155	34–35	70
157	105			34–40	70
162	66	*Quaest. in Exod.*		179–80	14
181	66	2.5	69, 93, 94	179	59
182	57	2.39–40	14	181–82	63
203	67			197	178
276–329	67	*Sacr.*		214	59
278	105	13	59		
317	105	76	59	*Vit. Cont.*	
337–38	67			3	65
346	67	*Somn.*		3–5	66
347	67	2.133–35	153	3–6	58
347–48	67			3–8	58, 64, 65,
350	178	*Spec. Leg.*			66, 75, 86,
		1.7	69		106
Migr. Abr.		1.12–20	62, 65, 66	4	65
28–40	14	1.12–31	58, 62, 63,	5	65
69	58		64, 65, 66,	6	65, 66
113–14	61		94, 106	7	65, 66
		1.13	62	8	65, 66
Omn. Prob. Lib.		1.15–16	62	18–21	57
26	155	1.16–18	62		
105	58	1.19	62	*Vit. Mos.*	
146	146	1.21–22	63, 66	1.54	70
		1.21–27	65	1.286	178
Op. Mund.		1.21–31	62, 66	1.296–99	70
3	58	1.22	63	1.303	178

Vit. Mos. (cont.)

2.26	69
2.161–73	60
2.162	161
2.189	61
2.193–96	58, 59
2.203–05	69, 93
2.205	58, 63, 69, 93
2.206	67
2.228	148

Josephus
Ant.

1.17	70
1.20	76
3.91	69, 131
3.91–2	36
4.12	71
4.126–30	70, 162
4.126–54	70
4.129	70
4.130	70
4.131–36	70
4.131–54	135
4.137	71, 135
4.139	71, 135
4.140	71, 72
4.141–44	71, 135
4.143	72
4.144	72
4.145–46	135
4.146	136
4.149	136
4.152	72
4.152–53	72
4.152–54	72
4.154	72
4.200	69
4.200–01	69
4.201	69, 73
4.202	93
4.207	93
4.207b	147
5.286–317	136
6.160	72
14.45	146
14.185–267	95
14.235	198
16.160–79	95
16.163	105, 106

16.167–68	198
18.65–80	163
18.159–60	121
19.276–77	121
20.100	121–22
20.100–203	121

Apion

1.227–50	95
1.304–11	95
2.66	72, 73, 95
2.66–67	72
2.73–74	75
2.73–77	72, 75
2.74	94
2.75–76	75
2.77	75
2.79	69
2.80	73
2.80–81	72
2.81	73
2.82	73
2.82–83	73
2.83–84	73
2.83–85	73
2.86	73
2.112–14	73
2.139	73
2.145	95
2.147	178
2.167	76
2.185	76
2.190	69, 76
2.190–93	69
2.191	70
2.192	70
2.193	70
2.237	69, 76, 93
2.237–38	94
2.238	69
2.239	73
2.239–49	72
2.239–54	72
2.240	74
2.241	74
2.242	74
2.244	74
2.245	74
2.246	74
2.249	74
2.250	75

2.251	75
2.252	75
2.254	75

Life

126–44	68
387–88	68
388–89	68

War

1.621	178
2.220	122
2.487–94	122
2.309	121
6.172	146
6.237	121
6.236ff	122

Classical Authors
Aristotle
Problemata

954a	83

Diodorus Siculus

1.16.1	114
1.89.5	113

Epictetus

3.22.38	176

Homer
Illiad

21.442–45	74
21.448–49	74

Joannes Lydus
De mens

4.53	**105**

Pausanias

2.2.6–2.5.4	149
2.4.6	149
2.2.8	110
5.15.5	**109**

Plato
Phdr.

274–75	114

Plutarch
Quaest. conviv.

4.5.3 73

Posidonius
34/35.1.3 73

Tacitus
Hist.
5.4.2 73

Early Christian Writings
Barn.
16.7 144

Clement
Paedogogus
2.1.8–10 144

Strom.
1.108.1 83

Dio Chrysostom
Or.
60–61 145

Eusebius
Praeparatio Evangelica
13.13.5 104
13.13.7 104

Origen
Contra Celsum
8.24 144
8.30 144

Tertullian
De Spectaculis
13 144

Papyri
CPJ
127a 120
127c 120
127d 120
127e 120
138 198
141 147
418a 121
1537 116
1538 116

CPJ III, Append.
1433 106
1443 106

Inscriptions
Inscriptions de Délos
2532 107, 108

CIJ
690 108, 110, 118
690a 118
709 119
710 119
711 118
711b 123
725 107, 108
726 107, 108
728 107
729 107

Horbury & Noy
121–24 117
123 117
124 117
154 123
155 123
156 123

OGIS
383 121
663 121
669 121

Aalen, S. 196
Adams, E. 142, 145
Albeck, S. 37
Albertz, R. 44
Allen, L.C. 138
Anderson, A.A. 138
Applebaum, S. 197
Attridge, H.W. 68, 69

Bar–Kochva, B. 73
Barclay, J.M.G. 51, 55, 57–58, 61–62, 68–
 69, 72, 77–80, 82–84, 87, 97–98, 101,
 103–104, 108, 111, 113, 117, 120–22,
 194, 198
Barrett, C.K. 5, 6, 9–11, 26, 127–28, 133–
 34, 141–46, 148, 150–51, 153, 155,
 157–61, 164–69, 173–74, 176, 178–79,
 182–84, 186–90, 192–97
Bartlett, J.R. 97–8
Batnitzky, L. 29
Baur, F.C. 6–8, 11, 201
Bertram, G. 105
Best, E. 147, 177–78
Bickermann, E. 96–97
Bilde, P. 68–70, 72
Boccaccini, G. 78, 96
Borgen, P. 57–63, 67, 135–36
Brownlee, W.H. 39–40, 45
Bruce, F.F. 147, 177
Büchsel, F. 4, 17, 130, 146
Burchard, C. 78–79, 81

Carroll, R.P. 39
Chesnutt, R. 77, 79
Cheung, A.T. 16–17, 25–26, 144, 152, 201
Childs, B.S. 37
Chow, J.K. 166, 175–76, 184
Clarke, A.D. 21, 166

Clark, E.G. 51
Collins, J.J. 51–56, 77–80, 82–84, 86, 96–
 97, 104, 111–14
Collins, R.F. 179
Conzelmann, H. 4–6, 13, 128, 130, 132,
 135, 141, 144–45, 148, 150–53, 155–
 56, 158, 160–61, 164–65, 168, 173–74,
 178–79, 183, 186, 190–94
Cook, A.B. 109
Craigie, P.C. 138
Cranfield, C.E.B. 146–47
Cullmann, O. 141

Dahl, N.A. 180–82
Dahood, M. 138
Davies, E.W. 38
Davies, G.H. 47
Davies, G.I. 42
Davies, M. 12
De Vries, S.J. 43
Downing, F.G. 12
Dungan, D.L. 189
Dunn, J.D.G. 147, 177, 207
Durham, J.I. 69

Ehrhardt, A. 8, 9, 11

Fee, G.D. 2, 4–6, 13–14, 19, 127–30, 132–
 34, 136, 141–42, 144–45, 148–68,
 173–75, 178–80, 182–84, 186–90,
 192–95
Feldman, L.H. 68, 70–73, 94–95, 119, 136
Ferguson, E. 74, 87, 112, 114, 118, 120–22
Finn, T.M. 110
Frame, J.E. 147
Fraser, P.M. 96, 111
Freudenthal, J. 113
Frey, J.-B. 118

Furnish, V.P. 142

Gager, J.G. 95
Gallas, S. 197
Gardner, P.D. 151, 154–56, 158–59, 163,
    168, 193, 201
Giblin, C.H. 128, 132
Gnuse, R.K. 37–38
Goldenberg, R. 59, 63, 69, 79, 93–95, 99,
    117
Gooch, P.D. 2, 19–20, 24–26, 127, 149, 201
Goodenough, E. R. 197
Goulder, M. 8, 11–12
Grabbe, L.L. 51–52, 83
Grant, R. 74, 131
Gray, J. 40
Greenberg, M. 36
Grosheide, F.W. 149–50
Gruen, E.S. 77, 80, 83–84, 96–98, 112
Guenther, H. O. 14
Gundry–Volf, J. M. 142, 153–55, 168

Halbertal, M. and Margalit, A. 27, 29–35,
    38, 46–48, 91, 162–64, 201
Halbertal, M. 35, 202, 207
Harrison, R.K. 44, 47
Hatch, E. and Redpath, H.A. 146
Hays, R.B. 2, 4–6, 127, 135, 141–42, 145,
    152–3, 156, 158–60, 162–63, 165–66,
    205
Hengel, M. 98, 198, 207
Héring, J. 4–6, 128, 132, 134, 141, 144,
    156–57, 160, 173, 177–78, 183, 187–
    88, 192, 196
Hobbs, T.R. 45
Hock, R.F. 176
Holladay, C.R. 111– 14
Hollander, H.W. 194
Holmberg, B. 176, 189–90
Horbury, W. 136
Horbury, W. and Noy, D. 107, 117–18, 123
Horrell, D.G. 3, 21, 173–74, 176, 187, 192–
    93, 195, 206
Horsley, R.A. 14–16, 129–32, 134, 136, 142
Hotz, T. 205
Houtman, C. 37
Hurd, J.C. 1, 2, 8, 14, 24–26, 128, 161, 163,
    166, 173

Hurtado, L.W. 76

Jones, D.R. 48

Käsemann, E. 189, 191–92
Kasher, A. 72
Klauk, Hans–Josef 145
Koester, H. 84
Kolarcik, M.F. 51
Kraabel, A.T. 110
Kraemer, R.S. 77
Kümmel, W.G. 7

Levinskaya, I. 104–105, 107–10
Liddell, H.G. and Scott, R. 39, 45, 47, 52–
    53, 56, 80, 85–87, 104, 152
Lietzmann, H. 141, 158
Lifshitz, B. 108, 118
Litfin, D. 8, 181–82, 184
Longenecker, R.N. 194

MacMullen, R. 74
Malherbe, A.J. 185, 191
Manson, T.W. 8–11
Marshall, P. 176, 189
Martin, D.B. 21, 23, 173–76, 191, 195
Martin, R.P. 143–44, 147
Mason, S. 68–69, 76
Meeks, W.A. 21, 160–62, 184
Meggitt, J.J. 22–23, 166, 191
Metzger, B.M. 4
Mitchell, M.M. 20, 150–51, 153, 173–74,
    176–77
Moo, D. 146
Muir, S.C. 8, 12
Munck, J. 180–81
Murphy–O'Connor, J. 4–5, 18–19, 128–33,
    154, 188–90, 193–94

Newton, D. 17, 29, 146, 149, 165, 201
Neyrey, J.H. 18
Nickelsburg, G.W.E. 140
Nilsson, M.P. 104
Nock, *et al.* 104, 109
Nowell, I. 140

Oropeza, B.J. 151, 154, 159
Overman, J.A. 110

Pascuzzi, M. 15
Pearson, B. A. 15–16, 128–29
Plummer, A. 144, 147
Price, S. 74, 87

Quell, G. and Foerster, W. 134

Reider, J. 51–57
Robertson, A. and Plummer, A. 4–6, 141–42, 145, 148–52, 158–60, 163–68, 173, 179
Rosner, B. 205–206

Sandmel, S. 57
Sawyer, W.T. 149
Schmithals, W. 12–14, 128, 173
Schnabel, E.J. 205–206
Schneider, J. 143
Schrage, W. 162, 164
Schürer, E. 52, 65, 68, 77, 82–83, 86, 95–97, 107–108, 113, 124, 140
Seland, T. 198
Segal, A.F. 144
Shutt, R.J.H. 99
Spilsbury, P. 76
Stambaugh, J.E. and Balch, D.L. 84
Stanley, D.M. 207
Stinespring, W.F. 97
Stuart, D. 39, 41–42
Swete, H. B. 94–95

Tcherikover, V. and Fuks, A. 98, 120–21
Theissen, G. 20–23, 189
Thiselton, A.C. 148, 151–58, 160, 162–65, 176, 187, 190
Thompson, J.A. 39
Thrall, M.E. 144
Tomson, P.J. 7, 25, 129, 205

Traub, v. R. 145
Trebilco, P.R. 104–10
Tromp, J. 77
Tuckett, C.M. 12
Turner, E.G. 122

Urbach, E.E. 37

Van der Horst, P.W. 92, 95
Van Unnik, W.C. 70–72, 136
Von Rad, G. 138
Von Soden, H.F. 151, 155

Watson, D.F. 207
Watts, J.D.W. 139, 152
Weinfeld, M. 36
Weiss, J. 24–25, 173, 187
Welborn, L.L. 181
Westerholm, S. 206
Westermann, W.L. 118–19
Wilcox, M. 110
Williams, M.H. 118–19
Willis, W.L. 16, 127–28, 131–32, 144–45, 157–58, 160, 164–66, 168, 173–75, 178, 194, 201
Wilson, R.M. 14
Winston, D. 51–55, 65
Witherington III, B. 17–18, 141, 144, 151, 174, 188–89, 201
Wolfson, H.A. 57–59, 62
Wright, N.T. 167

Yeo, K.K. 14, 20, 151, 154, 157, 161, 163, 165, 173
Young F. and Ford, D.F. 144

Zimmermann, F. 140